P9-CRE-337

Dickinson's
American Historical Fiction

Fifth Edition

by
VIRGINIA BROKAW GERHARDSTEIN

The Scarecrow Press, Inc.
Metuchen, N.J., & London
1986

Library of Congress Cataloging-in-Publication Data

Dickinson, A. T.
Dickinson's American historical fiction.

Includes indexes.
1. Historical fiction, American--Bibliography.
2. American fiction--20th century--Bibliography.
3. United States--History--Fiction--Bibliography.
4. United States in literature--Bibliography.
I. Gerhardstein, Virginia Brokaw, 1930- .
II. Title: American historical fiction.
Z1231.F4D47 1986 [PS374.H5] 016.813'081 85-27656
ISBN 0-8108-1867-1

Manufactured in the United States of America

"Fancy with fact is just one fact the more."

Robert Browning

PREFACE

American history in fiction is a fascinating and informative field for study, as evidenced by its popularity with the casual reader in library and bookstore, and its increasing use by teachers who recognize that fiction can bring to life for their students a particular period or event in history.

A. T. Dickinson Jr.'s interest in historical fiction grew out of an early interest in history, blossomed with the reading of Gone With the Wind and The Red Badge of Courage, and bore fruit in the form of a Master's thesis on the subject under the guidance of Professor Leon Carnovsky of the Graduate Library School, The University of Chicago.

My own interest in the field was nurtured when I majored in American Studies at Cornell University. I enjoyed a long friendship with Mr. Dickinson, worked with him for many years at the Mansfield-Richland County (Ohio) Public Library, and am happy to be associated with this continuation of his work.

Experience with the first edition revealed that its primary value was as a bibliography. Subsequent editions have been tailored to that usage. The basic list consists of novels published from 1917 to 1984, with the addition of those authors and titles from the past which have come to be standard names in historical fiction regardless of publication date.

A total of 3048 novels casting light on some aspect of American history are classified into natural chronological periods from Colonial days to the 1970's. The brief annotations are designed to place the books in historical perspective rather than to make any critical judgment of the quality or the historical accuracy of the writing.

A separate Author-Title Index and a Subject Index are keyed to an entry number assigned to each title in the body of the book.

TABLE OF CONTENTS

INTRODUCTION

Just what constitutes a historical novel is a question which either plagues the person who would write about it, or concerns him very little. At any rate, there are as many definitions as there are definers. Perhaps the most succinct statement has been made by Ernest E. Leisy in The American Historical Novel:

> In a sense all fiction has a preterit quality, a sense of having been lived. More specifically, historical fiction is concerned with historical truth, whatever that is. Whether such truth requires a spectacular historical figure or episode is a matter of controversy, as is the question of whether the term includes novels written contemporaneously with the events. Paul Leicester Ford once said, "An historical novel is one which grafts upon a story actual incidents or persons well enough known to be recognized as historical elements." This definition appears too restrictive, however, for manners, customs, and ideas may suffice to identify a period.... Owen Wister complicated the problem by asserting that "any narrative which presents a day and a generation is of necessity historical," a view concurred in by Brander Matthews when he said: "The really trustworthy historical novels are those which were a-writing while the history was a-making."

The statements of Owen Wister and Paul Leicester Ford represent opposite extremes in the academic approach to the definition of historical fiction. In practice, few would disagree with Leisy that the historical novel is one in which the action is laid in some identifiable past time. He suggests that a generation seems sufficient to make a preceding period historical, and he ends his discussion with the period of national expansion preceding World War I.

Robert A. Lively, in Fiction Fights the Civil War, is not concerned with past time as a prerequisite for the novels so ably analyzed in his study of the Civil War in fiction. His conclusion is that it is the "true residue of fact or color which determines the value of a work as a report from the past."

The criteria for judging whether a novel will, at a given point in time, present to the reader a feeling for the history potentially inherent in any peice of writing are: identifiable time, either by date or by approximate period; identifiable place, either by definite locality or general area; and historical agent, whether a person, an event, or a recognizable social, political, or economic phenomenon characteristic of a period. Such a definition may be interpreted with varying degrees of latitude and offers the reader interested in viewing our past through the novelist's eyes wide scope in selection, without concern about whether the author was sufficiently removed from his subject to rate the title of historical novelist.

American history, as rich and as varied as it is, falls into a natural chronological pattern corresponding to the periods of development of the nation from Colonial days to the present, and this seems to be a logical arrangement to follow.

Colonial America to 1775

The colonial period has been the inspiration for novels dealing with a variety of themes. The period covered is that of the colonization and settlement of the original colonies, and of their political, economic, social, and religious development up to the time of the Revolution. The ill-fated settlement on Roanoke Island, the struggle for survival of the first settlement at Plymouth, Bacon's Rebellion, the Pontiac Conspiracy, the Yemassee Wars, the Deerfield raid, the Salem witchcraft trials, conflict between Quakers and Puritans, the New Hampshire land-grant controversy, the attack on the French at Louisburg, Braddock's defeat, King Philip's War, and the siege of Fort Pitt are some of the more violent episodes in the history of the period which have been used in historical novels. Other novels have dealt with less violent, though not less crucial aspects of the period, such as the founding of Detroit, the French settlement of Mobile and New Orleans, social life at Williamsburg, the immigration of French Huguenots into the Carolinas and of the Scotch-Irish and Germans into Pennsylvania, the life of George Washington, and the social and mercantile life of the Dutch and the English in New York.

The American Revolution

The American Revolution has been well documented in historical fiction, from the tense political situation leading to the battles of Lexington and Concord, through the progress of the war southward to its culmination in Cornwallis' surrender at Yorktown, the war on the frontier, and the development of the American navy under Commodore John Paul Jones. The Boston Tea Party, the terrible winter at Valley Forge, Benjamin Franklin's diplomatic mission to France, the career of Benedict Arnold, the activities of George Rogers Clark on the frontier and of Francis Marion in South Carolina, the neutrality of Westchester County, New York and the conflict between English and rebel loyalties throughout the colonies, the separatist movement on the frontiers of Kentucky and Tennessee and the founding of the Transylvania Company and the State of Franklin, as well as action leading to various battles and campaigns of the war are some of the subjects of novels dealing with this period of history.

The Young Nation, 1783 to 1860

The period covered by this category extends from the end of the Revolution to the mid-1800's, thus overlapping in time parts of the two following categories. Novels dealing with political, social, cultural, and industrial development of the new young nation following the Revolution contribute to a fuller understanding of our history. Some of the themes found in fiction of this period are: the period of Confederation, the ratification of the Constitution, Shays' Rebellion, the Tripolitan War, the War of 1812, the beginnings of industrial and financial development, shipbuilding and the shipping industry, national and local politics in the 1830's and 1840's, musical life in New York in the 1830's, and American literary development in the early 1800's.

Expanding Frontiers, 1783 to 1893

The course of westward expansion from the Revolution to the closing of the American frontier in the 1890's offers the novelist a multitude of settings, periods, and characters from which to draw: simple tales of family life in a frontier cabin; heroic treks from the East to the wilderness of Western Pennsylvania, Ohio, Kentucky, and Tennessee; fur trade with the Indians and the founding of the cities on the Great Lakes and on the Ohio and Mississippi rivers; wagon trains pushing westward; the California gold rush; settlement of the plains states; and the development of the Old West. Daniel Boone, Buffalo Bill, General Custer, Aaron Burr, Marcus Whitman, William Bonney, Lewis and Clark, Abraham Lincoln, J. J. Hill, John Jacob Astor, Kit Carson, Santa Anna, David Crockett, and the Indians Pontiac, Sitting Bull, and Geronimo are among the many historical figures who appear in novels dealing with this phase of American history.

Eastern and Southern Frontiers

During the Colonial period the frontier was pushed slowly inland from the settlement along the Atlantic coast by hunters and fur traders, followed by settlers, until at the time of the Revolution the Appalachian Mountains had been breached; the Wautauga and Transylvania settlements had been made in Tennessee and Kentucky. George Rogers Clark's successful expedition against Hamilton in the Northwest Territory and the treaty setting the western boundary of the United States at the Mississippi River added impetus to the westward migration. However, frontier conditions did not cease to exist as the boundary of the frontier itself advanced. The New England states, and Western Pennsylvania and New York still had areas in which pioneer conditions existed in the mid-1800's. In the South, Florida, Georgia, the Mississippi Territory, and Louisiana furnish abundant sources for novels of frontier and pioneer life.

The Middle West

The settlement of the area comprising Ohio, Indiana, Illinois, Michigan, Wisconsin, Iowa, and Minnesota, has been treated in a large number of novels covering a wide range of time from the early settlements on the Ohio River to the immigration of Norwegians and Irish into Wisconsin and Minnesota in the 1870's.

The Southwest

The history of the American Southwest--Texas, New Mexico, Arizona, and Oklahoma--can be summed up in a relatively few subjects as far as historical fiction is concerned: the struggle for Texas' independence and the siege of the Alamo; the Mexican War; life along the Sante Fe Trail; conflict with the Indians, Indian life and customs; cattlemen versus homesteaders; and outlaws and characters.

California and the Pacific Northwest

California and Oregon became states in 1850 and 1858, respectively, thus being in the position of outposts separated from the rest of the United States by the Great American Desert, a vast expanse of mountains and plains considered unfit for white habitation, and it was to these outposts that pioneers looked for land to settle before turning to the plains for their rich soil and to the mountains for their rich mineral deposits. Episodes in the history of this region have been dealt with in novels centering around Spanish life and missionary activities in Mexico and California, the California gold rush and politics leading to statehood, the Lewis and Clark explorations, establishment of the early fur trading outposts and the settlement of Oregon, the British-American boundary dispute, and early Russian efforts to colonize the Northwest.

The Plains States and the Far West

The area west of the Mississippi River, consisting of the present states of Kansas, Nebraska, North and South Dakota, Colorado, Utah, Nevada, Wyoming, Montana, and Idaho were relatively late in being settled, but once started the process was fairly rapid. In the short space of fifty years was repeated the process of hunting and trapping, settling on new land, fighting the Indians and the hostile environment, and building communities where none had existed before. Themes which have appealed to historical novelists in this region are the pressing conflict with the Indians, life on the Oregon Trail, the daily life and hardships of the farmer-settlers of the plains, the mining boom and development of the mountain states, the migration and settling of the Mormons, homesteading and settling of the Indian lands, the Pony Express, and the extension of telegraph and railroad lines into the West.

The Civil War--Before and After

Among the novels dealing with the period of the Civil War are, of course, those which deal with specific battles and campaigns of the war and with the lives of military and government leaders on both sides. There is, however, a wide range of subject matter far removed from the battlefields. There are novels set against a background of the antebellum South, a South of manors, mammies, and mint juleps; novels of social life in the Eastern and Southern cities; stories of the abolitionist movement; stories of families, both North and South, torn between conflicting ideals and loyalties; and novels depicting the conflict between Southern sympathizers and those loyal to the Union in the struggle to influence the Western states. Blockade running and international diplomacy, spies, prison camps, and the activities of Copperheads furnish the motif for others. And there are novels dealing with the period of Reconstruction following the war. These novels are divided into the following sections: "The Old South," "Abolition," "The War Years, " and "Reconstruction."

The Old South

Life in the South before the Civil War, as reflected in the romantic school of historical fiction, was one of great plantations, loyal slaves, and a leisurely social life. During the 1930's and 1940's, a period during which there was a stream of reappraisals of Civil War history, a more complete picture of life in the South began to emerge. As a result of this revisionist trend, novelists took a fresh approach to the people of the South, concerning themselves with the pioneer-like daily existence of the small farmer, and the economic struggles of the planter and his relation with the Negroes.

Abolition

Novels of the abolitionist movement develop some exciting themes: the free-soil struggle for Kansas, John Brown's raid, the Underground Railroad, and the life and times of various real and fictitious leaders in the movement.

The War Years

Novels dealing with military and naval engagements range through the entire course of the war, from Fort Sumter to Appomattox, and through all phases of the conflict, from the drive down the Mississippi River to the final push against Richmond which culminated in Lee's surrender, anval warfare, and the plots to win the West over to one side or the other. No less important in the fictional literature of the period is the effect of the war on the home front. The occupation of the old plantation house by Yankee troops, conflicts in areas of neutrality, Copperhead activity in the North and in the West, the exciting life of spies on both side, the terrible conditions in prison camps, and the lives of political and military leaders are represented in novels of the Civil War.

Reconstruction

No less a part of the Civil War is its aftermath, the Reconstruction which followed. With few exceptions, the theme running through novels of this phase of history is the disintegration of an affluent mode of life and the rebuilding of a new South on the ashes of the old. The return of the soldier to his ruined plantation and his struggle to rebuild, the loyalty of the ex-slaves, political and social upheaval in the South aggravated by fanatic Southerners, insensitive occupation troops, carpetbaggers, the Ku Klux Klan, and the belligerence of some Negroes are threads running through these novels.

The Nation Grows Up, 1877 to 1917

The last decades of the nineteenth century and the first decade of the twentieth witnessed a major alteration in the manner of life in the United States. This changing social, political, and industrial scene is reflected in the background of novels set in the period from the end of the Civil War to World War I. The development of financial and industrial empires, the era of railroad expansion in the 1870's, the organization of labor and the growth of unions, local and national politics, the Spanish-American War, social life of the wealthy classes and life in the small town at the turn of the century, and such cultural themes as the birth of the movie industry, the assimilation of immigrants, Mormon life and customs, and the great world expositions held during the period are some of the subjects of novels in this group.

World War I

World War I is the first period in which the major events took place outside the United States. In addition to novels depicting actual warfare, however, there are novels based on the experiences of civilian noncombatants, nurses, telephone operators, ambulance drivers; novels depicting life in the training camps; stories of German spy activity and of anti-German feeling in American communities; novels dealing with the effects of the war on the home front; and novels dealing with politics before and during the war.

The Nineteen-Twenties

The United States during the decade of the twenties was characterized by an extravagance, a restlessness, and a lack of purpose which resulted in dramatic excesses, from the frantic boom in Florida real estate to the witch-hunting of the "red" scare. Several main themes predominate in the novels dealing with this period: the aftereffects of World War I; prohibition and gangsterism; further industrial expansion and the labor movement; mass hysteria and the red scare; life in the jazz age; and prosperity, speculation, and the market crash of 1929.

The Nineteen-Thirties

Novels dealing with the decade of the nineteen-thirties in United States history cover a wide range of dissimilar themes: The Depression and New Deal relief measures; labor union activity; the rise of Naziam and fascism and the approach of war; and contemporary family life in which one of the larger issues of the period is used as a background. Another theme unique to this period and closely related to the rise of fascism in its social implications deals with local politics and demagoguery, as exemplified, for example, by the rise to power of Huey Long in Louisiana.

World War II

United States participation in World War II has been covered in almost all its phases by the fiction dealing with that period of our history. In addition to novels concerned with specific battles and with naval warfare in both theaters, there are novels depicting various phases of the war on the home front and the plight of returning veterans. Among the themes developed in these novels are: American indifference to the war in Europe and the sharp reaction to the attack on Pearl Harbor; the treatment of Japanese-Americans in California internment camps; life in training camps and prisoner-of war camps; the role of women in the war effort; the effect of the war on civilian life--the fear of invasion, civil defense measures, rationing and price controls; and the efforts of returning veterans to find their place in life under changed conditions and attitudes.

The Tense Years--1945 to 1959

In the years following World War II a new phase of American history came into existence. Domestic and international crises erupted at the same time our complacency and standard of living rose to new heights. On the domestic scene the major force stimulating fiction of the period was the turmoil of the beginning of the fight for equal rights for the Negro. The voice of the conservative was heard again in the land, and is represented in fiction by novels based on the effects of the Congressional investigations and the fear aroused by the search for communists in our midst. This was just one aspect of our involvement in the Cold War, which has been used by novelists in a variety of settings: the interaction of U.S. servicemen and native populations in occupied countries all over the world; the Berlin Airlift; the Korean War; adventures behind the Iron Curtain; tales of spying and intrigue, and the operation of our diplomatic service in the tense spots around the world. Other novels set in this period deal with the character of the U.S. Senate, with the history of Alaska and Hawaii leading up to statehood, and the development of the United Nations.

The Turbulent Years--1960 to 1977

When Kennedy's inauguration opened the sixties the country was rich, powerful, and at peace. The catch phrases "Camelot" and "New Frontier" sounded a hopeful note. The violent shock of his assassination in 1963 was but the first of many that Americans would have to absorb in the years ahead. The Cold War eventually relaxed into détente, but the battles in Indochina would escalate to divide the country. The horror of the American experience in the Vietnam War is the somber theme of many novelists.

Others picked up other threads of discontent from the fabric of American life as the limits of power and growth became apparent. They wrote of the peaceful marches and movements that often ended in violence, as at Selma and Kent State; of the poverty and racism which provoked riots in Watts, Detroit, and Newark; of the 1968 assassinations of Robert Kennedy and Martin Luther King; of the unfolding scandals of Watergate that ended with the resignation of a president.

Minorities became militant in their demands for change, and novels showed the terrible inequities of life for the Black, the Chicano, and the American Indian. Environmentalists found a voice to decry the pollution of the environment that advanced with industrial and population growth. American women launched the fight to pass the Equal Rights Amendment. Some took a second look at their traditional role of wife and mother, found it stifling, and joined a sometimes-shrill Women's Liberation movement. And the young seemed bound to destroy every icon in the established pantheon. Many left home; some to be flower children in Haight-Ashbury; some to follow gurus of Eastern faiths strange to their fathers; some to seek expanded visions with drugs; and some to join hands in communes groping toward new Utopias.

But if novels illumined so many themes of dissatisfaction, they also recognized that ameliorating changes can occur in an open society, and writers joined in lauding the greatness in the history of the United States as her citizens enthusiastically celebrated the Bicentennial in 1976.

Chronicles

This group contains those novels which do not readily fall into a single chronological period of history; the epic stories which depict a whole slice of American life, or follow a family through generations, or tell the story of an individual whose life spanned several decades.

COLONIAL AMERICA TO 1775

1 Alderman, Clifford Lindsey. SILVER KEYS. Putnam, 1960. The adventures of William Phips in Boston, London, and the Caribbean before he became the first royal governor of Massachusetts under the charter of 1691.

2 Allen, Hervey. THE FOREST AND THE FORT. Farrar, 1943. The French and Indian War in the forests of Pennsylvania in the 1760's, and the founding of Fort Pitt.

3 ______. BEDFORD VILLAGE. Farrar, 1944. Picture of Pennsylvania frontier life from 1763 to 1764. Sequel to The Forest and the Fort.

4 ______. TOWARD THE MORNING. Rinehart, 1948. Life on the Pennsylvania frontier and in Philadelphia, 1764-1765. Sequel to Bedford Village.

5 Allis, Marguerite. NOT WITHOUT PERIL. Putnam, 1941. Pioneer hardships and folkways in the early settlement of Vermont.

6 Aswell, Mary Louise. ABIGAIL. Crowell, 1959. Background of colonial social and political life in Philadelphia in the story of a strong-willed woman who rebelled against her Quaker environment.

7 Bacheller, Irving. CANDLE IN THE WILDERNESS. Bobbs, 1930. Boston in stern colonial days; Reverend John Cotton, Sir Harry Vane, and others appear.

8 Barker, Shirley. PEACE, MY DAUGHTERS. Crown, 1949. Story of the witchcraft trials and persecutions in Salem in 1691.

9 ______. RIVERS PARTING. Crown, 1950. Settlement of New Hampshire, and the struggle with Massachusetts over control of the area.

10 ______. TOMORROW THE NEW MOON. Bobbs, 1955. Religious conflict in Puritan New England in the days of Cotton Mather in the early 1700's.

11 ______. SWEAR BY APOLLO. Random, 1958. Picture of

medical and social life in New Hampshire in the years leading up to the Revolution.

12 Barth, John. THE SOT-WEED FACTOR. Doubleday, 1960. A long, bawdy tale of many facets of life in colonial Maryland and England written in the style of the seventeenth-century novelists.

13 Borland, Barbara Dodge. THE GREATER HUNGER. Appleton, 1962. Story of hardship and romance in the life of the early Massachusetts Bay Colony.

14 Bowman, John Clarke. POWHATAN'S DAUGHTER. Viking, 1973. Historical romance traces the lives of Pocahontas and John Smith from her rescue of him in 1607 to her death in England in 1617. Based on Smith's narratives.

15 Boyce, Burke. MORNING OF A HERO. Harper, 1963. Picture of George Washington as a young man, surveying on the frontier, fighting in the French and Indian Wars, serving in the Virginia House of Burgesses, and bringing his bride home to Mount Vernon.

16 Breslin, Howard. THE SILVER OAR. Crowell, 1954. Story based on the revolt against Governor Andros in Boston in 1689, with Cotton Mather as one of the characters.

17 Buchan, John. SALUTE TO ADVENTURERS. Doran, 1917. Adventure tale of colonial Virginia in 1690.

18 Cannon, LeGrand. COME HOME AT EVEN. Holt, 1951. Story of four people who settle in the Puritan colony of Salem in the 1630's.

19 Cassel, Virginia. JUNIATA VALLEY. Viking, 1981. Shawnee and Mingo raid and harass settlers in western Pennsylvania during the French and Indian Wars. The forts are inadequate because the Quakers among the farmers refuse to finance war. Battle of Fort Duquesne.

20 Clark, Jean. UNTIE THE WINDS. Macmillan, 1976. This story of the early years of the New Haven, Connecticut colony centers on Anne Eaton, wife of the governor, whose religious inclinations did not fit the Puritan mold.

21 ________. MARRIAGE BED. Putnam, 1982. Dutch tenant farmers in the Hudson River valley are galled by the restrictions on their liberty under the manorial system. They organize under the leadership of William Prendergast to demand freedom.

22 Coatsworth, Elizabeth. SWORD OF THE WILDERNESS. Macmillan, 1936. Story of the French and Indian Wars in 1698 in New England.

23 Coleman, Terry. THANKSGIVING. Simon and Schuster, 1981. Wolsey Wheaton is left with two baby daughters when her husband, a Puritan intellectual, wanders into the wilderness outside the Massachusetts Bay Colony. She later moves to New Amsterdam. The lives of her adult children continue the story.

24 Colver, Alice. THE MEASURE OF THE YEARS. Dodd, 1954. Story of the white families who settled at Indian Town (later Stockbridge), Massachusetts during the French and Indian Wars. Pictures family life, religious controversy, and political events leading up to the Revolution.

25 _______. THERE IS A SEASON. Dodd, 1957. Picture of family life and frontier customs in Stockbridge, Massachusetts and Charles-Town, South Carolina from 1756 to 1770. Sequel to The Measure of the Years.

26 Cooper, James Fenimore. THE DEERSLAYER. Scribner, 1841. Story of warfare between the Iroquois Indians and white settlers around Lake Otsego, New York during King George's War, 1744. Followed by The Last of the Mohicans.

27 _______. THE LAST OF THE MOHICANS. Scribner, 1826. Story of wilderness warfare around Lake George, New York during the French and Indian Wars. Followed by The Pathfinder.

28 _______. THE PATHFINDER. Dodd, 1840. Tale of the French and Indian War in the area around Lake Ontario. Followed by The Pioneers.

29 _______. THE PIONEERS. Dodd, 1822. Pioneer life in the wilderness around Lake Otsego, New York in the years before the Revolution. Followed by The Prairie (Expanding Frontiers--Middle West).

30 Cooper, Kent. ANNA ZENGER, MOTHER OF FREEDOM. Farrar, 1946. Story of the first newspaper in New York and the first battle for freedom of the press, set against a background of life under the British governors.

31 Coryell, Hubert. INDIAN BROTHER. Harcourt, 1935. Adventures of a young colonist and his sister captured by the Indians; Maine in 1713.

32 _______. SCALP HUNTERS. Harcourt, 1936. Experiences of a young colonist and his Indian brother in Maine in the early 1700's.

33 Costain, Thomas B. HIGH TOWERS. Doubleday, 1949. Adventures of the LeMoyne brothers who explored the Mississippi River and founded New Orleans and Mobile in the early 1700's.

34 Cross, Ruth. SOLDIER OF GOOD FORTUNE. Banks Upshaw, 1936. Exploits of Louis de St. Denis on a trading expedition into Texas and Mexico for the French colony at Mobile in 1715.

35 Curwood, James Oliver. THE PLAINS OF ABRAHAM. Doubleday, 1928. Romance of the French and English Wars leading up to the capture of Quebec.

36 Davidson, L. S. THE DISTURBER. Macmillian, 1964. Story of Puritan persecution and the founding of Merry Mount by Thomas Morton.

37 Devon, John Anthony. O WESTERN WIND. Putnam, 1957. Story of the founding of Merry Mount and of its destruction by Miles Standish; emphasis on the bigotry and intolerance of the Puritans of the Pilgrim colony at Plymouth.

38 Dodge, Constance. IN ADAM'S FALL. Macrae, 1946. Story of the Salem witchcraft hysteria of the seventeenth century; recreates the life and spirit of the times.

39 Dowdey, Clifford. GAMBLE'S HUNDRED. Little, 1939. Tidewater Virginia around 1730; scene is mostly in Williamsburg.

40 Eaton, Evelyn. RESTLESS ARE THE SAILS. Harper, 1941. Historical romance centering around the fall of Louisburg in 1745.

41 _______. THE SEA IS SO WIDE. Harper, 1943. Story of French Acadians banished from their farmland in Nova Scotia during the French and English War who settle in the Southern colonies; pictures social life in Williamsburg.

42 Ethridge, Willie Snow. SUMMER THUNDER. Coward, 1959. Founding of Savannah and the early colonization of Georgia in the 1730's; picture of James Oglethorpe.

43 Farrar, Rowena Rutherford. BEND YOUR HEADS ALL. Holt, 1965. Emigration to Tennessee in 1770 and the settlement of Nashville, through the story of a pioneer family; pioneer life and Indian fighting before and during the Revolution.

44 Fletcher, Inglis. ROANOKE HUNDRED. Bobbs, 1948. Story of the first British settlement in America; scenes laid in England of Elizabethan time and in the wilderness of Roanoke Island, 1585-1586; Sir Richard Grenville, Walter Raleigh and others appear. Part of author's series on North Carolina history. (See other novels below and under "American Revolution" and "Young Nation.")

45 _______. BENNET'S WELCOME. Bobbs, 1950. Story of the first permanent settlement of North Carolina, still part of Virginia in 1651-1652.

46 ________. ROGUE'S HARBOR. Bobbs, 1964. North Carolina neighbors rebel against local British rule in 1677.

47 ________. MEN OF ALBEMARLE. Bobbs, 1942. The evolution of law and order in colonial North Carolina; 1710-1712.

48 ________. LUSTY WIND FOR CAROLINA. Bobbs, 1944. Story of the North Carolina plantation owners and of their attempts to establish communities and ward off pirates destroying their trade; 1718-1725.

49 ________. CORMORANT'S BROOD. Lippincott, 1959. Pictures the struggle of the colonists in the Albemarle region of North Carolina against their weak but greedy royal governors; 1725-1729.

50 ________. THE WIND IN THE FOREST. Bobbs, 1957. Story of the Regulators' Insurrection in North Carolina, an uprising of frontier farmers against the royal governor, William Tyron, and the Tidewater planters; ends in the Battle of Alamance in 1771.

51 Forbes, Esther. A MIRROR FOR WITCHES. Houghton, 1928. Amusing picture of a Massachusetts village during the witchcraft hysteria.

52 ________. PARADISE. Harcourt, 1937. Settlement of Canaan, near Boston, in the Massachusetts Bay Colony at the time of King Philip's War.

53 Fowler, Robert H. JASON MCGEE. Harper and Row, 1979. A family of settlers have lived in peace with the Pennsylvania Indians for many years; then sixteen-year-old Jason sees three strange tribesmen kill his mother and kidnap his brother. He and his father will make revenge their only purpose in life.

54 Frey, Ruby Frazier. RED MORNING. Putnam, 1946. Background of the struggle for the Ohio valley; warfare between Indians, French, and English in which George Washington began his career; Governor Dinwiddie, Franklin, and Braddock appear.

55 Fuller, Iola. THE GILDED TORCH. Putnam, 1957. Story of the explorations of LaSalle in the Great Lakes and Mississippi River areas and of his attempt to set up a French empire in America in the 1680's and 1690's.

56 Gebler, Ernest. PLYMOUTH ADVENTURE. Doubleday, 1950. Story of the Mayflower Pilgrims from Southampton across the Atlantic through the first few months on the New England coast.

57 Gerson, Noel B. THE HIGHWAYMAN. Doubleday, 1955. Story

built around the expedition against the French at Louisburg during the French and Indian War, 1744-1748.

58 _______. DAUGHTER OF EVE. Doubleday, 1958. Story of Captain John Smith and Pocahontas; picture of the life and customs of the Indians and the English in the early days of the Virginia colony at Jamestown.

59 _______. THE LAND IS BRIGHT. Doubleday, 1961. Portrait of William Bradford and the hardships of the first years of the Massachusetts Bay Colony.

60 _______. YANKEE DOODLE DANDY. Doubleday, 1965. Biographical novel of John Hancock, signer of the Declaration of Independence and governor of Massachusetts.

61 _______. GIVE ME LIBERTY. Doubleday, 1966. Biographical novel of the life of Patrick Henry.

62 Giles, Janice Holt. HANNAH FOWLER. Houghton, 1956. Story of pioneer settlers on the Kentucky River in the 1770's.

63 Gordon, Caroline. THE GREEN CENTURIES. Scribner, 1941. Pre-Revolutionary life in pioneer Kentucky and Tennessee; picture of the settlement of the Holston River area, and of the negotiations between the Indians and Judge Henderson.

64 Gould, John. NO OTHER PLACE. Norton, 1984. Lives of settlers in early Maine were complicated by the inadequate and sometimes fallacious land deeds issued by the rival English and French governments.

65 Hartog, Jan de. PEACEABLE KINGDOM. Atheneum, 1972. This tale of Quaker life opens in England in the seventeenth century, moves to Pennsylvania in the eighteenth century, where the Friends encounter slavery and Indian uprisings. They establish a settlement where for a time whites, blacks, and Indians live in harmony.

66 Hawthorne, Nathaniel. THE SCARLET LETTER. Dodd, 1850. Tale of sin and retribution in Puritan Boston.

67 Heidish, Marcy. WITNESSES. Houghton, 1980. Anne Hutchinson was twice tried for heresy in the Massachusetts Bay Colony in the 1630's. She eventually found freedom in Rhode Island. Mary Dyer, her friend in this novel, was hanged.

68 Houston, James. GHOST FOX. Harcourt, 1977. A young woman, kidnapped by Indians, moves from hatred and disgust to an appreciation of the culture; loves and marries one of her captors. Forcibly rescued and taken home, she soon escapes and returns to her Indian life.

69 Hughes, Rupert. STATELY TIMBER. Scribner, 1939. Life in Puritan New England and in Virginia and the Barbados Islands in the 1650's.

70 Jennings, John. NEXT TO VALOUR. Macmillan, 1939. Rogers' Rangers in New Hampshire during the French and Indian Wars; 1750's.

71 ________. GENTLEMAN RANKER. Reynal, 1942. Story of an English dandy tricked into joining Braddock's expedition against the French in 1755; settles in America and adapts to frontier life.

72 Johnston, Mary. CROATAN. Little, 1923. Story of the ill-fated Roanoke settlement in Virginia in 1587. Heroine is Virginia Dare.

73 ________. TO HAVE AND TO HOLD. Houghton, 1900. Story set in Virginia in 1621 centering on the first shipload of brides sent to the colony.

74 ________. PRISONERS OF HOPE. Houghton, 1898. Colonial life in Virginia centering on the deportation of convicts to the colony from England; 1649-1651.

75 ________. THE SLAVE SHIP. Little, 1924. Story of the colonial slave trade; 1660's.

76 ________. THE GREAT VALLEY. Little, 1926. Virginia before and during the French and Indian Wars; 1737-1759.

77 Jordon, Mildred. ONE RED ROSE FOREVER. Knopf, 1941. Pennsylvania of the mid-1700's; hero is Baron Stiegel, the German immigrant who became known as the maker of Stiegel glass.

78 King, Grace. LA DAME DE SAINTE HERMINE. Macmillan, 1924. Story of the settlement of New Orleans by Pierre LeMoyne in 1718.

79 Kotker, Zane. WHITE RISING. Knopf, 1981. Two sections of this book examine the motivation and battle style of Metacomet, the Wampanoag chief who waged war against the New England colonists in 1675 and 1676. The third section shows the settlers' side of King Philip's War.

80 Lide, Alice. DARK POSSESSION. Appleton, 1934. Charles-Town, South Carolina in the early 1700's; a tale of slaves and indentured servants, Indian wars, sorcery, and passion.

81 Lincoln, Victoria. A DANGEROUS INNOCENCE. Rinehart, 1958. Life in Salem, Massachusetts at the time of the witchcraft trials.

82 Linderholm, Helmer. LAND OF THE BEAUTIFUL RIVER. St. Martin's, 1963. Recollections of life in Peter Stuyvesant's settlement of New Amsterdam and adventures among the Susquehanna Indians.

83 Lofts, Norah. BLOSSOM LIKE THE ROSE. Knopf, 1939. Romance of a young Scotsman who joins a band of religious fanatics, sails to America, and battles Indians and Puritan intolerance.

84 Longstreet, Stephen. WAR IN THE GOLDEN WEATHER. Doubleday, 1965. French and Indian War in the 1750's and its effect on the Dutch settlers in New York State; characters are a young Dutch painter and Major George Washington as a young surveyor. Followed by <u>Eagles Where I Walk</u> (American Revolution).

85 Lovelace, Maud Hart. CHARMING SALLY. Day, 1932. Story of the first theatrical company to come to America; picture of brilliant social life in Virginia and more sedate Quaker life in Philadelphia in 1752.

86 McFarland, Philip. SEASONS OF FEAR. Schocken, 1983. Story is based on a historical incident of 1741, when rabid overreaction to a petty robbery in New York City led to the deaths of thirty-four blacks.

87 Malvern, Gladys. ERIC'S GIRLS. Messner, 1949. New Amsterdam, the Dutch city of Peter Stuyvesant at the time of the English siege and capture.

88 Mann, Helen. GALLANT WARRIOR. William B. Eerdmans, 1954. Fictionized biography of Hannah Duston, pioneer wife and mother who, with her baby and its nurse, was captured by Indians in 1697.

89 Marsh, George. ASK NO QUARTER. Morrow, 1945. Newport, Rhode Island at the end of the seventeenth century; reconstructs the speech and details of daily life of the period.

90 Marshall, Edison. THE LOST COLONY. Doubleday, 1964. Recreation of the fate of the settlers on Roanoke Island; based on the thesis that thdy fled to Florida to escape an Indian massacre and were assimilated into a friendly Indian tribe.

91 Mason, F. Van Wyck. THE YOUNG TITAN. Doubleday, 1959. Story of the hazards of frontier living during the French and Indian Wars; scenes set in Boston, in Bartholomey Mayhew's settlement on the Penobscot River, and on the wilderness march against Louisburg in 1745.

92 ________. THE SEA 'VENTURE. Doubleday, 1961. Story of the early years of Jamestown and the first colony in Bermuda.

93 ________. RASCALS' HEAVEN. Doubleday, 1964. Story of the settling of Georgia by General James Oglethorpe and of the colony's early enemies, the Indians, and the Spanish settlement at St. Augustine.

94 Matschat, Cecile Hulse. TAVERN IN THE TOWN. Farrar, 1942. A romance of plantation life in colonial Virginia.

95 Miers, Earl Schenck. VALLEY IN ARMS. Westminster, 1943. Clearing the land and fighting Indians in a Connecticut valley in the 1630's.

96 Miller, Helen Topping. DARK SAILS. Bobbs, 1945. Oglethorpe's colonization of Georgia in the 1730's and 1740's.

97 Moore, Ruth. A FAIR WIND HOME. Morrow, 1953. Story of Nathan Ellis of Massachusetts, Francis Carnavon of Cork, and Maynard Cantril, a shipbuilder of Somerset, Maine before the Revolution.

98 Murphy, Edward. A BRIDE FOR NEW ORLEANS. Hanover, 1955. Historical romance of the Casket girls sent to New Orleans from Paris in 1727 to marry and to help settle Louisiana.

99 Newton, John Edward. THE ROGUE AND THE WITCH. Abelard, 1955. Story of religious conflict between Puritans and Quakers in Boston, involving the Salem witchcraft trials; Increase Mather is one of the characters.

100 Oemler, Marie. THE HOLY LOVER. Boni and Liveright, 1927. Story of John Wesley, dealing with the three years he spent in the Georgia colony, 1735-1738; based on journals and letters from the period.

101 Page, Elizabeth. WILDERNESS ADVENTURE. Rinehart, 1946. A tale of the rescue of a young girl captured by Indians; rescuers follow her from Virginia to the Mississippi River, to New Orleans, and on to France and England.

102 Paradise, Jean. THE SAVAGE CITY. Crown, 1955. Story of colonial New York, based on the hysteria caused by a servant girl's tale of a Negro-Spanish plot to massacre the whites in the city.

103 Parker, Sir Gilbert. THE POWER AND THE GLORY. Harper, 1925. Achievements of LaSalle as pioneer and explorer; a novel of early Canadian and American history.

104 Peck, Robert Newton. FAWN. Little, 1975. Historically accurate novel about a French-Mohawk lad at Fort Ticonderoga during the French and Indian War. The young Benedict Arnold appears.

105 Pendexter, Hugh. WIFE-SHIP WOMAN. Bobbs, 1926. Louisiana and Virginia in the early 1700's; heroine is one of the Casket girls sent from France to be the wives of men in the Louisiana colony at New Orleans in 1727.

106 _______. THE RED ROAD. Bobbs, 1927. Tale of Braddock's defeat during the French and Indian War, 1754-1763.

107 Phillips, Alexandra. FOREVER POSSESS. Dutton, 1946. Picture of life on the feudal estates on the Hudson River in New York in the seventeenth century at the time of an uprising among the tenants.

108 Pinckney, Josephine. HILTON HEAD. Farrar, 1941. Story of the tribulations of a young doctor in South Carolina in the 1600's.

109 Pound, Arthur. THE HAWK OF DETROIT. Reynal, 1939. The founding of Detroit, and conflicting interests in the government monopoly of trade; Chief Cadillac is one of the characters.

110 Rees, Gilbert. I SEEK A CITY. Dutton, 1950. Fictional autobiography of Roger Williams, from his early life in England, his voyage to the colonies, his work as a minister in Salem, Massachusetts, his founding of Providence, Rhode Island, and his understanding of the Indians.

111 Richter, Conrad. FREE MAN. Knopf, 1943. Story of a young emigrant from the Palatinate who sought political freedom among the Pennsylvania-Dutch.

112 _______. THE LIGHT IN THE FOREST. Knopf, 1953. Settlers and Indians in Pennsylvania and Ohio at the time of Bouquet's expedition to free the captives of the Tuscaroras Indians in 1765. Followed by A Country of Strangers (Expanding Frontiers--Eastern).

113 Ritchie, Cicero T. THE WILLING MAID. Abelard, 1958. Boston and Nova Scotia during the French and Indian War; climax comes at the fall of Louisburg; 1740's.

114 Roberts, Kenneth L. NORTHWEST PASSAGE. Doubleday, 1937. Major Robert Rogers, and his expedition against the Indians of St. Francis in 1759. His dream was to find an overland passage to the Pacific.

115 _______. BOON ISLAND. Doubleday, 1956. Story of the harrowing experience of the survivors of a shipwreck on an island near Portsmouth, New Hampshire in 1710.

116 Rushing, Jane Gilmore. COVENANT OF GRACE. Doubleday, 1982. Anne Hutchinson is banished from the Bay Colony in

1637 for heresy. The title refers to the philosophical argument, opposed by the "covenant of works," which figured in her trials. See also Witnesses by Heidish.

117 Safford, Henry B. TRISTRAM BENT. Coward, 1940. Hero is an English agent sent to spy on the Dutch colonies in 1640; accurate historical details of the period and place.

118 Salvato, Sharon. FIRES OF JULY. Dell, 1983. The Manning family on their indigo plantation in South Carolina from 1767. The "Regulators" stir trouble, and the Revolution is near at the end of the story.

119 Sass, Herbert R. EMPEROR BRIMS. Doubleday, 1941. The Yemassee War in South Carolina in 1715; uprising of the Creek Indian Confederacy against the white settlements on the coast.

120 Schachner, Nathan. THE KING'S PASSENGER. Lippincott, 1942. Colonial Virginia at the time of Bacon's Rebellion and the burning of Jamestown in 1676.

121 Seifert, Shirley. RIVER OUT OF EDEN. M. S. Mill, 1940. Trip up the Mississippi River, from New Orleans to the settlement later known as St. Louis, in 1763; pictures political and economic rivalries on the frontier.

122 Seton, Anya. THE WINTHROP WOMAN. Houghton, 1958. Story of the Massachusetts Bay Colony and Connecticut, based on the life of Governor John Winthrop's niece; an account of life in early Boston.

123 ________. DEVIL WATER. Houghton, 1962. Biographical novel about the Radcliffe family and William Byrd of Westover in eighteenth century Virginia and England.

124 Settle, Mary Lee. O BEULAH LAND. Viking, 1956. Pictures the hardships of a group of Virginia settlers in the wilderness beyond the Allegheny Mountains and their struggles with the French and Indians; 1754-1774.

125 Simms, William Gilmore. THE YEMASSEE. American Book, 1835. Colonial expansion seen from the viewpoint of the Indians; story of the events leading up to the Yemassee War in South Carolina in the early 1700's.

126 Simons, Katherine. ALWAYS A RIVER. Appleton, 1956. Story of the clash of temperaments between a Puritan schoolmaster, who leaves Massachusetts during the witchcraft hysteria, and the French Huguenots in the Carolinas in 1695.

127 ________. THE LAND BEYOND THE TEMPEST. Coward, 1960. Story of a hazardous voyage from England to colonial Jamestown, Virginia.

128 Singmaster, Elsie. A HIGH WIND RISING. Houghton, 1942. Story of life in a Pennsylvania German-Dutch settlement at the time of the French and Indian War; based on the life of Conrad Weiser and his relations with the Indians.

129 Smith, Arthur Douglas. THE DOOM TRAIL. Brentano, 1922. Story built on the struggle for supremacy in the fur trade between the French and the English.

130 Snedeker, Caroline. UNCHARTED WAYS. Doubleday, 1935. Based on the life of Mary Dyer, a Quaker convert in Boston in the 1650's; pictures the religious tension of the period, and John Cotton's persecution of the Quakers.

131 Speare, Elizabeth. THE PROSPERING. Houghton, 1967. Story of the settling of Stockbridge, Massachusetts in the early 1700's by young missionary John Sergeant whose dream was to integrate the Indians and whites.

132 Stanford, Alfred B. THE NAVIGATOR. Morrow, 1927. Biography of Nathaniel Bowditch, creator of The American Practical Navigator, in Salem in the 1770's.

133 Stone, Grace Zaring. THE COLD JOURNEY. Morrow, 1934. Story of the 1704 raid on Deerfield, Massachusetts by French and Indians and the long journey of the captives to Quebec; contrasts life and manners of the French and the Puritans.

134 Stover, Herbert. SONG OF THE SUSQUEHANNA. Dodd, 1949. Story of a Pennsylvania-German's battle with Indians during the French and Indian War; Gouverneur Morris, John Bartram, and Conrad Weiser appear in the story.

135 Stowman, Knud. WITH CRADLE AND CLOCK. Harper, 1946. Struggles of a young doctor to establish an obstetrical practice in New York in 1702; background of New York social life and customs.

136 Sublette, Clifford. SCARLET COCKEREL. Little, 1925. Historical romance based on the French Huguenot colonization of the Carolinas in the 1690's.

137 ______. THE BRIGHT FACE OF DANGER. Little, 1926. Life in Henrico County, Virginia in the days of Bacon's Rebellion; 1676.

138 Swann, Lois. THE MISTS OF MANITOO. Scribner, 1976. The daughter of a wealthy landowner falls in love with the Indian who rescues her as she wanders lost and ill in the forest.

139 ______. TORN COVENANTS. Scribner, 1981. Romantic tragedy set in colonial Massachusetts. Elizabeth Dowland

marries the Indian Wakwa, but a conspiracy of his enemies force their separation. Sequel to The Mists of Manitoo.

140 Swanson, Neil. THE JUDAS TREE. Putnam, 1933. Pittsburgh besieged by the Indians during the Pontiac Conspiracy of 1763.

141 _______. THE FIRST REBEL. Farrar, 1937. Story of the uprising of the Scotch-Irish in Pennsylvania, led by James Smith against the British, and of Smith's capture by the Indians; 1763-1767.

142 _______. THE SILENT DRUM. Farrar, 1940. Life on the Pennsylvania frontier during the pre-Revolutionary period.

143. _______. THE UNCONQUERED. Doubleday, 1947. Story of the Pontiac Conspiracy of 1763 in the Ohio River region of the Pennsylvania frontier.

144 Van Every, Dale. BRIDAL JOURNEY. Messner, 1950. Story of life in the Ohio River valley when Indians, English, and Americans were fighting for the frontier lands prior to the Revolution.

145 Vaughan, Carter A (pseud.). THE INVINCIBLES. Doubleday, 1958. Financial scheming and frontier warfare during the French and Indian Wars, set in and around Boston and in the wilderness on the expedition against Louisburg; 1744-1745.

146 _______. THE SILVER SABER. Doubleday, 1967. Swash-buckling romance of an indentured servant in colonial Dela-ware and in Quebec.

147. _______. THE SENECA HOSTAGE. Doubleday, 1969. Life and adventures on the American frontier and as captive of the Seneca Indians in 1753.

148 White, Ethel. BEAR HIS MILD YOKE. Abingdon, 1966. Per-secution of the Quakers pictured in the story of Mary Dyer, a Quaker convert, who was hanged in Massachusetts in 1660; social and religious customs.

149 Widdemer, Margaret. LADY OF THE MOHAWKS. Doubleday, 1951. Story of French and English rivalry in the Mohawk Valley; the heroine is Molly Brant, who became the wife of Sir William Johnson, English Indian Commissioner.

150 _______. THE GOLDEN WILDCAT. Doubleday, 1954. His-torical romance depicting the struggle between British and French for the loyalty of the Mohawk and Iroquois Indians in upstate New York in the 1750's.

151 _______. BUCKSKIN BARONET. Doubleday, 1960. Story

of an English traveler in and around Albany, New York on the eve of the Revolution; picture of Indian customs and the political intrigues of the time.

152 Wilson, Dorothy Clarke. LADY WASHINGTON. Doubleday, 1984. Story of Martha Washington, first married at age eighteen to her godfather, Daniel Custis. Later, as a young widow, she marries George Washington, then commander of the Virginia militia.

153 Winwar, Frances. GALLOWS HILL. Holt, 1937. Story of early times in old Salem, chiefly concerned with the religious frenzy which took possession of the colony leading to the witchcraft trials and hangings; Cotton Mather appears.

154 Worsencroft, Mona Esty. AN ECHO FROM SALEM. Northwoods Press, 1981. A tale of Salem witch-hunting madness, written by a descendant of Mary Esty, hung on Gallows Hill after being accused by a feuding neighbor.

155 Zara, Louis. BLESSED IS THE LAND. Crown, 1954. Set in the days of Peter Stuyvesant when the first Jewish settlers came from Brazil to settle in New Amsterdam; picture of Jewish customs, language, and religion in the colonial period.

THE AMERICAN REVOLUTION

156 Allen Merrit Parmalee. BATTLE LANTERNS. Longmans, 1949. Exploits of Francis Marion, the Swamp Fox, and the war in South Carolina.

157 Arnow, Harriette Simpson. THE KENTUCKY TRACE. Knopf, 1974. A surveyor, an early settler in the Kentucky forest, returns from battle to find his farm deserted, and searches for his missing family.

158 Bacheller, Irving. IN THE DAYS OF POOR RICHARD. Bobbs, 1922. Shows the work of Franklin in the colonies, in England, and in France; comprehensive picture of the Revolution.

159 _______. MASTER OF CHAOS. Bobbs, 1932. Early days of the Revolution; George Washington and others appear.

160 Barker, Shirley. FIRE AND THE HAMMER. Crown, 1953. Story of Quaker outlaws in Bucks County, Pennsylvania harassing the Revolutionists.

161 _______. THE LAST GENTLEMAN. Random, 1960. Story of the conflicts facing the colonial-born Sir John Wentworth, royal governor of New Hampshire in 1774; climax comes when he sends aid to General Gage in Boston in 1775.

162 _______. THE ROAD TO BUNKER HILL. Duell, 1962. Two girls and their grandmother witness events leading up to the Battle of Bunker Hill.

163 _______. STRANGE WIVES. Crown, 1963. Life in the Jewish settlement at Newport, Rhode Island; persecution and hardship suffered before George Washington promised freedom of religion to the Jews.

164 Barry, Jane. THE CAROLINIANS. Doubleday, 1959. A Loyalist family in South Carolina becomes involved in the war when they help one of General Dan Morgan's men; action includes the battles of Cowpens and King's Mountain.

165 _______. THE LONG MARCH. Appleton, 1955. Portrait of General Dan Morgan in the campaign culminating in the Battle of Cowpens.

166 Beebe, Elswyth Thane. DAWN'S EARLY LIGHT. Duell, 1943.

The Carolina campaigns of the war, and politics and society in Williamsburg; 1774-1779.

167 Benét, Stephen Vincent. SPANISH BAYONET. Doran, 1926. Adventure tale set in New York and Spanish Florida at the time of the Revolution.

168 Beverley-Giddings, Arthur Raymond. THE RIVAL SHORES. Morrow, 1956. Story of an Englishman sent to the colonies to aid the escape of Loyalists from Tidewater Maryland in 1774.

169 Boyce, Burke. THE PERILOUS NIGHT. Viking, 1942. The war as it affected the prosperous Hudson River valley farmers, with firm convictions of loyalty either to king or to the colonies.

170 _______. MAN FROM MT. VERNON. Harper, 1961. Personal and family life of George Washington from his appointment as commander-in-chief of the Continental army to the surrender of the British at Yorktown.

171 Boyd, James. DRUMS. Scribner, 1925. The war in the southern colonies; John Paul Jones, generals Dan Morgan and Tarleton appear.

172 Boyd, Thomas Alexander. SHADOW OF THE LONG KNIVES. Scribner, 1928. Story of the Ohio frontier during the Revolution.

173 Brick, John. THE RAID. Farrar, 1951. The Mohawk chief Joseph Brant, leading his tribe in raids against the settlers in upstate New York.

174 _______. THE RIFLEMAN. Doubleday, 1953. Story of Tim Murphy, one of Morgan's riflemen, and of his grudge against the Indians; description of the Battle of Saratoga.

175 _______. THE KING'S RANGERS. Doubleday, 1954. Story of Butler's Rangers and Loyalists in the western Mohawk valley area of New York.

176 _______. STRONG MEN. Doubleday, 1959. Story of a company of rangers with Washington at Valley Forge in the winter of 1777-1778, and of Baron von Steuben's efforts to mold the survivors into an effective army.

177 Bristow, Gwen. CELIA GARTH. Crowell, 1959. Story of an orphan girl, who witnessed the siege of Charleston by the British and became a spy for the rebels during the occupation of the city; description of the fighting between General Tarleton and Francis Marion's raiders.

178 Cannon, LeGrand. LOOK TO THE MOUNTAIN. Holt, 1942. Frontier days in New Hampshire just before and after the Revolution.

179 Chambers, Robert W. CARDIGAN. Harper, 1901. First of a series of novels of frontier life in upstate New York, relations with the British and the Indians before and during the war, and life in New York City during the war; 1774 to 1782.

180 _______. MAID-AT-ARMS. Harper, 1902. Part of the author's New York series. See above.

181 _______. HIDDEN CHILDREN. Appleton, 1914. One of the author's New York novels. See above.

182 _______. LITTLE RED FOOT. Doran, 1921. Indian warfare in northeastern New York; 1774-1782.

183 _______. THE PAINTED MINX. Appleton, 1930. Life in New York City during the war; 1777-1781. See Cardigan above.

184 Chapman, Maristan (pseud.). ROGUE'S MARCH. Lippincott, 1949. Skirmishing in western Carolina and Tennessee, culminating in the Battle of King's Mountain in 1780.

185 Chidsey, Donald Barr. THE EDGE OF PIRACY. Crown, 1964. New England sea captain, impressed into service aboard a British man-of-war, escapes and takes up smuggling in the West Indies.

186 Churchill, Winston. RICHARD CARVEL. Macmillan, 1899. Set in Maryland and London before and during the Revolution. Hero fights with John Paul Jones in the battle between the Bonhomme Richard and the Serapis.

187 _______. THE CROSSING. Macmillan, 1904. Life on the Kentucky frontier during the Revolution; George Rogers Clark's expedition against Vincennes and Kaskaskia; life in early Louisville; and a picture of New Orleans during an epidemic.

188 Clague, Maryhelen. BEYOND THE SHINING RIVER. Coward, 1980. Accurate historical depiction of revolutionary New York City. An orphan girl is raised in a well-to-do Westchester family. Families and friends divide as the Revolution begins.

189 Coatsworth, Elizabeth. A TOAST TO THE KING. Coward, 1940. Boston at the time of the Boston Tea Party, seen from the Loyalists' viewpoint.

190 Cooper, James Fenimore. THE SPY. Dodd, 1821. Story of conflicting loyalties in New York City and the Hudson valley.

191 ______. THE PILOT. Dodd, 1824. Story of John Paul Jones and naval warfare during the Revolution.

192 ______. THE RED ROVER. Putnam, 1827. An adventure story of a former pirate fighting for his country during the Revolution.

193 Cormack, Maribelle, and William P. Alexander. LAND FOR MY SONS. Appleton, 1939. A surveyor and wilderness scout on the Pennsylvania frontier sees action as a member of the local militia when war breaks out.

194 Davis, Burke. THE RAGGED ONES. Rinehart, 1951. Southern campaign of 1781 with generals Morgan and Nathanael Greene engaging the forces under Cornwallis.

195 ______. YORKTOWN. Rinehart, 1952. Portrait of Washington, Lafayette, Clinton, and Cornwallis in the campaign leading up to Cornwallis' surrender at Yorktown.

196 Davis, Ellen. CLOUDS OF DESTINY. Putnam, 1978. A Connecticut smuggler tries to profit from the conflict between Patriot and Tory, but as the fighting intensifies, he will join those fighting for independence.

197 Davis, Mildred and Katherine. LUCIFER LAND. Random, 1977. Graphic portrayal of the horrors of war for Cassie Bedham and her family, at the mercy of British raiders in upstate New York.

198 Davis, William Stearns. GILMAN OF REDFORD. Macmillan, 1927. Story of Boston and Harvard College on the eve of the Revolution, 1770-1775; pictures life and customs in town and country, and revolves around famous men and events of the period; Paul Revere, Samuel Adams, and others appear.

199 Decker, Malcolm. THE REBEL AND THE TURNCOAT. McGraw, 1949. A young colonist torn between loyalty to the British and the American cause chooses sides with the help of Nathan Hale.

200 Dodge, Constance. DARK STRANGER. Penn, 1940. Son of Scotch settlers fights under John Paul Jones on the Bonhomme Richard.

201 Eaton, Evelyn. GIVE ME YOUR GOLDEN HAND. Farrar, 1951. Eighteenth-century England and America; events leading up to the Revolution are seen through the eyes of the hero who comes to the colonies as a bonded servant during the Revolution.

202 Edmonds, Walter D. DRUMS ALONG THE MOHAWK. Little, 1936. Effects of the Revolution on the farmers of the Mohawk valley in upstate New York; 1776-1784.

203 _______. WILDERNESS CLEARING. Dodd, 1944. Story of conflict and divided loyalties in the Mohawk valley in 1777.

204 _______. IN THE HANDS OF THE SENECAS. Little, 1947. Indian warfare on the frontier in 1778; story of the captivity of a group of children held by the Senecas.

205 Ellsberg, Edward. CAPTAIN PAUL. Dodd, 1941. John Paul Jones, from his days as a privateer to the engagement with the Serapis.

206 Erskine, John. GIVE ME LIBERTY. Stokes, 1940. Patrick Henry, George Washington, and Thomas Jefferson appear in a story of a young Virginian, from 1759 to the outbreak of the Revolution.

207 Fast, Howard. CONCEIVED IN LIBERTY. Simon and Schuster, 1939. Alexander Hamilton, von Steuben, Valley Forge; picture of the contrast between the ragged soldiers and the wealthy aristocrats in the Continental army.

208 _______. THE UNVANQUISHED. Duell, 1942. Portrays Washington, Knox, Putnam, Greene, and Hamilton and their part in the fight for freedom, from the retreat from Brooklyn to the crossing of the Delaware and the Battle of Trenton.

209 _______. CITIZEN TOM PAINE. Duell, 1943. Portrait of Tom Paine as a rabble-rouser.

210 _______. THE PROUD AND THE FREE. Little, 1950. Based on a revolt in the Continental army against injustices by the officers of the Pennsylvania militia.

211 _______. APRIL MORNING. Crown, 1961. Experiences of a 15-year-old farm boy in the battles of Lexington and Concord; April, 1775.

212 _______. THE HESSIAN. Morrow, 1972. Connecticut militia seek to try a young Hessian drummer boy for a war crime he was not responsible for. His is helped in hiding by the Quaker community, but in the end they cannot save him from the vindictive militiamen.

213 Fleming, Thomas J. LIBERTY TAVERN. Doubleday, 1976. Partisan passions run high in the neighborhood of a tavern on the road from Philadelphia to Perth Amboy.

214 Fletcher, Inglis. RALEIGH'S EDEN. Bobbs, 1940. Life in North Carolina from 1765 to 1782; part of the author's series

on the history of North Carolina (Colonial America and The Young Nation).

215 _______. TOIL OF THE BRAVE. Bobbs, 1946. The Albemarle district of North Carolina in the last years of the war, 1779-1780.

216 _______. THE SCOTSWOMAN. Bobbs, 1954. Flora Macdonald, who rescued Bonnie Prince Charlie after the Battle of Culloden, settles in the Carolinas and becomes involved in the American Revolution.

217 Flood, Charles Bracelen. MONMOUTH. Houghton, 1961. Story of events leading up to the Battle of Monmouth; some characters are George Washington, Alexander Hamilton, and generals Howe, Pulaski, and Lafayette.

218 Forbes, Esther. THE GENERAL'S LADY. Harcourt, 1938. Girl of a New England Tory family marries a rebel general to save her family's fortune, then falls in love with a British officer.

219 _______. JOHNNY TREMAIN. Houghton, 1943. Boston at the beginning of the Revolution; the Boston Tea Party, the Battle of Lexington; young hero is a courier for the rebel Committee of Public Safety.

220 Ford, Paul Leicester. JANICE MEREDITH. Dodd, 1899. Beginning in New Jersey in 1774, this spans the years of the Revolution and includes a picture of the character of George Washington.

221 Forman, James. COW NECK REBELS. Farrar, 1969. One colonial family faces the Revolution in different ways. The grandfather welcomes it, the mother is a pacifist, the father runs from it; one son sees himself as a swashbuckling hero, the second doubts his own courage but proves truly brave in the Battle of Long Island.

222 Fox, John. ERSKINE DALE, PIONEER. Scribner, 1920. Life on the Virginia and Kentucky frontier at the time of the Revolution.

223 Frye, Pearl. GALLANT CAPTAIN. Little, 1956. Story of John Paul Jones, from his days as an obscure British ship commander to being the hero of the American navy; authentic picture of the times.

224 Gerson, Noel B. I'LL STORM HELL. Doubleday, 1967. Life and career of General "Mad Anthony" Wayne.

225 _______. THE SWAMP FOX. Doubleday, 1967. Life of Francis Marion, the Swamp Fox, fighting the Cherokee

Indians and leading his guerrilla band in the battle for the Carolinas; scenes in Charleston, Boston, and Philadelphia.

226 Gessner, Robert. TREASON. Scribner, 1944. Fictional biography of Benedict Arnold.

227 Giles, Janice Holt. THE KENTUCKIANS. Houghton, 1953. Story of pioneer Kentucky when the Transylvania Company was agitating for separate statehood; 1769-1777.

228 Gordon, Charles William. THE REBEL LOYALIST. Dodd, 1935. Story of a Loyalist who fought on the side of the British in the war, and afterward took his bride to Canada.

229 Graves, Robert. SERGEANT LAMB'S AMERICA. Random, 1940. Experiences of an English soldier in the early years of the war.

230 _______. PROCEED, SERGEANT LAMB. Random, 1941. English soldier's experiences as a prisoner, his escape, service under Cornwallis, and the surrender at Yorktown. Sequel to Sergeant Lamb's America.

231 Gray, Elizabeth Janet. MEGGY MacINTOSH. Doubleday, 1930. Story of a young Scotch girl who joins Flora Macdonald in North Carolina in 1775.

232 _______. THE VIRGINIA EXILES. Lippincott, 1955. Story of the exile of a group of Philadelphia Quakers to Virginia when they refuse to sign a loyalty oath.

233 Green, Gerald. MURFY'S MEN. Seaview, 1981. The First Rhode Island Regiment, composed of freed slaves under the leadership of the Irish Murfy, defeats the Hessians at Barrington Hill.

234 Grey, Zane. BETTY ZANE. Grosset, 1903. Tale of hardships of life beyond the Allegheny Mountains on the Virginia frontier; fights with the Indians and the destruction of the settlement during the Revolution.

235 Groh, Lynn. CULPER SPY RING. Westminster, 1969. Story about the first intelligence service of the American army. "Culper, senior" and "Culper, junior" were spies, aided by a mysterious "lady," who pried secrets from Major André and other British officers, and who died without ever revealing her name.

236 Haines, Edwin. THE EXQUISITE SIREN. Lippincott, 1938. Historical novel about Peggy Shippen, Tory wife of Benedict Arnold, and her relations with Major André.

237 Haislip, Harvey. SAILOR NAMED JONES. Doubleday, 1957.

Story of John Paul Jones and of his financial difficulties and lack of support from the government; vivid re-creation of naval warfare, culminating in the battle of the Bonhomme Richard and the Serapis.

238 _______. THE PRIZE MASTER. Doubleday, 1959. Story of sea warfare during the Revolution through the adventures of a young seaman introduced in Sailor Named Jones (above).

239 _______. SEA ROAD TO YORKTOWN. Doubleday. 1960. Further adventures of the hero of The Prize Master (above) as a privateer and on duty with the fleet of Admiral de Grasse in Chesapeake Bay, blocking Cornwallis' escape from Yorktown.

240 Harris, Cyril TRUMPET AT DAWN. Scribner, 1938. New York social life and politics, 1776-1783.

241 _______. RICHARD PRYNE. Scribner, 1941. Story of a spy for General Washington in and around New York City.

242 Henri, Florette. KINGS MOUNTAIN. Doubleday, 1950. Story of the war in the southern colonies; Battle of Kings Mountain, South Carolina in 1780.

243 Hine, Al. BROTHER OWL. Doubleday, 1980. A novel in the form of the memoirs of Joseph Brant, the Mohawk Indian who helped the British fight. He also translated the Episcopal Book of Common Prayer into the Mohawk language, and traveled to London.

244 Hodge, Jane Aiken. JUDAS FLOWERING. Coward, 1976. The heroine and her father arrive in America in 1774. He is killed by a mob, but she is rescued and taken to Savannah, where she becomes a pamphleteer for the Patriot cause.

245 Hopkins, Joseph G. E. PATRIOT'S PROGRESS. Scribner, 1961. A Harvard-educated physician in a rural Massachusetts village is won over to the rebel cause while serving as a surgeon for the Continental militia at Lexington, Concord, and the siege of Boston.

246 _______. RETREAT AND RECALL. Scribner, 1966. Story of an American surgeon who is captured by the British, escapes from prison and becomes a secret agent operating in New York. Sequel to Patriot's Progress.

247 _______. PRICE OF LIBERTY. Scribner, 1976. An American surgeon cares for the many casualties of the Battle of Brandywine. The rapid spread of infectious disease among the wounded increases the horror. Sequel to Retreat and Recall.

248 Horan, James David. THE KING'S REBEL. Crown, 1953. Story of a British officer sent to study the Indians; captured

by the backwoodsmen, he comes to know them and joins their cause.

249 Horne, Howard. CONCORD BRIDGE. Bobbs, 1952. Story of the events preceding the battles of Lexington and Concord; sympathetic portrait of General Gage, commander of the English forces at Boston.

250 Hough, Frank Olney. RENOWN. Lippincott, 1938. Sympathetic account of Benedict Arnold, showing him as a brillant, extravagant, and frustrated man of action.

251 ________. IF NOT VICTORY. Lippincott, 1939. The war from the viewpoint of the common man; setting is the Hudson River valley of New York.

252 ________. THE NEUTRAL GROUND. Lippincott, 1941. The effects of the war on the neutral Westchester County region of New York.

253 Jahoda, Gloria. DELILAH'S MOUNTAIN. Houghton, 1963. Light romance set on the Tennessee frontier in the Clinch River valley where the settlers suffer from British and Indian raids and the heroine is captured by the Cherokees.

254 Jennings, John. THE SHADOW AND THE GLORY. Reynal, 1943. Centers around the campaigns leading up to the Battle of Bennington, 1774-1777.

255 ________. THE SEA EAGLES. Doubleday, 1950. Story of the young American navy and its part in the war.

256 Johnston, Mary. HUNTING SHIRT. Little, 1931. Life in a Cherokee Indian village in the Virginia wilderness, 1775-1780.

257 Kantor, MacKinlay. VALLEY FORGE. Evans, 1975. The book evidences sound historical research, combining fiction with fact in an account of the most desperate days of Washington's army.

258 Karig, Walter and Horace Bird. DON'T TREAD ON ME. Rinehart, 1954. Exploits of Commodore John Paul Jones; picture of early American politics, naval warfare, and social life.

259 Kelly, Eric. THREE SIDES OF AGIOCHOOK. Macmillan, 1935. Life on the New England frontier in 1775.

260 Lancaster, Bruce. GUNS OF BURGOYNE. Stokes, 1939. Story of the defeat of Burgoyne at the Battle of Saratoga from the viewpoint of a Hessian officer.

261 _______. TRUMPET TO ARMS. Little, 1944. Story of local militia companies in the campaigns of the war up to the Battle of Trenton.

262 _______. THE PHANTOM FORTRESS. Little, 1950. Story of the guerrilla warfare of Francis Marion, the Swamp Fox, in the Carolinas.

263 _______. THE SECRET ROAD. Little, 1952. Story of the part Washington's secret service played in exposing Benedict Arnold's treason and in the capture of Major André; picture of wartime life in New York City under British occupation.

264 _______. THE BLIND JOURNEY. Little, 1953. Benjamin Franklin sends money and supplies from France by a courier who lands near Yorktown in time for the campaign against Cornwallis.

265 _______. THE BIG KNIVES. Little, 1964. Lancaster's last novel follows a member of George Rogers Clark's expedition against the Indians and the British, culminating in the capture of Vincennes.

266 Leland, John Adams. OTHNEIL JONES. Lippincott, 1956. The war in the Carolinas as seen by a member of Francis Marion's raiders.

267 Linington, Elizabeth. THE LONG WATCH. Viking, 1956. Story of two colonial newspaper editors and of their struggle to keep their newspapers operating during the war; picture of life in New York City in the 1770's before the war and during the British occupation.

268 Longstreet, Stephen. EAGLES WHERE I WALK. Doubleday, 1961. Story of Dutch land-owning families in New York during the war; a young surgeon in Washington's army sees much of the war in New York State; ends with Benedict Arnold's treachery and the capture and execution of Major André. Sequel to War in the Golden Weather (Colonial).

269 _______. A FEW PAINTED FEATHERS. Doubleday, 1963. The war in the South through Yorktown to Washington's resignation from the Continental army. One of the main characters is Oxford-educated Peter Blue Feather, adopted son of Thomas Jefferson, who serves as a spy for the Americans. Sequel to Eagles Where I Walk.

270 Lynde, Francis. MR. ARNOLD. Bobbs, 1923. Story of Benedict Arnold centering around an attempt to kidnap Arnold and bring him back for trial after his escape.

271 Mason, F. Van Wyck. THREE HARBORS. Lippincott, 1938.

First in the author's series on the role of the American navy in the war; setting is Norfolk and Boston; 1774-1775.

272 ______. STARS ON THE SEA. Lippincott, 1940. Picture of the war in Rhode Island, Charleston, and the Bahamas; 1776-1777.

273 ______. RIVERS OF GLORY. Lippincott, 1942. Story centering around the siege of the British forces in Savannah; 1778-1779.

274 ______. EAGLE IN THE SKY. Lippincott, 1948. The role of the navy in the final campaign at Yorktown; 1780-1781.

275 ______. WILD HORIZON. Little, 1966. Story of life on the Tennessee frontier; pictures hardships of pioneer life, Indian raids, raids by the English under Col. Banastre Tarleton, and events leading to the American victory at the Battle of Kings Mountain in 1780.

276 ______. ROADS TO LIBERTY. Little, 1972. Combined edition of four earlier novels of the Revolution; Three Harbors, Stars on the Sea, Eagle in the Sky, and Wild Horizon. Mason terms them dramatic history, as the historical facts are never manipulated for the plot.

277 Melville, Herman. ISRAEL POTTER. Putnam, 1855. Based on the life of a Revolutionary War hero who fought at Bunker Hill, served as messenger to Benjamin Franklin, and served under John Paul Jones in the battle of the Bonhomme Richard and the Serapis.

278 Mercer, Charles E. ENOUGH GOOD MEN. Putnam, 1960. Picture of the political background of the war and of social life in Philadelphia.

279 Miller, Helen Topping. THE SOUND OF CHARIOTS. Bobbs, 1947. A Loyalist family flees from Augusta, Georgia to John Sevier's State of Franklin on the frontier, after the Battle of Kings Mountain.

280 ______. SLOW DIES THE THUNDER. Bobbs, 1955. Romance set against a background of the war in South Carolina in 1780; the bombardment of Charleston, Francis Marion's guerrilla warfare, and the Battle of Kings Mountain.

281 ______. CHRISTMAS AT MOUNT VERNON. Longmans, 1957. Short novel picturing the homecoming and Christmas celebration of George and Martha Washington at Mount Vernon in December, 1783.

282 Minnegerode, Meade. THE BLACK FOREST. Farrar, 1937. Story of life in the Northwest Territory from 1754 through the Revolution.

283 Mitchell, S. Weir. HUGH WYNNE, FREE QUAKER. Century, 1897. Life in Philadelphia during the war; hero serves as a spy for Washington and Lafayette.

284 Nutt, Frances. THREE FIELDS TO CROSS. Stephen-Paul, 1947. Spy story set in Staten Island, New York.

285 Page, Elizabeth. TREE OF LIBERTY. Farrar, 1939. A panorama of national events from 1754 to 1806.

286 Patterson, Emma. MIDNIGHT PATRIOT. Longmans, 1949. Heroic activities of a young colonist in the early days of the Revolution.

287 Peck, Robert Newton. HANG FOR TREASON. Doubleday, 1976. Ethan Allen's Green Mountain Boys in Vermont, and the capture of Ticonderoga from the British. The split between Tory and Rebel within the same family is another theme.

288 ________. THE KING'S IRON. Little, Brown. 1977. Based on fact. Washington orders sixty tons of cannon moved from Fort Ticonderoga, and Henry Knox leads a group of tough settlers in the prodigious task.

289 Pridgen, Tim. TORY OATH. Doubleday, 1941. Highland Scots of the Carolinas take the king's side in the Revolution.

290 Raddall, Thomas. HIS MAJESTY'S YANKEES. Winston, 1943. New Englanders living in Nova Scotia at the outbreak of the Revolution are torn between allegiance to the Crown and to the cause of the colonies.

291 Raynor, William. WORLD TURNED UPSIDE DOWN. Morrow, 1970. As the Revolution nears an end, a young British officer escapes an ambush and, by staining his skin, disguises himself as a Negro. Story makes clear the deplorable treatment of blacks by the colonists.

292 Ripley, Clements. CLEAR FOR ACTION. Appleton, 1940. John Paul Jones and the Bonhomme Richard.

293 Roberts, Kenneth L. ARUNDEL. Doubleday, 1930. Setting is Arundel, Maine; describes Benedict Arnold's expedition against Quebec.

294 ________. RABBLE IN ARMS. Doubleday, 1933. Story of the campaign leading up to the Battle of Saratoga; hero is Benedict Arnold; villain is Continental Congress.

295 ________. OLIVER WISWELL. Doubleday, 1940. Presents the Loyalists' side of the war.

296 Sabatini, Rafael. THE CAROLINIAN. Houghton, 1925. Historical romance set in South Carolina during the war.

297 Safford, Henry B. THAT BENNINGTON MOB. Messner, 1935. Story of the settlers in the New Hampshire grants, their relations with the Indians, and the actions leading to the Battle of Bennington in 1777.

298 Salvato, Sharon. DRUMS OF DECEMBER. Dell, 1983. Sequel to Fires of July (Colonial America) carries the story of the plantation family, now split in allegiance, through the Revolution.

299 Schoonover, Lawrence. THE REVOLUTIONARY. Little, 1958. Biographical novel of John Paul Jones, from boyhood in Scotland, through the Revolution, service in Russia under Catherine the Great, to his death in Paris in 1792.

300 Seifert, Shirley. WATERS OF THE WILDERNESS. Lippincott, 1941. Story of George Rogers Clark's expeditions in the Ohio wilderness and life in Spanish St. Louis; 1778-1780.

301 ______. LET MY NAME STAND FAIR. Lippencott, 1956. Light romance of the Revolution in which General Nathanael Greene, Light-Horse Harry Lee, Anthony Wayne, Alexander Hamilton, and George Washington appear.

302 Simons, Katherine. THE RED DOE. Appleton, 1953. Exploits of Francis Marion, the Swamp Fox.

303 Sinclair, Harold. WESTWARD THE TIDE. Doubleday, 1940. The war on the frontier; action centers around Fort Pitt and George Rogers Clark's expedition against Vincennes.

304 Singmaster, Elsie. RIFLES FOR WASHINGTON. Houghton, 1938. Story of a young colonist who joins Washington's ragged army.

305 Slaughter, Frank G. FLIGHT FROM NATCHEZ. Doubleday, 1955. Describes the flight of a group of Loyalists from Natchez in 1781.

306 Snow, Richard. FREELON STARBIRD. Houghton, 1976. Two young colonials join the Revolutionary army in the surge of patriotism that followed the signing of the Declaration of Independence in 1776; the hardships of the common soldier in Washington's command at Trenton and Princeton bring confusion, misery, and fear.

307 Spicer, Bart. BROTHER TO THE ENEMY. Dodd, 1958. Based on the attempt of Light-Horse Harry Lee's sergeant-major, John Champe, to capture Benedict Arnold by slipping into British-occupied New York.

308 Stackpole, Edouard A. NANTUCKET REBEL. Washburn, 1963. A neutral Quaker joins the colonial cause and becomes a successful privateer.

309 Stanley, Edward. THOMAS FORTY. Duell, 1947. Follows the career of a neutral Westchester County journeyman-printer through the war.

310 Sterne, Emma Gelders. DRUMS OF THE MONMOUTH. Dodd, 1935. Set in New Jersey and New York. Shows the part played by the Huguenots and Quakers in the war; central character is Philip Freneau.

311 Stone, Irving. THOSE WHO LOVE. Doubleday, 1965. Biographical novel of courtship and marriage of Abigail and John Adams.

312 Swanson, Neil. THE FORBIDDEN GROUND. Farrar, 1938. Detroit fur trade at the time of the Revolution.

313 Taylor, David. LIGHTS ACROSS THE DELAWARE. Lippincott, 1954. Story of a spirited farm girl torn between her devotion to the American cause and her pacifist Quaker lover; centers around Washington's campaign against Trenton; 1776-1777.

314 _______. FAREWELL TO VALLEY FORGE. Lippincott, 1955. General Charles Lee's plot to betray the colonial forces; the British evacuation of Philadelphia; and the Battle of Monmouth.

315 _______. SYCAMORE MEN. Lippincott, 1958. The war in South Carolina in 1880-1881; Francis Marion, the Swamp Fox, fights Cornwallis and Tarleton at the battle of Camden, Kings Mountain, and Eutaw Springs.

316 _______. STORM THE LAST RAMPART. Lippincott, 1960. Adventures of a colonial agent spying on the British in Tarrytown, New York, from the time of Arnold's treason to the surrender of Cornwallis at Yorktown; 1780-1781.

317 Thompson, Maurice. ALICE OF OLD VINCENNES. Bobbs, 1900. Indian warfare and pioneer life in the Northwest Territory, in and around Vincennes in 1778.

318 Turnbull, Agnes Sligh. THE DAY MUST DAWN. Macmillan, 1942. Western Pennsylvania and frontier warfare in the days of the Revolution.

319 Vail, Philip (pseud.). THE TWISTED SABRE. Dodd, 1963. Story of Benedict Arnold from his youth to his retirement; focuses on the military genius of his campaigns at Ticonderoga, Quebec, and Saratoga.

320 Van de Water, Frederic. THE RELUCTANT REBEL. Duell, 1948. Story of Ethan Allen and the Green Mountain Boys of New Hampshire; the Battle of Ticonderoga; fight over reapportionment of the New Hampshire grants.

321 _______. CATCH A FALLING STAR. Duell, 1949. Vermont in 1780; story of conflict and divided loyalties.

322 _______. WINGS OF THE MORNING. Washburn, 1956. Story of the struggle for independence and unity in Vermont; 1774-1791; picture of the political issues involved.

323 _______. DAY OF BATTLE. Washburn, 1958. Story of the rebel forces in Vermont from the Battle of Ticonderoga to the Battle of Bennington; 1777.

324 Vaughan, Carter A. (pseud.). SCOUNDREL'S BRIGADE. Doubleday, 1962. A former indentured servant becomes a spy to uncover a plot to undermine the colonial currency with counterfeit paper money.

325 _______. THE YANKEE RASCALS. Doubleday, 1963. Tale of espionage and intrigue in the Revolutionary War.

326 _______. DRAGON COVE. Doubleday, 1964. Romantic novel of action centering around Newport, Rhode Island during the war.

327 Wallace, Willard M. EAST TO BAGADUCE. Regnery, 1963. Based on a little-known episode, the siege of Bagaduce (now Castine), Maine, in 1779.

328 Wheeler, Guy. CATO'S WAR. Macmillan, 1980. A British view of the cruel internecine nature of the Revolution, through the eyes of an officer sent to aid Clinton and Cornwallis. Battles in the Carolinas and at Yorktown.

329 Wheelwright, Jere. KENTUCKY STAND. Scribner, 1951. A Baltimore boy on the Kentucky frontier, 1777, involved in politics and frontier warfare. Daniel Boone, Simon Kenton, and Thomas Jefferson appear.

330 Williams, Ben Ames. COME SPRING. Houghton, 1940. Life in a remote Maine settlement during the Revolution.

331 Wyckoff, Nicholas E. THE BRAINTREE MISSION. Macmillan, 1957. Based on the idea that England hoped to offer a title and a seat in Parliament to six colonial leaders to placate the colonies; this is the story of the offer made to John Adams.

THE YOUNG NATION, 1783 TO 1860

332 Adams, Samuel Hopkins. THE GORGEOUS HUSSY. Houghton, 1934. Washington social and political life from 1812 to the Civil War; story of Peggy Eaton, protégée of Andrew Jackson.

333 _______. CANAL TOWN. Random, 1944. Struggles of a young physician fighting ignorance and superstition in New York State in the 1820's; medical lore and customs of the times.

334 _______. BANNER BY THE WAYSIDE. Random 1947. A group of itinerant players tour the Erie Canal country of New York in the 1830's.

335 _______. SUNRISE TO SUNSET. Random, 1950. Early days in the shirt-making industry in Troy, New York, in the 1830's; centers around the struggle for better working conditions.

336 Allis, Marguerite. THE SPLENDOR STAYS. Putnam, 1942. Social and political developments during the first decades of the nineteenth century; birth of the Monroe Doctrine; Issac Hull, Simón Bolívar, and others appear; setting is Boston and New York.

337 _______. ALL IN GOOD TIME. Putnam, 1944. Beginnings of American industry at the turn of the century; a Connecticut clockmaker initiates the first steps toward mass production and faces the hard times of the Embargo Act of 1807.

338 _______. CHARITY STRONG. Putnam, 1945. Picture of the New York musical world in the 1830's.

339 _______. WATER OVER THE DAM. Putnam, 1947. Story of the fight for the Farmington Canal project in Connecticut in the 1820's.

340 _______. THE LAW OF THE LAND. Putnam, 1948. Story of the prejudice against public performers in early nineteenth century New England.

341 Bacheller, Irving. LIGHT IN THE CLEARING. Bobbs, 1917. Career of Silas Wright, governor of New York; 1840's and 1850's.

342 Benchley, Nathaniel. PORTRAIT OF A SCOUNDREL. Doubleday,

1979. A land-company syndicate creates a scandal in the 1790's. Two real men, the Bostonian John Greenleaf, and signer of the Declaration of Independence Robert Morris, turned speculators, bankrupting themselves, friends, and investors.

343 Bentley, Barbara. MISTRESS NANCY. McGraw, 1980. Court records and correspondence infuse the tenor of the period into this story of actual historical events. Nancy Randolph and her brother-in-law are accused of killing her newborn child. Acquitted at her trial, Nancy later married Gouverneur Morris, statesman and diplomat.

344 Bosworth, Allan R. STORM TIDE. Harper, 1965. An adventure tale of New England whaling ships at the turn of the century.

345 Bransford, Stephen E. RIDERS OF THE LONG ROAD. Doubleday 1984. A story of the circuit-riding clergy who brought Christianity to the scattered settlements in the wilderness in the late eighteenth century.

346 Breslin, Howard. TAMARACK TREE. McGraw, 1947. Story of the effects of a political convention on a small New England town, Stratton, Vermont, in 1840. William Henry Harrison and Daniel Webster appear.

347 ________. SHAD RUN. Crowell, 1955. Life of the shad fishermen in the Hudson River valley near Poughkeepsie at the time New York ratified the Constitution in 1788.

348 Cable, Mary. AVERY'S KNOT. Putnam, 1981. In 1832, Ephraim Avery, a real clergyman, is accused of killing Sarah Cornell, a young cotton-mill worker in Fall River, Massachusetts. See also Tragedy at Tiverton by Raymond Paul.

349 Caldwell, Janet Taylor. THE WIDE HOUSE. Scribner, 1945. Family story set against a background of social and political developments in a small New York town torn by the conflicts of the "Know-Nothing" party in the 1850's.

350 Carlisle, Henry. VOYAGE TO THE 1ST OF DECEMBER. Putnam, 1972. A historically accurate novel about the trial and punishment of the men accused of conspiring to mutiny on the U.S. Navy brig Somers in 1842. Philip Spencer, the son of Tyler's secretary of war, was hanged.

351 Carlisle, Henry. JONAH MAN. Knopf, 1984. Story of the luckless sailors involved in the case of murder and cannibalism that followed the wreck of the whaling ship Essex in 1819.

352 Carmer, Carl. GENESEE FEVER. Farrar, 1941. Background of fairs, horse racing, and political conflict when the Scotch-Irish in the Genesee valley of New York rebelled against Hamilton's excise law; Colonel Williamson, with Robert Morris and Aaron Burr, planned to establish landed estates in the valley.

353 Carr, John Dickson. PAPA LA-BAS. Harper, 1968. A mystery story set in New Orleans in 1858, involving Judah P. Benjamin, the British Consul, and some French voodoo.

354 Carse, Robert. GREAT CIRCLE. Scribner, 1956. Story of a whaling voyage out of Salem in the 1840's.

355 Case, Josephine. WRITTEN IN SAND. Houghton, 1945. Story of the Tripolitan War, 1801-1805; centering around General Eaton's campaigns in Africa.

356 Chapman, Maristan (pseud). TENNESSEE HAZARD. Lippincott, 1953. Tennessee frontier in 1788 in a story of the effort to ratify the Constitution and of General Wilkinson's conspiracy to turn the frontier lands over to the Spanish in Louisiana.

357 Chase, Mary Ellen. SILAS CROCKETT. Macmillan, 1935. Chronicle of a Maine seafaring family as steam begins to replace sail, and the New England shipbuilding industry declines.

358 Chase-Riboud, Barbara. SALLY HEMMINGS. Viking, 1979. Love story of Thomas Jefferson and Sally Hemmings, his slave and mistress. The social life and fashions of two continents are accurately portrayed as Sally goes to Paris with Ambassador Jefferson.

359 Coatsworth, Elizabeth. HERE I STAY. Coward, 1938. Story of Maine in 1817, and the beginning of the rush to the Ohio wilderness.

360 Cochran, Louis. THE FOOL OF GOD. Duell, 1958. Fictional biography of the life and times of Alexander Campbell, founder of the Disciples of Christ, president of Bethany College, and friend of John Brown, Henry Clay, James Madison, and Thomas Jefferson.

361 Coffin, Robert Peter Tristram. JOHN DAWN. Macmillan, 1936. Maine during the shipbuilding era following the Revolution.

362 Colver, Anne. LISTEN FOR THE VOICES. Farrar, 1939. Concord during the years 1848 to 1851; picture of small-town life and literary activity; Thoreau, Emerson, and the Alcotts mingle with the characters.

363 Cowdrey, A. E. ELIXIR OF LIFE. Doubleday, 1965. Story of a patent-medicine hawker who develops a remedy for yellow fever during the epidemic in New Orleans in 1850.

364 Crabb, Alfred Leland. HOME TO THE HERMITAGE. Bobbs, 1948. Story of Andrew and Rachel Jackson, from his return from the War of 1812 to the time he leaves for Washington and the presidency.

365 ______. HOME TO KENTUCKY. Bobbs, 1953. Fictional biography of Henry Clay.

366 Cummings, Betty Sue. SAY THESE NAMES (REMEMBER THEM) Pineapple Press, 1984. A young squaw sees her tribe nearly exterminated in the second Seminole War in 1830's Florida. She follows Apayaka, the real Indian leader who continued to defy the whites, hiding deep in the Everglades.

367 David, Evan John. AS RUNS THE GLASS. Harper, 1943. Story of a Maine seafaring family at the time of the French Revolution.

368 Davidson, Louis B. and Edward J. Doherty. CAPTAIN MAROONER. Crowell, 1952. Based on an actual mutiny on the whaler Globe out of Nantucket in 1822.

369 Davis, Dorothy. MEN OF NO PROPERTY. Scribner, 1956. Irish immigrants in conflict with the "Know-Nothing" faction in New York City in the 1850's.

370 Degenhard, William. THE REGULATORS. Dial, 1943. Story of Shays' Rebellion in Massachusetts.

371 Dolbier, Maurice. BENJY BOONE. Dial, 1967. Life with a traveling theatrical troupe in the early 1800's with scenes in New England, Philadelphia, and in the frontier country.

372 Edmonds, Walter D. YOUNG AMES. Little, 1942. Social political, and economic life in New York City in the 1830's.

373 Ehle, John. THE ROAD. Harper, 1967. Story of the first railroad construction in the North Carolina mountains in the 1870's; characters are descendants of The Land Breakers (Expanding Frontiers--Frontiers--Southern).

374 Falkner, Leonard. PAINTED LADY. Dutton, 1962. Story of Eliza Jumel, wife of Aaron Burr, against a background of social life in New York and Paris in the early 1800's.

375 Field, Rachel. ALL THIS AND HEAVEN TOO. Macmillan, 1938. Novel of the American literary scene in the 1850's. Harriet Beecher Stowe, Samuel Morse, William Cullen Bryant, and others appear.

376 Fletcher, Inglis. THE QUEEN'S GIFT. Bobbs, 1952. Albemarle County, North Carolina in 1788. Story of the debates about the ratification of the Constitution.

377 Forbes, Esther. THE RUNNING OF THE TIDE. Houghton, 1948. Novel of Salem's great shipbuilding days and the beginning of their decline.

378 ________. RAINBOW ON THE ROAD. Houghton, 1954. Story of an itinerant portrait painter in New England in the 1830's.

379 Gerson, Noel B. OLD HICKORY. Doubleday, 1964. Biographical novel of the life and career of Andrew Jackson.

380 ________. THE SLENDER REED. Doubleday, 1965. Biographical novel of James K. Polk, eleventh president of the U.S.; covers the period of the Mexican War, the annexation of Texas, and the Oregon boundary dispute. Martin Van Buren, Daniel Webster, and John Tyler appear.

381 Grebenc, Lucile. THE TIME OF CHANGE. Doubleday, 1938. Customs and daily life of a Connecticut family in the years following 1812.

382 Hackney, Louise. WING OF FAME. Appleton, 1934. Fictional biography of the founder of the Smithsonian Institution. Historical characters are Smithson, Franklin, Blake, Cavendish, and Lavoisier.

383 Hawthorne, Nathaniel. THE BLITHEDALE ROMANCE. Dutton, 1852. Story of George Ripley's Brook Farm socialistic experiment in 1841; associated with the venture were Emerson, Hawthorne, Margaret Fuller, and other Transcendentalists.

384 Heidish, Marcy. MIRACLES. New American Library, 1984. Subtitled: A Novel About Mother Seton, the First American Saint. Elizabeth Seton's life is told from her own point of view, and from that of a fictional Father John. Born an Episcopalian, Elizabeth converted to Catholicism after her husband died. She later established the order of the Sisters of Charity of St. Vincent de Paul.

385 Hergesheimer, Joseph. JAVA HEAD. Knopf, 1919. Story of a Salem shipowning family in the 1840's.

386 ________. BALISAND. Knopf, 1924. Political developments in Virginia from Washington's second inauguration to Jefferson's election.

387 Hough, Henry Beetle. THE NEW ENGLAND STORY. Random, 1958. Three generations of a New England whaling family in the 1800's.

388 Houston, Robert. NATION THIEF. Pantheon, 1984. Episodes in the life of William Walker, the American adventurer who proclaimed himself King of Nicaragua in 1856. Supported by some southerners, he hoped to establish a slave economy, but the opposing economic interests of Commodore Vanderbilt eventually doomed his scheme.

389 Hulme, Kathryn. ANNIE'S CAPTAIN. Little, 1961. Story of the long, happy marriage of the author's grandparents as a background for the description of the progress from sail to steam in the 1800's.

390 Hurwood, Bernhardt J. MY SAVAGE MUSE. Everest, 1979. Imaginary memoirs of Edgar Allan Poe. He is presumed to be writing in 1847, the year of Virginia's death, and two years before his own.

391 Idell, Albert. ROGER'S FOLLY. Doubleday, 1957. New Jersey, 1844; picture of social and economic life in the period when steam was replacing sail and the railroad empires were being formed. Followed by Centennial Summer (Nation Grows Up).

392 James, Henry. WASHINGTON SQUARE. Modern Library, 1881. Social life in New York City in the early 1800's.

393 Jennings, John. SALEM FRIGATE. Doubleday, 1946. Adventurous sea story of the early years of the young nation; action centers around the African coast during the Tripolitan War.

394 _______. BANNERS AGAINST THE WIND. Little, 1954. Biographical novel of Dr. Samuel Gridley Howe, his interest in the struggle for Greek independence, founding a school for the blind, and marriage to Julia Ward.

395 Kane, Harnett. NEW ORLEANS WOMAN. Doubleday, 1946. Biographical novel of Myra Clark Gaines and a picture of the New Orleans scene.

396 _______. THE AMAZING MRS. BONAPARTE. Doubleday, 1963. Story based on the life of Betsy Patterson, Jerome Bonaparte's Baltimore-born wife; settings in America and Europe.

397 Kelland, Clarence Budington. HARD MONEY. Harper, 1930. Son of a Dutch peddler becomes one of the financial leaders in New York. First in the author's series on the economic development of the United States (Civil War and The Nation Grows Up).

398 Kennedy, Lucy. MR. AUDUBON'S LUCY. Crown, 1957. Story of Lucy Bakewell Audubon and of her life with the naturalist-painter John James Audubon.

399 Laing, Alexander. JONATHAN EAGLE. Duell, 1955. Picture of American politics from 1786 to 1801; banking policies of Hamilton, reaction to the Alien and Sedition Laws, and the election of Jefferson.

400 ________. MATHEW EARLY. Duell, 1957. Story of New England and the slave trade; heroine is active in a move to abolish slavery.

401 LeMay, Alan. PELICAN COAST. Doubleday, 1929. New Orleans with its varied characters and the contrast of sea, town, and river life in the early 1800's.

402 Longstreet, Stephen. A MAST TO SPEAR THE STARS. Doubleday, 1967. Story of shipbuilding days in Nantucket, and sailing in the China trade.

403 MacDonald, Kay L. VISION OF THE EAGLE. Crowell, 1977. Set in the trans-Appalachian wilderness. A young couple venture into Indian country. Their son will be raised in the Indian culture but will reenter the white world when he is grown.

404 McKee, Ruth Eleanor. THE LORD'S ANOINTED. Doubleday, 1934. Story of the missionaries from Boston who sailed to Hawaii in 1820.

405 Malm, Dorothea. THE WOMAN QUESTION. Appleton, 1958. Amusing novel of the women's rights movement culminating in a women's rights convention in New York in 1853. Lucretia Mott, Lucy Stone, and others appear.

406 Mason, F. Van Wyck. HARPOON IN EDEN. Doubleday, 1969. A seafaring tale of whaling ships out of Nantucket in the 1830's, involving adventures in Mexico and New Zealand.

407 Miller, Heather Ross. GONE A HUNDRED MILES. Harcourt, 1968. Story of a German doctor who settles in rural North Carolina and raises his only daughter alone, after his wife dies.

408 Minnigerode, Meade. COCKADES. Putnam, 1927. New York and New Orleans at the time of the French Revolution; story of the Dauphin's supposed escape to America.

409 Moore, Barbara. THE FEVER CALLED LIVING. Doubleday, 1976. The story of the final five years of the life of Edgar Allan Poe, a period when his young wife sickened and died, his literary reputation was sliding, and he was addicted to opiates.

410 Morrow, Honoré. BLACK DANIEL. Morrow, 1931. Romance of Daniel Webster and Caroline LeRoy and her influence on his career.

411 Muir, Robert. THE SPRIG OF HEMLOCK. Longmans, 1957. Story of Shays' Rebellion in Massachusetts in 1786-1787, when Daniel Shays led an uprising against high land taxes and debtors' prisons.

412 Murphy, Edward. ANGEL OF THE DELTA. Hanover, 1958. Based on the life of Margaret Haughery, who worked to establish a home for orphan children in New Orleans; follows her struggles during the Union occupation after the Civil War.

413 O'Neal, Cothburn. THE VERY YOUNG MRS. POE. Crown, 1956. Based on the life of Virginia Clemm, wife of Edgar Allan Poe; describes the unsettled, emotional life of the poet and his dependence upon his wife.

414 O'Neill, Charles. MORNING TIME. Simon and Schuster, 1949. Based on the supposed plot of General Wilkinson to sell out to the Spanish at New Orleans during the period of the Confederation, 1783-1789.

415 Paradise, Viola. TOMORROW THE HARVEST. Morrow, 1952. Small-town life in Maine just after the Revolution.

416 Parker, Cornelia Stratton. FABULOUS VALLEY. Putnam, 1956. Romance set against a background of the oil rush in Western Pennsylvania in the mid-1800's.

417 Partridge, Bellamy. THE BIG FREEZE. Crowell, 1948. Story of the political skulduggery connected with the development of New York's water supply in the 1840's.

418 Paul, Raymond. THOMAS STREET HORROR. Viking, 1982. Novel based on a true crime that was committed in New York City in 1835. Helen Jewett, a prostitute, has been murdered. The defense attorney for the accused man helps to find the real murderer.

419 _______. TRAGEDY AT TIVERTON. Viking, 1984. Accused of killing a young mill worker and her unborn child, the Reverend Ephraim Avery becomes the first clergyman in America to stand trial for murder. Based on historical incident. See also Avery's Knot by Mary Cable.

420 Rikhoff, Jean. BUTTE'S LANDING. Dial, 1973. An early settler in the Adirondacks claims land and wrests a living in the wilderness. His son will marry an Indian. Two sons of the third generation will choose divergent paths. One will become a politician in Albany, the second will return to his grandfather's land after fighting in the Civil War. Followed by Sweetwater (Expanding Frontiers) and One of the Raymonds (Civil War).

421 Roark, Garland. THE LADY AND THE DEEP BLUE SEA. Doubleday, 1958. A sea story set around the clipper-ship trade out of Boston; plot revolves around a race from Melbourne to Boston.

422 Roberts, Carey and Rebecca Seely. TIDEWATER DYNASTY. Harcourt, 1981. The earliest generations of the famous Lee family of Virginia. Thomas, who settled there in 1718, his sons, two of whom (Francis Lightfoot and Richard Henry) were signers of the Declaration of Independence, and their cousin "Light-horse Harry," a Revolutionary War hero and the father of Robert E. Lee.

423 Roberts, Kenneth L. LYDIA BAILEY. Doubleday, 1947. Story of Americans in the Haitian revolution and in the Tripolitan War.

424 Rossner, Judith. EMMELINE. Simon and Schuster, 1980. Tragic story of the seduction of Emmeline Mosher, a real woman who was sent from her poor farm home to work in the fabric mills of Lowell, Massachusetts.

425 Schaeffer, Susan Fromberg. TIME IN ITS FLIGHT. Doubleday, 1978. Details of the way of life of medical doctors and their families in the mid-nineteenth century, when typhoid, diphtheria, and influenza were epidemic.

426 Seifert, Shirley. THE THREE LIVES OF ELIZABETH. Lippincott, 1952. Follows the heroine from her youth on the Missouri River frontier in the 1820's to maturity as a leader in Washington society just before the Civil War.

427 Seton, Anya. DRAGONWYCK. Houghton, 1944. Manners and customs of the early 1800's in a baronial family home in the Hudson River valley.

428 Shine, Francis L. CONJUROR'S JOURNAL. Dodd, 1978. This tale of a traveling magician touring the Northeast in the 1790's accurately pictures details of the popular culture of the times.

429 Stewart, Ramona. CASEY. Little, 1968. Picture of life among the immigrant Irish in New York City in the 1850's and '60's; politics in the Tweed ring, Boss Kelly, the Draft Riots of 1863, the Molly Maguires, and fire fighting.

430 Stone, Irving. THE PRESIDENT'S LADY. Doubleday, 1951. Sympathetic account of Rachel and Andrew Jackson, against a background of American politics at the beginning of the nineteenth century.

431 Stowe, Harriet Beecher. OLDTOWN FOLKS. Belknap, 1966. Saga of life in Oldtown (South Natick), Massachusetts in the years following the Revolutionary War. First published in 1869.

432 Taylor, David. MISTRESS OF THE FORGE. Lippincott, 1964. Social and political life and industrial development in Pennsylvania in the 1790's, at the time of the Alien and Sedition Laws.

433 Taylor, Robert Lewis. NIAGARA. Putnam, 1980. In the 1850's Niagara Falls was a magnet for an endless parade of crackpots who ran rapids, walked tightropes, and sealed themselves into barrels. They attracted crowds of tourists who came to gawk. In this story a reporter from New York comes to find out if they are being fleeced.

434 Thorp, Roderick. JENNY & BARNUM. Doubleday, 1981. The love affair between Jenny Lind and P. T. Barnum which developed when the Swedish singer toured the U. S. for the showman in 1860.

435 Turnbull, Agnes Sligh. THE KING'S ORCHARD. Houghton, 1963. Fictional biography of James O'Hara, Irish immigrant, who settled at Fort Pitt, served as an officer in the Revolution, as Indian agent, and as Quartermaster General of the United States. Saga of the social, political, and industrial development of the period.

436 Vidal, Gore. BURR. Random House, 1973. A revisionist look at Burr's role in history. Told as a memoir left by the aging Burr, commented on by the young journalist in whom he confides. Composes a trilogy together with 1876 (The Nation Grows Up) and Washington, D. C. (Chronicles).

437 Wellman, Paul I. THE BUCKSTONES. Trident, 1967. A light tale of a picaresque scoundrel whose daughter seeks his release from a Tennessee debtors' prison by appealing to President Andrew Jackson.

438 Whitney, Janet. JUDITH. Morrow, 1943. Philadelphia in 1792 is the background for the love story of two young people; Washington's second inauguration, Blanchard's balloon ascent, troubled international relations, and the yellow fever epidemic are historical highlights.

439 Whitney, Phyllis A. SEA JADE. Appleton, 1965. Romantic tale of life in a New England seaport town, with glimpses of the sailing and shipping industry.

440 Widdemer, Margaret. THE RED CASTLE WOMEN. Doubleday, 1968. Life, manners, dress and customs in a mansion on the Hudson River and in New York City in the period between the Mexican War and the Civil War.

441 Wilson, Dorothy Clarke. LINCOLN'S MOTHERS. Doubleday, 1981. Nancy Hanks, Lincoln's mother, and Sarah Bush Johnston, his stepmother, both grew up in Elizabethtown, Kentucky. This novel envisions a friendship between the two.

442 Zaroulis, Nancy. CALL THE DARKNESS LIGHT. Doubleday, 1979. Story of the plight of the women mill workers in pre-Civil War Lowell, Massachusetts.

War of 1812

443 Banks, Polan. BLACK IVORY. Harper, 1926. Story of Jean Lafitte, pirate and slave runner, and of the conflict involved in his decision to join the Americans in the defense of New Orleans against the British in the War of 1812.

444 Beebe, Ralph. WHO FOUGHT AND BLED. Coward, 1941. Pioneering in Ohio and General Isaac Hull's campaigns around Detroit.

445 Bell, Sallie. MARCEL ARMAND. Page, 1935. Intrigue of Lafitte's lieutenant with the British.

446 Chambers, Robert W. THE HAPPY PARROT. Appleton, 1929. Story of naval warfare during the War of 1812.

447 ________. THE RAKE AND THE HUSSY. Appleton, 1930. Story of Jackson's defense of New Orleans.

448 Chidsey, Donald Barr. STRONGHOLD. Doubleday, 1948. Connecticut and Martinique during the War of 1812. Hero is impressed into the British navy.

449 Finger, Charles. CAPE HORN SNORTER. Houghton, 1939. New England shippers in the years leading up to the War of 1812.

450 Forester, C. S. CAPTAIN FROM CONNECTICUT. Little, 1941. Blockade-running out of Long Island during Jefferson's administration.

451 Gordon, Charles William. THE RUNNER. Doubleday, 1929. Fighting around the Niagara peninsula.

452 ________. ROCK AND THE RIVER. Dodd, 1931. Set in Quebec and on the Canadian-American border during the War of 1812. Canadian point of view.

453 Harper, Robert S. TRUMPET IN THE WILDERNESS. M. S. Mill, 1940. Story of frontier warfare, the surrender of Detroit, the Battle of Erie, and pioneer newspaper work in Ohio.

454 Hepburn, Andrew. LETTER OF MARQUE. Little, 1959. Vivid account of sea warfare; story of an American privateer in the War of 1812.

455 Hodge, Jane Aiken. HERE COMES A CANDLE. Doubleday, 1967. A young British widow is taken into the home of a Boston merchant who saved her from American militiamen in the raids against Canada in the War of 1812.

456 Jennings, John. THE TALL SHIPS. McGraw, 1958. Story of the American navy in the period before and during the War of 1812.

457 La Farge, Oliver. THE LONG PENNANT. Houghton, 1933. Rhode Island privateer harasses British shipping in the Caribbean.

458 Lane, Carl. THE FLEET IN THE FOREST. Coward, 1943. Life around Erie, Pennsylvania; the building of Perry's fleet at Presque Isle, and the Battle of Erie.

459 Lincoln, Joseph Crosby and Freeman Lincoln. THE NEW HOPE. Coward, 1941. Cape Codders launch a privateer through the British blockade.

460 Marshall, Bernard Gay. OLD HICKORY'S PRISONER. Appleton, 1925. Story of a boy too young to join the army in the War of 1812, who serves as a messenger, earning a commendation and promotion from General Andrew Jackson.

461 Moore, John. HEARTS OF HICKORY. Cokesbury, 1926. The defense of New Orleans; Andrew Jackson, David Crockett, Jean Lafitte.

462 Mudgett, Helen. THE SEAS STAND WATCH. Knopf, 1944. Follows the ups and downs of the New England sea trade and politics, from the Revolution through the War of 1812.

463 O'Daniel, Janet. O GENESEE. Lippincott, 1957. A tale of pioneer settlers in the Genesee valley near present Rochester, New York and the conflicts building up to the War of 1812.

464 Orr, Myron. THE CITADEL OF THE LAKES. Dodd, 1952. Story of Astor's fur-trading empire around Mackinac Island during the War of 1812.

465 Roberts, Kenneth L. THE LIVELY LADY. Doubleday, 1931. Privateering against British shipping, and life in Dartmoor prison.

466 ________. CAPTAIN CAUTION. Doubleday, 1934. Maine merchant ship captured by the British; seamen impressed into British service.

467 Root, Corwin. AN AMERICAN, SIR. Dutton, 1940. Privateering, impressment into British service, and life in Boston, split between Federalists and Republicans during the War of 1812.

468 Rowland, Henry C. HIRONDELLE. Harper, 1922. Adventure on the high seas. Privateering on the eve of the war.

469 Shepard, Odell and Willard Shepard. HOLDFAST GAINES. Macmillan, 1946. Panorama of national events from the end of the Revolution to the War of 1812; includes the Fort Mims Massacre and Battle of New Orleans; Tecumseh, Jean Lafitte, and Andrew Jackson appear.

470 Speas, Jan Cox. MY LOVE, MY ENEMY. Morrow, 1961. Light story of a young American girl in live with a British spy; background of politics and battles culminating in the burning of Washington.

471 Sperry, Armstrong. THE BLACK FALCON. Winston, 1949. Son of a New Orleans planter sails with Jean Lafitte in his privateering raids against the English in 1814.

472 Tracy, Don. CRIMSON IS THE EASTERN SHORE. Dial, 1953. The war around the shores of Eastern Maryland.

473 Vail, Philip (pseud.). THE SEA PANTHER. Dodd, 1962. Fictionalized account of the life of William Bainbridge, commander of the U.S.S. Constitution; action centers around Stephen Decatur's campaign against Algiers in 1815.

474 Wallace, Willard M. JONATHAN DEARBORN. Little, 1967. Story of a young law student who ships as a privateer in the War of 1812.

475 Williams, Ben Ames. THREAD OF SCARLET. Houghton, 1939. Nantucket privateer fights a British frigate during the War of 1812.

476 Wilson, Margaret. THE VALIANT WIFE. Doubleday, 1934. Story of the imprisonment of a young American in Dartmoor prison in 1812.

EXPANDING FRONTIERS, 1783 TO 1893

Eastern and Southern Frontiers

477 Atkinson, Oriana. THE TWIN COUSINS. Bobbs, 1951. The Catskill country of New York in the days when it was still frontier; story of the construction of the Susquehanna Turnpike.

478 Barnes, Percy Raymond. CRUM ELBOW FOLKS. Lippincott, 1938. Country life and customs of a Quaker settlement on the Hudson River in 1838.

479 Best, Allena. HOMESPUN. Lothrop, 1937. Family life on the New York frontier in the 1820's.

480 Best, Herbert. YOUNG'UN. Macmillan, 1944. Picture of daily living in the frontier region of Northern New York State in the early 1800's.

481 Boyd, James. THE LONG HUNT. Scribner, 1930. Life on the frontier from North Carolina to the Mississippi River at the time of Daniel Boone.

482 Bristow, Gwen. DEEP SUMMER. Crowell, 1937. Evolution of a great Louisiana plantation from a frontier cabin in the wilderness. Followed by The Handsome Road (Civil War).

483 Clagett, John. BUCKSKIN CAVALIER. Crown, 1954. Story of a young woman captured by Indians near Fort Pitt; covers much of the frontier region including a description of the Wilderness Road.

484 Cochran, Louis. RACCOON JOHN SMITH. Duell, 1963. Authentic frontier background in a fictional biography of the Campbellite preacher in Kentucky in the early 1800's.

485 Colver, Anne. THEODOSIA, DAUGHTER OF AARON BURR. Farrar, 1941. Fictionized biography in which his schemes are treated casually.

486 Crabb, Alfred Leland. JOURNEY TO NASHVILLE. Bobbs, 1957. Story of the founding of Nashville, retracing the journey of a group of settlers from the Wautauga Settlement of East Tennessee through the wilderness to the site of the new town.

487 Davis, Julia. EAGLE ON THE SUN. Rinehart, 1956. Story of Virginia plantation life and the Mexican War. Sequel to Bridle the Wind (Civil War--Abolition).

488 Dowdey, Clifford. TIDEWATER. Little, 1943. Panoramic story of the migration from the old Virginia Tidewater plantations to new lands in the West in 1837.

489 Downes, Anne Miller. THE PILGRIM SOUL. Lippincott, 1952. Life in the wilderness area of New Hampshire in 1820.

490 _______. THE QUALITY OF MERCY. Lippincott, 1959. Family affairs and politics in Philadelphia and on the Tennessee frontier at the time of Andrew Jackson's war against the Creek Indians in 1813.

491 Eckert, Allen W. JOHNNY LOGAN. Little, 1983. Story of the Indian boy Spemica Lawba, adopted and educated by the American General Benjamin Logan. In adulthood he sought to have his people acculturate with the whites; Tecumseh, his uncle, saw survival for the Indian only if the whites could be defeated.

492 Edmonds, Walter D. ROME HAUL. Little, 1929. Life and manners along the banks of the Erie Canal in the 1850's.

493 _______. THE BIG BARN. Little, 1930. Story of farm life in the Black River valley of New York in the 1860's.

494 _______. ERIE WATER. Little, 1933. Story of the building of the Erie Canal from 1817 to 1825.

495 _______. CHAD HANNA. Little, 1940. A circus story set in the Erie Canal region of New York in the 1850's; depicts the struggle of small business in competition with big business.

496 _______. WEDDING JOURNEY. Little, 1947. Story of a honeymoon couple traveling through the Erie Canal on the way to Buffalo and Niagara Falls in the 1830's.

497 Ehle, John. THE LAND BREAKERS. Harper, 1964. Life and hardships of the settlers in a remote mountain valley in North Carolina in 1779.

498 Fleischmann, Glen. WHILE RIVERS FLOW. Macmillan, 1963. Story of the removal of the Cherokee Indians from their homes in Georgia and Tennessee in the 1830's.

499 Forrest, Williams. TRAIL OF TEARS. Crown, 1958. Story of the Cherokee Indians and of their leader, John Ross, at the time of their enforced migration from their home in Georgia to new lands in Oklahoma Territory in the 1830's.

500 Fort, John. GOD IN THE STRAW PEN. Dodd, 1931. Story of a Methodist revival meeting in a Georgia backwoods community in the 1830's.

501 Gabriel, Gilbert Wolf. I THEE WED. Macmillan, 1948. Story of a group who came to America during the French Revolution to build a refuge for Marie Antoinette at the site of Asylum, in Pennsylvania.

502 Gerson, Noel B. THE CUMBERLAND RIFLES. Doubleday, 1952. Story of the frontier State of Franklin, its struggle for recognition, and the admission of Tennessee as a state in 1796.

503 Giles, Janice Holt. THE BELIEVERS. Houghton, 1957. Story of religious beliefs and social customs of a Shaker colony in Kentucky in the early 1800's.

504 ________. LAND BEYOND THE MOUNTAINS. Houghton, 1958. Story of the settling of Kentucky from 1783 to 1792 and the fight for separate statehood, introducing General James Wilkinson's schemes for an empire on the frontier.

505 Ham, Tom. GIVE US THIS VALLEY. Macmillan, 1952. Story of a Pennsylvania couple moving to new land in a Georgia valley in 1837.

506 Harris, Cyril. STREET OF KNIVES. Little, 1950. Follows Aaron Burr's journey westward on his way to Mexico.

507 Hatcher, Harlan H. THE PATTERNS OF WOLFPEN. Bobbs, 1934. Family chronicle from pioneer days in Eastern Kentucky to the encroachment of industry after about 1885.

508 Holt, Felix. THE GABRIEL HORN. Dutton, 1951. Frontier life along the Tennessee River.

509 Johnson, Gerald White. BY REASON OF STRENGTH. Minton, 1930. Chronicle of the Campbell clan of North Carolina, from just after the Revolution through the Civil War.

510 Jones, Madison. FOREST OF THE NIGHT. Harcourt, 1960. Story of an idealistic school teacher facing the brutal reality of frontier life in Tennessee in the early 1800's.

511 Jordan, Mildred. ASYLUM FOR THE QUEEN. Knopf, 1948. Story of a group of aristocrats who plot to rescue the French royal family, imprisoned in Paris, and bring them to a Pennsylvania colony which they named Asylum.

512 Kendrick, Bayard H. THE FLAMES OF TIME. Scribner, 1948. Story of life in Northern Florida preceding its acquisition by the United States.

513 Kroll, Harry Harrison. ROGUE'S COMPANION. Bobbs, 1943. Story of John Murrell's outlaw band and life on the Natchez Trace in the 1820's and 1830's.

514 ________. DARKER GROWS THE VALLEY. Bobbs, 1947. Pioneer life in the Tennessee River valley from 1778 to the advent of the T. V. A. in the 1930's.

515 Linney, Romulus. HEATHEN VALLEY. Atheneum, 1962. Story of the religious mission of Bishop Ames and William Starns and their effect on the isolated inhabitants of a mountain valley in North Carolina in the 1850's.

516 Loomis, Noel. THE TWILIGHTERS. Macmillan, 1955. Frontier Kentucky and lands west of the Mississippi in the early nineteenth century.

517 McCutcheon, George B. VIOLA GWYN. Dodd, 1922. Frontier Kentucky and Indiana in the early 1800's.

518 MacKinnon, Mary Linehan. ONE SMALL CANDLE. Crown, 1956. Story of family life in a New York farming community during the mid-1800's.

519 McMeekin, Clark (pseud). RECKON WITH THE RIVER. Appleton, 1941. Life on the Kentucky frontier and on the Ohio River; Johnny Appleseed, Aaron Burr, the Blennerhassets, and others appear. Early 1800's.

520 Markey, Gene. THAT FAR PARADISE. McKay, 1960. Story of the eventful journey of a Virginia Blue Ridge family to the Kentucky wilderness beyond the Alleghenies in 1794.

521 Meigs, Cornelia. CALL OF THE MOUNTAIN. Little, 1940. Vermont backwoods in the 1830's.

522 Miller, Caroline. LEBANON. Doubleday, 1944. Story of pioneer life, of hunting and trapping in the Georgia swamplands, and on the Mississippi River frontier.

523 Myers, John. THE WILD YAZOO. Dutton, 1947. Life on the Mississippi frontier as lived by a Virginia aristocrat in the Indian lands above the Yazoo River in the 1780's and 1790's.

524 Nicholson, Meredith. THE CAVALIER OF TENNESSEE. Bobbs, 1928. Story of Andrew Jackson, 1789 to 1824; Tennessee in pioneer days.

525 Palmer, Bruce and John Clifford Giles. HORSESHOE BEND. Simon and Schuster, 1962. Authentic reconstruction of events leading up to the Battle of Horseshoe Bend during the Creek Indian Wars in Alabama in 1814; characters include

Andrew Jackson, Sam Houston, Davy Crockett, and William Weatherford--Chief Red Eagle of the Creek Indians.

526 Pendexter, Hugh. RED BELTS. Doubleday, 1920. Story of the settling of the Tennessee frontier.

527 _______. A VIRGINIA SCOUT. Bobbs, 1922. Story of Indian warfare on the Virginia frontier.

528 Poole, Ernest. THE NANCY FLYER. Crowell, 1949. A New Hampshire lad witnesses the end of an era as railroads replace the stagecoach; 1835 through the Civil War.

529 Pope, Edith. RIVER IN THE WIND. Scribner, 1954. Scouting, fighting, and social life in the Florida towns during the Seminole Wars, 1835-1842.

530 Price, Eugenia. MARIA. Lippincott, 1977. Colonial Florida under the British through the years of struggle for control with Spain, and the following period of Spanish rule in the late 1700's.

531 Pridgen, Tim. WEST GOES THE ROAD. Doubleday, 1944. Story of a frontiersman fighting Indians, Spaniards, and Frenchmen for the lands between the Alleghenies and the Mississippi River, and opposing Wilkinson and Burr's scheme.

532 Pryor, Elinor. THE DOUBLE MAN. Norton, 1957. Story of Indian life on the American frontier and England in the mid-1800's, as seen by a white man raised by the Cherokees and educated in England, who returns to live with the Indians.

533 Richter, Conrad. A COUNTRY OF STRANGERS. Knopf, 1966. Story of a white girl who grows up as a captive of the Tuscarawas Indians and is rejected by her own family when she is unwillingly returned to Pennsylvania, following Bouquet's expedition in 1765. Sequel to Light in the Forest (Colonial America).

534 Roberts, Elizabeth Maddox. THE GREAT MEADOW. Viking, 1930. Pioneer life as settlers move from Virginia over the Wilderness Road to Harrod's Fort, Kentucky.

535 Seifert, Shirley. NEVER NO MORE. Lippincott, 1964. Rebecca Boone endures Indian raids, the death of her oldest son, and the marriage of a daughter in western Virginia in 1773-1774 before she and Daniel move on to Kentucky.

536 Seton, Anya. MY THEODOSIA. Houghton, 1941. Story of Aaron Burr's daughter, of her relations with her father and his schemes, and of her love for Meriwether Lewis.

537 Skinner, Constance. BECKY LANDERS, FRONTIER WARRIOR.

Macmillan, 1926. Story of a pioneer girl on the Kentucky frontier. Daniel Boone and George Rogers Clark appear.

538 Slate, Sam J. AS LONG AS THE RIVERS RUN. Doubleday, 1972. White man joins the Cherokees fighting with Andrew Jackson in Tennessee in 1813 against the Creek Indians. Later tries to help the Cherokees remain in their homes, only to find Jackson as president betraying his former allies.

539 Slaughter, Frank G. THE WARRIOR. Doubleday, 1956. The Seminole War of 1835, describing contemporary feeling, and the Indian fighting culminating in the capture of Osceola.

540 Stanley, Edward. THE ROCK CRIED OUT. Duell, 1949. The Blennerhassets develop a homestead on an island in the Ohio River and become involved in Aaron Burr's plot.

541 Sterne, Emma Gelders. SOME PLANT OLIVE TREES. Dodd, 1937. Napoleonic exiles form the Vine and Olive colony at Demopolis, Alabama in the early 1800's.

542 Street, James. OH, PROMISED LAND. Dial Press, 1940. Frontier life in the Mississippi Territory (Alabama and Mississippi) from the founding of Natchez to the War of 1812.

543 Sublette, Clifford and Harry Harrison Kroll. PERILOUS JOURNEY. Bobbs, 1943. A tale of the Mississippi River and the Natchez Trace; 1821.

544 Taylor, Robert Lewis. TWO ROADS TO GUADALUPE. Doubleday, 1964. The journals of a teenaged drummer and his older brother tell of their adventures in the Mexican War, 1845-48.

545 Van Every, Dale. WESTWARD THE RIVER. Putnam, 1945. Trip by flatboat down the Ohio River from Pittsburgh to Louisville in 1794.

546 _______. CAPTIVE WITCH. Messner, 1951. Scout for George Rogers Clark escorts prisoners from Vincennes to Virginia, then strikes out for new land in Kentucky.

547 _______. THE VOYAGERS. Holt, 1957. Life on the frontier in the 1780's; centers around the Ohio River valley below Pittsburgh, and the Mississippi River to New Orleans.

548 _______. SCARLET FEATHER. Holt, 1959. Story of a Virginia family who make their way down the Ohio River and settle in the Kentucky wilderness near Louisville in 1785.

549 Vaughan, Carter A. (pseud.). THE RIVER DEVILS. Doubleday,

1968. An adventure tale centering on the politics leading up to the Louisiana Purchase; New Orleans under Spanish and French rule; Thomas Jefferson; James Madison.

550 Ward, Christopher. STRANGE ADVENTURES OF JONATHAN DREW. Simon and Schuster, 1932. Itinerant peddler wanders through the New England and Middle Western frontier; 1821-1824. See author's Yankee Rover (Expanding Frontiers --Southwest).

551 Warren, Robert Penn. WORLD ENOUGH AND TIME. Random, 1950. Story of a Kentucky murder trial of 1820's showing the social and political life of the period.

552 Welty, Eudora. THE ROBBER BRIDEGROOM. Doubleday, 1942. Fanciful tale of a bandit who steals his bride. Set in the Natchez country on the Mississippi River in the early 1800's.

553 Wilder, Robert. BRIGHT FEATHER. Putnam, 1948. Fictional history of the Seminole Wars, 1835-1842. The Seminole leader Osceola is one of the characters.

554 Wylie, I. A. R. HO, THE FAIR WIND. Random, 1945. Narrow-minded religion versus personal integrity. Setting is Martha's Vineyard at the end of the Civil War.

555 Young, Stanley. YOUNG HICKORY. Farrar, 1940. The early years of Andrew Jackson from his boyhood in Waxhaw, North Carolina to his days as a circuit lawyer on the Tennessee frontier.

The Middle West

556 Aldrich, Bess Streeter. SONG OF YEARS. Appleton, 1939. Details of home life in pioneer Iowa; 1854-1865.

557 Allee, Marjorie. JUDITH LANKESTER. Houghton, 1930. Story of a Quaker settlement in Indiana; 1840.

558 _______. A HOUSE OF HER OWN. Houghton, 1934. Frontier life in Indiana; 1850's and 1860's.

559 Allis, Marguerite. NOW WE ARE FREE. Putnam, 1952. Story of the westward migration from Connecticut to Ohio, just after the Revolution.

560 _______. TO KEEP US FREE. Putnam, 1953. Development of the Ohio country from 1797 to 1815; settlement at Marietta; founding of Cleveland; the first census; the Burr-Blennerhassett conspiracy; and the War of 1812.

561 _______. BRAVE PURSUIT. Putnam, 1954. Story of the difficulties of acquiring an education on the frontier; set in Southern Ohio. Followed by The Rising Storm (The Civil War--Abolition).

562 Altrocchi, Julia. WOLVES AGAINST THE MOON. Macmillan, 1940. Fur trading in the Great Lakes region; 1794-1834.

563 Atkinson, Eleanor. HEARTS UNDAUNTED. Harper, 1917. Story of pioneer hardships in the Middle West, life among the Iroquois Indians, and the founding of Chicago.

564 Atkinson, Oriana. THE GOLDEN SEASON. Bobb, 1953. New England seafaring life and the rush to Ohio in the 1790's.

565 Auslander, Joseph. MY UNCLE JAN. Longmans, 1948. Old World customs and festivals among an ebullient family of Czech immigrants in Wisconsin in the 1800's.

566 Babcock, Bernie. THE SOUL OF ANN RUTLEDGE. Lippincott, 1919. Romance of Abe Lincoln and Ann Rutledge; Illinois from 1831 to 1835.

567 Bacheller, Irving. EBEN HOLDEN. Lothrop, 1900. Story of simple life in the Adirondack Mountain region of New York in the 1850's; introduces Abraham Lincoln and Horace Greeley.

568 _______. A MAN FOR THE AGES. Bobbs, 1919. Pioneer days and the formative years of Abraham Lincoln; 1831-1847.

569 Baldwin, Leland. THE DELECTABLE COUNTRY. Lee Furman, 1939. Story of the Ohio River keelboat age, the Whiskey Rebellion, and Pittsburgh in the 1790's.

570 Barney, Helen Corse. FRUIT IN HIS SEASON. Crown, 1951. Story of a Quaker boy who goes to the Ohio wilderness a few years after the Revolution.

571 Benson, Ramsey. HILL COUNTRY. Stokes, 1928. Story of James J. Hill and the settling of the northwest Minnesota country.

572 Brigham, Johnson. THE SINCLAIRS OF OLD FORT DES MOINES. Torch Press, 1927. Pioneer life around Fort Des Moines, Iowa in the early 1840's; Sioux Indians, bootleggers, and squatters.

573 Brink, Carol. CADDIE WOODLAWN. Macmillan, 1935. Pioneer Wisconsin in the 1860's.

574 Carnahan, Walter. HOFFMAN'S ROW. Bobbs, 1963. Account of an incident in the courtship of Abraham Lincoln and Mary

Todd, when he was challenged to duel by a rival for her affections.

575 Colby, Merle. ALL YE PEOPLE. Viking, 1931. Social history of a group of migrants from Vermont to Ohio in 1810.

576 ______. THE NEW ROAD. Viking, 1933. Traces the development of a settlement on the Maumee River in Ohio from about 1820 to 1840.

577 Cook, Roberta St. Clair. THE THING ABOUT CLARISSA. Bobbs, 1958. Contrasts life in a ladies' seminary in Philadelphia with the manners and customs on the Ohio frontier in 1837.

578 Cooper, James Fenimore. THE PRAIRIE. Dodd, 1827. Story of life on the prairies beyond the Mississippi River at the time of Jefferson's administration. Sequel to The Pioneers (Colonial America).

579 Cooper, Jamie Lee. THE HORN AND THE FOREST. Bobbs, 1963. A tale of frontier life in the Indiana Territory and of the events leading to General Benjamin Harrison's campaign against the Indians at the Battle of Tippecanoe in 1811.

580 Daviess, Maria. THE MATRIX. Century, 1920. The love story of Nancy Hanks and Thomas Lincoln.

581 Derleth, August. WIND OVER WISCONSIN. Scribner, 1938. The Black Hawk Wars and the transition from fur trading to farming in Wisconsin in the 1830's.

582 ______. STILL IS THE SUMMER NIGHT. Scribner, 1937. Sac Prairie, Wisconsin in the 1880's when lumber rafts were floated down the Wisconsin River.

583 ______. RESTLESS IS THE RIVER. Scribner, 1939. Story of the early settlement of Wisconsin; 1839-1850.

584 ______. BRIGHT JOURNEY. Scribner, 1940. Adventures of Hercules Dousman, an agent of John Jacob Astor in the Northwest Territory; 1812-1843.

585 ______. THE HOUSE ON THE MOUND. Duell, 1958. Continues the story of Hercules Dousman, fur trader and railroad builder, begun in Bright Journey (above).

586 ______. THE HILLS STAND WATCH. Duell, 1960. Pioneer life in a small lead-mining town in Wisconsin in the 1840's; local politics and the movement toward statehood, trouble with the Indians, and details of lead mining.

587 ______. THE SHADOW IN THE GRASS. Duell, 1963.

Biographical novel of Nelson Dewey, first governor of Wisconsin, who came to Wisconsin Territory from New York in 1836.

588 Duncan, Thomas W. BIG RIVER, BIG MAN. Lippincott, 1959. Story of the Wisconsin logging industry with many characters and with settings in the North Woods, New Mexico, New England, and the Civil War South.

589 _______. THE LABYRINTH. Doubleday, 1967. Family and farm life in Iowa in the 1800's.

590 Eggleston, Edward. THE HOOSIER SCHOOL-MASTER. Scribner, 1871. Tale of Indiana backwoods life and education in the 1850's.

591 _______. THE CIRCUIT RIDER. Scribner, 1874. Daily life and customs and frontier religion in Ohio; 1800-1825.

592 _______. THE HOOSIER SCHOOL-BOY. Scribner, 1883. Life in Indiana and Ohio about 1840, showing the difficulties of acquiring an education on the frontier.

593 _______. THE GRAYSONS. Scribner, 1887. Picture of daily life and customs in rural Illinois about 1850.

594 Ellis, William D. THE BOUNTY LANDS. World, 1952. Story of conflict between speculators and settlers in Ohio after the Revolution, involving lands granted to the veterans for their war service.

595 _______. JONATHAN BLAIR, BOUNTY LANDS LAWYER. World, 1954. Story of a lawyer on the Ohio frontier; picture of daily life and customs; sequel to The Bounty Lands.

596 _______. THE BROOKS LEGEND. Crowell, 1958. Story of medical practice and daily life on the Ohio frontier in the years following the War of 1812; continues the story of some of the characters of The Bounty Lands.

597 Faralla, Dana. CIRCLE OF TREES. Lippincott, 1955. Story of the prairies of Minnesota in 1880, and of the Danes who settled there.

598 Finney, Gertrude E. THE PLUMS HANG HIGH. Longmans, 1955. Story of family life on a pioneer farm in the American Midwest; 1868 to 1890.

599 Fuller, Iola. THE LOON FEATHER. Harcourt, 1940. Fictionized autobiography of Tecumseh's daughter. Setting is the Mackinac region in the early 1800's.

600 _______. THE SHINING TRAIL. Duell, 1943. Centers around

the life of the Sauk Indians and their struggles leading up to the Black Hawk Wars; 1820's to the 1830's.

601 Furnas, Joseph C. THE DEVIL'S RAINBOW. Harper, 1962. Biographical novel centering around Joseph Smith and the Mormons, from his arrival in Kirtland, Ohio in 1831, through the exodus to Nauvoo, Illinois, and to his death in 1844.

602 Garth, David. FIRE ON THE WIND. Putnam, 1951. Story of the Upper Michigan peninsula in the 1860's; logging, mining and railroading.

603 Gay, Margaret Cooper. HATCHET IN THE SKY. Simon and Schuster, 1954. Life with the Ojibway Indians under Chief Pontiac in the Northwest Territory; scenes in early Detroit.

604 Grierson, Francis. VALLEY OF SHADOWS. Harper, 1966. (Reprint of 1909 edition.) Frontier portraits of the Sangamon country, infused with the forboding sense of the coming Civil War.

605 Hallet, Richard. MICHAEL BEAM. Houghton, 1939. Story of the Black Hawk Wars and life on the Illinois and Wisconsin frontier; 1820's and 1830's.

606 Harris, Laura B. BRIDE OF THE RIVER. Crowell, 1956. Story of the adjustment of a Louisiana plantation belle to life in a small Ohio River town in the late 1830's, including slave traffic on the Underground Railroad.

607 Havighurst, Walter. QUIET SHORE. Macmillan, 1937. Homesteading on Lake Erie just after the Civil War, and the growth of industry in Ohio.

608 ________. WINDS OF SPRING. Macmillan, 1940. The settling of Wisconsin; 1840's to 1870's.

609 Havill, Edward. BIG EMBER. Harper, 1947. Norwegian immigrants and the uprising of the Sioux in Southern Minnesota in 1862.

610 Kantor, MacKinlay. SPIRIT LAKE. World, 1961. Story of the settlers and the Indians involved in the Spirit Lake massacre in Iowa in 1857; picture of social and economic life on the frontier in the 1850's.

611 Krause, Herbert. THE OXCART TRAIL. Bobbs, 1954. Story of settlers and traders pushing into the Minnesota Territory in the 1850's.

612 Lancaster, Bruce. FOR US THE LIVING. Stokes, 1940. Abraham Lincoln in Indiana and Illinois.

613 Lockwood, Sarah. FISTFUL OF STARS. Appleton, 1947. Northern Wisconsin in the 1880's.

614 Lovelace, Maud Hart. THE BLACK ANGELS. Day, 1926. Story of a musical family touring small towns of the Minnesota Territory; local color and social history.

615 _______. EARLY CANDLELIGHT. Day, 1929. Frontier life along the Minnesota and the Mississippi rivers; Fort Snelling (St. Paul), Minnesota in the 1830's.

616 _______. ONE STAYED AT WELCOME. Day, 1934. Pioneering in Minnesota in the 1850's.

617 _______, and D. W. Lovelace. GENTLEMEN FROM ENGLAND. Macmillan, 1937. Picture of life in Minnesota; 1860's-1870's.

618 Lutes, Della. GABRIEL'S SEARCH. Little, 1940. Details of daily life in Michigan in the early 1800's.

619 McLean, Sydney. MOMENT OF TIME. Putnam, 1945. Seventy years in the life of a pioneer woman, from girlhood before the Revolution to the 1840's.

620 McLeod, LeRoy. THE YEARS OF PEACE. Appleton, 1932. Story of daily life in the Wabash River valley of Indiana after the Civil War.

621 McMahon, Thomas. McKAY'S BEES. Harper, 1979. In 1855, a Bostonian, his wife, and his brother-in-law set forth to Kansas to found a community devoted to apiculture and honey production. The naturalist Agassiz appears in the story. Part of the plot concerns the Missourians who come to battle the free-staters.

622 McNeil, Everett. DANIEL DULUTH. Dutton, 1926. Story of the exploration of the Great Lakes, from Montreal to Lake Superior, by Daniel DuLuth.

623 Magnuson, James and Dorothy Petrie. ORPHAN TRAIN. Dial, 1978. Based on historical fact. In 1853 the first group of orphans are loaded on a train in New York, heading for the rural Midwest where new homes might be found. The Reverend Edward Symms and his daughter Anne are their caretakers in transit.

624 Masters, Edgar Lee. CHILDREN OF THE MARKET PLACE. Macmillan, 1922. Story of an English immigrant in Illinois; 1833-1861.

625 Matschat, Cecile Hulse. PREACHER ON HORSEBACK. Farrar, 1940. Story of a circuit-riding preacher in Michigan and northern New York in the 1870's.

626 Matthews, Jack. SASSAFRAS. Houghton, 1983. Phrenology was a popular pseudo-science in the early nineteenth century. This fictional practitioner took his skill on the road, reading skulls in small towns from Ohio to Kansas.

627 Mayer, Albert I. FOLLOW THE RIVER. Doubleday, 1969. A long tale of frontier settlement and Indian fighting in the Ohio country in the 1790's. The hero journeys down the Ohio River to Cincinnati to teach; later joins General Josiah Harmar's expedition against the Indians along the Maumee River.

628 Meader, Stephen. BOY WITH A PACK. Harcourt, 1939. Tale of a young itinerant peddler wandering from New Hampshire to the Ohio frontier, 1837.

629 Means, Florence. CANDLE IN THE MIST. Houghton, 1931. Minnesota in the 1870's.

630 Meigs, Cornelia. SWIFT RIVERS. Little, 1932. Minnesota in the early 1800's. Floating logs down the Mississippi River to St. Louis.

631 Miller, Helen Topping. BORN STRANGERS. Bobbs, 1949. Picture of life in Michigan from pioneer days to the Civil War.

632 Moberg, Vilhelm. UNTO A GOOD LAND. Simon and Schuster, 1954. Story of Swedish immigrants pioneering in the Minnesota Territory in the 1850's.

633 ________. LAST LETTER HOME. Simon and Schuster, 1961. Picture of the growth of frontier communities in the Minnesota Territory, the Sioux uprising, and the Civil War; details of family life up to 1890. Sequel to Unto a Good Land (above).

634 Orr, Myron David. MISSION TO MACKINAC. Dodd, 1956. Story of English-French conflict in the area of Mackinac Island prior to the War of 1812.

635 Oskison, John. BROTHERS THREE. Macmillan, 1935. Farm life in the Indian Territory after 1873.

636 Ostenso, Martha. O RIVER, REMEMBER. Dodd, 1943. Irish and Norwegian pioneers in the Red River valley of the Minnesota country; 1870-1941.

637 Peattie, Donald Culross. A PRAIRIE GROVE. Simon and Schuster, 1938. Saga of missionaries, traders, Indians, settlers, and the founding of Chicago.

638 Quick, Herbert. VANDEMARK'S FOLLY. Bobbs, 1922.

Pioneering in Iowa, 1840's to 1860's; claim jumping, frontier law, and the Underground Railroad.

639 _______. THE HAWKEYE. Bobbs, 1923. Political, social, and farm life in Iowa, 1857-1878. Sequel to Vandemark's Folly.

640 Reed, Warren. SHE RODE A YELLOW STALLION. Bobbs, 1950. Farming and horse raising in Southeastern Wisconsin, 1840's-1890's; picture of German, Irish, and Scottish settlers, and the development of the cheese industry.

641 Richter, Conrad. THE TREES. Knopf, 1940. First of a series on the development of the Ohio wilderness.

642 _______. THE FIELDS. Knopf, 1946. Story of the development of a community in the Ohio wilderness. Sequel to The Trees.

643 _______. THE TOWN. Knopf, 1950. Emergence of a frontier town and the trappings of civilization in the Ohio wilderness. Sequel to The Fields.

644 Sanders, Scott. WILDERNESS PLOTS. Morrow, 1983. A series of sketches of pioneer life in the Ohio valley. Arranged in chronological order from 1781 to 1861.

645 Seifert, Shirley. THE WAYFARER. M. S. Mill, 1938. Fictional biography of John Cotter; whaling, trading in the West, fighting in the Civil War, and stock farming in Missouri.

646 _______. THE MEDICINE MAN. Lippincott, 1971. Based on the real-life story of Antoine Saugrain, the physician who escaped the French Revolution, settled in St. Louis in 1800 and successfully introduced the widely feared new smallpox vaccination.

647 Selby, John. ELEGANT JOURNEY. Rinehart, 1944. Southerner frees slaves and starts out anew in Wisconsin; 1840's.

648 Sinclair, Harold. AMERICAN YEARS. Doubleday, 1938. History of a small Illinois town; 1830 to the Civil War.

649 Skelton, Jess. MARTIN'S LAND. Chilton, 1961. Life among the Osage Indians and on a Spanish land grant on the Missouri frontier in 1785.

650 Snedeker, Caroline. SETH WAY. Houghton, 1917. Life in the New Harmony settlement in Indiana in the 1840's.

651 _______. BECKONING ROAD. Doubleday, 1929. Story of the New Harmony settlement in Indiana in the 1840's.

652 _______. THE TOWN OF THE FEARLESS. Doubleday, 1931. European background and the founding of the New Harmony community in Indiana. Robert Owen, Pestalozzi, and others appear.

653 Spicer, Bart. THE WILD OHIO. Dodd, 1953. Settlement of French émigrés at Gallipolis, Ohio.

654 Stong, Philip. BUCKSKIN BREECHES. Farrar, 1937. Westward migration from Ohio to Iowa, 1837.

655 Suchow, Ruth. COUNTRY PEOPLE. Knopf, 1924. Family chronicle of pioneer hardships of a group of German-Americans who settled in Iowa in the 1850's.

656 Swanson, Neil. THE PHANTOM EMPEROR. Putnam, 1934. Based on an attempt to form a separate empire in the Northwest Territory in 1836.

657 Teilhet, Darwin. STEAMBOAT ON THE RIVER. Sloane, 1952. Story of the first steamboat on the Sangamon River in Illinois in the 1830's; introduces Abe Lincoln, who pilots the boat to safety around New Salem.

658 Titus, Harold. BLACK FEATHER. Macrae, 1936. Story of the Astor fur-trading enterprise around Mackinac Island.

659 Todd, Helen. SO FREE WE SEEM. Reynal, 1936. Story of a pioneer woman on the Missouri frontier.

660 Troyer, Howard. THE SALT AND THE SAVOR. Wyn, 1950. Chronicles the development of Indiana from pioneer days to the Civil War; development of the Grange movement, daily life and customs.

661 Van Every, Dale. THE TREMBLING EARTH. Messner, 1953. Lead mining in southeast Missouri at the time of the New Madrid earthquake of 1811.

662 Voelker, John Donaldson. LAUGHING WHITEFISH. McGraw, 1965. Follows the course of a law suit of an Indian girl against a powerful mining company; Marquette, Michigan in 1873.

663 Walker, Mildred. IF A LION COULD TALK. Harcourt, 1970. Based on real persons. A tragic tale of a minister and his wife who go from Massachusetts to the wilderness of Missouri to convert the Indians. Frightened, unsuccessful, they return in defeat and the man loses his congregation and his wife.

664 West, Jessamyn. THE FRIENDLY PERSUASION. Harcourt, 1945. Episodes in the life of a Quaker family in Indiana, including a minor Civil War encounter.

665 _______. LEAFY RIVERS. Harcourt, 1967. Life on a midwestern homestead and in Cincinnati around 1818.

666 _______. EXCEPT FOR ME AND THEE. Harcourt, 1969. Earlier episodes in the courtship and marriage of the Birdwells' of Friendly Persuasion, as they settle a farm on the Indiana frontier, cooperate with the Underground Railroad, and raise their family in good Quaker tradition.

667 _______. THE MASSACRE AT FALL CREEK. Harcourt, 1975. Story based on a true incident Four white men and a boy are tried for the 1824 massacre of nine Seneca Indians in frontier Indiana.

668 Whitlock, Brand. THE STRANGERS ON THE ISLAND. Appleton, 1933. Story of the exiled group of Mormons on Beaver Island in Lake Michigan in 1850.

669 Wilson, Margaret. ABLE McLAUGHLINS. Harper, 1923. Midwestern Scotch community in the 1860's.

670 Wyckoff, Nicholas. THE CORINTHIANS. Macmillan, 1960. Story of small-town life in Illinois and Missouri in the 1850's; pictures the effect of the Mormons on the places and people they meet on their westward movement.

671 Zara, Louis. THIS LAND IS OURS. Houghton, 1940. Story of American frontier life from the Susquehanna to the Mississippi River, 1755 to 1835; Chief Pontiac, George Rogers Clark, and General Anthony Wayne appear.

The Southwest

672 Adams, Andy. LOG OF A COWBOY. Houghton, 1903. Picture of western ranch life; daily journal of a cattle drive from Texas to Wyoming.

673 Allen, Henry. MACKINNA'S GOLD. Random, 1963. Dramatic story of a young prospector leading a group of outlaws to a hidden treasure in Arizona in 1897.

674 _______. ONE MORE RIVER TO CROSS. Random, 1967. An Arkansas Negro escapes to freedom in Texas; after a career of rustling, he settles on an Oklahoma cotton farm.

675 _______. CHIRICAHUA. Lippincott, 1972. Difficulties of an Apache Indian who recognizes the inevitable supremacy of the white civilization in Arizona of the 1880's. He is regarded as a turncoat by other Indians, while white men distrust him.

676 Arnold, Elliot. BLOOD BROTHER. Duell, 1947. Account of

the Apache wars in New Mexico and Arizona; sympathetic with the Indians.

677 _______. TIME OF THE GRINGO. Knopf, 1953. Story of New Mexico under the Mexican governor, Don Manuel Armijo, just before the Mexican War.

678 _______. CAMP GRANT MASSACRE. Simon and Schuster, 1976. Arizona in the 1870's. A fragile peace based on the friendship between an army officer and an Apache chief is ended when fearful settlers raid the Indian village.

679 Aydelotte, Dora. TRUMPETS CALLING. Appleton, 1938. Story of the Cherokee Strip and the settling of Oklahoma in the 1890's.

680 _______. RUN OF THE STARS. Appleton, 1940. Picture of life in the Oklahoma Territory at the time of its settlement in the 1890's.

681 Baker, Karle. STAR OF THE WILDERNESS. Coward, 1942. Story of the struggle for Texas' independence; set chiefly in Nacogdoces.

682 Barrett, Monte. THE TEMPERED BLADE. Bobbs, 1946. Fictional biography of James Bowie from 1815 to his death at the Alamo in 1836.

683 Barry, Jane. A TIME IN THE SUN. Doubleday, 1962. Story of two women, captured by the Apaches, who witness the Indians' struggle against the encroachment of the Americans and Mexicans in Arizona Territory in the 1870's; introduces the Indian leaders Cochise, Victorio, and Nane.

684 _______. A SHADOW OF EAGLES. Doubleday, 1964. Life on a cattle ranch in southwestern Texas and on a cattle drive to Montana in the 1870's.

685 _______. MAXIMILIAN'S GOLD. Doubleday, 1966. A band of Southerners search for a cache of gold, supposedly hidden by Emperor Maximilian; set in Missouri, Texas, and Mexico in post-Civil War days.

686 Bass, Milton R. JORY. Putnam, 1969. Adventures of a young cowboy and gunslinger in Texas of the 1870's.

687 Bean, Amelia. THE FEUD. Doubleday, 1960. Violent story of sheep and cattle ranching, based on the Graham-Tewksbury feud in Arizona in the 1880's.

688 _______. TIME FOR OUTRAGE. Doubleday, 1967. Tale of the Lincoln County War in New Mexico in 1878; hero is a boyhood friend of William Bonney (Billy the Kid).

689 Bennett, Dwight. CHEROKEE OUTLET. Doubleday, 1961. Opening of the Cherokee Strip in Northern Oklahoma in 1893; shows the change from open prairie to farmland and the development of towns.

690 Blacker, Irwin R. TAOS. World, 1959. Revolt of the Pueblo Indians against the Spaniards in New Mexico in 1680; climaxed by the bloody massacre at Santa Fe.

691 Blake, Forrester. JOHNNY CHRISTMAS. Morrow, 1948. American Southwest from 1836 to 1846, when Mexicans opposed the incoming Americans.

692 ________. THE FRANCISCAN. Doubleday, 1963. A Franciscan priest works to protect the Pueblo Indians from the Spaniards in early New Mexico in 1675.

693 Bosworth, Allan Bernard. THE LONG WAY NORTH. Doubleday, 1959. Story of character, played out during a cattle drive from Texas to Montana Territory.

694 Boyd, James. BITTER CREEK. Scribner, 1939. Incidents of ranch life and Indian warfare in the story of a young boy making his way to the West in the 1870's.

695 Brackett, Leigh. FOLLOW THE FREE WIND. Doubleday, 1963. Based on the life of James Beckwourth, son of a slave, who went West as a blacksmith, was adopted by the Crow Indians, and lived and fought with them against the whites.

696 Brand, Max. THE LONG CHANCE. Dodd, 1941. The Old West in the days before the Civil War.

697 Bristow, Gwen. JUBILEE TRAIL. Crowell, 1950. Story of a trading and honeymoon trip over the Santa Fe Trail from New York to California in 1845.

698 Brown, Dee. WAVE HIGH THE BANNER. Macrae, 1942. The life of Davy Crockett, from boyhood to death at the Alamo.

699 Bryan, Jack Y. COME TO THE BOWER. A New Orleans lawyer becomes involved in the war for Texas' independence in 1835-36; Santa Anna, the Battle of the Alamo, the Battle of San Jacinto.

700 Burnett, William Riley. SAINT JOHNSON. Longmans, 1930. Story of lawless Tombstone, Arizona and the Earp-Clanton feud.

701 ________. ADOBE WALLS. Knopf, 1953. Story of the last Apache uprising in the 1880's and of the tactics used by generals Crook and Miles in defeating the Indians.

702 _______. MI AMIGO. Knopf, 1959. Based on the Lincoln County wars in New Mexico in 1878 and the story of Billy the Kid (William Bonney).

703 Busch, Niven. DUEL IN THE SUN. Morrow, 1944. Texas in the 1880's with wide-open towns and cattlemen fighting the railroad and the homesteaders.

704 Campbell, Walter Stanley. DOBE WALLS. Houghton, 1929. Life on the Santa Fe Trail in the days of Kit Carson.

705 Capps, Benjamin. THE TRAIL TO OGALLALA. Duell, 1964. Story of the rough life on a cattle drive from Texas to Nebraska.

706 _______. SAM CHANCE. Duell, 1965. A Civil War veteran becomes a Texas cattle rancher and creates an empire before his death in 1922.

707 _______. A WOMAN OF THE PEOPLE. Duell, 1966. A white girl captured by the Indians in 1854 witnesses the daily life and customs of the Comanche Indians and their struggle against the encroachment and raids by the white man; Texas from the 1850's to the 1870's.

708 _______. WHITE MAN'S ROAD. Harper, 1969. Indian life in the 1890's in the story of a young Comanche searching for identity in a society taken over by the white man.

709 Carter, Forrest. GONE TO TEXAS. Delacorte Press/Eleanor Freide, 1975. The Union Army has trouble subduing Confederate rebels, Indians, and bandits in Texas in the period during and just after the Civil War. First published in 1973 under the title The Rebel Outlaw.

710 _______. WATCH FOR ME ON THE MOUNTAIN. Delacorte, 1978. Novel about the life of Geronimo, the Chiricahua Apache chief who fought a long hit-and-run war against American settlers in the Southwest.

711 Cather, Willa. DEATH COMES FOR THE ARCHBISHOP. Knopf, 1927. Story of two French priests in New Mexico soon after the Mexican War.

712 Comfort, Will. APACHE. Dutton, 1931. Story of Mangas Colorados, famous Apache chieftain, and of his efforts to unite the Indians.

713 Constant, Alberta. OKLAHOMA RUN. Crowell, 1955. Pioneer life and homesteading in the Oklahoma Territory in the 1890's.

714 Cook, Will. ELIZABETH BY NAME. Dodd, 1958. Life on a

frontier trading post on the Texas prairie in the post-Civil War period.

715 Cooke, David Coxe. THE POST OF HONOR. Putnam, 1958. Authentic picture of Indian-white relations and details of Apache Indian fighting on an isolated outpost in the Arizona Territory.

716 Cooper, Courtney Ryley. OKLAHOMA. Little, 1926. Epic tale of the opening of the Oklahoma Territory to homesteading, the rush of settlers, and the development of the state.

717 Cooper, Jamie Lee. SHADOW OF A STAR. Bobbs, 1965. Three brothers from the Basque country come to Spanish New Mexico in the 1680's; one becomes a trader, another turns to renegade fur trapping, the other becomes a priest among the Indians.

718 Corle, Edwin. BILLY THE KID. Duell, 1953. Fictional biography of the famous outlaw William Bonney.

719 Culp, John H. BORN OF THE SUN. Sloane, 1959. Life on a Texas cattle ranch in the 1870's; picture of the cattle drives to Kansas. Followed by The Restless Land.

720 _______. THE MEN OF GONZALES. Sloane, 1960. Story of the hurried march of 32 men from Gonzales to San Antonio in 1836 to reinforce the besieged garrison at the Alamo.

721 _______. THE RESTLESS LAND. Sloane, 1962. Life in a frontier community in northwest Texas in the 1870's depicting range wars, cattle drives, and conflicts with the Comanche Indians. Sequel to Born of the Sun.

722 _______. A WHISTLE IN THE WIND. Holt, 1968. Story of the lives of white captives of the Comanche Indians as the Indians are dispersed and the land is settled; Texas in the 1870's.

723 _______. TIMOTHY BAINES. Holt, 1969. Outlaws, Indians, and medicine on the Texas frontier in the 1870's.

724 _______. TREASURE OF THE CHISOS. Holt, 1971. Adventure of a young man in search of fortune as he travels down the Mississippi on a whiskey-runner, across Indian Territory, to the southwestern tip of Texas.

725 _______. OH, VALLEY GREEN. Holt, 1972. Father and son, engaged in an espionage plot concerning the annexation of Texas in 1842, travel from their Virginia home to Santa Fe.

726 Davis, James F. THE ROAD TO SAN JACINTO. Bobbs, 1936.

Sam Houston and the struggle for Texas' independence; 1835-1836. Bowie, Crockett, and Travis appear.

727 Dawkins, William Cecil. THE LIVE GOAT. Ultramarine, 1971. Pre-Civil War period; a posse rides through the West, from Carolina to Texas, to hunt down a mentally defective murderer. They meet adventurers, pioneering settlers, and runaway slaves in the raw frontier country.

728 Di Donato, Georgia. WOMAN OF JUSTICE. Doubleday, 1980. Temperance Smith, a real-life ancestor of the author, was the first woman judge in the West. In 1875 she was appointed an assistant to the famous Isaac Parker, at Fort Smith in the Arkansas Territory.

729 Dodge, Louis. THE AMERICAN. Messner, 1934. Saga of the American West in the 1850's; the gold rush, homesteading, fur trading, fighting the Indians, and life on the Santa Fe Trail.

730 Duffus, Robert L. JORNADA. Covici, 1935. A romance of the Southwest; wagon trains to Santa Fe; Indian raids; and and the Mexican War.

731 Erdman, Loula. THE EDGE OF TIME. Dodd, 1950. Story of a wagon journey to the Texas panhandle and life on an isolated farm on the prairie in 1885.

732 _______. THE FAR JOURNEY. Dodd, 1955. Overland trip from Missouri to Texas in the 1890's.

733 Evarts, Hal. TUMBLEWEEDS. Little, 1923. The Cherokee Strip and the Oklahoma frontier in the 1890's.

734 Ferber, Edna. CIMARRON. Doubleday, 1930. Oklahoma from the opening of the Cherokee Strip in the 1890's to the striking of oil; picture of the development of the state.

735 Fergusson, Harvey. THE CONQUEST OF DON PEDRO. Morrow, 1954. Social history of a frontier town in New Mexico soon after the Civil War.

736 _______. IN THOSE DAYS. Knopf, 1929. Story of the development of a small town on the Rio Grande River, from the days of wagon trains and Indian raids to the 1920's.

737 Flynn, Robert. NORTH TO YESTERDAY. Knopf, 1967. Life on a Texas cattle drive after the Civil War.

738 Foreman, Leonard. THE ROAD TO SAN JACINTO. Dutton, 1943. Story of Davy Crockett on the way to join the Texans in defense of the Alamo.

739 Gerson, Noel B. THE GOLDEN EAGLE. Doubleday, 1953. The Mexican War, 1845-1848; secret agent draws maps of Vera Cruz for General Winfield Scott.

740 _______. SAM HOUSTON. Doubleday, 1968. Fictional biography of Sam Houston from his childhood in Tennessee, service under Andrew Jackson, leading the war for Texas' independence, action at the battles of the Alamo and San Jacinto, to governor of Texas and U. S. senator.

741 Giles, Janice Holt. JOHNNY OSAGE. Houghton, 1960. Story of a young trader living among the Osage Indians in Arkansas Territory in the 1820's.

742 _______. SAVANNA. Houghton, 1961. Story of a woman facing life alone in Arkansas Territory in the 1830's; plot involves competition between trading posts around Fort Gibson and the activities of Sam Houston.

743 _______. VOYAGE TO SANTA FE. Houghton, 1962. Johnny Fowler and his young wife leave the Arkansas Territroy in 1823 bound for Santa Fe with a 20-man mule train carrying trading supplies. Sequel to Johnny Osage.

744 Gipson, Fred. OLD YELLER. Harper, 1956. Boy's life on a prairie farm in Texas in the 1860's.

745 Glidden, Frederick. AND THE WIND BLOWS FREE. Macmillan, 1945. Story of the cattlemen evicted from the Indian grasslands, later a part of Oklahoma, by order of President Cleveland in the 1880's.

746 Gorman, Herbert. THE WINE OF SAN LORENZO. Farrar, 1945. Presents the Mexican viewpoint of the Mexican War; an American boy, captured at the Alamo, fights with Santa Anna in the war.

747 Grant, Blanch. DOÑA LONA. Funk, 1941. Santa Fe and Taos, New Mexico in the 1830's and 1840's.

748 Grey, Zane. THE HERITAGE OF THE DESERT. Harper, 1910. Mormons, Indians, and cowboys in a story of life on the Arizona desert during the early days of the settlement of the Southwest.

749 _______. FIGHTING CARAVANS. Harper, 1929. The West at the time of the Civil War.

750 Hall, Oakley. WARLOCK. Viking, 1958. Story of the violent life in a frontier mining town in the Southwest Territory in the 1880's.

751 Hogan, Pendleton. THE DARK COMES EARLY. Washburn,

1934. Events leading up to the fight for Texas' independence and to the Mexican War.

752 Hooker, Forrestine. WHEN GERONIMO RODE. Doubleday, 1924. Life in a frontier army post during the last campaign against the Apache Indians in Arizona.

753 Horgan, Paul. A DISTANT TRUMPET. Farrar, 1960. Life on a remote army post, Fort Delivery, in the Arizona Territory in the 1880's in the face of a constant threat of attack by the Apaches.

754 Hough, Emerson. NORTH OF 36. Appleton, 1923. Story of the beginnings of the great cattle drives from Texas north to the railroad markets in Kansas.

755 Houston, Margaret Bell. COTTONWOODS GROW TALL. Crown, 1958. Family life and tragedy on a Texas ranch in the 1890's.

756 Irving, Clifford. THE VALLEY. McGraw, 1961. A story of father-son conflict and life on a cattle ranch in New Mexico in post-Civil War years.

757 James, Will. THE AMERICAN COWBOY. Scribner, 1942. Picture of cattle ranching in the Southwest, through three generations of cowhands.

758 Jayne, Mitchell. OLD FISH HAWK. Lippincott, 1970. An Osage Indian is driven to alcoholism as his wilderness world is converted to settlers' farms in the Ozarks. But the tragic death of a friend catalyzes his coming to terms with himself, and his friendship enriches the life of a young white settler.

759 Jennings, John. SHADOWS IN THE DUSK. Little, 1955. A tale of Apache revenge for the plot of unscrupulous whites to collect the government bounty on Indian scalps; picture of copper mining in the Southwest.

760 Jones, Douglas C. WINDING STAIR. Holt, 1979. A novel about a real group of desperadoes who commit a series of murders in the Winding Stair Mountains during the 1890's. The lawmen who pursue them are fictional, but they are brought to trial before the real Isaac Parker, history's "hanging judge."

761 ________. SEASON OF THE YELLOW LEAF. Holt, 1983. The ten-year-old daughter of settlers is captured by Comanches, acculturated, and later marries within the tribe. The Comanche are doomed, and eventually fate returns her to the now alien world of the white man.

762 ________. GONE THE DREAMS AND THE DANCING. Holt,

1984. Sequel to Season of the Yellow Leaf. The Indian son of the heroine of that novel, now chief of his tribe, surrenders them at Fort Sill. Based on the real Quanah Parker's life.

763 Kelland, Clarence Budington. VALLEY OF THE SUN. Harper, 1940. Tale of Arizona and the beginnings of Phoenix in the 1870's.

764 Kirkland, Elithe. DIVINE AVERAGE. Little, 1952. Theme of racial tolerance and the conflict between Americans, Indians, and Mexicans in Texas in 1838.

765 ______. LOVE IS A WILD ASSAULT. Doubleday, 1959. Daily life, politics, and brutality in early Texas; a biographical novel based on the life of Harriet Ann Moore, a Texas pioneer.

766 Knaggs, John R. THE BUGLES ARE SILENT. Shoal Creek, 1977. Texas War for Independence of 1835-1836 as seen by participants on both sides.

767 Krey, Laura. ON THE LONG TIDE. Houghton, 1940. Story of the American settlement of Texas, 1812-1836; Sam Houston, Stephen Austin, Bill Travis, Andrew Jackson, and others appear.

768 Lafferty, R. A. OKLA HANNALI. Doubleday, 1972. Story of a Choctaw Indian who lived through the uprooting of his civilization when the Choctaws were forced from their southeastern homes to the Oklahoma Territory.

769 Lanham, Edwin. THE WIND BLEW WEST. Longmans, 1935. Political, economic, and social development of a small Texas town from 1875 to 1885.

770 Laughlin, Ruth. THE WIND LEAVES NO SHADOW. Whittlesey, 1948. Santa Fe in the years before the Mexican War.

771 Lea, Tom. THE WONDERFUL COUNTRY. Little, 1952. Story of the people who helped build Puerto, Texas in the 1880's; includes Texas Rangers, railroad promoters, Mexicans, and Indians.

772 LeMay, Alan. THE SEARCHERS. Harper, 1954. Life on the Texas frontier just after the Civil War, when the Comanche were opposing encroachment by white settlers.

773 ______. THE UNFORGIVEN. Harper, 1957. Pioneer life under the threat of a Kiowa Indian attack in Texas in the 1870's.

774 Loomis, Noel. A TIME FOR VIOLENCE. Macmillan, 1960.

Story of the struggles between ranchers and outlaws in the Texas panhandle in the 1880's.

775 Lott, Milton. BACKTRACK. Houghton, 1965. Story of a cattle drive from Texas to Montana.

776 McCague, James. FORTUNE ROAD. Harper, 1965. An itinerant newspaperman and two children share adventures as they travel west in the 1860's.

777 McCarter, Margaret. VANGUARDS OF THE PLAINS. Harper, 1917. Story of an expedition from Kansas City to Santa Fe in the 1840's.

778 McMurtry, Larry. LEAVING CHEYENNE. Harper & Row, 1963. A woman and two men share life on a Texas ranch for 50 years.

779 Morgan, Speer. BELLE STARR. Atlantic, 1979. The final months of life of outlaw Belle, who will be murdered in 1889 in the Oklahoma Territory.

780 Mulford, Clarence E. BRING ME HIS EARS. McClure, 1922. Adventures on the Missouri River and the Santa Fe Trail in the 1840's.

781 Myers, John. I, JACK SWILLING. Hastings House, 1961. Story of the founding of Phoenix, Arizona following the discovery of a prehistoric waterway in the middle of the desert.

782 Newsom, Ed. WAGONS TO TUCSON. Little, 1954. Story of a wagon train crossing the plains to Arizona at the close of the Civil War. Picture of Apache raids and life at Fort Reno in Oklahoma Territory.

783 Ogden, George Washington. THE LAND OF LAST CHANCE. McClurg, 1919. Story of the land run and the settling of the Oklahoma Territory in the 1890's.

784 ________. SOONER LAND. Dodd, 1929. Story of pioneering and homesteading in Oklahoma Territory in the 1890's.

785 O'Meary, Walter. SPANISH BRIDE. Putnam, 1954. The Spanish struggling to maintain control in the Southwest; story of the mistress of the Spanish governor in Santa Fe.

786 O'Rourke, Frank. FAR MOUNTAINS. Morrow, 1959. An orphan Irish-American boy grows up as a Spanish-Mexican in Taos, New Mexico; story of the decline of Spanish influence, culminating in the U.S. annexation of Texas and the invasion of Mexico during the Mexican War; 1801-1848.

787 Oskison, John Milton. BLACK JACK DAVY. Appleton, 1926.

Story of life among pioneer settlers who move from Arkansas to the Indian territory of the Southwest in the 1800's.

788 Owens, William A. LOOK TO THE RIVER. Atheneum, 1963. Adventures of a young runaway in the Texas Red River plains in 1910.

789 Pearce, Richard. THE IMPUDENT RIFLE. Lippincott, 1951. Life in a frontier fort in the Arkansas Territory during the Jackson administration; pictures the migration of the Choctaw, and war with the Commanche.

790 _______. THE RESTLESS BORDER. Lippincott, 1953. Comanche warfare and fights with Santa Anna at an army outpost on the Red River in the 1840's.

791 Portis, Charles. TRUE GRIT. Simon & Schuster, 1968. A girl and a U.S. Marshal set out to revenge her father's death; Arkansas to the Indian Territory in the 1880's.

792 Prebble, John. SPANISH STIRRUP. Harcourt, 1958. Story of one of the first great cattle drives from Texas to market in Kansas, depicting hardships of the drive and the savage attack of the Comanche.

793 _______. THE BUFFALO SOLDIERS. Harcourt, 1959. Story of a patrol of Negro recruits accompanying a group of Comanches on their last buffalo hunt.

794 Putnam, George Palmer. HICKORY SHIRT. Duell, 1949. Story of the hazards encountered by a wagon train struggling through Death Valley.

795 Richter, Conrad. TACEY CROMWELL. Knopf, 1942. Daily life and society in a frontier mining town in Arizona in the 1890's; pictures the importance of miners and bankers in the life of the mining towns of the period.

796 _______. THE LADY. Knopf, 1957. Tale of violence and revenge in the Mexican-American society of northern New Mexico in the 1880's; rivalry between cattlemen and sheepmen.

797 Roark, Garland. BUGLES AND BRASS. Doubleday, 1964. Story of the U.S. Cavalry fighting Apaches in Arizona in the 1870's.

798 Robson, Lucia St. Clair. RIDE THE WIND. Ballantine, 1982. Another version of the story of the white girl kidnapped by Comanche who became devoted to her new family. See also Season of the Yellow Leaf by Douglas C. Jones.

799 Rushing, Jane. WALNUT GROVE. Doubleday, 1964. Life in

a West Texas frontier community in the early 1900's as the young hero matures and leaves home for college and a teaching career.

800 _______. TAMZEN. Doubleday, 1972. A family moves west to homestead in Texas in the 1890's, when cattlemen, railroads, and homesteaders were in competition for the land.

801 _______. MARY DOVE. Doubleday, 1974. Set in western Texas; the late nineteenth century. Story of a young mulatto girl raised in isolation by her father who wanted to protect her from racial prejudice.

802 Santee, Ross. COWBOY. University of Nebraska Press, 1977. A naturalistic description of the hardships of daily life for a Texas cowboy; based on recollections of the author. This classic tale of life in the saddle was first published in 1928.

803 Schaefer, Jack. COMPANY OF COWARDS. Houghton, 1957. Eight Union soldiers, assigned to a punishment battalion, redeem themselves in a frontier battle.

804 _______. MONTE WALSH. Houghton, 1963. Accurate picture of life in the Western cattle country in a story of a cowboy working and enjoying life on the open range.

805 Seifert, Shirley. THE TURQUOISE TRAIL. Lippincott, 1950. Overland from Independence, Missouri to Santa Fe in 1846.

806 _______. DESTINY IN DALLAS. Lippincott, 1958. Story of Alexander and Sarah Cockrell, centering around their part in the early development of Dallas, Texas; 1858.

807 _______. BY THE KING'S COMMAND. Lippincott, 1962. A Spanish rancher leads a group of villagers on a long trek to San Antonio, and eventually on to the founding of Nacogdoches; picture of Texas under Spanish rule in the 1770's.

808 Shelton, Jess. HANGMAN'S SONG. Chilton, 1960. Story of family pride and revenge set in frontier Missouri, Arkansas, and Indian Territory in the 1850's.

809 Smith, William Fielding. DIAMOND SIX. Doubleday, 1958. Fictional biography of Wesley Smith, Texas Ranger, Southern soldier in the Civil War, Indian fighter, sheriff, and owner of the Diamond Six ranch.

810 Swarthout, Glendon. THE SHOOTIST. Doubleday, 1975. End of the era of gunslingers. A famous outlaw is helpless, ill with cancer in El Paso in 1901; journalists, sensing money in the drama of his story, move in for a deathwatch.

811 Taylor, Ross. THE SADDLE AND THE PLOW. Bobbs, 1942. Conflict between cattlemen and farmers in Texas in the 1880's.

812 Thomason, John. GONE TO TEXAS. Scribner, 1937. Danger and excitement in a fort on the Rio Grande River after the Civil War.

813 Vane, Norman T. and R. Rude. THE CAVES. Major Books, 1977. Based on fact. Apache warriors and the 4th U.S. Cavalry are trapped together in the Huachuca Mountains in Arizona; they battle nature and each other in a desperate struggle to survive.

814 Venable, Clarke. ALL THE BRAVE RIFLES. Reilly and Lee, 1929. Life in Tennessee, in Washington, and in Texas and the events leading up to the Texas War for independence; fall of the Alamo; Santa Anna, Sam Houston, David Crockett, and others appear.

815 Vliet, R. G. ROCKSPRING. Viking, 1974. A daughter of poor white pioneers is kidnapped from her East Texas home by Mexican bandits in the 1830's.

816 ________. SOLITUDES. Harcourt, 1977. A drifter wanders across Texas in the 1880's. The speech patterns of the largely uneducated settlers are well rendered, as is the distinctive, harsh beauty of the countryside.

817 Ward, Christopher. YANKEE ROVER. Simon & Schuster, 1932. Itinerant New England peddler wanders through the Southwest; 1824-1829. See also The Strange Adventures of Jonathan Drew (Expanding Frontiers--Eastern and Southern).

818 Ward, John. DON'T YOU CRY FOR ME. Scribner, 1940. Story of the American West; 1846-1847.

819 Wellman, Paul. BRONCHO APACHE. Macmillan, 1936. Story of Massai, one of Geronimo's warriors, captured and sent to a Florida prison after Geronimo's surrender, and of his escape and revenge.

820 ________. THE IRON MISTRESS. Doubleday, 1951. Fictionalized biography of James Bowie.

821 ________. THE COMANCHEROS. Doubleday, 1952. A New Orleans gambler becomes a Texas Ranger and tracks down Comancheros leading Indians in attacks against settlers on the Texas border.

822 ________. RIDE THE RED EARTH. Doubleday, 1958. Set in the Southwest and Mexico in the early 1700's at the time of the struggle between France and Spain for the Texas territory; pictures Louis Juchereau de St. Denis' role in the struggle.

823 _______. MAGNIFICENT DESTINY. Doubleday, 1962. Sweeping story of friendship that led to the annexation of Texas; follows the careers of Andrew Jackson and Sam Houston from 1813 to 1843; includes descriptions of the Battle of New Orleans in the War of 1812, the Battle of San Jacinto, and the death of Rachel Jackson.

824 Western Writers of America. RAWHIDE MEN. Doubleday, 1965. A collection of stories about frontier scouts, cattle drives, and settlers on the open ranges of the Old West.

825 Woolley, Bryan. SAM BASS. Corona, 1983. Bass was a real Texas outlaw who progressed from gambling on horses to bank and train heists. He was betrayed by a companion when he robbed a Union Pacific train in Nebraska.

826 Wormser, Richard Edward. BATTALION OF SAINTS. McKay, 1960. Story of a battalion of Mormons from Council Bluffs, Iowa who marched to New Mexico to join the U.S. troops in the Mexican War in 1846.

California and the Pacific Northwest

827 Adleman, Robert H. SWEETWATER FEVER; McGraw, 1984. An eighteen year old and his friends find adventure aplenty in an Oregon gold-mining town in 1853, including Tong wars among the Chinese laborers.

828 Ainsworth, Edward. EAGLES FLY WEST. Macmillan, 1946. Picture of New York and California in the 1840's and 1850's; story of a newspaperman who takes part in the fighting between U.S. troops and Spanish Californians; the discovery of gold, and the struggle for statehood.

829 Allen, Henry. THE GATES OF THE MOUNTAINS. Random, 1963. Story based on the disappearance of Francois Rivet, a young boatman with the Lewis and Clark expedition.

830 Allen, T. D. (pseud). DOCTOR IN BUCKSKIN. Harper, 1951. Story of Marcus and Narcissa Whitman, among the Indians in Oregon and the Northwest.

831 Andersen, Richard. MUCKALUCK. Delacorte, 1980. Muckalucks are facing starvation on an Oregon reservation in 1873. They finally fight and win a desperate battle with the U.S. Cavalry on the lava flats.

832 Ballard, Todhunter. GOLD IN CALIFORNIA. Doubleday, 1965. Experiences of a boy in a wagon train, from Wilmington, Ohio to California, and life in the mining camps around Sutter's Mill during the gold rush of 1848.

833 Bartlett, Lanier. ADIOS! Morrow, 1929. California just after the American acquisition in 1846, when a band of desperadoes refuse to recognize U.S. control and harass the settlers.

834 Beach, Rex. THE WORLD IN HIS ARMS. Putnam, 1946. Competition between Russian and American sealers off Alaska; scenes in Russian Alaska and in San Francisco.

835 Bedford, Donald (pseud.). JOHN BARRY. Creative Age, 1947. Hero rises from clerk to financier and prominent citizen; the gold rush starts, and Yerba Buena becomes San Francisco.

836 Berry, Don. TRASK. Viking, 1960. Story of the first homesteaders in the Oregon Territory in the 1840's, and of their troubles with the Indians. Based on the life of Elbridge Trask, an early settler.

837 ________. MOONTRAP. Viking, 1962. Picture of the conflict between the trappers and the settlers who want to establish law and order in the Oregon Territory in the 1840's.

838 ________. TO BUILD A SHIP. Viking, 1963. Homesteading hardships in the Oregon Territory in the 1850's.

839 Binns, Archie. MIGHTY MOUNTAIN. Scribner, 1940. Story of pioneer hardships in Washington in the 1850's and of the campaigns against the Indians.

840 ________. YOU ROLLING RIVER. Scribner, 1947. Life in the port town of Astoria at the mouth of the Columbia River about 1865.

841 ________. THE HEADWATERS. Duell, 1957. Story of a young couple struggling against the hardships of pioneering in the wilderness of the Northwest in the 1890's.

842 Blacker, Irwin R. DAYS OF GOLD. World, 1961. Adventures of an ex-teacher who joins the gold prospectors in the rush to the Yukon territory during the Alaska gold rush days of the 1890's.

843 Bretherton, Vivien. ROCK AND THE WIND. Dutton, 1942. Frontier life of the early settlers in the Pacific Northwest, and the development of the area with the coming of the railroad.

844 Bristow, Gwen. CALICO PALACE. Crowell, 1970. Adventures of two women during the California gold rush of 1849, one of whom later runs the San Francisco gambling tent referred to by the title.

845 Cameron, Margaret. JOHN DOVER. Harper, 1924. Picturesque details of life in California at the time of the gold rush.

846 Campbell, Patricia. THE ROYAL ANNE TREE. Macmillan, 1956. Romantic novel set on an isolated homestead in Washington Territory in the 1850's.

847 _______. CEDARHAVEN. Macmillan, 1965. Life in Washington Territory during and after the Civil War.

848 Case, Victoria. THE QUIET LIFE OF MRS. GENERAL LANE. Doubleday, 1952. Fictionized biography of Polly and Joseph Lane. Contrasts Polly's life at home raising ten children with that of General Lane in the legislature, the Mexican War, and fighting for statehood for Oregon.

849 _______. A FINGER IN EVERY PIE. Doubleday, 1963. Pioneering in Oregon Territory in the 1840's and 1850's.

850 Cheshire, Giff. STRONGHOLD. Doubleday, 1963. Sad tale of the efforts of the U.S. Army to displace the Modoc Indian tribe in California.

851 Coolidge, Dane. GRINGO GOLD. Dutton, 1939. Life of the Mexican bandit Joaquin Murrietta; a story of California in the gold rush days of 1849.

852 Cranston, Paul. TO HEAVEN ON HORSEBACK. Messner, 1952. Based on the lives of Narcissa and Marcus Whitman, missionaries and pioneers in Oregon in the 1830's.

853 Davis, Harold Lenoir. THE DISTANT MUSIC. Morrow, 1957. Poetic story of the development of the Columbia River country in Washington Territory from wilderness to settled country, and the founding of towns.

854 Downes, Anne Miller. NATALIA. Lippincott, 1960. Picture of Russian-American relations in Alaska through the story of a Civil War veteran sent to study the country at the time of the purchase of Alaska in 1867.

855 Easton, Robert. PROMISED LAND. Capra, 1982. A story of the Spanish in eighteenth-century California, beginning with General Caspar Portolo's Sacred Expedition to convert the natives.

856 Elwood, Muriel. AGAINST THE TIDE. Bobbs, 1950. Los Angeles in 1879. Conflict between the old Spanish heritage and the new American ways.

857 Emmons, Della. SACAJAWEA OF THE SHOSHONES. Binfords and Mort, 1943. Fictional account of the life of the Shoshone woman who guided Lewis and Clark, from her childhood to later years in St. Louis and her return to the reservation.

858 Evansen, Virginia B. NANCY KELSEY. McKay, 1965. Fictional account of the life of Nancy Kelsey, one of the first women to travel by wagon train from Missouri to California, in 1841.

859 Evarts, Hal. FUR BRIGADE. Little, 1928. Story of fur trading in the Northwest; 1815-1835.

860 Fisher, Vardis. TALE OF VALOR. Doubleday, 1958. Story of the Lewis and Clark expedition.

861 Footner, Hulbert. THE FURBRINGERS. McCann, 1920. Fur trading in the Northwest.

862 Frazier, Neta Lohnes. ONE LONG PICNIC. McKay, 1962. Pioneer story based on the diary of an eleven-year-old boy who made the covered-wagon journey from Wisconsin to Oregon in 1851.

863 Gabriel, Gilbert Wolf. I, JAMES LEWIS. Doubleday, 1932. Story of John Jacob Astor's trading post expedition to the Pacific Northwest in 1810-1811; founding of Astoria; massacre of the crew of the Tonquin.

864 Giles, Janice Holt. THE GREAT ADVENTURE. Houghton, 1966. Based on the journals of Captain Benjamin Bonneville, the story follows the grandson of Hannah Fowler as he leads a trapping party from Santa Fe to Oregon where Captain Bonneville is assigned to spy on the British in the Pacific Northwest.

865 Gulick, Bill. THE LAND BEYOND. Houghton, 1958. Settlement of the Oregon country, the explorations of Captain Bonneville, the English-American boundary dispute, and the plight of the Nez Percé Indians.

866 Hargreaves, Sheba. THE CABIN AT THE TRAIL'S END. Harper, 1928. Indian customs and pioneer life during a family's first year in Oregon; 1843-1844.

867 Haycox, Ernest. THE EARTHBREAKERS. Little, 1952. Story of settlers in the Oregon Territory, 1845.

868 ______. THE ADVENTURERS. Little, 1954. Picture of colonization of the Northwest; Oregon in the mid-1860's; development of the lumber industry.

869 Horan, James David. THE SHADOW CATCHER. Crown, 1961. Story of life on the trail to the Oregon Territory in the 1830's and of the American effort to break the British monopoly of the fur trade; based on first-hand contemporary accounts.

870 Hough, Emerson. 54-40 OR FIGHT. Bobbs, 1909. Story of the political and personal conflicts behind the Northwest boundary treaty and the annexation of Texas; introduces the English minister Pakenham, John C. Calhoun, and the Russian Baroness von Ritz in major roles.

871 Hueston, Ethel. STAR OF THE WEST. Bobbs, 1935. Story of the Lewis and Clark expedition of 1803-1806.

872 Huffman, Laurie. A HOUSE BEHIND THE MINT. Doubleday, 1969. A tale based on the exploits of Black Bart, outlaw and stagecoach robber; San Francisco, 1875-1883.

873 Hunter, Evan. THE CHISHOLMS. Harper, 1976. A family leaves their worn-out farmland in a mountainous section of Virginia and journeys to California in search of a better life; 1844.

874 Jackson, Helen Hunt. RAMONA. Little, 1884. Story of relations between Indians and Spanish-Mexicans in California at the time of the American conquest.

875 Jennings, John. RIVER TO THE WEST. Doubleday, 1948. Dangers of frontier exploration contrasted with the picture of New York society in the days of John Jacob Astor and his friend Washington Irving; centers around the Astor fur-trading scheme in the Northwest; 1808-1811.

876 Johnston, Terry C. CARRY THE WIND. Caroline House, 1982. Beaver trappers and fur traders bargain and skirmish with the Indians in the Oregon Territory; 1820's to 1840's.

877 Jones, Edwal. VERMILLION. Prentice, 1947. A hundred years of California history centered in the story of the Five Apostles Mine, started in 1846.

878 Jones, Nard. SWIFT FLOWS THE RIVER. Dodd, 1940. Oregon and the Columbia River region, 1856.

879 Kesey, Ken. SOMETIMES A GREAT NATION. Viking, 1964. Lusty novel of three generations of loggers in the Wakonda River region of Oregon.

880 Kyne, Peter B. TIDE OF EMPIRE. Cosmopolitan, 1928. California during the gold rush.

881 Lauritzen, Jonreed. CAPTAIN SUTTER'S GOLD. Doubleday, 1964. Fictional biography of John Augustus Sutter, Swiss immigrant to California in the 1830's, who developed a flourishing trading post and precipitated the gold rush in the 1840's.

882 ______. THE CROSS AND THE SWORD. Doubleday, 1965

Story of the military and the missionary settlement of Spanish California in the 1700's, contrasting the careers of Father Junipero Serra, who established a chain of missions in his conquest for the Church, and General Juan de Anza, who was dedicated to military conquest for Spain.

883 Lee, C. Y. LAND OF THE GOLDEN MOUNTAIN. Meredith, 1967. Picture of life among the Chinese laborers in the gold fields and in San Francisco's Chinatown in the 1850's.

884 Lee, Virginia Chin-lan. THE HOUSE THAT TAI MING BUILT. Macmillan, 1963. Story of four generations of a Chinese-American family who divide their time between China and San Francisco, building the family fortune during the gold rush and the growth of a thriving import business.

885 McDonald, Kay L. THE BRIGHTWOOD EXPEDITION. Liveright, 1976. Story of a group of adventurous pioneers in Oregon in the 1850's, including their troubles with the Indians.

886 MacDonald, William. CALIFORNIA CABALLERO. Covici, 1936. California in the late 1860's when the Americans were supplanting the old Spanish families.

887 McKay, Allis. THE WOMEN AT PINE CREEK. Macmillan, 1966. Story of two sisters who settle in the apple-growing region of the Columbia River valley in Washington State in 1910.

888 McKee, Ruth Eleanor. CHRISTOPHER STRANGE. Doubleday, 1941. Growth of San Francisco, 1853-1901; young lawyer involved in the social and business life and the development of the railroads; state politics, vigilantes, and life on an old Spanish ranch.

889 McNeilly, Mildred. HEAVEN IS TOO HIGH. Morrow, 1944. Russian America in the days when Aleksandr Baranov was seeking to open the Pacific Northwest to the Russian fur trade and to establish colonies there; 1780-90's.

890 ________. EACH BRIGHT RIVER. Morrow, 1950. Oregon in 1845. South Carolina girl goes to Oregon, finds her sweetheart dead, and adjusts to frontier life.

891 Marius, Richard. BOUND FOR THE PROMISED LAND. Knopf, 1976. Saga of a wagon train in the 1850's, as the travelers hurry across the plains to cash in on the gold rush.

892 Marshall, Edison. SEWARD'S FOLLY. Little, 1924. Romance built around the purchase of Alaska by the U.S. in 1867.

893 Matthews, Greg. FURTHER ADVENTURES OF HUCKLEBERRY FINN. Crown, 1983. An imaginative continuation of the beloved Twain novel. In this story, Huck and Jim journey to California as forty-niners.

894 Miller, May. FIRST THE BLADE. Knopf, 1938. First part set in Missouri during the Civil War; second part deals with settling in the San Joaquin Valley in California. Coming of the railroad and digging irrigation ditches.

895 Moffat, Gwen. BUCKSKIN GIRL. Victor Gollancz, 1982. An intrepid young woman on a wagon train discards her ruffled dresses in favor of buckskin trousers and helps lead the way over the treacherous Rockies.

896 Morrow, Honoré. WE MUST MARCH. Stokes, 1925. Marcus Whitman crosses the Rockies.

897 ________. BEYOND THE BLUE SIERRA. Morrow, 1932. Story of Juan de Anza and the first overland route from Mexico to the Spanish colony at the site of San Francisco.

898 Mulvihill, William. NIGHT OF THE AXE. Houghton, 1972. Conflict develops between leaders of a band of settlers moving across the mountains to California in 1846. Those who choose to linger are endangered by the coming of winter.

899 Nevin, David. DREAM WEST. Putnam, 1984. Novel about John Fremont, California explorer, senator, Civil War officer, and the first presidential nominee of the Republican Party.

900 Norris, Kathleen. CERTAIN PEOPLE OF IMPORTANCE. Doubleday, 1922. Fictional history of the life and times of San Francisco; the days of the gold rush, Spanish ranch life, growth of the tea and spice business, and the development of the city.

901 O'Dell, Scott. HILL OF THE HAWK. Bobbs, 1947. Story of California under Spanish rule about the time Captain Fremont led the Americans in the conquest of the territory.

902 Older, Cora. SAVAGES AND SAINTS. Dutton, 1936. Story of Spanish California after the American conquest.

903 Paul, Charlotte. GOLD MOUNTAIN. Random, 1953. Story of hop ranching, teaching in a small town, and the effects of smallpox on the Indians; set in a small farming community near Seattle in the late 1800's.

904 ________. THE CUP OF STRENGTH. Random, 1958. Logging operations and life in the lumber camps of the Northwest in the 1890's.

905 Peattie, Donald Culross. FORWARD THE NATION. Putnam, 1942. The Lewis and Clark expedition, 1805.

906 Peeples, Samuel Anthony. THE DREAM ENDS IN FURY. Harper, 1949. Based on the life of Joaquin Murrietta, Mexican bandit in California in gold rush days.

907 Pendexter, Hugh. OLD MISERY. Bobbs, 1924. California in 1853 with its mining camps, gambling houses, robber bands, and hostile Indians.

908 Pettibone, Anita. JOHNNY PAINTER. Farrar, 1944. Story of the settling of the Washington Territory in the years after the Civil War.

909 Ripley, Clements. GOLD IS WHERE YOU FIND IT. Appleton, 1936. California in the 1870's during the second gold boom. Conflict between miners and ranchers.

910 Roark, Garland. RAINBOW IN THE ROYALS. Doubleday, 1950. Story of a race in 1850 from Boston around the Horn to San Francisco.

911 Ross, Lillian. THE STRANGER. Morrow, 1942. Pioneering in the Big Sur country of California in the 1870's.

912 Schoell, Yvonne. THE ARGONAUTS. Prentice Hall, 1972. Characters in the story arrive by clipper ship and wagon train to join the 1849 gold rush.

913 Scott, Reva. SAMUEL BRANNAN AND THE GOLDEN FLEECE. Macmillan, 1944. Fictional biography of the Mormon leader Samuel Brannan, who first reported California's gold discovery to the world.

914 Shaftel, George. GOLDEN SHORE. Coward, 1943. Rivalry between the United States, Russia, and Mexico over the colonizing of California in the 1840's.

915 Small, Sidney. THE SPLENDID CALIFORNIANS. Bobbs, 1928. California in the early nineteenth century; details of the life of Spanish rancheros in a new country.

916 Spearman, Frank. CARMEN OF THE RANCHO. Doubleday, 1937. Romance of Spanish California; a Texas scout rescues the daughter of a Spanish don from the Indians.

917 Sperry, Armstrong. NO BRIGHTER GLORY. Macmillan, 1942. John Jacob Astor's fur-trading expedition into the Northwest, 1810.

918 Steinbeck, John. EAST OF EDEN. Viking, 1952. Chronicle of a family who moves from Connecticut to California. Details of country and small-town life; Civil War to World War I.

919 Stewart, George Rippey. EAST OF THE GIANTS. Holt, 1938. Chronicle of the development of California from 1837 to 1861. Indian fighting, the American conquest, the gold rush, the rise of San Francisco, and the beginnings of big business.

920 Stone, Irving. IMMORTAL WIFE. Doubleday, 1944. Fictional biography of Jessie Benton Fremont, wife of John Fremont, covering his part in the conquest and development of California, politics in Washington, and action in the Western campaigns in the Civil War.

921 Stong, Philip. FORTY POUNDS OF GOLD. Doubleday, 1951. Panorama of frontier life from Iowa to California during the gold rush, by way of St. Louis, New Orleans, the Isthmus of Panama, and the sea voyage to San Francisco.

922 ________. THE ADVENTURE OF "HORSE" BARNSBY. Doubleday, 1956. Romanticized story of a teenager's adventures in the California gold fields in the 1850's.

923 Teilhet, Darwin. THE ROAD TO GLORY. Funk and Wagnall, 1956. Story of the Spanish missions in California in 1783; and of the work of Father Junipero Serra among the Indians; set in and near San José.

924 Terrell, John. PLUME ROUGE. Viking, 1942. Trek of a fur-trading expedition from St. Louis to the Pacific Northwest.

925 Turner, William Oliver. CALL THE BEAST THY BROTHER. Doubleday, 1973. Missionaries to the Haida Indians are captured and held as slaves. Good description of Indian customs.

926 Van Every, Dale. THE SHINING MOUNTAINS. Messner, 1948. Scout for Lewis and Clark crosses the Rockies and is captured by the Indians.

927 Wells, Evelyn. A CITY FOR ST. FRANCIS. Doubleday, 1967. Background of General Juan de Anza's expedition in 1775 to found San Francisco; trials of the journey through Apache country; building of the Mission Dolores; and Anza's dismissal by Governor Rivera. Includes an episode with Father Junipero Serra.

928 Wetherell, June. THE GLORIOUS THREE. Dutton, 1951. Pioneering in the Puget Sound region at the time of the boundary dispute between England and the United States.

929 White, Helen. DUST ON THE KING'S HIGHWAY. Macmillan, 1947. Story of early Spanish missionaries in Mexico and California in 1771.

930 White, Leslie Turner. WAGONS WEST. Doubleday, 1964. Story of a young doctor who joins a family on their journey from Boston to Mississippi and on to San Bernardino, California in a Conestoga wagon.

931 White, Stewart Edward. ROSE DAWN. Doubleday, 1920. Story of California's development from the land boom of the 1880's to 1910. Sequel to Gold (1913) and The Gray Dawn (1915).

932 _______. LONG RIFLE. Doubleday, 1932. Exploring in the Rockies in the 1820's. First in author's second series on California history.

933 _______. RANCHERO. Doubleday, 1933. Hero of The Long Rifle crosses the Sierras to Southern California.

934 _______. FOLDED HILLS. Doubleday, 1934. Continues the history of California through the American conquest; ranch life, and conflict with the Mexicans.

935 _______. STAMPEDE. Doubleday, 1942. Conflict between landowners and squatters after California became a state in 1850; sequel to The Folded Hills.

936 _______. WILD GEESE CALLING. Doubleday, 1940. Lumbering in the Pacific Northwest in 1895; scenes in Seattle and Alaska.

937 Young, Gordon. DAYS OF '49. Doran, 1925. Graphic picture of the color and excitement of the California gold rush.

The Plains States and the Far West

938 Adleman, Robert H. THE BLOODY BENDERS. Stein and Day, 1970. Story based on the real Kate Bender, who helped rob and kill visitors to the family's inn on the Kansas frontier.

939 Aldrich, Bess Streeter. A LANTERN IN HER HAND. Appleton, 1928. Trek of a pioneer family from Iowa to Nebraska.

940 _______. A WHITE BIRD FLYING. Appleton, 1931. Second and third generation of a pioneer family in Nebraska. Sequel to Lantern in Her Hand.

941 _______. SPRING CAME ON FOREVER. Appleton, 1935. Chronicle of pioneering on the Nebraska prairie from 1866 to the Depression in 1933.

942 _______. LIEUTENANT'S LADY. Appleton, 1942. Omaha, Nebraska just after the Civil War.

943 Allen, Henry. NO SURVIVORS. Random, 1950. Background of General Custer's campaign against the Sioux in the 1870's, sympathetic toward the Indians; white man adopted by Chief Crazy Horse rejoins Custer at the Battle of Little Big Horn.

944 ______. THE LAST WARPATH. Random, 1966. Story of forty years of struggles of the Cheyenne Indians against the white man; pictures events leading to the Sand Creek Massacre, the battles of the Washita, Rosebud, Little Big Horn, and Powder River, and the final tragedy at the Battle of Wounded Knee.

945 ______. THE BEARPAW HORSES. Lippincott, 1973. Based on historical incident. Group of Sioux steal horses from whites and deliver them to the Nez Percé in the Bearpaw mountains, a journey of almost 600 miles. This enables the Nez Percé to escape to Canada; 1877.

946 Ames, Francis H. THAT CALLAHAN SPUNK. Doubleday, 1965. A Massachusetts family settles in Montana in 1908; picture of life in a sod house on the prairie.

947 Aydelotte, Dora. ACROSS THE PRAIRIE. Appleton, 1941. Story of frontier settlers in Kansas in the 1890's.

948 Babson, Naomi. I AM LIDIAN. Harcourt, 1951. Theatrical troupe, heading west from Massachusetts in 1856, settles down in Montana two years later.

949 Bailey, Paul Dayton. FOR TIME AND ALL ETERNITY. Doubleday, 1964. Mormon life in Utah in the 1870's and 1880's, centers around the government's struggle to abolish the principle of polygamy.

950 Barton, Del. GOOD DAY TO DIE. Doubleday, 1980. Author is the grandson of Grey Wolf, the last holdout among the Dakota Sioux against white encroachment. This is the narrative of the old Indian's action-packed life over its 107-year span.

951 Bean, Amelia. THE FANCHER TRAIN. Doubleday, 1958. Based on the massacre of a California-bound wagon train at Mountain Meadows, Utah by Mormon Danites and Indians in 1857.

952 Berger, Thomas. LITTLE BIG MAN. Dial, 1964. Story of frontier and Indian life among the Cheyennes at the time of the Washita Massacre, and events leading up to the Battle of the Little Big Horn; characters include General Custer, Wild Bill Hickok, Calamity Jane, and Wyatt Earp.

953 Binns, Archie. THE LAND IS BRIGHT. Scribner, 1939. Adventures along the Oregon Trail in the 1850's.

954 Birney, Hoffman. GRIM JOURNEY. Minton, 1934. Story of the ill-fated trek of the Donner party on the way to California in 1846.

955 ________. THE DICE OF GOD. Holt, 1956. Fictional biography of General Custer and events leading up to the Battle of Little Big Horn.

956 Blackburn, Thomas W. A GOOD DAY TO DIE. McKay, 1967. Story of the massacre of the Sioux Indians by the U.S. Cavalry at the Battle of Wounded Knee in 1890; characters include Chief Sitting Bull, Buffalo Bill Cody, John J. Pershing, and Frederic Remington, the artist.

957 ________. THEY OPENED THE WEST. Doubleday, 1967. A collection of stories dealing with the development of transportation and communications in the opening of the West.

958 Blake, Forrester. WILDERNESS PASSAGE. Random, 1953. Pioneering, hunting, and trapping in the Utah Territory and along the Oregon Trail. Conflict between whites and Indians, and between the Mormons and the United States government.

959 Bojer, Johan. THE EMIGRANTS. Appleton, 1925. Story of the colony of Norwegians who settled the Red River valley of North Dakota, and their fight with drought, frost, poverty, and isolation.

960 Borland, Hal. THE SEVENTH WINTER. Lippincott, 1959. Authentic picture of cattle ranching in Colorado in the 1870's.

961 ________. WHEN THE LEGENDS DIE. Lippincott, 1963. Story of the life and customs of a Ute family in Wyoming at the turn of the century; when his parents die, a young Indian boy faces conflict at a reservation school and later as a bronc rider on the rodeo circuit; he eventually finds himself by accepting his Indian heritage.

962 Breneman, Mary Worthy. THE LAND THEY POSSESSED. Macmillan, 1956. Story of farm and small-town life in the Dakota Territory during the late 1800's.

963 Brink, Carol. BUFFALO COAT. Macmillan, 1944. Story of small-town life in Opportunity, Idaho in the 1890's.

964 ________. SNOW IN THE RIVER. Macmillan, 1964. Life of Scottish immigrants settling in Idaho at the turn of the century.

965 Brown, Dee Alexander. KILLDEER MOUNTAIN. Holt, 1983. A reporter travels by steamboat to the Dakota Territory. He is trying to determine the truth among conflicting reports about the army's attempt to subdue hostile Indians.

966 Bryant, Will. THE BIG LONESOME. Doubleday, 1971. A young boy and his father, a deserter from the Civil War, are prospecting in the west. A grizzly attacks the boy, and Blackfoot Indians rescue and treat him. Indian ways and the companionship of a grizzly cub change his life.

967 Burgess, Jackson. PILLAR OF CLOUD. Putnam, 1957. Story of an expedition of six men from Kansas to the Rockies to break a new trail to the West in 1858.

968 Capps, Benjamin. TRUE MEMOIRS OF CHARLEY BLANKENSHIP. Lippincott, 1972. Realistic account of the life of a cowboy from 1880 to 1890; based on the memoirs of a real man.

969 Cather, Willa. O PIONEERS! Houghton, 1913. Pioneer farming on the Nebraska prairie in the 1800's.

970 _______. MY ANTONIA. Houghton, 1918. Life on the Nebraska prairie.

971 Chapman, Arthur. JOHN CREWS. Houghton, 1926. Story of life on the frontier around old Fort Laramie, Wyoming, involving a rescue from a group of Mormon Danites, fights with the Indians, and Indian ceremonial life and customs.

972 Chay, Marie. PILGRIMS PRIDE. Dodd, 1961. Family life of an Italian immigrant family in a Colorado mining town in the 1890's.

973 Christgau, John. SPOON. Viking, 1978. Tragi-comic adventures of Alexander Featherstone, the artist-narrator of the story, and his Indian interpreter, Spoon, as they observe the action of the Dakota Indian wars in Minnesota in 1862.

974 Clark, Walter Van Tilburg. THE OX-BOW INCIDENT. Random, 1940. A frontier Nevada town in 1885 is the scene of the lynching of three men accused of murder and cattle rustling.

975 Cockrell, Marian. THE REVOLT OF SARAH PERKINS. McKay, 1965. Story of a schoolteacher in a frontier Colorado Territory community; 1869-70.

976 _______. THE MISADVENTURES OF BETHANY PRICE. Times Books, 1979. A picaresque tale of an adventurous young woman who escapes an unhappy marriage by disguising herself as a boy and taking to the road.

977 Cooper, Courtney Ryley. THE LAST FRONTIER. Little, 1923. Opening of the Kansas Indian lands after the Civil War; Buffalo Bill, General Custer, and others appear.

978 _______. THE GOLDEN BUBBLE. Little, 1928. Discovery of gold in the Pike's Peak region in 1859, organization of a People's Court in Denver, and life in the lawless frontier towns.

979 _______. THE PIONEERS. Little, 1938. Kit Carson and the Oregon Trail; 1842.

980 Cooper, Jamie Lee. RAPAHO. Bobbs, 1967. Reminiscences of an old trapper, reliving his past as a preacher's son, buffalo hunter, and Indian fighter.

981 Corcoran, William. GOLDEN HORIZONS. Macrae, 1937. Traces the agricultural development of Kansas from frontier days to the introduction of winter wheat.

982 Culp, John H. THE BRIGHT FEATHERS. Holt, 1965. Three young cattle drovers take their first train ride, their first steamboat ride, and see their first "civilized" Indians on a vacation trip through Kansas in 1871.

983 Cunningham, John. WARHORSE. Macmillan, 1956. Story of ranch life in Montana in 1882.

984 Cushman, Dan. THE SILVER MOUNTAIN. Appleton, 1957. Story of a man's rise to wealth and power by way of the mining industry in Montana in the 1880's and 1890's.

985 Davis, Clyde Brion. NEBRASKA COAST. Farrar, 1939. Journey to Nebraska from the Erie Canal, in 1861.

986 Davis, Harold Lenoir. BEULAH LAND. Morrow, 1949. Westward journey of a small group from North Carolina in 1851. Their journey carries them into the Southwest, to Kansas, and on to Oregon.

987 _______. WINDS OF MORNING. Morrow, 1952. An old-timer tells the story of his early life as a settler in the American Northwest, looking back from the 1920's.

988 Dieter, William. WHITE LAND. Knopf, 1970. Men and animals endangered by a terrifying blizzard on the winter rangeland of Montana in the 1880's.

989 Downing, J. Hyatt. HOPE OF LIVING. Putnam, 1939. Tribulations of homesteading in the Dakotas.

990 Drago, Harry Sinclair. MONTANA ROAD. Morrow, 1935. Early days in the opening of the Dakota Territory; General Custer's campaigns against the Indians and the Battle of the Little Big Horn.

991 _______. SINGING LARIAT. Morrow, 1939. Life in Nebraska just before and after admission of the Territory to

statehood in 1867. Deals with the problem of whiskey runners to the Indians and the conflicts over statehood.

992 ______. BOSS OF THE PLAINS. Morrow, 1940. Opening of the West, 1840's to 1860's; Mormons, General Fremont, and the Pony Express.

993 Durham, Marilyn. MAN WHO LOVED CAT DANCING. Harcourt, 1972. Grobart killed three Indians who had raped and murdered his Shoshone wife. Now out of prison he robs a train to get money to free his son. The action is in the Wyoming Territory in the 1880's.

994 Egan, Ferol. THE TASTE OF TIME. McGraw, 1977. An elderly widower in New York State, his children grown and gone, decides to join a wagon train and head for California in 1859.

995 Ertz, Susan. THE PROSELYTE. Appleton, 1933. Story of the hardships endured by Brigham Young's Mormon colony in Utah.

996 Evarts, Hal. THE SHAGGY LEGION. Little, 1930. Story of the passing of the buffalo; generals Sheridan and Custer, Wild Bill Hickok, and Buffalo Bill appear.

997 Farris, John. ME AND GALLAGHER. Simon and Schuster, 1982. The Gallagher of the title is a tough wagon master and lawman; the "me" is the thirteen-year-old orphan boy he informally adopts. The pair ride west in 1863.

998 Fast, Howard. THE LAST FRONTIER. Duell, 1941. Flight of 300 Cheyennes from Oklahoma to Montana in 1878; picture of the hardships of the Indians' life on the reservation.

999 Fish, Rachel Ann. THE RUNNING IRON. Coward, 1957. Story of frontier life in Wyoming in the years after the Civil War.

1000 Fisher, Richard. JUDGMENT IN JULY. Doubleday, 1962. Story of conflict between gold miners and Indians in the Dakotas, and life in Deadwood, S.D. in the period following Custer's defeat at the Battle of the Little Big Horn in 1876.

1001 Fisher, Vardis. CHILDREN OF GOD. Harper, 1939. An account of the background of the Mormon movement, persecution in Illinois and Missouri, and the heroic migration to Utah and the founding of an empire in the desert; Joseph Smith and Brigham Young are major characters.

1002 ______. CITY OF ILLUSION. Harper, 1941. The Comstock Lode gold boom; picture of life in Virginia City, Nevada in 1859.

1003 ________. THE MOTHERS. Vanguard, 1943. Story of the Donner party trapped in the Sierras in 1846.

1004 ________. MOUNTAIN MAN. Morrow, 1965. Trapping, fishing, and fighting Crow Indians in the Rocky Mountains in the 1850's.

1005 Foreman, Leonard. THE RENEGADE. Dutton, 1942. A white man adopted by the Sioux Indians faces a decision at the Battle of the Little Big Horn.

1006 Frazee, Steve. SHINING MOUNTAINS. Rinehart, 1951. Story of a mixed group of Civil War veterans thrown together in a gold rush at the close of the war; picture of life in a mining boomtown.

1007 Fulton, Len. THE GRASSMAN. Thorp Springs Press, 1974. Scarcity of water in nineteenth-century Wyoming brings range wars over the rights to the Ten Smoke River.

1008 Furnas, Marthedith. THE FAR COUNTRY. Harper, 1947. Follows a group on the long journey from Kentucky to California in 1845.

1009 Galloway, David. TAMSEN. Harcourt, 1983. George Donner and his wife, Tamsen, lead the ill-fated group of California-bound settlers through the Sierra Nevada, where winter storms entrap them.

1010 Gardiner, Dorothy. GOLDEN LADY. Doubleday, 1936. Gold mining in a Colorado town, from the 1880's to the Depression.

1011 ________. SNOW-WATER. Doubleday, 1939. Saga of a small Colorado town and its founder from 1868 to 1934; pictures the irrigation projects necessary for life on the plains, and the growth of a town from prairie land to city.

1012 ________. THE GREAT BETRAYAL. Doubleday, 1949. Based on the treacherous Sand Creek Massacre of Chief Black Kettle's Cheyenne tribe near Fort Lyon, Colorado Territory in 1864 under the leadership of Col. Chivington.

1013 Giles, Janice Holt. RUN ME A RIVER. Houghton, 1964. A Kentucky steamboat captain faces the tribulations of riverboating on the Green River in the West at the time of the Civil War.

1014 ________. SIX-HORSE HITCH. Houghton, 1969. More about the Fowler clan in this story of the overland stage routes in Utah, Colorado, and the Northwest in the 1850's; includes descriptions of the stage-line business, and life as a captive of the Indians.

1015 Gold, Douglas. A SCHOOLMASTER WITH THE BLACKFEET INDIANS. Caxton, 1963. Stories and anecodotes based on the author's experiences with the Siksika Indians on the Blackfoot Reservation in Montana from 1914 to 1934.

1016 Grey, Zane. RIDERS OF THE PURPLE SAGE. Harper, 1913. Story of Mormon vengeance in southwestern Utah in 1871.

1017 _______. THE U. P. TRAIL. Harper, 1918. The building of the Union Pacific Railroad in the 1860's.

1018 _______. WESTERN UNION. Harper, 1939. Romance of the West and the construction of the first telegraph lines across the plains.

1019 Gulick, Bill. THE HALLELUJAH TRAIL. Doubleday, 1965. The temperance league, hijackers, and Indians attempt to stop a wagon train loaded with whiskey and champagne; based on the actual incident of the Walshingham train near Denver in the 1860's. First published in 1963.

1020 Guthrie, A. B. THE BIG SKY. Sloane, 1947. Fur trapping in the Upper Mississippi River country in the 1830's.

1021 _______. THE WAY WEST. Sloane, 1949. Follows a wagon train from Independence, Missouri through the wilderness to Oregon, on the Oregon Trail in the 1840's. Follows The Big Sky (above).

1022 _______. THESE THOUSAND HILLS. Houghton, 1956. Story of cattle ranching in Montana in the 1880's. Follows The Way West (above).

1023 _______. FAIR LAND, FAIR LAND. Houghton, 1982. An authentic picture of the West in the period from 1845 to 1870. Dick Summers, his wife, Teal Eye, and other friendly Indians live in the Teton Valley. Sequel to The Big Sky, and The Way West.

1024 Haines, William Wister. THE WINTER WAR. Little, 1961. A superior novel of the campaign against Chief Sitting Bull and the Sioux Indians in Montana during the blizzards of 1876.

1025 Haldeman-Julius, Emanuel. DUST. Brentano, 1921. A story of pioneer life in Kansas.

1026 Hall, Oakley. BADLANDS. Atheneum, 1978. Set in South Dakota in the 1880's, when free-rangers battled against fences. A transplanted Scot builds a slaughterhouse to break the monoply interests of the Chicago meat-packers.

1027 Hanes, Frank Borden. THE FLEET RABBLE. Rage, 1961. Story of Chief Joseph and the Nez Percé Indians in their epic flight in 1877 when the U.S. Army attempted to force them onto an Idaho reservation.

1028 Hargreaves, Sheba. HEROINE OF THE PRAIRIES. Harper, 1930. Picture of life along the Oregon Trail in 1848.

1029 Harris, Margaret and John Harris. MEDICINE WHIP. Morrow, 1953. Wyoming in post-Civil War days; wagon trains out of Fort Laramie, and battles with the Indians.

1030 Haruf, Kent. TIE THAT BINDS. Holt, 1984. Daily life was often burdensome for the turn-of-the-century homesteader in Colorado. A mother's early death makes inescapable for her only daughter a life spent caring for her father and brothers.

1031 Haycox, Ernest. TROUBLE SHOOTER. Doubleday, 1937. Construction of the Union Pacific Railroad out of Cheyenne, Wyoming in the spring of 1868.

1032 ________. BUGLES IN THE AFTERNOON. Little, 1944. The Dakota frontier and Indian-white relations preceding the campaigns of Custer against the Sioux in the 1870's.

1033 Heinzman, George. ONLY THE EARTH AND THE MOUNTAINS. Macmillan, 1964. Story of the destruction of the Cheyenne Indians in the 1860's and 70's, from the massacres at Sand Creek and Washita to the final blow at the Battle of Wounded Knee, witnessed by an army scout married to an Indian woman.

1034 Hill, Ruth Beebe. HANTO YO. Doubleday, 1979. Fiction elaborated from records kept by a Sioux from 1794 to 1835, a period when the arrival of whites threatened them and corrupted their indigenous lifestyle.

1035 Hotchkiss, Bill. THE MEDICINE CALF. Norton, 1981. Based on the life of the Virginia mulatto Jim Beckwourth, who was abducted and then adopted by a Crow tribe. He later became their chief. See also Follow the Free Wind by Leigh Brackett.

1036 ________. AMMAHABAS. Norton, 1983. Sequel to The Medicine Calf. Beckwourth, still a Crow chief, travels to California in 1844, visits relatives in Missouri, and settles in Colorado.

1037 Hough, Emerson. THE COVERED WAGON. Appleton, 1922. Wagon train from Missouri to Oregon along the Oregon Trail in 1848.

1038 Hueston, Ethel. THE MAN OF THE STORM. Bobbs, 1936.

Story of John Colter, member of the Lewis and Clark expedition, who discovered Yellowstone; scenes in old St. Louis under Spanish, French, and American flags.

1039 _______. CALAMITY JANE OF DEADWOOD GULCH. Bobbs, 1937. Story of early days in Deadwood, South Dakota in the 1870's; based on the life of Martha Jane Burke (Calamity Jane).

1040 Jackson, Donald. VALLEY MEN. Houghton, 1983. Thomas Jefferson laid plans for an expedition up the Arkansas River, extending the exploration of the lands of the Louisiana Purchase. The plans were scuttled, but the author imagines the journey as if it had taken place, peopling the story with historical characters.

1041 Jarrett, Marjorie. WIVES OF THE WIND. Seaview, 1980. Polygamy among the Mormons in Utah in the decade following 1875, when the U.S. government was fighting the now illegal practice.

1042 Jennings, William Dale. THE COWBOYS. Stein and Day, 1971. When a nearby gold strike empties the Montana ranches of hands, a cattleman recruits a dozen boys, 11 to 15 years old, to drive his 500 steers to market. The difficulties of the drive mature the young cowboys.

1043 Jones, Cleo. SISTER WIVES. St. Martin's, 1983. This novel focuses on the tribulations of the multiple wives of the Mormon men. The story begins with the arrival of the daughters of a Mormon family in Utah, just before the Civil War.

1044 Jones, Douglas. THE COURT-MARTIAL OF GEORGE ARMSTRONG CUSTER. Scribner, 1976. Starting with the assumption that Custer survived Little Big Horn, the author imagines him brought before a court-martial to answer charges of having lost the lives of his men through military incompetence.

1045 _______. ARREST SITTING BULL. Scribner, 1977. Based on an actual incident. Leery of further Indian uprisings, the government orders the arrest of the aging Sitting Bull. The Indian agent in charge is dismayed, as are the Indians employed by the U.S., who must carry out the order.

1046 _______. CREEK CALLED WOUNDED KNEE. Scribner, 1978. The 7th Cavalry and the Dakota Sioux face each other at Wounded Knee in 1890. Also present are reporters eager to cover the excitement for Eastern readers; their ardor inflames both sides.

1047 Kerns, Frances Casey. THIS LAND IS MINE. Crowell, 1974.

A white man is adopted by an Indian tribe on the Montana frontier.

1048 Kilpatrick, Terrence. SWIMMING MAN BURNING. Doubleday, 1977. A white man, whose Indian wife was murdered by whites, travels to Washington with braves from several tribes, seeking an audience with President Grant.

1049 Kjelgaard, Jim. THE LOST WAGON. Dodd, 1955. A lone family with six children make their way along the Oregon Trail, from Missouri to Oregon.

1050 Klem, Kaye. TOUCH THE SUN. Doubleday, 1971. An Irish immigrant heads to Virginia City, Nevada in 1875 to seek a fortune in silver mines others thought were played out.

1051 Laird, Charlton. WEST OF THE RIVER. Little, 1953. Story of the fur trade in an Upper Mississippi town in the late 1830's.

1052 L'Amour, Louis. COMSTOCK LODE. Bantam, 1981. A silver miner, the son of an English coal miner who was killed during the California gold rush, seeks revenge. The story exposes the crooked financial deals that sprang from silver fever.

1053 Lane, Rose Wilder. LET THE HURRICANE ROAR. Longmans, 1933. Story of pioneering days on the North Dakota prairie.

1054 _______. FREE LAND. Longmans, 1938. Homesteading in South Dakota in the 1880's.

1055 Lathrop, West. KEEP THE WAGONS MOVING. Random, 1949. Two young boys join a wagon train on the Oregon Trail; pictures life of the Indians and of the adventurous pioneers.

1056 Lauritzen, Jonreed. THE EVERLASTING FIRE. Doubleday, 1962. Story of the persecution of the Mormons in Nauvoo, Illinois; the murder of Joseph Smith, the leadership of Brigham Young, and the beginning of the exodus to Utah.

1057 Lavender, David B. RED MOUNTAIN. Doubleday, 1963. Story of road building during the Colorado silver boom in the 1880's.

1058 Laxness, Halldor. PARADISE RECLAIMED. Crowell, 1962. An Icelandic farmer, persuaded by a Mormon missionary to make a pilgrimage to Utah, settles in the new country and brings his family to join him.

1059 Leasure, Robert. BLACK MOUNTAIN. Purnam, 1975. A determined group of men set out to kill a marauding grizzly; civilization impinged on wilderness in Colorado in the late nineteenth century.

1060 Lockwood, Sarah. ELBOW OF THE SNAKE. Doubleday, 1958. Story of homesteading in the Snake River valley of Idaho in the 1890's.

1061 Lofts, Norah. WINTER HARVEST. Doubleday, 1955. A California-bound group trapped by snow in the Sierras; based on the story of the Donner party.

1062 Lott, Milton. THE LAST HUNT. Houghton, 1954. Story of a big hunt for the last of the buffalo herds in the 1880's.

1063 ______. DANCE BACK THE BUFFALO. Houghton, 1959. Based on the rise of the Ghost Dance of the Plains Indians in 1889 and the incidents leading up to the Battle of Wounded Knee in 1890.

1064 Lund, Robert. THE ODYSSEY OF THADDEUS BAXTER. Day, 1957. An amusing story of the adventures of a young Texan, drifting in Wyoming in the 1870's.

1065 Lutz, Giles A. THE LONG COLD WIND. Doubleday, 1962. Story of cattle ranching and a family feud in Montana in the 1880's.

1066 Mabie, Mary Louise. LONG KNIVES WALKED. Bobbs, 1932. Hardships of a California-bound wagon train over the plains and the mountains.

1067 McDonald, Kay L. VISION IS FULFILLED. Walker, 1983. Sequel to Vision of the Eagle (Young Nation). Ross Ches-nut is leading settlers from Missouri to Oregon when a smallpox epidemic hits.

1068 McKeown, Martha. MOUNTAINS AHEAD. Putnam, 1961. Hardships of life on an overland wagon train on the Oregon Trail, from Independence, Missouri to Oregon in 1847.

1069 MacLean, Alistair. BREAKHEART PASS. Doubleday, 1974. An adventure story of an army relief train dispatched to a fort in Indian territory where cholera is reported. A secret-service agent in disguise is among the passengers.

1070 McNames, James. MY UNCLE JOE. Viking, 1963. Recollections by a 12-year-old boy of a scouting trip with his uncle into Montana in 1884.

1071 Manfred, Frederick F. LORD GRIZZLY. McGraw, 1954. Story of frontier revenge in the Upper Missouri River country in the 1820's.

1072 ______. CONQUERING HORSE. McDowell, 1959. Story of a Sioux boy's search for a vision for his initiation into manhood; picture of Indian life, customs, lore, and religion.

1073 Meigs, Cornelia. RAILROAD WEST. Little, 1937. Story of the difficulties encountered in the laying of the Northern Pacific Railroad from Minnesota to Yellowstone.

1074 Morrow, Honoré. ON TO OREGON. Morrow, 1926. Life on the Oregon Trail in early pioneer days as a wagon train makes its way from Missouri to Oregon.

1075 Newton, Dwight Bennett. LEGEND IN THE DUST. Doubleday, 1970. Law and order are brought to a western Kansas town in the late 1860's.

1076 Olsen, Theodore V. MISSION TO THE WEST. Doubleday, 1973. Col. Henry Dodge and artist George Catlin appear in this story of an army regiment sent to intimidate the Plains Indians in the 1830's. Disease, Indian attacks, and water shortages complicate their mission.

1077 Parkhill, Forbes. TROOPERS WEST. Farrar, 1945. Story of a Ute Indian rebellion in Wyoming in 1879; sympathetic to the Indians' grievances.

1078 Patten, Lewis B. PROUDLY THEY DIE. Doubleday, 1964. A French half-breed joins the Sioux Indians and participates in the struggle against Custer's troops, culminating in the Battle of the Little Big Horn.

1079 ________. THE RED SABBATH. Doubleday, 1968. A civilian Army scout, sympathetic to the Indians, describes events leading up to the Battle of the Little Big Horn.

1080 Payne, Robert. THE CHIEFTAIN. Prentice, 1953. Sympathetic account of the resistance of the Nez Percé Indians under Chief Joseph and of their valiant effort to escape to Canada in 1877.

1081 Pendexter, Hugh. KINGS OF THE MISSOURI. Bobbs, 1921. The Northwest, from St. Louis to the Yellowstone country, in the days of the fur trappers.

1082 ________. HARRY IDAHO. Bobbs, 1926. Discovery of gold in Idaho and the activities of the "avenging angels," the Danite sect of the Mormons; 1860's.

1083 Prescott, John. JOURNEY BY THE RIVER. Random, 1954. Journey of a wagon train through Missouri and Kansas to Fort Laramie, Wyoming in 1848.

1084 Pryor, Elinor. AND NEVER YIELD. Macmillan, 1942. Mormons in Illinois and Missouri; Joseph Smith's death.

1085 Rhodes, Richard. THE UNGODLY. Charterhouse, 1973. Retelling of the tale of the starving Donner party, trapped by the Sierra winter of 1864, forced to cannibalism for survival.

1086 Rikhoff, Jean. SWEETWATER. Dial, 1976. Sequel to Buttes Landing (Young Nation) and One of the Raymonds (Civil War). John Buttes and his cousin Mason Raymond face dangers on the Oregon Trail in 1876.

1087 Rogers, Gayle. THE SECOND KISS. McKay, 1972. A wagon train is ambushed, all but one massacred. The surviving woman is taken captive by, and later becomes the second wife of, a Blackfoot brave. Details of the Indian culture.

1088 Rolvaag, Ole. GIANTS IN THE EARTH. Harper, 1927. Picture of the Norwegian immigrant as a pioneer on the Dakota prairie.

1089 Roripaugh, Robert A. HONOR THY FATHER. Morrow, 1963. Story of conflict between ranchers and homesteaders in the Sweetwater valley of Wyoming in the 1880's.

1090 Rush, William. RED FOX OF THE KINAPOO. Longmans, 1949. Story of Chief Joseph and the Nez Percé Indians from 1872 to 1877.

1091 Sandoz, Mari. MISS MORISSA, DOCTOR OF THE GOLD TRAIL. McGraw, 1955. Life on the Nebraska frontier in the 1870's; historical background of a frontier settlement in the North Platte River country as seen by a woman doctor.

1092 ______. SON OF THE GAMBLIN' MAN. Potter, 1960. Pioneer days in Nebraska centered around the lives of a family who go west to found a town, enduring hardships of climate, financial difficulties, and conflicts with cattlemen and fellow townsmen.

1093 Schaefer, Jack. SHANE. Houghton, 1949. Life on a homestead farm in Wyoming; picture of the conflict between farmer and rancher.

1094 Seelye, John. THE KID. Viking, 1972. Racial hatred flares into violent death in the old Wyoming Territory.

1095 Seidman, Robert J. ONE SMART INDIAN. Putnam, 1977. A Cheyenne Indian youth is captured and adopted by a U.S. army officer. He is educated at Yale, works in Washington, D.C. for the Indian Bureau, but eventually decides to return to his tribe in Nebraska.

1096 Seifert, Shirley. THOSE WHO GO AGAINST THE CURRENT. Lippincott, 1943. Set against the background of the founding of St. Louis, the Louisiana Purchase, and the exploration of the Upper Mississippi and Missouri River country in the early 1800's.

1097 Sinclair, Harold. THE CAVALRYMAN. Harper, 1958. Based on the campaign against the Sioux in 1864; follows an army of Civil War veterans through the Dakota Bad Lands in pursuit of the Indians. Sequel to The Horse Soldiers (Civil War).

1098 Snow, Donald. THE JUSTICER. Rinehart, 1960. Story of a young lawyer's defense of an Indian on trial under a tyrannical Federal District Court judge in Kansas in Indian Territory in 1889.

1099 Sorensen, Virginia. A LITTLE LOWER THAN THE ANGELS. Knopf, 1942. Story of the Mormons in Nauvoo, Illinois.

1100 ______. THE EVENING AND THE MORNING. Harcourt, 1949. Scotch-Irish immigrants move out across the Western plains to Utah.

1101 Stark, Joshua. BREAK THE YOUNG LAND. Doubleday, 1964. Story of conflict between wheat farmers and cattle ranchers in post-Civil War Kansas.

1102 Steele, Wilbur. DIAMOND WEDDING. Doubleday, 1950. Chronicle of a typical mountain man and frontier scout in Colorado, and the founding of Denver; 1835 to 1919.

1103 Stewart, Ramona. THE STARS ABIDE. Morrow, 1961. Two generations of family life in the Nevada ranching and mining country.

1104 Storm, Hyemeyohsts. SEVEN ARROWS. Harper, 1972. The story, which takes place in the Old West, is interspersed with "teaching stories" from the oral history of the Cheyenne. First book of the publisher's American Indian Publishing Program.

1105 Straight, Michael. CARRINGTON. Knopf, 1960. Based on the Fetterman Massacre in northern Wyoming in 1866, when the Sioux ambushed and killed Col. Fetterman and his men, who were marching against the orders of Col. Carrington; story of Carrington's life and of the events leading up to the massacre.

1106 ______. A VERY SMALL REMNANT. Knopf, 1963. Accurate account of Col. Chivington's massacre of the Cheyenne, under Chief Black Kettle, at Sand Creek near Fort Lyon, Colorado Territory, in 1864.

1107 Swain, Virginia. THE DOLLAR GOLD PIECE. Farrar, 1942. Background of the livestock industry in Kansas City in the boom years, 1887 to 1888.

1108 Taylor, Robert Lewis. THE TRAVELS OF JAMIE McPHEETERS.

Doubleday, 1958. Hair-raising adventures are encountered by an adolescent boy and his father as they make their way from Louisville to the California gold fields in 1849; capture by bandits, torture by Indians, a short stay with the Mormons, and settling on a ranch in California.

1109 _______. A ROARING IN THE WIND. Putnam, 1978. Story of miners, prostitutes, and vigilantes in a Montana boomtown, before the territory became a state in 1864.

1110 Thom, James Alexander. FROM SEA TO SHINING SEA. Ballantine, 1984. Anne Rogers Clark narrates this story of her famous sons--George, the hero of the Revolution, and William, who explored the West with Meriwether Lewis.

1111 Ulyatt, Kenneth. NORTH AGAINST THE SIOUX. Prentice, 1965. Based on the building of Fort Phil Kearny and of its eventual destruction under siege by the Sioux, Cheyenne, and Arapaho under Chief Red Cloud.

1112 Van Every, Dale. THE DAY THE SUN DIED. Little, 1971. The story of the events of the 1890 campaign against the Indians. An officer incites a battle by falsely suggesting that the Sioux Ghost Dance is a war dance. Sitting Bull, General Nelson Miles, and Frederic Remington appear in the story.

1113 Wagoner, David. WHERE IS MY WANDERING BOY TONIGHT? Farrar, 1970. Tale of a small town in Wyoming in the 1890's. Told in the first person, with the sense of fun and freshness of the young narrator.

1114 _______. THE ROAD TO MANY A WONDER. Farrar, 1974. Triumph of love and innocence as a young man and his sweetheart leave home in the Nebraska Territory and seek their fortune in the Colorado gold fields.

1115 _______. WHOLE HOG. Atlantic, 1976. A family heads for California with a drove of hogs. The parents die en route, leaving son Zeke to continue his travels with an adventurer whose trade is in whiskey.

1116 Waters, Frank. THE WILD EARTH'S NOBILITY. Liveright, 1935. Settling of Colorado after the Civil War; the mining boom; the development of Colorado Springs.

1117 Webb, Lucas. ELI'S ROAD. Doubleday, 1971. Kansas in the days of the Free Soil debate is the setting for the first part of this book. The hero, a restless pioneer, then leaves his settled wife and family to go to Montana Territory, where he becomes a U.S. Marshal.

1118 Wellman, Manly Wade. CANDLE OF THE WICKED. Putnam, 1960. Story of a Civil War veteran and his search for land in Kansas in 1873; action centers around a wilderness tavern on the road from Fort Scott to Independence.

1119 Wellman, Paul. THE BOWL OF BRASS. Lippincott, 1944. Settling of the range country of Western Kansas in 1889, and the growth of county politics and land promotion.

1120 Wheeler, Richard. WINTER GRASS. Walker, 1983. Life on a Montana cattle ranch in the days when installing barbed-wire fences meant war with neighboring ranchers.

1121 Whipple, Maurine. GIANT JOSHUA. Houghton, 1941. Story of the settlement of the Dixie Mission in the desert of Utah by a band of Mormons in the 1860's.

1122 Winsor, Kathleen. WANDERERS EASTWARD, WANDERERS WEST. Random, 1965. Epic story of the development of Montana Territory in post-Civil War days.

1123 Yerby, Frank. WESTERN. Dial, 1982. A transplanted New Englander faces new challenges homesteading in Kansas in 1866.

THE CIVIL WAR--BEFORE AND AFTER

The Old South

1124 Bontemps, Arna. BLACK THUNDER. Macmillan, 1936. Story of Gabriel's Insurrection in 1810, when 1,100 slaves plotted to seize Richmond.

1125 Brown, Joe David. THE FREEHOLDER. Morrow, 1949. Follows the fortunes of a Carolina plantation overseer through immigration to Alabama and on to the time when his slavery-hating sons leave to join the Union army in 1861.

1126 Campbell, Thomas. OLD MISS. Houghton, 1929. A chronicle of Virginia life from the days of the great plantations, loyal slaves, and leisurely social life to the days of poverty brought on by war and Reconstruction.

1127 Cather, Willa. SAPPHIRA AND THE SLAVE GIRL. Knopf, 1940. Relations of the mistress of a Virginia plantation and an intelligent slave girl; 1850's.

1128 Coleman, Lonnie. BEULAH LAND. Doubleday, 1973. Plantation life in antebellum Georgia, 1800-1861.

1129 Courlander, Harold. THE AFRICAN. Crown, 1967. Story of a young African sold into slavery in Georgia in 1802; pictures the effect of the African cultural heritage on the American Negro in his relation with the white man.

1130 Delaney, Martin R. BLAKE. Beacon, 1970. A novel, chapters of which originally appeared in The Weekly Anglo-African in 1861 and 1862, by a black author; discusses slavery and slave revolution in the 1850's.

1131 Ehle, John. JOURNEY OF AUGUST KING. Harper, 1971. A middle-aged white farmer on the way to market meets and befriends a 15-year-old runaway slave girl. His humanitarian decision is not easily made in the culture of rural North Carolina in pre-Civil War days.

1132 Ford, Jesse Hill. THE RAIDER. Atlantic-Little, 1975. Story of a man who built a plantation from the Tennessee wilderness. He joined the Confederate Army as the war erupted; a war that took the lives of his wife, his son, and destroyed his home and livelihood.

1133 Forrest, Leon. TWO WINGS TO VEIL MY FACE. Random, 1984. The aged black Greatmama Sweetie Reid Witherspoon recollects her beginnings as a slave.

1134 Gaither, Frances. FOLLOW THE DRINKING GOURD. Macmillan, 1940. Plantation life in Georgia and Alabama; the drinking gourd is the Big Dipper which guides the Negroes on their way north on the Underground Railroad.

1135 ________. THE RED COCK CROWS. Macmillan, 1944. A young Northerner sympathetic to the slaves is forced to take part in suppressing a slave rebellion in Mississippi in the 1830's.

1136 ________. DOUBLE MUSCADINE. Macmillan, 1949. Plantation life in Mississippi in the 1850's, exposed in the trial of a young kitchen slave accused of poisoning the plantation owner's family.

1137 Gordon, Caroline. PENHALLY. Scribner, 1931. Family chronicle of plantation life from 1826 through the Civil War and on into the "new South" of this century.

1138 Graham, Alice Walworth. CIBOLA. Doubleday, 1961. Picture of life on a Louisiana plantation on the Mississippi River near Natchez in 1839.

1139 Gray, Elizabeth. JANE HOPE. Viking, 1934. Picture of home life in the South just before the Civil War; Chapel Hill, North Carolina.

1140 Griswold, Francis. TIDES OF MALVERN. Morrow, 1930. Chronicle showing scenes from each generation, from Colonial times through World War I, set at a plantation house on the river above Charleston, South Carolina.

1141 ________. SEA ISLAND LADY. Morrow, 1939. Long chronicle of a Southern family near Beaufort, South Carolina from the Civil War to the 1920's.

1142 Henkle, Henrietta. DEEP RIVER. Harcourt, 1944. Pictures differences between land-owning aristocrats in the lowlands and the mountaineers in Georgia in 1859.

1143 ________. FIRE IN THE HEART. Harcourt, 1948. The heroine's debut in Covent Garden is followed by her unsuccessful marriage to the slave-holding owner of a Sea Island, Georgia plantation; picture of the temper of the times in England and America in the years preceding the Civil War. Based on the life of Fanny Kemble.

1144 Howe, Fanny. WHITE SLAVE. Avon, 1980. Based on the life of a real man. Peter McCutcheon was an illegitimate white infant given to a slave family on a small Missouri farm, to hide the scandal of his birth. He loves his new family and marries a black woman. After the Civil War, free people, they homestead in Kansas.

1145 Jakes, John. NORTH AND SOUTH. Harcourt, 1982. The first novel of a trilogy follows the fortunes of two families during the two decades preceding the Civil War. The son of an industrialist in Pennsylvania meets the son of a South Carolina plantation owner, as both are en route to West Point.

1146 Jennings, Gary. SOW THE SEEDS OF HEMP. Norton, 1976. Based on a historical incident. In 1834, the horse thief John Murrel devises a grandiose scheme to overthrow the wealthy planters in Mississippi and rule an empire. To this end he steals slaves, and, hidden in the swamps, he trains them for his army. See also Rogue's Companion (Expanding Frontiers) by Harry Kroll.

1147 Kane, Harnett T. PATHWAY TO THE STARS. Doubleday, 1950. Fictional biography of John McDonough, who made a fortune in New Orleans in the 1840's and left it all to his pet projects, a plan for the slaves to earn their freedom and a public school system for the children of Louisiana.

1148 _______. THE GALLANT MR. STONEWALL. Doubleday, 1957. Life of Anna Morrison, Southern belle who later married Stonewall Jackson.

1149 Kantor, MacKinlay. BEAUTY BEAST. Putnam, 1968. Long novel of slave and plantation life on the Mississippi Gulf Coast in the 1850's.

1150 McMeekin, Clark (pseud.). SHOW ME A LAND. Appleton, 1940. Horse racing, gypsies, tobacco raising, and politics in Virginia and Kentucky from 1816 to 1875.

1151 _______. RED RASKALL. Appleton, 1943. Romance of Tidewater Virginia, beginning in 1816; plantation life and horse racing. Introduces some characters from Show Me a Land.

1152 Miller, Caroline. LAMB IN HIS BOSOM. Harper, 1933. Pioneer life on a Georgia farm from 1810 through the Civil War.

1153 Olsen, Theodore. THERE WAS A SEASON. Doubleday, 1972. Novel about Jefferson Davis and his romance with Sarah Knox Taylor, second daughter of Zachary. The young West Point graduate sees duty in the Black Hawk War in this period.

1154 Price, Eugenia. NEW MOON RISING. Lippincott, 1969. Southern white and Negro life on St. Simons Island, Georgia, from the 1830's through the Civil War. The hero returns from Yale, spends seven years on a Mississippi riverboat, marries his childhood sweetheart on the island plantation, and suffers hardships during the war.

1155 ______. MARGARET'S STORY. Lippincott, 1980. Story of a real family who settled on the Saint John River in Florida in 1832, built a home, and ran a hotel for travelers. The story continues through the war years, which brought tragedy and miserable times for the survivors.

1156 ______. SAVANNAH. Doubleday, 1983. Picture of the graceful city in Georgia and its society and customs between 1812 and 1822.

1157 Price, Nancy. A NATURAL DEATH. Little, 1973. Antebellum South Carolina plantation life seen through the eyes of both a black girl raised in freedom and later sold into bondage, and the wife of the planter whose first look at slavery came with her marriage.

1158 Rice, Anne. FEAST OF ALL SAINTS. Simon and Schuster, 1979. The unique culture of antebellum New Orleans included "free people of color." Their position in that society was always shaky: this is the story of one such man, trying to maintain his rights and dignity.

1159 Roberts, Walter. ROYAL STREET. Bobbs, 1944. Sectionalism and conflicting ideals leading to the Civil War are indicated in the conflict between Creoles and encroaching Northern business men in New Orleans in the 1840's.

1160 Seifert, Shirley. PROUD WAY. Lippincott, 1948. Natchez plantation life during the years 1843-1844; story of the courtship of Varina Howell and Jefferson Davis.

1161 Settle, Mary Lee. KNOW NOTHING. Viking, 1960. Story of plantation family life and politics in the twenty years before the Civil War, in the area which became West Virginia; authentic picture of the South in that period.

1162 Stevenson, Janet. THE ARDENT YEARS. Viking, 1960. Based on the life of Fanny Kemble, English actress who married a wealthy American planter; picture of Southern social life and conflicting views about slavery in the years before the war.

1163 Styron, William. THE CONFESSIONS OF NAT TURNER. Random, 1967. An account of the slave insurrection led by Nat Turner in Virginia in 1831.

1164 Upchurch, Boyd. THE SLAVE STEALER. Weybright and Talley, 1968. Story of a Jewish merchant in a Southern city who becomes involved in the efforts of a young Negro slave girl to escape the horrors of slavery.

1165 Walker, Margaret. JUBILEE. Houghton, 1966. Story of Negro life on a Georgia plantation from the early days of slavery through the Civil War and Reconstruction, told from the viewpoint of a slave woman.

1166 Warren, Lella. FOUNDATION STONE. Knopf, 1940. Chronicle of the South from 1823 through the Civil War; pictures the migration to Alabama from worn-out land in South Carolina, and the planters' economic struggles and relations with the Negroes.

1167 Young, Stark. HEAVEN TREES. Scribner, 1926. Picture of lavish hospitality, genial conversation, and light-hearted romance on a Mississippi plantation in the years before the Civil War.

Abolition

1168 Allis, Marguerite. THE RISING STORM. Putnam, 1955. Operations of the Underground Railroad in Cincinnati. Fourth in the author's series on Ohio history (see Expanding Frontiers--the Middle West).

1169 ______. FREE SOIL. Putnam, 1958. Continues the story of the Cincinnati Fields, one of whom marries a Southern belle, moves to Kansas Territory and becomes involved in the struggle over the slavery versus free-soil issue in the 1840's.

1170 Barney, Helen Corse. GREEN ROSE OF FURLEY. Crown, 1953. A Quaker girl on a farm near Baltimore helps runaway slaves on the Underground Railroad.

1171 Brown, Katharine. THE FATHER. Day, 1928. A New England abolitionist settles in Illinois and publishes an anti-slavery newspaper which attracts the attention of Abraham Lincoln.

1172 Burnett, William Riley. THE DARK COMMAND. Knopf, 1938. Picture of the warfare between free-soil Kansans and Quantrill's guerrillas and the burning of Lawrence, Kansas.

1173 Buster, Greene B. BRIGHTER SUN. Pageant, 1954. Story of slavery on a Kentucky plantation, and of the escape to freedom with the help of the Underground Railroad.

1174 Cannon, LeGrand. A MIGHTY FORTRESS. Farrar, 1937. Growth of the abolitionist movement in New England; set in Boston and New Hampshire in the 1850's.

1175 Carrighar, Sally. THE GLASS DOVE. Doubleday, 1962. Vivid and authentic picture of life on an Ohio farm, station on the Underground Railroad; 1860 through the Civil War.

1176 Davis, Julia. BRIDLE THE WIND. Rinehart, 1953. Struggle of a plantation owner's wife to regain acceptance in her home after helping a slave escape to freedom in the 1840's. Followed by Eagle on the Sun (Expanding Frontiers--Southwest).

1177 Dell, Floyd. DIANA STAIR. Farrar, 1932. Heroine takes part in the feminist, socialist, and abolitionist movements; Boston in the 1840's.

1178 Ehrlich, Leonard. GOD'S ANGRY MAN. Simon and Schuster, 1932. Biographical novel of the turbulent life of John Brown.

1179 Fuller, Edmund. STAR POINTED NORTH. Harper, 1946. Fictional biography of Frederick Douglass, escaped slave who became an outstanding Negro leader in the abolitionist movement.

1180 Gruber, Frank. THE BUSHWACKERS. Rinehart, 1959. Story of the aftermath of the raid and massacre of abolitionists at Lawrence, Kansas, by Quantrill's Raiders in 1863.

1181 Heidish, Marcy. A WOMAN CALLED MOSES. Houghton, 1976. Biographical novel about Harriet Tubman, who, born a slave, escaped to freedom and helped hundreds of others escape via the Underground Railroad.

1182 Howard, Elizabeth. NORTH WIND BLOWS FREE. Morrow, 1949. Story of a Michigan girl in the days of the Underground Railroad, and the founding of a community in Ontario for the fugitives.

1183 Lewis, Sinclair. THE GOD-SEEKER. Random, 1949. A carpenter doing missionary work among the Sioux Indians later becomes a builder in St. Paul, organizes a union, and fights for the rights of Negroes to join; Minnesota in the 1840's.

1184 Longstreth, Thomas. TWO RIVERS MEET IN CONCORD. Westminster, 1946. Abolitionist sentiment in Massachusetts; 1840's-1850's. Thoreau and Emerson appear.

1185 Lynn, Margaret. FREE SOIL. Macmillan, 1920. History of the free-soil struggle in Kansas.

1186 _______. LAND OF PROMISE. Little, 1927. Settling of Kansas and the conflict between free- and slave-state supporters.

1187 Nelson, Truman. THE SIN OF THE PROPHET. Little, 1952. The trial of an escaped slave under the Fugitive Slave Law in Boston in 1854; introduces many notable abolitionists of the day including Theodore Parker and Wendell Phillips.

1188 _______. THE SURVEYOR. Doubleday, 1960. Story of John Brown and the Development of the free-soil movement in Kansas in the years following the Kansas-Nebraska Act of 1854.

1189 Niles, Blair. EAST BY DAY. Farrar, 1941. Story of the mutiny of the crew of a slave ship captured off Long Island in 1839. Heroine with abolitionist sympathies discovers her grandfather's fortune was made in the slave trade.

1190 Parrish, Anne. CLOUDED STAR. Harper, 1948. Story of a small slave boy, sold away from his parents, who joined others on the journey to the North by way of the Underground Railroad, under the guidance of Harriet Tubman.

1191 Robertson, Constance. FIRE BELL IN THE NIGHT. Holt, 1944. Abolition and the Underground Railroad in Syracuse, New York in the 1850's.

1192 Seifert, Shirley. THE SENATOR'S LADY. Lippincott, 1967. Five years in the marriage of Addie and Stephen A. Douglas, with scenes in Kansas and Washington and events leading to the Lincoln-Douglas debates.

1193 Sherburne, James. HACEY MILLER. Houghton, 1971. Story of the abolitionist movement in Kentucky; Cassius Marcellus Clay; and the founding of Berea College.

1194 Stern, Philip Van Doren. THE DRUMS OF MORNING. Doubleday, 1942. Panoramic picture of the abolitionist movement from the 1830's to the 1860's; John Brown, the Underground Railroad, the free-soil struggle in Kansas, and scenes of life in Andersonville Prison.

1195 Stevenson, Janet. SISTERS AND BROTHERS. Crown, 1966. Fictionalized biography of the abolitionists Angelina and Sara Grimke and their Negro nephew Archibald Grimke, who became an author and crusader for Negro advancement.

1196 Strachey, Rachel. MARCHIN' ON. Harcourt, 1923. The feminist and abolitionist movements in Michigan in the 1840's and later in Kansas.

1197 Swift, Hildegard. RAILROAD TO FREEDOM. Harcourt,

1932. Story of Harriet Tubman, Negro slave who escaped in Maryland about 1821 and became a leader in the Underground Railroad.

1198 Wills, Grace. MURPHY'S BEND. Westminster, 1946. Frontier settlement on the Susquehanna River becomes a station on the Underground Railroad.

The War Years

1199 Allen, Henry. JOURNEY TO SHILOH. Random, 1960. Seven young Texans who set out in 1862 for Richmond are recruited into the Army of the Mississippi and see action under General Bragg at the battles of Corinth and Shiloh.

1200 Allen, Hervey. ACTION AT AQUILA. Farrar, 1938. Picture of the war in the Shenandoah Valley in 1864.

1201 Andrews, Robert. GREAT DAY IN THE MORNING. Coward, 1950. Southern conspirators working for the South in Colorado in the 1850's; growing bitterness between Northern and Southern sympathizers in the West.

1202 Auchincloss, Louis. WATCHFIRES. Houghton, 1982. An upper-class New York City man and wife aid the Underground Railroad, serve the Union in the Civil War, and in postwar years are absorbed in the early struggles for women's rights.

1203 Babcock, Bernie. SOUL OF ABE LINCOLN. Lippincott, 1923. Story of Lincoln's influence on the lives of a Union soldier and his Southern fiancée.

1204 Bacheller, Irving. FATHER ABRAHAM. Bobbs, 1925. Story of conflicting ideals in the North; Lincoln does not appear, but his influence is felt.

1205 Bannister, Don. LONG DAY AT SHILOH. Knopf, 1981. Story of the bloody battle which began at dawn, when Grant's army, camped along the Tennessee River, is surprised by the Confederate attack.

1206 Basso, Hamilton. THE LIGHT INFANTRY BALL. Doubleday, 1959. Southern traditions and Confederate politics seen through the experiences of a South Carolina rice planter, from his college days at Princeton, service through the war as assistant in the Confederate cabinet at Richmond, and after the war when everything is lost.

1207 Becker, Stephen D. WHEN THE WAR IS OVER. Random, 1969. A Union officer, wounded by a teenaged Kentucky soldier, tries unsuccessfully to save him from being shot as a spy.

1208 Beebe, Elswyth Thane. YANKEE STRANGER. Duell, 1944. Williamsburg, Virginia in the 1860's. Sequel to Dawn's Early Light (American Revolution); followed by Ever After (The Nation Grows Up).

1209 Bellah, James. THE VALIANT VIRGINIANS. Ballantine, 1953. Story of the Virginia cavalry in the Army of the Shenandoah, under Jubal Early, and of their defeat by Sheridan.

1210 Borland, Hal. THE AMULET. Lippincott, 1957. Confederate sympathizers making their way from Denver to join the Confederacy in 1861 become involved in the Battle of Wilson's Creek, Missouri.

1211 Boyd, James. MARCHING ON. Scribner, 1927. The war as seen by a Southern soldier on the march; in battle against Sherman's March to the Sea, through Georgia, and in a Federal prison camp. Hero is a descendant of the characters in Drums (American Revolution).

1212 Boyd, Thomas Alexander. SAMUEL DRUMMOND. Scribner, 1925. Life on an Ohio farm before and after the Civil War.

1213 Bradford, Roark. KINGDOM COMING. Harper, 1933. Negro life on a Louisiana plantation during the war.

1214 _______. THREE-HEADED ANGEL. Harper, 1937. Family sketches of various types living in Western Tennessee during the war.

1215 Branson, Henry C. SALISBURY PLAIN. Dutton, 1965. Written in the form of a legend, this relates the experiences of a young Union officer in the war.

1216 Brick, John. TROUBLED SPRING. Farrar, 1950. A Union soldier returns to his Hudson Valley home to find it a growing commercial center.

1217 _______. JUBILEE. Doubleday, 1956. Follows a regiment of New York volunteers through the campaigns and battles at Gettysburg, Lookout Mountain and the siege of Chattanooga, the capture and burning of Atlanta, and Sherman's March to the Sea.

1218 _______. THE RICHMOND RAID. Doubleday, 1963. Story of the Kilpatrick-Dahlgren raid on Richmond in February, 1864.

1219 _______. ROGUES' KINGDOM. Doubleday, 1965. Story of an outlaw family in upstate New York, who vindicated themselves in the Civil War.

1220 Brier, Royce. BOY IN BLUE. Appleton, 1937. The war in the Cumberland valley and the Battle of Chickamauga as it appeared to a Union soldier.

1221 Bristow, Gwen. THE HANDSOME ROAD. Crowell, 1938. Life in a small river town in Louisiana before, during, and after the war; 1859-1885. Sequel to Deep Summer (Expanding Frontiers--Southern).

1222 Bromfield, Louis. WILD IS THE RIVER. Harper, 1941. Story of life in New Orleans during the occupation by Union troops under General Butler.

1223 Burchard, Peter. RAT HELL. Coward, 1971. Twenty Yankee officers, captive in Libby Prison, tunnel to freedom. Story based on historical incident.

1224 Burress, John. BUGLE IN THE WILDERNESS. Vanguard, 1958. Life on a farm in the Missouri wilderness during the Civil War.

1225 Castor, Henry. THE SPANGLERS. Doubleday, 1948. Details of soldiering in the Union army and of life in Andersonville Prison.

1226 Catton, Bruce. BANNERS AT SHENANDOAH. Doubleday, 1955. Story of General Phil Sheridan's Union cavalry operations in the Shenandoah valley; the battles of Boonville, Missionary Ridge, and Cedar Creek.

1227 Chambers, Robert W. THE WHISTLING CAT. Appleton, 1932. Experiences of two young Texans serving as telegraph operators in the Union army.

1228 ______. SECRET SERVICE OPERATOR 13. Appleton, 1934. Adventures of a woman spy for the Union who falls in love with her opponent.

1229 Churchill, Winston. THE CRISIS. Macmillan, 1901. Story peopled by carpetbaggers, abolitionists, and Southern gentlemen, including a Confederate spy; hero is an antislavery New Englander, heroine is a descendant of the hero of Richard Carvell (American Revolution).

1230 Cochran, Hamilton. THE DRAM TREE. Bobbs, 1961. Efforts of a sea captain to run the Confederate blockade to get to the cotton exports in Wilmington, North Carolina.

1231 Coker, Elizabeth. INDIA ALLAN. Dutton, 1953. Charleston, South Carolina during the war and Reconstruction.

1232 ______. BLOOD RED ROSES. Dutton. 1977. Young Southern woman manages a plantation when her husband enlists in the Civil War; her trials as Yankee soldiers arrive.

1233 Coleman, Lonnie. LOOK AWAY, BEULAH LAND. Doubleday, 1977. The wise mistress of a Georgia plantation runs its affairs during and right after the war. Sequel to Beulah Land (The Old South).

1234 Colver, Anne. MR. LINCOLN'S WIFE. Holt, 1964. Biographical novel of Mary Todd Lincoln from the days of courtship in Springfield, Illinois, through the trying years in the White House, to the assassination of Lincoln. First published by Farrar, 1943.

1235 Corbett, Elizabeth. FAYE'S FOLLY. Appleton, 1941. Romance of the Civil War and politics on an Illinois farm.

1236 Crabb, Alfred Leland. DINNER AT BELMONT. Bobbs, 1942. Nashville, Tennessee before and during the war; action takes place in and near the city under siege.

1237 ______. LODGING AT THE SAINT CLOUD. Bobbs, 1946. Three Southern spies elude the Yankees in Nashville in the summer of 1862 when the Union army was occupying the city.

1238 ______. MOCKINGBIRD SANG AT CHICKAMAUGA. Bobbs, 1949. The war around Chattanooga in 1863; battles of Chickamauga, Missionary Ridge, and Lookout Mountain.

1239 ______. HOME TO TENNESSEE. Bobbs, 1952. Effort of the Confederates, under General Hood and Nathan Bedford Forest, to recapture Nashville.

1240 ______. PEACE AT BOWLING GREEN. Bobbs, 1955. Picture of life in the South and the development of Bowling Green, Kentucky, from the early 1800's through the Civil War.

1241 Crane, Stephen. THE RED BADGE OF COURAGE. Appleton, 1895. Psychological study of a young Union soldier in his first action at the Battle of Chancellorsville in 1863.

1242 Daley, Joseph A. EXIT WITH DRUMS. St. Martin's, 1970. Commanders of two rival army camps in Georgia have established an unofficial truce until two Union soldiers are found dead. Confederates are blamed and the Northern soldiers stage a bloody attack.

1243 Davis, Maggie. THE FARSIDE OF HOME. Macmillan, 1963. Moving story of a Georgia soldier and his young bride facing the hardships of the war.

1244 Deland, Margaret. THE KAYS. Harper, 1926. Experiences of a conscientious objector during the Civil War.

1245 Delmar, Viña. BELOVED. Harper, 1956. Life of Judah P. Benjamin, Confederate secretary of state, from his boyhood in Charleston to his death in Paris in 1884.

1246 Denuziere, Maurice. BAGATELLE. Morrow, 1978. A French author looks at the Civil War in Louisiana. The heroine of his story is a French orphan girl sent to live with a plantation owner.

1247 Devon, Louis. AIDE TO GLORY. Crowell, 1952. Fictionized biography of John Rawlins, Grant's aide-de-camp and later his secretary of war.

1248 Dixon, Thomas. THE MAN IN GRAY. Appleton, 1921. Portrait of Robert E. Lee.

1249 Doneghy, Dagmar. THE BORDER; A MISSOURI SAGA. Morrow, 1931. Picture of the ravages of war on the Missouri-Kansas border.

1250 Dowdey, Clifford. BUGLES BLOW NO MORE. Little, 1937. Richmond, Virginia, from secession to the evacuation of the city in the last year of the war.

1251 ______. WHERE MY LOVE SLEEPS. Little, 1945. Picture of the last year of fighting in and around Petersburg and Richmond.

1252 ______. THE PROUD RETREAT. Doubleday, 1953. Story of the attempt to save some of the Confederate treasury in a wagon train, in the retreat from Richmond.

1253 ______. LAST NIGHT THE NIGHTINGALE. Doubleday, 1962. Vivid picture of the desolation following the war in a story of family life on a Virginia plantation in 1865.

1254 Duncan, Harley. WEST OF APPOMATTOX. Appleton, 1961. Story of the Confederate Iron Brigade, a group of volunteers led by General Joseph Shelby, who march to Mexico to avoid surrender at the end of the Civil War.

1255 Eberhart, Mignon G. THE CUP, THE BLADE, OR THE GUN. Random, 1961. The Connecticut wife of a Confederate officer faces alone the hostility and suspicion of the community at the old family plantation while her husband is away at war in 1863.

1256 ______. FAMILY FORTUNE. Random, 1976. As West Virginia is becoming a separate state, the Civil War divides a family when two brothers enlist in opposing armies.

1257 ______. BAYOU ROAD. Random, 1979. War romance set

in New Orleans. A belle falls in love with the Yankee officer billeted in her home.

1258 Edgerton, Lucille. PILLARS OF GOLD. Knopf, 1941. The West in Civil War days; the gold rush in Arizona, and secessionist activities in the Southwest.

1259 Edmonds, Walter D. CADMUS HENRY. Dodd, 1949. Soldier, on desk detail and scout duty for Robert E. Lee, floats over enemy lines in a balloon.

1260 Eliot, George Fielding. CALEB PETTINGILL, U.S.N. Messner, 1956. Story of a Union officer commanding a ship blockading Southern ports.

1261 Erdman, Loula. MANY A VOYAGE. Dodd, 1960. Biographical novel of Edmund G. Ross, as an antislavery newspaper editor in Kansas during the free-soil movement, serving in the Civil War, as senator from Kansas, casting the deciding vote in Andrew Johnson's impeachment trial, as promoter of western railroad expansion, and as territorial governor of New Mexico; 1848 to 1889.

1262 ________. ANOTHER SPRING. Dodd, 1966. Union and Confederate raiders force rich and poor, black and white into exile from their burned-out homes in the border region of Missouri in 1863.

1263 Fairbank, Janet Ayer. THE CORTLANDS OF WASHINGTON SQUARE. Bobbs, 1922. New York City social life in the early days of the war.

1264 ________. BRIGHT LAND. Houghton, 1932. Story of life in Galena, Illinois, showing the effect of the Mississippi River trade, the California gold rush, and the Civil War on the town.

1265 Ferrel, Elizabeth and Margaret Ferrel. FULL OF THY RICHES. M. S. Mill, 1944. Growth of oil companies, politics, and Confederate raids in the new state of West Virginia; John D. Rockefeller, as a young man, appears.

1266 Feuille, Frank. THE COTTON ROAD. Morrow, 1954. A crippled Southern boy and a young Englishman transport cotton by wagon train to Brownsville, Texas for shipment to the Glasgow cotton mills.

1267 Foote, Shelby. SHILOH. Dial, 1952. Centers around the Battle of Shiloh in the spring of 1862.

1268 Fowler, Robert H. JIM MUNDY. Harper, 1977. Sergeant of North Carolina volunteers enlists at the outbreak of the Civil War, is wounded at Gettysburg, captured and imprisoned by the Union army, escapes, rejoins doomed Confederates in time to surrender at Appomattox.

1269 Fox, John. LITTLE SHEPHERD OF KINGDOM COME. Scribner, 1903. Kentucky mountain people before and during the war; description of college life, the conflicting feelings about the war in Kentucky, and Morgan's raiders.

1270 Frederick, Harold. THE COPPERHEAD. 1893. Story of the problems of an upstate New York farmer with pro-Southern sympathies.

1271 Garland, Hamlin. TRAIL-MAKERS OF THE MIDDLE BORDER. Macmillan, 1926. Fictional biography of the author's father who met Grant as a businessman in Galena, Illinois, joined the Union army, and participated in Grant's Vicksburg campaign.

1272 Garth, David. GRAY CANAAN. Putnam, 1947. Spy story centering around the revelation of Southern war plans.

1273 Glasgow, Alice. TWISTED TENDRIL. Stokes, 1928. Biographical novel of John Wilkes Booth.

1274 Glasgow, Ellen. BATTLE-GROUND. Doubleday, 1920. Picture of Virginia plantation life before secession, contrasted with the hardships imposed by war.

1275 Gordon, Caroline. NONE SHALL LOOK BACK. Scribner, 1937. The Western campaigns in 1862-1863; Ft. Donelson and Chickamauga; central figure is Nathan Bedford Forrest.

1276 Grubb, Davis. A DREAM OF KINGS. Scribner, 1955. Story of young love in Western Virginia from 1855 to 1864.

1277 Haas, Ben. THE FORAGERS. Simon & Schuster, 1962. An idealistic Confederate officer rounding up supplies for his retreating army encounters resistance on a Virginia plantation.

1278 Hart, Scott. EIGHT APRIL DAYS. Coward, 1949. Story of the campaign of Robert E. Lee in the days preceding the surrender at Appomattox.

1279 Haycox, Ernest. THE LONG STORM. Little, 1946. Fight of the Copperheads to take Oregon out of the Union.

1280 Heyward, Du Bose. PETER ASHLEY. Farrar, 1932. Story of a sensitive young Southerner witnessing events leading to secession and war in Charleston, South Carolina.

1281 Horan, James David. SEEK OUT AND DESTROY. Crown, 1958. Based on the raiding trip of the Confederate ship

Shenandoah in the last months of the war; describes the hardships of the voyage and the conflicts leading to mutiny during the trip.

1282 Hutchens, Jane. TIMOTHY LARKIN. Doubleday, 1942. Story of an adventurer who returns from the California gold fields, settles in Missouri, and joins the Union army as a scout; 1852 through the war.

1283 Jakes, John. LOVE AND WAR. Harcourt, 1984. Sequel to North and South. The stories of the Hazard and Main families are carried through the war years.

1284 Johnston, Mary. THE LONG ROLL. Houghton, 1911. Military biography of Stonewall Jackson, vividly describing his campaigns from the Confederate point of view.

1285 _______. MISS DELICIA ALLEN. Little, 1933. Life on a Virginia plantation before and during the war.

1286 _______. DRURY RANDALL. Little, 1934. Study of a Virginia gentleman from 1850 to just after the war.

1287 Jones, Douglas C. ELKHORN TAVERN. Holt, 1980. The Confederate and Union armies destroy a settlement in Arkansas as they wage a battle. The Hasford family watch as the war rolls over their farm.

1288 _______. BAREFOOT BRIGADE. Holt, 1983. Story of the common soldiers of the Third Arkansas Infantry as they endure hard marches, tedious encampments, then fight in four major battles before surrendering at Appomattox.

1289 Jordan, Jan. DIM THE FLARING LAMPS. Prentice Hall, 1971. Novel about the life of John Wilkes Booth, who combined his career as an itinerant actor with espionage for Jefferson Davis. Offers a theory of the motivation for Lincoln's assassination.

1290 Kane, Harnett T. BRIDE OF FORTUNE. Doubleday, 1948. Story of Varina Howell Davis, from the time she first met Jefferson Davis to the time he is released from prison after the war.

1291 _______. LADY OF ARLINGTON. Doubleday, 1953. Based on the life of Mary Custis, wife of Robert E. Lee.

1292 _______. THE SMILING REBEL. Doubleday, 1955. Story of Belle Boyd, Confederate spy.

1293 Kantor, MacKinlay. AROUSE AND BEWARE. Coward, 1936. Escape of two Union prisoners from Belle Isle, Virginia prison camp.

1294 _______. LONG REMEMBER. Coward, 1945. Picture of life in Gettysburg, Pennsylvania on the day of the great battle.

1295 _______. ANDERSONVILLE. World, 1955. Story of the Confederacy's largest prison camp, at Andersonville, Georgia.

1296 Kelland, Clarence Budington. ARIZONA. Harper, 1939. Arizona in Civil War days; gamblers and desperadoes, robberies, and Indian raids.

1297 Kelly, Eleanor. RICHARD WALDEN'S WIFE. Bobbs, 1950. Pioneer days in Wisconsin before and during the Civil War; Southern wife loyal to her husband even after his death.

1298 Keneally, Thomas. CONFEDERATES. Harper, 1979. In 1862 the Confederate army was pushing back the Union forces until the second battle at Antietam made a decisive change. Here are four stories of common soldiers in Stonewall Jackson's command during that crucial summer.

1299 Kennelly, Ardyth. THE SPUR. Messner, 1951. Story of John Wilkes Booth, of his life in the theater, and of the forces that drove him to the assassination of Lincoln.

1300 Keyes, Frances Parkinson. THE CHESS PLAYERS. Farrar, 1960. Family affairs and social life in New Orleans in the mid-1800's; centered around Paul Charles Morphy, chess expert, and the activities of the Confederate representatives in Paris during the Civil War.

1301 _______. MADAM CASTEL'S LODGER. Farrar, 1962. Picture of Louisiana plantation life and Southern politics leading up to the war in a fictional biography of Pierre Beauregard, Confederate general who ordered the first shot fired at Fort Sumter.

1302 Knox, Rose Bell. GREY CAPS. Doubleday, 1932. Story of two children on a Southern plantation, showing the attitude of the South to the war.

1303 Kroll, Harry Harrison. THE KEEPERS OF THE HOUSE. Bobbs, 1940. Conflict between two brothers on a Mississippi plantation before and during the war.

1304 Lancaster, Bruce and Lowell Brentano. BRIDE OF A THOUSAND CEDARS. Stokes, 1939. Story of Southern blockade running.

1305 Lancaster, Bruce. THE SCARLET PATCH. Little, 1947. Story of the Rochambeau Rifles, a New York company, in the fighting during the first year of war.

1306 _______. NO BUGLES TONIGHT. Little, 1948. Campaigns in the Tennessee Valley from 1862 to the relief of Nashville; Union spy is among the secret Union sympathizers in the city.

1307 _______. ROLL, SHENANDOAH. Little, 1956. Story of the Shenandoah valley campaign of 1864 with description of General Sheridan's victories at Opequon and Cedar Creek and the Confederates' burning of Chambersburg; narrator is a newspaper reporter.

1308 _______. NIGHT WATCH. Little, 1958. Based on the Kilpatrick-Dahlgren raid to free Union prisoners in Richmond in 1863; two cavalrymen are captured, imprisoned in Libby Prison, escape and make their way to Tennessee where they participate in the Battle of Franklin.

1309 LeMay, Alan. BY DIM AND FLARING LAMPS. Harper, 1962. Story of violence and conflicting loyalties on the Missouri frontier at the beginning of the Civil War.

1310 Lentz, Perry. THE FALLING HILLS. Scribner, 1967. Story of the Battle of Fort Pillow in Tennessee and the massacre of Negro soldiers and white Tennessee Union sympathizers in 1864.

1311 Lincoln, Joseph Crosby. STORM SIGNALS. Appleton, 1935. Story of Cape Cod in the early days of the war.

1312 Longstreet, Stephen. GETTYSBURG. Farrar, 1961. Story of the daily life of the people of Gettysburg, Pennsylvania as the battle develops nearby.

1313 Lytle, Andrew. THE LONG NIGHT. Bobbs, 1936. Story of revenge set in Georgia and Alabama; protagonist participates in the Battle of Shiloh.

1314 _______. THE VELVET HORN. McDowell, 1957. Story of complex family relationship and of a boy growing up in the Cumberland Mountains on the Tennessee wilderness frontier during and after the Civil War.

1315 McDonald, Robert S. THE CATHERINE. Petrocelli, 1982. The Rhode Island ship Catherine and her sailors were in Charleston harbor when Fort Sumter was fired on. This naval adventure story tells of the Union blackade of the Confederacy.

1316 McGehee, Thomasine. JOURNEY PROUD. Macmillan, 1939. Pictures the declining fortunes of a large tobacco plantation in Virginia during the war.

1317 McMeekin, Clark (pseud.). CITY OF TWO FLAGS. Appleton,

1950. Story of the conflict between Union and Confederate sympathizers in Louisville, who refused to accept Kentucky's neutrality.

1318 McNeilly, Mildred. PRAISE AT MORNING. Morrow, 1947. International diplomacy, when England decides not to recognize the Confederacy and the Russians stage naval demonstrations at New York and San Francisco in 1863.

1319 Mally, Emma Louise. THE MOCKING BIRD IS SINGING. Holt, 1944. New Orleans and Texas during the war; picture of city and frontier life.

1320 Markey, Morris. THE BAND PLAYS DIXIE. Harcourt, 1927. Fredericksburg, Richmond, and Savannah in the last years of the war.

1321 Mason, F. Van Wyck. PROUD NEW FLAGS. Lippincott, 1951. Story of naval warfare; efforts of the South to build a navy, the Baltimore riots, and the capture of New Orleans.

1322 _______. BLUE HURRICANE. Lippincott, 1954. Naval warfare in the West in 1862; the Union drive down the Mississippi River.

1323 _______. OUR VALIANT FEW. Little, 1956. Story of a Southern blockade runner and a newspaperman who exposes war profiteers; set in Charleston, South Carolina.

1324 _______. ARMORED GIANTS. Little, 1980. Life on the ironclads _Monitor_ and _Merrimack_.

1325 Medary, Marjorie. COLLEGE IN CRINOLINE. Longmans, 1937. Story of a girl in an Iowa college during the Civil War.

1326 Miller, Helen Topping. NO TEARS FOR CHRISTMAS. Longmans, 1954. A tale of Christmas at a Tennessee plantation house, used by Union troops as headquarters.

1327 _______. CHRISTMAS FOR TAD. Longmans, 1956. Vignette of Christmas with the Lincolns in the White House in 1863.

1328 _______. SING ONE SONG. Appleton, 1956. Story of persecution, guerrilla raids, and divided loyalties in neutral Kentucky during the Civil War.

1329 _______. CHRISTMAS WITH ROBERT E. LEE. Longmans, 1958. Short novel depicting the Lee family's first Christmas together after the war at Lexington, Virginia, where General Lee had accepted the presidency of Washington College.

1330 Minnegerode, Meade. CORDELIA CHANTRELL. Putnam, 1926. The effects of the war on social life in Charleston, South Carolina.

1331 Mitchell, Margaret. GONE WITH THE WIND. Macmillan, 1936. Panorama of the war and Reconstruction in Georgia; plantation life, hardships of war at home, Sherman's siege of Atlanta, carpetbaggers, Ku Klux Klan, and the rebuilding of business after the war.

1332 Montgomery, James Stuart. TALL MEN. Greenberg, 1927. Story of Confederate blockade running during the war.

1333 Morrison, Gerry. UNVEXED TO THE SEA. St. Martin's, 1960. Story of the war from both sides, centering around the siege and capture of Vicksburg.

1334 Morrow, Honoré. FOREVER FREE. Morrow, 1927. Abraham Lincoln from his inauguration to the Emancipation Proclamation; 1861-1863.

1335 _______. WITH MALICE TOWARD NONE. Morrow, 1928. Story of the conflict between Lincoln and Charles Sumner over Reconstruction policy during the last two years of the war.

1336 _______. LAST FULL MEASURE. Morrow, 1930. Picture of the last days of the war and of Lincoln's plans for Reconstruction; full treatment of John Wilkes Booth and the assassination plot.

1337 _______. LINCOLN STORIES. Morrow, 1934. Collection of three stories, each focused on a different phase of Lincoln's career.

1338 Noble, Hollister. WOMAN WITH A SWORD. Doubleday, 1948. Story of Anna Ella Carroll, newspaperwoman and writer who is credited with planning the Tennessee campaign.

1339 O'Connor, Richard. COMPANY Q. Doubleday, 1957. Story of the men of one of the punishment battalions, composed of demoted Union officers, who redeem themselves in heavy fighting; hero undertakes an undercover spying mission into besieged Atlanta.

1340 O'Neal, Cothburn. UNTOLD GLORY. Crown, 1957. Based on the spy activities of Felicia Shover, who made friends with Union officers in occupied Memphis in order to smuggle medical supplies to the Confederacy.

1341 O'Toole, G. J. A. COSGROVE REPORT. Rawson Wade, 1979. A Pinkerton detective investigates the Booth conspiracy after Lincoln's assassination.

1342 Palmer, Bruce. MANY ARE THE HEARTS. Simon & Schuster, 1961. Four short episodes with various aspects of the war as a background.

1343 Perenyi, Eleanor. THE BRIGHT SWORD. Rinehart, 1955. Picture of Richmond society and the story of General John B. Hood's campaign in Tennessee in 1864; battles of Franklin and Nashville.

1344 Plain, Belva. CRESCENT CITY. Delacorte, 1984. A Jewish family fleeing old world pogroms settles in New Orleans. They are divided by conflicting loyalties in the Civil War.

1345 Price, Eugenia. LIGHTHOUSE. Lippincott, 1971. Saga of the real James Gould and his family, set mainly on St. Simons Island, Georgia. Originally published in three volumes, Beloved Invader, New Moon Rising, and Lighthouse, now here in chronological order, covering the periods before, during, and after the Civil War.

1346 Pulse, Charles. JOHN BONWELL. Farrar, 1952. Ohio and Kentucky frontier before and during the war.

1347 Reno, Marie R. WHEN THE MUSIC CHANGED. New American Library, 1980. Romance set in the accurately described wartime atmosphere of New York and Washington.

1348 Rhodes, James A. JOHNNY SHILOH. Bobbs, 1959. Story of a nine-year-old Ohio boy, John Clem, who ran away to join the Union army, won his nickname at the Battle of Shiloh, and after the war became a major in the regular army.

1349 Roberts, Walter. BRAVE MARDI GRAS. Bobbs, 1946. After the Battle of Bull Run, a Confederate soldier returns to occupied New Orleans to organize a spy ring; picture of life under the occupation forces of General Benjamin Butler.

1350 Robertson, Constance. THE UNTERRIFIED. Holt, 1946. Copperheads in upstate New York; a senator's son involved with a group spying for the South.

1351 ______. THE GOLDEN CIRCLE. Random, 1951. Story of the Copperhead movement in Ohio under the leadership of Clement Vallandigham; plot to form the Northwest Confederacy; Morgan's raids into Ohio; the Dayton riot; and the Ohio gubernatorial race in 1863.

1352 Robertson, Don. THE THREE DAYS. Prentice, 1959. Realistic story of the three days of the Battle of Gettysburg in June, 1863.

1353 ______. BY ANTIETAM CREEK. Prentice, 1960. Story

of the Battle of Antietam in September, 1862, points up the blunders of General McClellan.

1354 _______. THE RIVER AND THE WILDERNESS. Doubleday, 1962. Raw picture of army life and action at the battles of Antietam, Fredericksburg, and Chancellorsville.

1355 Russell, Pamela Redford. THE WOMAN WHO LOVED JOHN WILKES BOOTH. Putnam, 1978. Story based on fact. Anne Suratt, the daughter of Mary, relates the romance between her mother and John Wilkes Booth, who boarded at their Washington home just before he shot Lincoln.

1356 Sass, Herbert R. LOOK BACK TO GLORY. Bobbs, 1933. South Carolina in the days preceding the Civil War; story of the political events leading to the firing on Fort Sumter.

1357 Schachner, Nathan. BY THE DIM LAMPS. Stokes, 1941. Life on New Orleans and on a Louisiana plantation during the war and Reconstruction.

1358 Scott, Evelyn. THE WAVE. Cape and Smith, 1929. Sweeping picture of the whole war.

1359 Seifert, Shirley. CAPTAIN GRANT. Lippincott, 1946. Ulysses Grant, from his entrance at West Point to the beginning of the war; service in Mexico and California; his retirement to business in Galena, Illinois; beginning of his Civil War service as a colonel of Illinois volunteers.

1360 _______. FAREWELL, MY GENERAL. Lippincott, 1954. Fictional account of the life of J. E. B. Stuart from his days on the Western frontier in 1855 to his death while defending Richmond against Custer in 1864.

1361 Shaara, Michael. THE KILLER ANGELS. McKay, 1974. The opposing armies and their generals endure the bloody horrors of the Battle of Gettysburg.

1362 Sherburne, James. THE WAY TO FORT PILLOW. Houghton, 1972. Sequel to Hacey Miller (Abolition). Opening with the evacuation of Berea College in 1859, the story follows the Kentucky emancipationist through his career in the Union army, climaxing at the massacre of the all-black unit at Fort Pillow.

1363 Shuster, George. LOOK AWAY. Macmillan, 1939. Kentuckian moves to Wisconsin during a mining boom; becomes a Confederate spy during the war.

1364 Sinclair, Harold. THE HORSE SOLDIERS. Harper, 1956. Story of a Union cavalry mission behind Southern lines, based on Grierson's raid. Followed by The Cavalryman (Expanding Frontiers--Plains States).

1365 Singmaster, Elsie. BOY AT GETTYSBURG. Houghton, 1924. Story of a young boy who aids the Union cause at the Battle of Gettysburg.

1366 _______. SWORDS OF STEEL. Houghton, 1933. Story of Gettysburg, Pennsylvania and the events leading up to the battle, including John Brown's raid on Harper's Ferry.

1367 _______. LOVING HEART. Houghton, 1937. Story of the Underground Railroad in Gettysburg and of events moving up to the Battle of Gettysburg.

1368 Slaughter, Frank G. IN A DARK GARDEN. Doubleday, 1946. Spies, counterspies, and a medical student fighting for the Confederacy.

1369 _______. STONEWALL BRIGADE. Doubleday, 1975. Adventures of a medical officer serving with the Confederacy's crack Stonewall Brigade through the war years.

1370 _______. PASSIONATE REBEL. Doubleday, 1979. Spying and adventure mix with historical military strategy in this tale of a Southern woman, returned from living in France, who reports the war for a Paris newspaper.

1371 Slotkin, Richard. CRATER. Atheneum, 1980. A black regiment in the Union army participates in a scheme to lay and explode mines behind Confederate lines. Based on the Battle of the Crater, which took place in Virginia in 1864.

1372 Smith, Chard. ARTILLERY OF TIME. Scribner, 1939. Upstate New York farm and business life from the 1850's to the end of the war.

1373 Stacton, David. THE JUDGES OF THE SECRET COURT. Pantheon, 1961. Story of the assassination of Abraham Lincoln, showing the effects of the assassination on the people involved; unsympathetic portrait of John Wilkes Booth.

1374 Stern, Philip Van Doren. THE MAN WHO KILLED LINCOLN. Random, 1939. The story of John Wilkes Booth and his part in the assassination.

1375 Sterne, Emma Gelders. NO SURRENDER. Dodd, 1932. Life on an Alabama plantation during the war.

1376 Stevenson, Janet. WEEP NO MORE. Viking, 1957. Based on the life of Elizabeth Van Lew, a Southern abolitionist in Richmond, who served as a spy for the North, helped Union soldiers escape from Libby Prison, and evolved a master plan for the capture of Richmond.

1377 Steward, Davenport. SAIL THE DARK TIDE. Tupper and

Love, 1954. Blockade running for the Confederacy between British Nassau and Wilmington, Delaware.

1378 Stover, Herbert. COPPERHEAD MOON. Dodd, 1952. Pennsylvania soldier, returning home, tangles with Copperheads.

1379 Street, James. TAP ROOTS. Dial, 1942. Story of the neutral Dabney clan in Jones County, Mississippi; 1858-1865.

1380 ______. BY VALOUR AND ARMS. Dial, 1944. Naval warfare on the Mississippi River; with the Confederate ironclad Arkansas; Natchez and Vicksburg under Union occupation. More about the Dabney clan.

1381 ______. CAPTAIN LITTLE AX. Lippincott, 1956. Story of the actions of a company of teenaged Confederates, from the Battle of Shiloh to Chickamauga.

1382 Stribling, T. S. THE FORGE. Doubleday, 1931. Alabama before and during the Civil War and the era of Reconstruction. Followed by The Store (Nation Grows Up).

1383 Sullivan, Walter. SOJOURN OF A STRANGER. Holt, 1957. Story of a part-Negro plantation owner who finds bitterness in the plantation society, but who comes to terms with himself after service in the war.

1384 Tate, Allen. THE FATHERS. Putnam, 1938. Conflicting ideas in Virginia, just across the Potomac from Washington; 1850's-1860's.

1385 Thomsen, Robert. CARRIAGE TRADE. Simon and Schuster, 1972. At the time of the Battle of Gettysburg, a madam of a brothel turns her house into a field hospital. An alcoholic doctor regains his sobriety and self-respect, the girls are able nurses, and many wounded are saved.

1386 Toepfer, Ray Grant. THE SCARLET GUIDON. Coward, 1958. Follows a group of Confederate soldiers from their enlistment in the 43rd Alabama Infantry through four years of war; action in the Shenandoah Valley campaign, and the battles of Gettysburg, Fisher's Hill, and Cold Harbor.

1387 ______. THE SECOND FACE OF VALOR. Chilton, 1966. A young Southern artillery man and guerrilla fighter comes of age in the Shenandoah Valley campaign in 1864.

1388 Toepperwein, Herman. REBEL IN BLUE. Morrow, 1963. Story of a group of German settlers, staunch Union supporters, in Fredericksburg, Texas; 1861-64.

1389 Townsend, George A. KATY OF CATOCTIN. Appleton, 1886.

A romance involving the German-American settlers of the Blue Ridge mountains of Maryland. Story opens with John Brown's raid and ends with Booth's conviction.

1390 Tracy, Don. LAST BOAT OUT OF CINCINNATI. Trident, 1970. Adventures of a young boy sent from Louisiana to Cincinnati by riverboat to buy horses for his father, on eve of the outbreak of the Civil War.

1391 Vaughan, Matthew. MAJOR STEPTON'S WAR. Doubleday, 1978. Terrible violence of the war is emphasized in this story of the real Gervase Stepton, advisor to Jefferson Davis, staff member for Robert E. Lee, and commander of a raiding force.

1392 Vidal, Gore. LINCOLN. Random, 1984. The president, as he wrestles with the issues of war, conflicts within his cabinet, and his role as commander-in-chief.

1393 Wagner, Constance. ASK MY BROTHER. Harper, 1959. Civil War background in a story of a Southern aristocrat with a Yankee husband.

1394 Waldman, Emerson. BECKONING RIDGE. Holt, 1940. Story of a neutral Virginia hill farmer caught between two armies.

1395 Wallace, Willard M. THE RAIDERS. Little, 1970. A Union navy man disguised as a crew member of the rebel cruiser _Alabama_. Story describes the draft riots in New York, the sinking of the _Alabama_, and the capture of Fort Fisher by the Union.

1396 Warren, Robert Penn. BAND OF ANGELS. Random, 1955. Kentucky and Louisiana plantation life before, during, and after the Civil War.

1397 _______. WILDERNESS. Random, 1961. Story of a crippled German Jew who finds his courage and his manhood on the battlefield.

1398 Weaver, Ward (pseud.). HAND MY WREATH. Funk and Wagnall, 1941. Campaign of Jeb Stuart in Maryland and Virginia, culminating in the Battle of Antietam.

1399 Weber, William. JOSH. A young Southerner tracks down his horse, stolen by a band of Union soldiers who shot his father. Less about the war, more about his growing self-awareness.

1400 Wheelwright, Jere. GENTLEMEN, HUSH! Scribner, 1948. Story of three young Southern soldiers in the war, and of the conditions they find when they return home.

1401 _______. GRAY CAPTAIN. Scribner, 1954. Story of the 2nd Maryland Infantry of the Army of Northern Virginia in the summer of 1864.

1402 Whitney, Janet. INTRIGUE IN BALTIMORE. Little, 1951. Political developments and the presidential election of 1860, in Baltimore and Illinois.

1403 Whitney, Phyllis. STEP TO THE MUSIC. Crowell, 1953. Story of a divided family on Staten Island during the war.

1404 _______. THE QUICKSILVER POOL. Appleton, 1955. Story of Copperhead intrigue and rebellion on Staten Island; 1862-1863.

1405 Wicker, Tom. UNTO THIS HOUR. Viking, 1984. The Battle of Bull Run was full of gore and bloodshed. This book looks at the effect of its horrors on battle leaders, common soldiers, and the civilians in the vicinity.

1406 Williams, Ben Ames. A HOUSE DIVIDED. Houghton, 1947. Saga of an aristocratic Virginia family with conflicting loyalties, and of the full sweep of the war. Followed by The Unconquered (Reconstruction).

1407 Willsie, Honoré McCue. BENEFITS FORGOT. Stokes, 1917. Story of a young army surgeon presumed dead by his neglected mother.

1408 Wilson, William. THE RAIDERS. Rinehart, 1955. Story of conflicting loyalties and the efforts to defend an Ohio River town under threat of a Confederate raid.

1409 Yerby, Frank. THE FOXES OF HARROW. Dial, 1946. Plantation life and politics in New Orleans; 1825-1865.

1410 Young, Stark. SO RED THE ROSE. Scribner, 1934. Plantation life near Natchez, Mississippi before and during the war.

1411 Zara, Louis. REBEL RUN. Crown, 1951. Story of the daring theft of a railroad engine, and the race to burn the bridges south of Chattanooga, by the Union spy Andrews.

Reconstruction

1412 Anderson, Alston. ALL GOD'S CHILDREN. Bobbs, 1965. A Virginia-born slave escapes to Philadelphia on the Underground Railroad, is later captured and returned to a Georgia plantation, joins the Union army, settles in New Orleans during Reconstruction and meets a violent end after an affair with a white teacher.

1413 Andrews, Annulet. MELISSA STARKE. Dutton, 1935. Story of impoverished life on a once-prosperous Georgia plantation after the war.

1414 Cain, James M. MIGNON. Dial, 1962. Adventures of a Union army veteran in postwar New Orleans.

1415 Campbell, Marie. A HOUSE WITH STAIRS. Rinehart, 1950. Problems of adjustment faced by whites and Negroes on an Alabama plantation during Reconstruction; carpetbaggers, occupation troops, and the Ku Klux Klan enter the plot.

1416 Cheney, Brainard. LIGHTWOOD. Houghton, 1939. Story of the farmers' struggle against a Yankee-owned corporation in post-Civil War years in Georgia.

1417 Coleman, Lonnie. LEGACY OF BEULAH LAND. Doubleday, 1979. Sequel to <u>Beulah Land</u> (The Old South) and <u>Look Away, Beulah Land</u> (The War Years). Carries the story of the Georgia family through the Reconstruction period to 1895.

1418 Corrington, John William. AND WAIT FOR THE NIGHT. Putnam, 1964. Shreveport, Louisiana under occupation during the last days of the war and the beginning of Reconstruction in 1865.

1419 Crabb, Alfred Leland. SUPPER AT THE MAXWELL HOUSE. Bobbs, 1943. Sympathetic portrait of impoverished Southern gentry's efforts to rebuild a shattered culture; plot centers around a Southerner's determination to regain his family home; set in Nashville.

1420 Dykeman, Wilma. THE TALL WOMAN. Holt, 1962. Story of a strong woman whose life was affected by the war and its aftermath, through Reconstruction and later as she works for tax-supported public schools; set in the Smoky Mountains, backwoods country of North Carolina, 1864 to the 1890's.

1421 Fast, Howard. FREEDOM ROAD. Duell, 1944. Story of a freed slave who guides former slaves and poor-white tenant farmers in founding a cooperative community in the face of local opposition.

1422 Gersen, Noel B. YANKEE FROM TENNESSEE. Doubleday, 1960. Fictionized biography of Andrew Johnson, centering on the problems he faced with Reconstruction policies after the assassination of Abraham Lincoln.

1423 Gordon, Armistead. OMMIRANDY. Scribner, 1917. Amusing story of an old Southern Negro sharing privations with her ex-master's family.

1424 Harben, William. THE TRIUMPH. Harper, 1917. Story of an abolitionist in a small Georgia town and his troubles with the Ku Klux Klan.

1425 Herbst, Josephine. PITY IS NOT ENOUGH. Harcourt, 1933. Story of easy money and political graft in the South in Reconstruction days. Followed by The Executioner Waits (The Twenties).

1426 Krey, Laura. AND TELL OF TIME. Houghton, 1938. Picture of the confusing social, political, and economic problems faced by Southerners after the war; Ku Klux Klan, relations with Negro servants, rebuilding a prosperous plantation, and the struggle to establish law and order in Georgia and Texas from 1865 to 1888.

1427 McMeekin, Clark (pseud.). TYRONE OF KENTUCKY. Appleton, 1954. Story of the conflicting attitudes and the problems of Reconstruction in a divided Kentucky, as they were faced by a Confederate veteran and his Alabama bride.

1428 Miller, Helen Topping and John Dewey. REBELLION ROAD. Bobbs, 1954. Search for a new way of life by a Confederate soldier who returns to find his family's plantation in ruins.

1429 Miller, Helen Topping. AFTER THE GLORY. Appleton, 1958. Story of the conflicts between ex-Confederates and Union sympathizers in eastern Tennessee during the Reconstruction period.

1430 Page, Thomas Nelson. RED ROCK. Scribner, 1898. Social life in the South during Reconstruction in the late 1860's, including carpetbaggers and the Ku Klux Klan.

1431 Pierce, Ovid William. ON A LONESOME PORCH. Doubleday, 1960. A young widow, her small son, and mother-in-law return to their North Carolina plantation in 1865 to begin a new life.

1432 Price, Eugenia. THE BELOVED INVADER. Lippincott, 1965. Fictional biography of Anson Dodge, a Union veteran who devoted himself to rebuilding a church on St. Simons Island, Georgia, after the war.

1433 Rhodes, James A. TRIAL OF MARY TODD LINCOLN. Bobbs, 1959. Based on the sanity trials of Lincoln's wife in 1875 and 1876.

1434 Rikhoff, Jean. ONE OF THE RAYMONDS. Dial, 1974. Sequel to Buttes Landing (Young Nation). A member of a later generation is an urban intellectual, but he feels compelled to prove himself brave and strong for his macho uncle. Set in the period of Reconstruction.

1435 Ripley, Alexandra. CHARLESTON. Doubleday, 1981. A new way of life is a necessity for an old Charleston family after the war has destroyed home and fortune.

1436 Sims, Marian. BEYOND SURRENDER. Lippincott, 1942. An ex-Confederate officer sets out to rebuild his ruined plantation with the aid of his mother and a few loyal ex-slaves.

1437 Slaughter, Frank G. THE STUBBORN HEART. Doubleday, 1950. A romance centering around the plantation of a young doctor and his wife, who is a Union spy; has the usual elements of Ku Klux Klan, scalawags, carpetbaggers, honest Union men, and loyal Southerners.

1438 ______. LORENA. Doubleday, 1959. A strong-willed Southern belle manages her husband's plantation during the war and faces the problems of Reconstruction and the Ku Klux Klan after the war.

1439 Stewart, Catherine Pomeroy. THREE ROADS TO VALHALLA. Scribner, 1948. A sweeping novel of Reconstruction in Jacksonville, Florida; carpetbaggers, the Freedmen's Bureau, and the social and political turmoil of the times.

1440 Taylor, Robert Lewis. A JOURNEY TO MATECUMBE. McGraw, 1961. Adventure-packed story of the flight of a 14-year-old boy, his uncle, and a Negro servant, from Kentucky after a run-in with the Ku Klux Klan; includes a stint with a quack doctor's medicine show on a Mississippi River barge en route to New Orleans, a harrowing experience at a Tennessee plantation, a dangerous crossing of the Everglades with the guidance of friendly Seminole Indians, and various economic schemes in Key West; authentic picture of life in the time and places involved.

1441 Tourgee, Albion W. A FOOL'S ERRAND. Harbard, 1961. Difficulties faced by a Union officer who settles his family in the South; social and political life during Reconstruction; first published in 1879.

1442 Twain, Mark (pseud.). THE ADVENTURES OF COLONEL SELLERS. Doubleday, 1965. Twain's satire on the Reconstruction era. First published in 1874 as part of The Golden Age.

1443 Weekley, Robert S. THE HOUSE IN RUINS. Random, 1958. Story of a guerrilla band carrying on the war in a small Mississippi community; theme is the responsibility one bears to rebuild for the future.

1444 Wellman, Paul. ANGEL WITH SPURS. Lippincott, 1942. Story of General Jo Shelby and the group of Confederate volunteers that he led to Mexico to join Maximilian, rather than accept surrender at the end of the war.

1445 White, Leslie. LOOK AWAY, LOOK AWAY. Random, 1943. Story of the group of Southerners who migrated to Brazil after the war rather than stay on under Reconstruction, and of their unsuccessful efforts to pioneer on the Amazon River.

1446 Williams, Ben Ames. THE UNCONQUERED. Houghton, 1953. Picture of political, social, and economic strife in New Orleans during Reconstruction, 1865 to 1874; development of the cotton-seed oil industry, and the temperate attitude promoted by General James Longstreet.

1447 Yerby, Frank. THE VIXENS. Dial, 1947. Story of New Orleans plantation life and Reconstruction legislation.

1448 _______. GRIFFIN'S WAY. Dial, 1962. Romantic novel of political and social life in Mississippi following the Civil War.

THE NATION GROWS UP, 1877 TO 1917

1449 Adams, Henry. DEMOCRACY. 1879. Story of Washington social life, and political corruption during the second administration of U.S. Grant.

1450 Adams, Samuel Hopkins. TENDERLOIN. Random, 1959. New York City in the 1890's. A clergyman undertakes a crusade against gambling and prostitution in spite of corrupt police and politicians.

1451 Allen, Henry. SAN JUAN HILL. Random, 1962. An Arizona cowboy joins Teddy Roosevelt's Rough Riders and sees action in the Spanish-American War.

1452 Anderson, Sherwood. WINDY McPHERSON'S SON. Cape, 1916. Story of a Midwestern small-town boy who becomes a successful Chicago financier in the years following the Spanish-American War.

1453 Angoff, Charles. JOURNEY TO THE DAWN. Yoseloff, 1951. A Russian family migrates to America and settles in Boston at the turn of the century. Followed by <u>In the Morning Light</u> (World War I).

1454 Asch, Sholem. EAST RIVER. Purnam, 1946. Story of conflicts between Jews and Irish-Catholics in New York's East Side at the turn of the century.

1455 Atherton, Sarah. MARK'S OWN. Bobbs, 1941. Industrial history of a Pennsylvania coal mine from 1849 to 1929, through the story of the mine owner, his descendants, laborers and labor organizers.

1456 Aydelotte, Dora. LONG FURROWS. Appleton, 1935. Picture of country social life in the 1890's; Fourth of July picnics, quilting bees, revival meetings, school exercises, and other local affairs.

1457 ________. MEASURE OF A MAN. Appleton, 1942. Business and social life in a small Illinois town in the 1890's; effects of mail-order houses on small business, the coming of the automobile, and the depression of 1893.

1458 Barber, Elsie. HUNT FOR HEAVEN. Macmillan, 1950. Picture of labor developments in the 1890's and an experiment in communal living on a Pennsylvania farm; Chicago's Haymarket Riots; Samuel Gompers.

1459 Barker, Squire Omar. A LITTLE WORLD APART. Doubleday, 1966. Story of boyhood life on a New Mexico ranch in the years before World War I.

1460 Barnes, Margaret Ayer. YEARS OF GRACE. Houghton, 1930. Background of changing social life from the 1890's to 1930's; settling is Chicago.

1461 _______. WITHIN THIS PRESENT. Houghton, 1933. Two decades in the life of a wealthy Chicago family from 1914 to the 1930's; World War I; Depression; flashbacks show the development of Chicago from 1840.

1462 _______. EDNA, HIS WIFE. Houghton, 1935. Social and business life in Chicago suburb and in Washington, D. C., through the Gibson Girl days and World War I to the Depression.

1463 Beebe, Elswyth Thane. EVER AFTER. Duell, 1945. The Spanish-American War, the Rough Riders, and the Battle of San Juan Hill, as seen by a Virginia war correspondent. Part of the author's Williamsburg series.

1464 Beer, Thomas. SANDOVAL. Knopf, 1924. New York social scene in the 1870's.

1465 Bell, Thomas. OUT OF THIS FURNACE. Little, 1941. The steel industry in Homestead, Pennsylvania from 1881 to the 1930's; development of the labor movement and the organizing of the Congress of Industrial Organizations; Hungarian immigrant family.

1466 Bellamann, Henry. KINGS ROW. Simon and Schuster, 1940. Life in a small Midwestern town at the turn of the century.

1467 Belland, F. W. TRUE SEA. Holt, 1984. Turn-of-century picture of life in the Florida Keys. Flagler's proposed railway anticipated a boom period, but the reality was exploitation and hard times for the residents.

1468 Benasutti, Marion. NO STEADY JOB FOR PAPA. Vanguard, 1967. Nostalgic story of the happy life of a poor Italian immigrant family in Philadelphia.

1469 Benson, Sally. MEET ME IN ST. LOUIS. Random, 1942. Typical Midwestern family at the St. Louis Exposition, 1903-1904.

1470 Berlin, Ellin. LACE CURTAIN. Doubleday, 1948. Long Island, New York, and Paris society in the first decade of the century. Story of prejudice in the marriage of a Protestant and an Irish-Catholic.

1471 _______. THE BEST OF FAMILIES. Doubleday, 1970. Picture of life in a wealthy family in New York City in the early part of the twentieth century, as remembered by the youngest daughter.

1472 Betts, Doris. THE SCARLET THREAD. Harper, 1964. Life in a North Carolina textile mill town at the turn of the century.

1473 Bickham, Jack M. DINAH, BLOW YOUR HORN. Doubleday, 1979. Life in a small Ohio railroad center in the heyday of the steam locomotive.

1474 Bisno, Beatrice. TOMORROW'S BREAD. Liveright, 1938. Story of the sweatshop conditions in the Chicago garment-making industry in the 1890's; and of the effort to organize labor.

1475 Bissell, Richard. JULIA HARRINGTON. Little, 1969. A nostalgic, Sears Roebuck catalog-of-life in a small town in Iowa in 1913.

1476 Bjorn, Thyra Ferre. PAPA'S WIFE. Rinehart, 1955. Large Swedish family migrates to America and settles in New England where Papa becomes a minister. Story of family life and customs.

1477 _______. PAPA'S DAUGHTER. Rinehart, 1958. Story of a Swedish immigrant's daughter's ambition and struggle to be a writer; set in New England in the early 1900's. Sequel to Papa's Wife.

1478 Black, David. MINDS. Wyden, 1982. Early development of psychiatry in the United States. An MD hears Freud lecture, then opens a clinic in Nebraska. The story resembles that of the Menninger Clinic.

1479 Blanton, Margaret. THE WHITE UNICORN. Viking, 1961. Family life and the story of a girl growing up in Nashville at the turn of the century.

1480 Blassingame, Wyatt. HALO OF SPEARS. Doubleday, 1962. Brutal story of life on a chain gang in Georgia and Florida in the early 1900's.

1481 Blickle, Katrinka. DARK BEGINNINGS. Doubleday, 1978. Story of Southern girl who takes a brave and unusual path when she attends Bellevue Hospital's medical school and pursues her career as a physician.

1482 Block, Robert. AMERICAN GOTHIC. Simon and Schuster, 1974. Horror story, loosely based on a scandalous series of murders discovered in Chicago at the time of the 1893 World's Fair.

1483 Blum, Carol O'Brien. ANNE'S HEAD. Dial, 1981. An Irish family in St. Louis copes with tragedy, even as the World's Fair in their city promises progress and light in the new century.

1484 Boles, Paul Darcy. THE LIMNER. Crowell, 1975. Adventures of an itinerant portrait painter in Pennsylvania who elopes with one of his subjects, is falsely accused of murder; 1870's.

1485 Brace, Gerald Warner. THE WORLD OF CARRICK'S COVE. Norton, 1957. Nostalgic view of a young boy's life in a Maine seafaring-farming community near the turn of the century.

1486 Brinig, Myron. THE SISTERS. Farrar, 1937. Life in Silver Bow, Montana, San Francisco, and New York, as seen by the daughters of a small-town druggist; 1904-1910.

1487 _______. MAY FLAVIN. Farrar, 1938. Chicago, New York, and Hollywood from the 1890's to the 1930's.

1488 Brink, Carol Ryrie. STRANGERS IN THE FOREST. Macmillan, 1959. Story of homesteading in Idaho in the early 1900's; centers around a Forest Service agent sent to find out if the settlers were actually farming the land or selling the timber.

1489 Bristow, Gwen. THIS SIDE OF GLORY. Crowell, 1940. Life on a Louisiana plantation from about 1885 to the period following World War I. Sequel to The Handsome Road (Civil War).

1490 Bromfield, Louis. MRS. PARKINGTON. Harper, 1943. Daughter of a Nevada mining-town hotel keeper marries a rich robber baron and becomes famous on two continents.

1491 Brough, James. MISS LILLIAN RUSSELL. McGraw, 1978. The imaginary memoirs of the great entertainer. She describes her relationship with Diamond Jim Brady and brings back the heady atmosphere of New York's bright lights around the turn of the century.

1492 Budd, Lillian. LAND OF STRANGERS. Lippincott, 1953. Story of the struggles of a young Swedish couple to make a life for themselves in their new country.

1493 _______. APRIL HARVEST. Duell, 1959. Story of the

daughter of Swedish immigrant parents in Chicago, from the early 1900's through the outbreak of World War I, as she struggles to support herself and get an education. Sequel to Land of Strangers.

1494 Burke, J. F. NOAH. Sherbourne, 1968. A love story with a background of the I. W. W. movement in a small town in Illinois and in New York City in 1910; brief glimpses of Theodore Dreiser, Emma Goldman, small-town life, and radical politics of the day.

1495 Byron, Gilbert. THE LORD'S OYSTERS. Little, 1957. Story of a boy's life among the oyster men of Chester River in the eastern-shore region of Maryland, about the turn of the century.

1496 Caldwell, Janet Taylor. THIS SIDE OF INNOCENCE. Scribner, 1946. Social novel set in upstate New York, 1868-1880's.

1497 ______. NEVER VICTORIOUS, NEVER DEFEATED. McGraw, 1954. Pictures the rise of American capitalism and the exploitation of labor in the one hundred years from Jackson's administration to 1935.

1498 ______. A PROLOGUE TO LOVE. Doubleday, 1961. Story of an ambitious woman who rises from poverty to great wealth, set in Boston, 1880-1914.

1499 ______. TESTIMONY OF TWO MEN. Doubleday, 1968. Problems of an outspoken medical doctor in a small town in Pennsylvania in 1901 following the abortion death of his wife.

1500 Carroll, Gladys Hasty. A FEW FOOLISH ONES. Macmillan, 1935. Depicts the lives of a few Maine farmers from the 1870's to the 1930's.

1501 ______. WEST OF THE HILL. Macmillan, 1949. Village life in Maine in the late 1800's.

1502 Carson, Katharine. MRS. PENNINGTON. Putnam, 1939. Social picture of a small Kansas town in the 1880's.

1503 Carson, Robert. THE MAGIC LANTERN. Holt, 1954. Growth of the movie industry from silent to sound movies in New York and Hollywood; 1907-1927.

1504 Carter, Isabel. SHIPMATES. W. R. Scott, 1934. Story of a seafaring family in Maine in the 1870's.

1505 Castor, Henry. THE YEAR OF THE SPANIARD. Doubleday, 1950. The Spanish-American War and its impact on the United States; Cuba, Puerto Rico, and the Philippines.

1506 Catto, Max. KING OIL. Simon and Schuster, 1970. Ordeals and disasters in the dusty oil fields outside Amarillo, Texas, when the industry was just beginning to mean wealth for the state.

1507 Chase, Mary Ellen. THE LOVELY AMBITION. Norton, 1960. Story of the family of an English Methodist minister which emigrates to Pepperell, Maine around 1900.

1508 Chevalier, Elizabeth Pickett. DRIVIN' WOMAN. Macmillan, 1942. Life on a Kentucky plantation from the end of the Civil War to 1905; teaching school, development of tobacco-growing enterprise, and the Kentucky tobacco war of 1905.

1509 Clune, Henry W. THE BIG FELLA. Macmillan, 1956. Story of machine politics in an Eastern state in the early 1900's.

1510 Corbett, Elizabeth. THE LANGWORTHY FAMILY. Appleton, 1937. Family life in a Midwestern city at the turn of the century.

1511 _______. SHE WAS CARRIE EATON. Appleton, 1938. Re-creates the life of a small Ohio city in the 1870's. Part of the author's Mrs. Meigs series.

1512 _______. THE FAR DOWN. Appleton, 1939. Story of a large family living on the outskirts of a Midwestern city in 1877.

1513 _______. MR. AND MRS. MEIGS. Appleton, 1940. Family life in a Midwestern city of the 1880's.

1514 _______. EARLY SUMMER. Appleton, 1942. Rural Illinois in post-Civil War days.

1515 _______. THE HEAD OF APOLLO. Lippincott, 1956. Light romance set in a small Illinois town in the 1890's.

1516 _______. HAMILTON TERRACE. Appleton, 1960. Story of a woman at the turn of the century, cut off from the social life of her small Wisconsin community by her wealth.

1517 Cordell, Alexander. THE RACE AND THE TIGER. Doubleday, 1963. Story of labor agitation and violence and the Molly Maguire movement in the steel industry in Pittsburgh when the new Bessemer process throws many Irish immigrants out of work in the 1870's.

1518 Corey, Paul. THREE MILES SQUARE. Bobbs, 1939. Picture of agricultural America through the story of an Iowa farm family; 1910-1916.

1519 Crabb, Alfred Leland. BREAKFAST AT THE HERMITAGE. Bobbs, 1945. Story of the development of Nashville and the rebuilding of the Hermitage in the period following Reconstruction.

1520 _______. REUNION AT CHATTANOOGA. Bobbs, 1950. Social and economic developments in post-Reconstruction Chattanooga; 1876-1890.

1521 Crabtree, Lou V. SWEET HOLLOW. Louisiana State Univ. Press, 1984. Vignettes of the past in the Appalachian hills, expressing the importance of folk tale and myth to the hill folk. Well-rendered native idiom.

1522 Curry, Peggy. SO FAR FROM SPRING. Viking, 1956. Story of ranch life in the cattle country of the Colorado Rockies in the early 1900's.

1523 Davenport, Marcia. THE VALLEY OF DECISION. Scribner, 1942. Rise of the steel industry from 1873, told through the story of a Pennsylvania steel manufacturer's family.

1524 Davis, Burke. THE SUMMER LAND. Random, 1965. Story of one summer in the life of an adolescent boy in the North Carolina tobacco country in 1916, with sidelights on the tobacco wars going on at the time.

1525 Davis, Christopher. A PEEP INTO THE 20th CENTURY. Harper, 1971. The final months of life of Rupert Weber, the first man to die in the electric chair. Based on fact. Edison and Westinghouse appear as characters.

1526 Davis, Clyde Brion. JEREMY BELL. Rinehart, 1947. Life in a small Illinois town, in Chicago, in an Arkansas lumber camp, in the army, and in various other places in 1897.

1527 _______. SHADOW OF A TIGER. Day, 1963. Story of a boy growing up in Denver from the turn of the century to World War I.

1528 Davis, Harold Lenoir. HONEY IN THE HORN. Harper, 1935. Oregon homesteading in the early 1900's.

1529 Dawson, Cleo. SHE CAME TO THE VALLEY. Morrow, 1943. Saga of a Texas border town in the years prior to World War I. Small-town life, droughts, and Mexican raids.

1530 De Capite, Raymond. A LOST KING. McKay, 1961. Family life of Italian immigrants in the industrial section of Cleveland, Ohio.

1531 De Forest, J. W. PLAYING THE MISCHIEF. Bald Eagle Press, 1961. Washington, D. C. in the 1870's. Story of a fraudulent claim for a barn destroyed in the War of 1812. Originally published in 1875.

1532 Deal, Borden. THE TOBACCO MEN. Holt, 1965. Story of the tobacco industry in Kentucky; pictures the tobacco war of 1905 and the struggle to form cooperatives.

1533 Deasy, Mary. O'SHAUGHNESSY'S DAY. Doubleday, 1957. Story of the family relationships of a corrupt Irish politician in Corioli, Ohio, from the turn of the century to 1922.

1534 Dempsey, David. ALL THAT WAS MORTAL. Dutton, 1957. Novel of the social and economic struggles of a family in a small Illinois town from 1889 to 1924; conveys the manners and customs of the period.

1535 Denker, Henry. HEALERS. Morrow, 1982. A story of an immigrant Jewish doctor and his American wife, one of the first female physicians. Together they fight the epidemics of cholera, diptheria, and tuberculosis that plagued New York in the years after the Civil War.

1536 Di Donato, Georgia. FIREBRANDS. Doubleday, 1982. At the turn of the century a newspaperwoman, working for real Seattle editor Colonel Alden Blethen, covers stories about the Chinese immigrants, the plight of the cannery workers, and the Yukon gold rush.

1537 Doctorow, E. L. RAGTIME. Random, 1957. Houdini, Henry Ford, Freud, Booker T. Washington, and many other well-known people of the day appear in this story of a fictional family living in New Rochelle, New York in the first decade of the century.

1538 Dowdey, Clifford. SING FOR A PENNY. Little, 1941. Unscrupulous financial dealings in Richmond in the 1880's and 1890's.

1539 Downing, J. Hyatt. SIOUX CITY. Putnam, 1940. Picture of the growth of Sioux City, Iowa up to the year 1884.

1540 Dreiser, Theodore. SISTER CARRIE. 1900. Depicts life of the lower middle classes in New York and Chicago with insights into the business world.

1541 _______. JENNIE GERHARDT. Harper, 1911. Pictures the materialism of American society at the turn of the century through the lives of two families, German and Irish immigrants.

1542 _______. THE FINANCIER. Harper, 1912. Story of the love affairs and business career of a Philadelphia financier whose enterprises lead finally to his arrest and conviction for embezzlement in the late 1800's. Followed by The Titan.

1543 _______. THE TITAN. Lane, 1914. Continues the story of Frank Cowperwood in the financial world in Chicago in the 1870's.

1544 Ducharme, Jacques. THE DELUSSON FAMILY. Funk and Wagnall, 1939. Social and industrial developments around Holyoke, Massachusetts in the years after 1874.

1545 Edmonds, Walter D. THE BOYDS OF BLACK RIVER. Dodd, 1953. Upstate New York is the setting of a story about a horse-loving family who look with disdain at the coming of the horseless carriage.

1546 _______. THE NIGHT RAIDER AND OTHER STORIES. Little, 1980. Four short stories set in upstate New York. Two stories concern the Erie Canal, and two are about farm life in the first decade of the twentieth century.

1547 Elfman, Blossom. STRAWBERRY FIELDS OF HEAVEN. Crown, 1983. Life in the utopian Oneida Community, whose distinctive mores resulted in an unusual amount of freedom and independence for the Victorian woman.

1548 Ellsberg, Edward. MID WATCH. Dodd, 1954. Story of the pre-World War I navy, based on the explosion aboard the cruiser Manhattan on its trial run in 1909.

1549 Emerson, Elizabeth. THE GARNERED SHEAVES. Longmans, 1948. Quaker farmers in Illinois at the turn of the century.

1550 Erdman, Loula Grace. THE SHORT SUMMER. Dodd, 1958. Life in a Missouri town during the summer of 1914, with church socials, the Chautauqua, band concerts, family gatherings, and a faint echo of the trouble brewing in Europe.

1551 Eyre, Katherine Wigmore. THE CHINESE BOX. Appleton, 1959. Life in the upper social circles in San Francisco in the 1880's.

1552 Fairbank, Janet Ayer. THE SMITHS. Bobbs, 1925. Life in growing Chicago, from early 1860's to the 1920's.

1553 Fall, Thomas. ORDEAL OF RUNNING STANDING. McCall, 1970. Violent tragedy befalls a young Indian, given an education at a white man's college around the turn of the century, when he cannot reconcile the opposing cultures.

1554 Falstein, Louis. LAUGHTER ON A WEEKDAY. Obelensky, 1965. Story of a Jewish family's escape from the Russian pogroms in the early twentieth century, and of their difficulties in establishing themselves in a small town in the American Middle West.

1555 Faralla, Dana. THE MADSTONE. Lippincott, 1958. Story of character conflict between three children and their stern mother during a summer vacation at a lake in Minnesota in 1914.

1556 Fast, Howard. THE AMERICAN. Duell, 1946. Sympathetic portrait of Peter Altgeld, governor of Illinois during the Haymarket Riots; a one-sided picture of the struggle between capital and labor in the 1890's.

1557 _______. THE IMMIGRANTS. Houghton, 1977. Son of immigrants, orphaned by the San Francisco earthquake in 1906, builds a fortune from a fishing fleet, only to be wiped out by the crash of '29.

1558 _______. MAX. Houghton, 1982. A story of pre-Hollywood days of the fledgling movie industry when the flicks were shown in store-front theaters and the films were produced in New York studios.

1559 Federspiel, J. F. BALLAD OF TYPHOID MARY. Dutton, 1983. A Swiss novelist recounts the story of Mary Mallon, the immigrant girl who came to these shores on the ship Leibnitz in 1868. Many of the passengers had typhoid; Mary, herself immune, carried the germ and spread the disease throughout New York.

1560 Ferber, Edna. SHOW BOAT. Doubleday, 1926. Life on a Mississippi River showboat, in New Orleans and St. Louis, in the 1870's and after.

1561 _______. SARATOGA TRUNK. Doubleday, 1941. Background of social and business life in New Orleans, Louisiana, and Saratoga, New York in the 1880's.

1562 _______. GREAT SON. Doubleday, 1945. Chronicle of the Melendy clan and the growth of Seattle, Washington from early Alaska gold-rush days to 1941.

1563 Field, Rachel. TIME OUT OF MIND. Macmillan, 1935. Story of the declining fortunes of a New England shipbuilding family, with the passing of the sailing ship, the coming of steam, and the beginning influx of summer colonists.

1564 Fischer, Marjorie. MRS. SHERMAN'S SUMMER. Lippincott, 1960. Story of events in the household of the matriarch of a large Jewish family on Long Island in 1911.

1565 Ford, Elizabeth. NO HOUR OF HISTORY. Ives Washburn, 1940. Politics, theater, fashions, songs, and books as seen by a girl growing up in a small town of Iowa from 1859 to World War I.

1566 Ford, James. HOT CORN IKE. Dutton, 1923. Politics and political bosses in New York City; 1880's-1900.

1567 Ford, Paul Leicester. THE HONORABLE PETER STIRLING. Holt, 1894. A story of politics, based on the career of Grover Cleveland; set in New York in the 1870's.

1568 Gabriel, Gilbert Wolf. BROWNSTONE FRONT. Century, 1924. Social background of New York City in the 1890's.

1569 Gardiner, John Rolfe. GREAT DREAM FROM HEAVEN. Dutton, 1974. Tennessee mine owners and the miners at odds in the late 1880's. One man tries unsuccessfully to organize the fiercely independent workers in this story of the halting beginnings of labor unions.

1570 Gerson, Noel B. T. R. Doubleday, 1970. Biographical novel about Theodore Roosevelt, the sickly boy who became a strong outdoorsman, powerful political leader, and popular president.

1571 Giles, Barbara. THE GENTLE BUSH. Harcourt, 1947. Louisiana plantation life at the turn of the century, showing the conflicts in the transition from the old society to new customs and economics.

1572 Giles, Janice Holt. THE PLUM THICKET. Houghton, 1954. Farm and village life in Arkansas at the turn of the century, with religious revivals, Confederate reunions, and baseball.

1573 Goertz, Arthemise. NEW HEAVEN, NEW EARTH. McGraw, 1953. Doctor in New Orleans in 1909 faces conflict between his loyalty to the past and his desire to progress with the times.

1574 Grant, Ozro F. KICK THE DOG GENTLY. Bobbs, 1965. Memories of a young man's boyhood days, centering on life in the family hotel in a small Oklahoma town in 1914.

1575 Guthrie, A. B. ARFIVE. Houghton, 1971. Fourth in the author's Northwestern chronicles series. An unruly Western town, in the first years of this century, is gradually civilized by the arrival of the principal of its first high school. He is a cultured man and a dedicated teacher.

1576 Hagedorn, Hermann. THE ROUGH RIDERS. Harper, 1927. The Spanish-American War and the United States in the

1890's; emphasizes the disorder and mismanagement of our entry into the war.

1577 Hansen, Ron. ASSASSINATION OF JESSE JAMES BY THE COWARD ROBERT FORD. Knopf, 1983. Jesse James was already a mythical hero to the young Bob Ford when they met. The author tries to unravel some complex truths about both James and his killer, who found himself pardoned for his crime but never respected.

1578 ______. DESPERADOES. Knopf, 1979. The lives of the Dalton boys, peace officers turned outlaws, here recalled by the elderly Emmett Dalton, the only brother to survive the aftermath of their robbery of the bank at Coffeyville, Kansas.

1579 Hart, Alan. IN THE LIVES OF MEN. Norton, 1937. Panorama of national events and life in a logging town on Puget Sound from 1890 to 1907. The depression of 1893; Spanish-American War; the Alaska gold rush, and labor unrest.

1580 Hayden, Sterling. VOYAGE. Putnam, 1976. Dangers of life on the sea aboard a square-rigger. Story follows Neptune's Car on her maiden voyage from Maine, around the Horn to San Francisco in 1896. Politics of the day, the McKinley-Bryan election are part of the story.

1581 Hergesheimer, Joseph. THREE BLACK PENNYS. Knopf, 1917. The development of the steel industry in Pennsylvania, told through the chronicle of a manufacturing family.

1582 Hollingsworth, Mary H. HOW LONG THE HEART REMEMBERS. Houghton, 1976. A proudly independent family struggles for livelihood on a hardscrabble farm in the rocky hills of north Georgia from 1914 to 1923.

1583 Holt, Isabella. RAMPOLE PLACE. Bobbs, 1952. A period piece of the American Middle West from 1906 to 1912.

1584 Horan, Kenneth. A BASHFUL WOMAN. Doubleday, 1944. Growth of the automobile industry as a background of family life in a Michigan city; 1890's to World War II.

1585 Horgan, Paul. THINGS AS THEY ARE. Farrar, 1964. Picture of childhood and growing up in a town in New York in the early 1900's.

1586 Howard, Elizabeth. BEFORE THE SUN GOES DOWN. Doubleday, 1946. Life in a small Pennsylvania town in 1880, from the mansions to the hovels, from the viewpoint of a kindly doctor.

1587 Howells, William Dean. A HAZARD OF NEW FORTUNES. Dutton, 1890. Story of the exploitation of labor and the unionization of industry, set around the streetcar strike in New York City in the late 1800's.

1588 Hunter, Evan. STREETS OF GOLD. Harper, 1974. Story of a blind jazz pianist, a member of an Italian immigrant family in the early years of the twentieth century.

1589 _______. LIZZIE. Arbor House, 1984. Author finds a motive for Lizzie Borden's crime, assuming that her stepmother had discovered her in a lesbian relationship. The story of this presumed love affair alternates with sections of court records from Lizzie's trial.

1590 Hurling, John. THE BOOMERS. Vanguard, 1979. A group of itinerant steelworkers, whose dangerous job it was to construct and repair huge oil tanks, work together in Billings, Montana in 1919.

1591 Idell, Albert. CENTENNIAL SUMMER. Holt, 1943. Political and social issues of the period of 1876; Philadelphia family witnesses the opening of the Centennial Exposition, and visits New York City.

1592 _______. BRIDGE TO BROOKLYN. Holt, 1944. Picture of the period 1877 to 1883, centering around construction of the Brooklyn Bridge. Sequel to Centennial Summer.

1593 _______. THE GREAT BLIZZARD. Holt, 1948. Brooklyn and New York from 1884 to the "Blizzard of 1888." Some of the same characters who appear in Centennial Summer.

1594 _______. STEPHEN HAYNE. Sloane, 1951. Picture of social and financial dealings in the Pennsylvania coal-mining region; 1870's-1880's; conflict between the established Dutch and immigrant Irish.

1595 James, Henry. THE BOSTONIANS. 1886. Satirical view of Boston society in the 1870's.

1596 Johnston, Mary. MICHAEL FORTH. Harper, 1919. Emergence of the new economic and social order in the South at the turn of the century.

1597 Jones, Nard. WHEAT WOMEN. Duffield, 1933. Three generations of Oregon wheat growers, from the arrival of the pioneers to the crash of the market in 1930.

1598 Kapstein, Israel. SOMETHING OF A HERO. Knopf, 1941. Life in a small Midwestern industrial city in the early 1900's; bankers, bootleggers, iron workers, politicians, and labor agitators.

1599 Kaup, Elizabeth. NOT FOR THE MEEK. Macmillan, 1941. Rise of the Pittsburgh steel industry through the story of a Danish immigrant who rose to the top under Andrew Carnegie.

1600 Kazan, Elia. THE ANATOLIAN. Knopf, 1982. Greek traditional life quickly ceased to govern the members of an immigrant family in New York in the early twentieth century. Old ways crumbled against the desire to succeed in urban America.

1601 Kelland, Clarence Budington. GOLD. Harper, 1931. High finance and struggle for control of the railroads; 1860's to 1870's. Sequel to Hard Money (The Young Nation).

1602 ______. JEALOUS HOUSE. Harper, 1934. Business, finance, and politics; 1880's to World War I. Sequel to Gold.

1603 Kelly, Wallace. DAYS ARE AS GRASS. Knopf, 1941. Depicts the changes in the social structure of a small Kentucky town, from the late 1870's to the early 1900's.

1604 Kelton, Elmer. THE DAY THE COWBOYS QUIT. Doubleday, 1971. Based on the actual cowboy strike in Texas in 1883. When Eastern banks demanded changes in business management on the part of the landowners as a prerequisite to lending money, the cowhands reacted angrily to the threat to their traditional independence.

1605 Kennelly, Ardyth. THE PEACEABLE KINGDOM. Houghton, 1949. Salt Lake City, Utah in the 1890's and the difficulties which beset the Mormons after the death of Brigham Young.

1606 ______. UP HOME. Houghton, 1955. Sequel to the Peaceable Kingdom presents further events in the lives of a Mormon family in Salt Lake City in the 1890's.

1607 ______. MARRY ME, CARRY ME. Houghton, 1956. Story of the nomadic life of a young couple in the West in the early 1900's.

1608 Keyes, Frances Parkinson. HONOR BRIGHT. Messner, 1936. Story of an aristocratic Boston family from 1890 to 1925. Washington politics and Boston and Virginia social life.

1609 ______. BLUE CAMELLIA. Messner, 1957. Story set in the rice-growing Cajun country of Louisiana, from the 1880's to the early 1900's; description of life in New Orleans and the customs of the Cajuns.

1610 Kluge, P. F. SEASON FOR WAR. Freundlich, 1984. Story of a former Civil War hero, a career army man, determined to climb the military ladder. He fights the Apache, then in the Philippines, taking advantage of the period in American history when imperialism propelled U.S. policies.

1611 Kluger, Richard. MEMBERS OF THE TRIBE. Doubleday, 1977. Based on historical incident. A Jew who settled in Savannah, Georgia in the 1880's thrived until his defense of a fellow Jew accused of murder in 1913, when the anti-Semitism of his neighbors surfaced.

1612 Knowles, John. A VEIN OF RICHES. Little, 1978. West Virginia in the coal industry's boom-days in 1909. The unions struggle to organize workers. At the story's end, in 1924, oil has signaled the end of prosperity for the miners.

1613 LaFontaine, George. SCOTT-DUNLAP RING. Coward, 1978. Story of the real nineteenth-century Chicago criminals Robert Scott and Jim Dunlap, whose safecracking skills threatened the security of all banks.

1614 Laman, Russell. MANIFEST DESTINY. Regnery, 1963. Story of forty years in the life of a rural Kansas community from the 1880's to 1920's; a bankrupt Eastern financier becomes a farmer, supporting the Populist Party of William Jennings Bryan.

1615 LaPiere, Richard. WHEN THE LIVING STRIVE. Harper, 1941. Life in San Francisco's Chinatown; 1875-1929. Tong wars, the earthquake, and Chinese and American social customs.

1616 Latham, Edythe. THE SOUNDING BRASS. Little, 1953. Chronicle of three generations of a powerful North Carolina family, following the Civil War.

1617 Leonard, Jonathan. BACK TO STAY. Viking, 1929. Portrays the life and spirit of an isolated New England village in the 1870's.

1618 Leslie, Aleen. THE SCENT OF ROSES. Viking, 1963. Light romance evoking a nostalgic view of life in a German-American family in Pittsburgh at the turn of the century.

1619 Levin, Meyer. THE ARCHITECT. Simon and Schuster, 1981. Protagonist Andrew Lane is an architect. His story is patterned after the early years of the American genius Frank Lloyd Wright.

1620 Lewisohn, Ludwig. THE ISLAND WITHIN. Harper, 1928. Saga of a family of Polish Jews who migrate to New York

City in the 1870's; story of the son's medical education at Columbia and the cultural conflicts between his Jewish heritage and Americanization.

1621 Lion, Hortense. THE GRASS GROWS GREEN. Houghton, 1935. Changing social scene in New York from the 1840's to 1918.

1622 Lipsky, Eleazar. THE DEVIL'S DAUGHTER. Meredith, 1969. Story based on a scandal/trial in San Francisco in the 1880's; gives a good feeling of the time and place.

1623 Lord, Eda. CHILDSPLAY. Simon and Schuster, 1961. Story of a girl's childhood in Evanston, Illinois at the turn of the century.

1624 McCall, Dan. BEECHER. Dutton, 1979. Story about Henry Ward Beecher centers on his 1875 adultery trial, which took place after Victoria Woodhull made public her charges against the respected clergyman.

1625 McDonald, Julie. AMALIE'S STORY. Simon and Schuster, 1970. An appealing picture of family life and customs in a Danish community in nineteenth century Iowa, and of the difficulties of adjusting to life in the new country.

1626 McDonald, N. C. SONG OF THE AXE. Ballantine, 1957. Adventure tale of lumbering, and smuggling of Chinese workers into the country; setting is an island in Puget Sound in the early 1900's.

1627 MacDougall, Ruth Doan. FLOWERS OF THE FOREST. Atheneum, 1981. Story of immigrants who flee from the Scottish Clearances to New Hampshire. They hope to raise sheep, their familiar way of life, but their children must go to work in a cotton mill.

1628 McGehee, Florence. BRIDE OF KING SOLOMON. Macmillan, 1958. Story of a woman raising her children in the Ozarks; details of daily life covering the period from 1871 through the turn of the century.

1629 McKay, Allis. THEY CAME TO A RIVER. Macmillan, 1941. The development of the apple-growing industry in the Columbia River region, from the early 1900's through World War I.

1630 McMeekin, Clark (pseud.). THE OCTOBER FOX. Putnam, 1956. Family conflict on an estate in the Kentucky bluegrass country in the 1890's.

1631 ________. THE FAIRBROTHERS. Putnam, 1961. Family life, horse breeding and racing, in post-Civil War Kentucky; the first running of the Kentucky Derby in 1875.

1632 McMillion, Bonner. SO LONG AT THE FAIR. Doubleday, 1964. An orphan and his older brother join a touring theatrical company and settle into the insurance business in Dallas, Texas at the turn of the century.

1633 McSorley, Edward. OUR OWN KIND. Harper, 1946. Picture of life in the Irish section of Providence, Rhode Island in the early 1900's.

1634 Marius, Richard. THE COMING OF RAIN. Knopf, 1969. A traditional novel of the Old South, set in Tennessee in 1885, with mystery in the background of a genteel white family, violence, and murder.

1635 Marshall, Catherine. CHRISTY. McGraw, 1967. Story of a Quaker teacher in a mission school in Appalachia in 1912; moonshine, feuding, and religion among the hill people.

1636 Masterton, Graham. MAN OF DESTINY. Simon and Schuster, 1981. The building of the transcontinental railroad. The fictional developer and his railway follow closely on the historical tracks of the Central Pacific.

1637 Mathewson, Janet. A MATTER OF PRIDE. Dodd, 1957. Romance of post-Civil War South Carolina and Connecticut, dealing with the Yankee wife of a Southerner connected with the invention of a cotton loom.

1638 Meeker, Arthur. PRAIRIE AVENUE. Knopf, 1949. The changing social scene in Chicago's South Side from 1885 to 1918.

1639 Meggs, Brown. WAR TRAIN. Atheneum, 1981. Tale based on the memories of the grandfather of the writer. He journied, a mere teenager, on a cavalry train that rolled from North Dakota to the Mexican border, bringing troops and horses to aid Pershing in his pursuit of Pancho Villa.

1640 Mian, Mary Lawrence. YOUNG MEN SEE VISIONS. Houghton, 1958. Social life and customs in a New England town at the turn of the century; episodes of church bazaars, carriage rides, and Decoration Day parades.

1641 Miller, Mary Britton. THE WHIRLIGIG OF TIME. Crown, 1971. Life in the genteel society of New York City after the turn of the century, as recalled by one of the characters after his return home from years of expatriation.

1642 Morrell, David. LAST REVEILLE. Evans, 1977. Story of an elderly Georgian, helping Pershing pursue Pancho Villa. In his past, he had joined the victorious Yankees after he saw them destroy his home, then moved on to fight the Sioux, and then the Spanish with the Rough Riders.

1643 Morris, Ira Victor. THE CHICAGO STORY. Doubleday, 1952. Story of a German immigrant family in the meat-packing industry in Chicago from 1905 to the present.

1644 Murphy, Robert William. A CERTAIN ISLAND. Lippincott, 1967. A boy growing up in a small Iowa town in the early 1900's joins a scientific expedition to a Pacific island, to study the birds and wildlife. Based on an actual incident.

1645 Norris, Frank. McTEAGUE. Doubleday, 1899. Picture of the depressing poverty of the laboring classes and of the evils of the lust for money; set in California.

1646 _______. THE OCTOPUS. Doubleday, 1901. Story of the war between California wheat growers and the railroads they depend upon to reach their markets.

1647 _______. THE PIT. Doubleday, 1903. Novel of protest, dealing with the Chicago wheat market, an attack on the financiers' manipulations on the wheat exchange, with no regard for the welfare of the producers.

1648 Norris, Kathleen. THE VENABLES. Doubleday, 1941. Family life in San Francisco before and after the great earthquake.

1649 Nyburg, Sidney. THE GATE OF IVORY. Knopf, 1920. A romance with a political background, laid in Baltimore in the 1890's.

1650 O'Connor, Richard. OFFICERS AND LADIES. Doubleday, 1958. Story of two brothers serving with the American occupation forces in the Philippines in the 1890's.

1651 O'Daniel, Janet. THE CLIFF HANGERS. Lippincott, 1961. Story of the early motion-picture industry, set in Ithaca, New York in 1915.

1652 Ondaatje, Michael. COMING THROUGH SLAUGHTER. Norton, 1977. Novel about the real Buddy Bolden, the great black cornetist, whose colorful life ended in 1907 in a Louisiana hospital for the insane.

1653 O'Neal, Cothburn. PA. Crown, 1962. Saga of the rise of a Texas family from poor farmers in 1910 to wealth in the oil boom.

1654 Osterman, Marjorie K. DAMNED IF YOU DO, DAMNED IF YOU DON'T. Chilton, 1962. A German-Jewish immigrant family achieves success as department store owners in New York in the early 1900's.

1655 Owens, William. FEVER IN THE EARTH. Putnam, 1958.

Story of the first oil well and of the oil-boom towns in the Texas Spindletop oil region in 1901.

1656 Page, Evelyn. THE CHESTNUT TREE. Vanguard, 1964. Social and business life of a wealthy Philadelphia family, summering at a resort hotel in 1916.

1657 Parmenter, Christine. A GOLDEN AGE. Crowell, 1942. Life in a small New England town in the 1880's and 1890's.

1658 Parrish, Anne. PERENNIAL BACHELOR. Harper, 1925. Panorama of American manners, fads, and fashions from 1860 to 1920's.

1659 Pound, Arthur. ONCE A WILDERNESS. Reynal, 1934. Family life on a Michigan farm from 1890 to about 1913.

1660 _______. SECOND GROWTH. Reynal, 1935. Development of the automobile industry, 1913-1930's, told through the story of the Michigan family of Once a Wilderness.

1661 Prose, Francine. ANIMAL MAGNETISM. Berkley, 1978. Mesmerism was a fad in the late nineteenth century. A practictioner tours New England, accompanied by a woman he treated, exhibiting her as evidence of his curative powers.

1662 Quick, Herbert. THE INVISIBLE WOMAN. Bobbs, 1924. Politics and the rise of the railroad interests in Iowa in the 1890's. Sequel to The Hawkeye (Expanding Frontiers--Middle West).

1663 Reniers, Percival. ROSES FROM THE SOUTH. Doubleday, 1959. Social life in and around the famous resorts of the 1880's; setting in White Sulphur Springs, West Virginia; Saratoga, New York; and New York City.

1664 Richter, Conrad. ALWAYS YOUNG AND FAIR. Knopf, 1947. Life in a Pennsylvania town, from the Spanish-American War to World War I.

1665 _______. A SIMPLE HONORABLE MAN. Knopf, 1962. Story of the daily life and activities of a preacher-storekeeper in the Dutch-Pennsylvania country at the turn of the century.

1666 Ritner, Ann Katherine. SUMMER BRINGS GIFTS. Lippincott, 1956. Light romance picturing small-town life in Fidelia, Colorado during the summer of 1915.

1667 Roberts, Dorothy James. MISSY. Appleton, 1957. Picture of small-town life at the turn of the century; story of a girl growing up in West Virginia.

1668 Robertson, Don. PARADISE FALLS. Putnam, 1968. Robust tale of business and social life and corruption in an Ohio town in the years following the Civil War.

1669 Rölvaag, Ole. THIRD LIFE OF PER SMEVIK. Dillon Press, 1971. Letters home to Norway describe the bewilderment at the strange ways of the new country felt by an immigrant to South Dakota at the turn of the century.

1670 Roscoe, Theodore. ONLY IN NEW ENGLAND. Scribner, 1959. New England atmosphere and folkways pictured in the story of a murder committed in 1911.

1671 ________. TO LIVE AND DIE IN DIXIE. Scribner, 1961. Southern and Victorian mores portrayed in the story based on an actual murder trial in Amityburg, Virginia in 1902.

1672 Ross, Zola Helen. CASSY SCANDAL. Bobbs, 1954. Business and social life and the growth of Seattle in the 1880's.

1673 Rubins, Harold. DREAM MERCHANTS. Knopf, 1949. Picture of the movie industry from penny arcade to serials and sound, and the financial deals behind it.

1674 Sandburg, Helga. THE WIZARD'S CHILD. Dial, 1967. Poetic picture of harsh life in the North Carolina mountain country in 1915.

1675 Schaeffer, Susan Fromberg. MADNESS OF A SEDUCED WOMAN. Dutton, 1983. Invented details fill out the real-life story of Agnes Dempster, a woman who murdered the woman who replaced her in the affections of her lover. The crime took place in Vermont in the last years of the nineteenth century. Agnes was acquitted on her plea of insanity.

1676 Selby, John. ISLAND IN THE CORN. Rinehart, 1941. Period novel of a Wisconsin town on the Fox River in the 1880's and 1890's. Sequel to Elegant Journey (Expanding Frontiers--Middle West).

1677 Seton, Anya. THE TURQUOISE. Houghton, 1946. Pictures the social climb of the beautiful heroine, from a Mexican hovel to a Fifth Avenue mansion in the 1870's.

1678 Settle, Mary Lee. THE SCAPEGOAT. Random House, 1980. Events of one day of a coal miners' strike in West Virginia in 1912. An accurate picture of the miners' world, their clothes, food, and homes.

1679 Shellabarger, Samuel. TOLBECKEN. Little, 1956. Story of American life at the turn of the century in which old traditional family values are in conflict with rising commercialism.

1680 Shenkin, Elizabeth. BROWNSTONE GOTHIC. Holt, 1961. Family story set in a Fifth Avenue mansion in New York City in 1871; shows the cultural and social background of the period.

1681 Sherburne, James. A POOR BOY A LONG WAY FROM HOME. Houghton, 1984. Picaresque journey of a young man who travels in 1909 to Washington and Oregon, where he is attracted to the radical labor movement. A later move takes him to California, and he finds work as a stuntman in the early movies.

1682 Sinclair, Harold. YEARS OF GROWTH. Doubleday, 1940. Life in a small Illinois town from 1861 to 1893.

1683 Sinclair, Upton. THE JUNGLE. Viking, 1906. Pictures the oppressed life of the workingman in and around the Chicago stockyards at the turn of the century.

1684 Smith, Betty. MAGGIE-NOW. Harper, 1958. Story of immigrant Irish and Germans in Brooklyn at the turn of the century.

1685 Smith, Chard. LADIES DAY. Scribner, 1941. Social conditions in a New York manufacturing town in the 1880's-1890's; exploitation of labor and the movement for women's rights.

1686 Smith, Larry. THE ORIGINAL. Herder and Herder, 1972. Picture of the grim, unremitting labor that was the reality of farm life at the turn of the century. Set in Michigan.

1687 Snow, Richard. THE BURNING. Doubleday, 1981. Vivid picture of a terrible fire that destroyed a Minnesota lumber town in 1894.

1688 Sorensen, Virginia. MANY HEAVENS. Harcourt, 1954. Mormon life and customs at the turn of the century.

1689 Steegmuller, Francis. THE CHRISTENING PARTY. Farrar, 1960. Social life and customs as observed by a six-year-old boy at a christening party in Connecticut in 1906.

1690 Steele, Wilbur. THEIR TOWN. Doubleday, 1952. Business and social development of a Colorado town from 1897 to the 1930's.

1691 Steelman, Robert. CALL OF THE ARCTIC. Coward, 1960. Adventures of a young Harvard man who joined the Arctic expeditions of Charles Francis Hall in the years between 1860 and 1873.

1692 Stegner, Wallace. THE PREACHER AND THE SLAVE.

Houghton, 1950. Fictional biography of Joseph Hillstrom, songwriter and labor organizer for the Industrial Workers of the World, 1910-1916.

1693 _______. ANGLE OF REPOSE. Doubleday, 1971. Life in California, at the turn of the century, for an engineer who moved west with his strong, artistic wife, to what he hoped would be a land of opportunity.

1694 Stein, Harry. HOOPLA. Knopf, 1983. The infamous baseball scandal of 1919, when George Weaver and other Chicago White Sox players took bribes to throw the World Series.

1695 Stephenson, Howard. GLASS. Claude Kendall, 1933. Struggle between agriculture and industry in Ohio at the turn of the century, and the development of gas wells and the glass industry.

1696 Steuber, William. THE LANDLOOKER. Bobbs, 1957. Adventures of the sons of a Chicago harness-maker, in 1871, on a selling trip in Wisconsin; life in the small towns, isolated farms, and lumber camps, punctuated by a forest fire and the great Chicago fire.

1697 Stevens, James. BIG JIM TURNER. Doubleday, 1948. Labor agitation and the I. W. W. in the Pacific Northwest; 1900 to 1903.

1698 Stone, Irving. ADVERSARY IN THE HOUSE. Doubleday, 1947. Based on the life of Eugene V. Debs.

1699 Street, James and James Childers. TOMORROW WE REAP. Dial, 1949. Lumber industry and political corruption in a Mississippi valley in the 1890's. Sequel to By Valour and Arms (Civil War).

1700 _______. MINGO DABNEY. Dial, 1950. Member of the Mississippi Dabney clan becomes involved in the Cuban revolt; 1895. Sequel to Tomorrow We Reap.

1701 Stribling, T. S. THE STORE. Doubleday, 1932. Picture of Southern life in the 1880's. Traces the transformation of the Old South into the new. Sequel to The Forge (Civil War).

1702 Suchow, Ruth. THE JOHN WOOD CASE. Viking, 1959. Story of small-town life in Iowa at the turn of the century, and the effects on a high school senior when he learns his father has been embezzling company funds.

1703 Sugrue, Thomas. SUCH IS THE KINGDOM. Holt, 1940. Everyday life in an Irish community in a Connecticut factory town in 1909.

1704 Swarthout, Glendon. THEY CAME TO CORDURA. Random, 1958. Story of a small band of Americans making their way to a rear base following action against Mexican revolutionists who attacked across the border in 1916.

1705 ________. THE TIN LIZZIE TROOP. Doubleday, 1972. Based on an actual event in the Mexican-American border skirmishes of 1916. The Philadelphia Light Horse Brigade of the National Guard arrives for duty equipped with automobiles and champagne. Pursuing bandits across the border in their gas buggies, the green soldiers misread a surrender signal and provoke a battle.

1706 Synon, Mary. GOOD RED BRICKS. Little, 1941. Politics, horse racing, and prize-fighting in Chicago in the 1890's.

1707 Taber, Gladys. SPRING HARVEST. Putnam, 1959. Life on the campus of a small college in Wisconsin in the spring of 1914.

1708 Tarkington, Booth. THE MAGNIFICENT AMBERSONS. Doubleday, 1918. Rise and decline of a typical Midwestern family in the 1870's.

1709 Tax, Meredith. RIVINGTON STREET. Morrow, 1982. The women of the Levy family on New York's Lower East Side survive the inferno at the Triangle Waist factory in 1911 and help organize a union to alleviate conditions for the garment workers.

1710 Taylor, R. S. IN RED WEATHER. Holt, 1961. Story of the varied political reactions produced by a catastrophic fire in a New England city in 1871.

1711 Taylor, Robert, Jr. LOVING BELLE STARR. Algonquin, 1984. The first story in this book explores Belle's relationships with the father of her children, and with Sam Starr, whom she later married. The second concerns Jesse James, his family relationships, and also the motivations of his slayer.

1712 Telfer, Daniel. THE NIGHT OF THE COMET. Doubleday, 1969. A simple family story set in a Midwestern city at the time of Halley's Comet.

1713 Thompson, Ariadne. THE OCTAGONAL HEART. Bobbs, 1956. Nostalgic memories of a Greek-American family living in an octagonal house in St. Louis at the turn of the century.

1714 Tippett, Thomas. HORSE SHOE BOTTOMS. Harper, 1935. The early labor movement and the problems of Illinois mine workers in the 1870's and after.

1715 Towne, Charles H. GOOD OLD YESTERDAYS. Appleton, 1935. Picture of a Southern family growing up and finding a place in life in New York in the 1880's and 1890's.

1716 Train, Arthur Cheney. TASSLES ON HER BOOTS. Scribner, 1940. New York society and politics in the days of Boss Tweed and the Grant administration.

1717 Turnbull, Agnes Sligh. GOWN OF GLORY. Houghton, 1952. Life of a minister and his family in a small Pennsylvania town at the turn of the century.

1718 _______. THE NIGHTINGALE. Houghton, 1960. Nostalgic, romantic picture of life in the United States in the early 1900's.

1719 Vidal, Gore. 1876. Random, 1976. Picture of growing industrial fortunes in New York and politics in Washington in Grant's last term and during the Tilden-Hayes campaign. Comprises a trilogy with Burr (Young Nation) and Washington, D. C. (Chronicles).

1720 Walker, Mildred. LIGHT FROM ARCTURUS. Harcourt, 1935. Development of a girl's character built around the Philadelphia Centennial Exposition, 1876, the Chicago Columbian Exposition, 1893, and the Chicago World's Fair, 1933.

1721 _______. THE QUARRY. Harcourt, 1947. Life in Vermont from just before the Civil War to the beginning of World War I.

1722 Wall, Roy. THIS WAS MY VALLEY. Naylor, 1964. Autobiographical story of childhood life on a Texas ranch at the turn of the century.

1723 Warren, Lella. WHETSTONE WALLS. Appleton, 1952. Struggles of a young doctor in Alabama at the turn of the century. Sequel to Foundation Stone (Civil War--Old South).

1724 Warren, Robert Penn. NIGHT RIDER. Houghton, 1939. Story of the Kentucky tobacco war of 1905 and the development of the tobacco cooperatives.

1725 Watts, Mary. THE NOON-MARK. Macmillan, 1920. Picture of life in a prosaic American city in the 1880's.

1726 Wellman, Manly Wade. NOT AT THESE HANDS. Putnam, 1962. Portici, North Carolina in 1916 is the setting for the story of the personal and business feuds, the social and educational institutions, and the life of the citizens of the community.

1727 Wellman, Paul. THE WALLS OF JERICHO. Lippincott, 1947. Story of social and political life in a small town in Kansas from 1901 to the 1940's.

1728 ________. JUBAL TROOP. Doubleday, 1953. Story of the rise and decline of an adventurer in the Southwest and a picture of the oil industry; set in Texas, Mexico, the Dakotas, and Oklahoma from 1886 to the 1920's.

1729 West, Jessamyn. THE WITCH DIGGERS. Harcourt, 1951. Picture of life on a farm in Southern Indiana in 1899.

1730 ________. SOUTH OF THE ANGELS. Harcourt, 1960. Pictures the daily life and drama of the families who settle in a new farming community near Los Angeles in 1916.

1731 Wharton, Edith. AGE OF INNOCENCE. Appleton, 1920. Study of American manners and of New York's original 400 in the 1870's.

1732 ________. THE BUCCANEERS. Appleton, 1938. Social life in the New York and Newport in the 1870's.

1733 White, Leslie Turner. LOG JAM. Doubleday, 1959. Story of the days of the lumber barons of Michigan's lower peninsula in the 1870's, and of the conflicts resulting in the first attempts to break the monopoly and to introduce new methods and machinery to the logging operation.

1734 White, Victor. PETER DOMANIG IN AMERICA: STEEL. Bobbs, 1954. Story of a young Austrian immigrant and the steel industry in Pittsburg about 1919.

1735 White, William Allen. IN THE HEART OF A FOOL. Macmillan, 1918. Pictures the growth of a Kansas town from the 1870's to World War I; story of political corruption and conspicuous consumption following a mining boom.

1736 Whitlock, Brand. J. HARDIN & SON. Appleton, 1923. Picture of the political, social, and industrial life of a small Ohio town in 1880's.

1737 Whitney, Phyllis A. THE TREMBLING HILLS. Appleton, 1956. Light romance set in San Francisco at the time of the 1906 earthquake.

1738 ________. SKYE CAMERON. Appleton, 1957. Creole society in New Orleans in the 1880's.

1739 ________. WINDOW ON THE SQUARE. Appleton, 1962. Social customs observed in a light romance set in the opulent social circles of New York in the 1870's.

1740 Wilder, Thornton. THE EIGHTH DAY. Harper, 1967. Introspective picture of life in a small Illinois town about 1910.

1741 Wiley, John W. ABBIE WAS A LADY. St. Martin's, 1962. Pleasant recollections of social life and customs in New England and New York, fictionalized account of the life of the author's grandmother.

1742 Williams, Ben Ames. SPLENDOR. Houghton, 1927. Picture of American family life and interests from 1872 to 1916 in the life of a newspaperman.

1743 _______. OWEN GLEN. Houghton, 1950. The development of the United Mine Workers union, and the American social and political scene, from the viewpoint of a boy in a small town in the Southern Ohio coal fields in the 1890's.

1744 Williams, Elva. SACRAMENTO WALTZ. McGraw, 1957. A romance set in Sacramento, San Francisco, and Paris, from about 1910 to the Prohibition era.

1745 Williams, Vinnie. GREENBONES. Viking, 1967. Story of a mother and her son, a boy evangelist, on the revival trail; set in Georgia from 1912 to the beginning of World War I.

1746 Winslow, Anne Goodwin. IT WAS LIKE THIS. Knopf, 1949. A love story set in Southern Mississippi after the Civil War.

1747 _______. THE SPRINGS. Knopf, 1949. Gentle story of a beautiful girl and her beaux at a resort hotel in a Southern town in the late 1800's.

1748 Yarnall, Sophia. CLARK INHERITANCE. Walker, 1981. A picture of the technical workings of coal mines in the last quarter of the nineteenth century. Story also explores the attitudes of the mine owners toward their workers' rights.

1749 Yellen, Samuel. THE WEDDING BAND. Atheneum, 1961. Story of cultural conflict in the marriage of a hard-working Jewish immigrant and a sensitive Gentile woman; Cleveland, Ohio at the turn of the century.

1750 Yerby, Frank. PRIDE'S CASTLE. Dial, 1949. New York social and business rivalry in the 1870's.

1751 _______. SERPENT AND THE STAFF. Dial, 1958. Picture of medical and social life in New Orleans at the turn of the century.

1752 Young, Agatha. I SWEAR BY APOLLO. Simon and Schuster, 1968. Story of the medical profession in the 1870's; scenes at Harvard Medical School in Boston.

1753 Zara, Louis. DARK RIDER. World, 1961. Fictional biography of Stephen Crane, journalist and author of The Red Badge of Courage.

1754 Zaroulis, Nancy. LAST WALTZ. Doubleday, 1984. The protected but restricted lives of society women in Back Bay Boston, around the turn of the century.

WORLD WAR I

1755 Adams, Samuel Hopkins. COMMON CAUSE. Houghton, 1919. A newspaperman tried to promote patriotism in a Midwestern city in wartime; conflicts created by large German-American population.

1756 Allen, Hervey. IT WAS LIKE THIS. Farrar, 1940. Two stories describing what war was actually like in July and August, 1918.

1757 Andrews, Mary Shipman. HER COUNTRY. Scribner, 1918. Story of a girl singer who gave her talents to the patriotic cause of singing for the Liberty Bond drives.

1758 _______. HIS SOUL GOES MARCHING ON. Scribner, 1922. The spirit of Theodore Roosevelt inspires a young soldier in the Rainbow Division in France.

1759 Angoff, Charles. IN THE MORNING LIGHT. Yoseloff, 1952. Follows a family of Russian Jews in Boston up through World War I and after; development of the young son in the public school system, the war years, and some of the bad times afterward. Followed by The Sun at Noon (The Twenties).

1760 Anonymous. CONSCRIPT 2989. Dodd, 1918. Amusing experiences in training camp, related by a young draftee.

1761 Babson, Naomi. LOOK DOWN FROM HEAVEN. Reynal, 1942. New England village at the time of the war.

1762 Bacheller, Irving. THE PRODIGAL VILLAGE. Bobbs, 1920. Story of the beginning of flapper society during the inflated days of 1917-1918.

1763 Bailey, Temple. THE TIN SOLDIER. Penn, 1918. Story of a young millionaire of draft age whose promise to his dying mother prevents his enlistment. Set in wartime Washington.

1764 Beebe, Elswyth Thane. LIGHT HEART. Duell, 1947. Williamsburg, New York, and London customs and traditions at the time of the war. In the author's Williamsburg series (see other categories).

1765 _______. KISSING KIN. Duell. 1948. Williamsburg, Virginia,

London and the continent at the time of the war. Sequel to Light Heart.

1766 Binns, Archie. THE LAURELS ARE CUT DOWN. Reynal, 1937. The American army in the Siberian campaign and the indifference of people at home, in the Puget Sound area of Washington.

1767 Bonner, Charles. LEGACY. Knopf, 1940. Family life and war service of five brothers; 1905-1918.

1768 Boyd, Thomas Alexander. THROUGH THE WHEAT. Scribner, 1923. Describes the maturing experiences of a young marine in the war.

1769 Bromfield, Louis. GREEN BAY TREE. Stokes, 1924. Saga of a Midwestern city growing from farmland to industrial center at the time of the war.

1770 Brown, Alice. BROMLEY NEIGHBORHOOD. Macmillan, 1917. Life in a New England village, showing the effect of the war on everyone in the community.

1771 Caldwell, Janet Taylor. BALANCE WHEEL. Scribner, 1951. Story of a munitions family in a Pennsylvania town.

1772 Campbell, W. M. COMPANY K. Smith and Haas, 1933. Experiences of a company, from training camp to action in France and return.

1773 Cather, Willa. ONE OF OURS. Knopf, 1922. A frustrated Nebraska farm boy prefers life as a soldier in France to farm life.

1774 Corey, Paul. THE ROAD RETURNS. Bobbs, 1940. Farm life through the difficult years of the war and after; 1917-1923.

1775 Dawson, William James. THE WAR EAGLE. Lane, 1918. Story of the indifference of Americans to the war, until the sinking of the Lusitania brings the United States into active involvement.

1776 Di Donato, Pietro. THREE CIRCLES OF LIGHT. Messner, 1960. Story of family life in the Italian community of West Hoboken, New Jersey during the war.

1777 Dinneen, Joseph. WARD EIGHT. Harper, 1936. Politics in the North End of Boston before and during the war.

1778 Dodge, Henry Irving. THE YELLOW DOG. Harper, 1918. Short tale of a plan to hand out a "yellow dog" card to complainers who undermine morale by finding fault with the war effort.

1779 Dos Passos, John. THREE SOLDIERS. Doran, 1921. Military history of three men, from training camp through the war, and the disillusionment following demobilization.

1780 _______. 1919. Houghton, 1932. Camera-eye view of the United states in 1919; catches the spirit of the period.

1781 _______. CHOSEN COUNTRY. Houghton, 1951. Chicago and its suburbs in wartime.

1782 Downes, Anne Miller. HEARTWOOD. Lippincott, 1945. Love story of a mountain boy who takes a wife to his mountain home after serving in the war.

1783 Downey, Fairfax. WAR HORSE. Dodd, 1942. Story of a Texas mare attached to an American artillery regiment in France.

1784 Ellsberg, Edward. PIGBOATS. Dodd, 1931. Story of submarine and destroyer warfare in the war.

1785 Fee, Mary Helen. PLAIN AMERICANS. McClurg, 1926. Story of a provincial family at the time of World War I. After the death of her husband at the end of the war, the heroine joins a "Save-America" movement.

1786 Fredenburgh, Theodore. SOLDIERS MARCH! Harcourt, 1930. Combat experiences of a young American soldier.

1787 Goodrich, Marcus. DELILAH. Rinehart, 1941. Story of a destroyer of the U.S. battle fleet in the six months before the declaration of war.

1788 Grey, Zane. DESERT OF WHEAT. Harper, 1919. Story of German-inspired labor troubles with the I. W. W. in the Washington wheat fields, life in training camp, and the horrors of the war in France.

1789 Harrison, Henry. SAINT TERESA. Houghton, 1922. Picture of anti-German feeling during the war; story of a steel manufacturer who refused to make munitions.

1790 Hemingway, Ernest. A FAREWELL TO ARMS. Scribner, 1929. Love story of an American soldier and a Swiss nurse on the Italian front in 1917.

1791 Heth, Edward H. TOLD WITH A DRUM. Houghton, 1937. Effects of anti-German feeling in a German-American community in the Midwest.

1792 Hobson, Laura Keane. FIRST PAPERS. Random, 1964. Russian-Jewish immigrant family becomes involved with unpopular causes before and during World War I.

1793 Hodson, James. GREY DAWN--RED NIGHT. Doubleday, 1930. Picture of army life from training camp to battlefield.

1794 ________. RETURN TO THE WOOD. Morrow, 1955. Story of a veteran who returns to the battlefields of his youth and relives his wartime experiences.

1795 Houston, Robert. BISBEE, '17. Pantheon, 1979. The strike at Phelps Dodge in Bisbee, Arizona where the I. W. W. faced mine owners backed by lawmen, and lost, effectively ending the movement.

1796 Hunt, Frazier. BLOWN IN BY THE DRAFT. Doubleday, 1918. Character sketches of life in an army camp, showing the variety of races and nationalities thrown together by the draft.

1797 Ingram, Bowen. MILBRY. Crown, 1972. Story of a child, the daughter of a wealthy Tennessee family, before and during World War I. Her mother's gentility of manners and mores contrasts with her father's willingness to accept the accelerating social changes in the new century.

1798 Knox, James. SUNDAY'S CHILDREN. Houghton, 1955. Small-town parsonage life in the Shenandoah Valley before and during World War I.

1799 Kyne, Peter B. THEY ALSO SERVE. Cosmopolitan, 1927. Wartime experiences of a U.S. army horse.

1800 Lardner, Ring. TREAT 'EM ROUGH. Bobbs, 1918. Humorous letters on life in an army training camp written by an illiterate Chicago baseball player.

1801 Lee, Mary. IT'S A GREAT WAR. Houghton, 1929. War and its effects on the individuals as seen by a New England girl in the hospital, in a Y. M. C. A. hut, and with the army of occupation in Germany.

1802 Lewis, Flannery. BROOKS TOO BROAD FOR LEAPING. Macmillan, 1938. A young child's experiences while his father is serving in France.

1803 Lewis, Herbert C. SPRING OFFENSIVE. Viking, 1940. Reflections of his life in Indiana by a young soldier trapped in the no-man's-land of the Maginot Line during a German offensive.

1804 Lutes, Della Thompson. MY BOY IN KHAKI. Harper, 1918. Emotional story of a mother whose son is in the army; shows his life in training camp, his war wedding, and his departure for France.

1805 Lutz, Grace Livingston Hill. THE SEARCH. Lippincott, 1919. Story of the Salvation Army in the war.

1806 McClure, Robert E. THE DOMINANT BLOOD. Doubleday, 1924. Dilemma of a young German-American with conflicting loyalties between his German heritage and love for his new country.

1807 _______. SOME FOUND ADVENTURE. Doubleday, 1926. Story of the life and love of an American soldier in France during the war.

1808 McCutcheon, George B. SHOT WITH CRIMSON. Dodd, 1918. Story of German agents in the U.S., spying and sabotoging the war effort, aided by a New York society woman.

1809 McKee, Ruth. THREE DAUGHTERS. Doubleday, 1938. Story of the civilian role behind the front lines; nurse, telephone operator, and Red Cross representatives. Shows the waste and horror of war.

1810 Manfred, Frederick. GREEN EARTH. Crown, 1977. A realistic picture of the lives of Iowa farmers just before and after WW I. Evocative of the endless toil, and of their feeling for the earth that kept them going through economic cycles that seldom brought prosperity.

1811 Martin, Mrs. George. MARCH ON. Appleton, 1921. Presents the reaction of the South to the war.

1812 Montague, Margaret. UNCLE SAM OF FREEDOM RIDGE. Doubleday, 1920. Eccentric old man leads the patriotic spirit of his small Virginia community; loses faith when the United States refuses to join the League of Nations.

1813 Murphy, Robert William. THE POND. Dutton, 1964. Virginia in 1917 is the background for the adventures of a 14-year-old boy during several visits to his soldier-father's hunting and fishing camp.

1814 Nason, Leonard. CHEVRONS. Doran, 1926. The account of a soldier and his buddies on the front lines in France.

1815 _______. SERGEANT EADIE. Doubleday, 1928. Humorous account of a doughboy's experience in the A. E. F. (American Expeditionary Forces).

1816 _______. A CORPORAL ONCE. Doubleday, 1930. Adventures of a soldier through the ups and downs of war time.

1817 North, Sterling. NIGHT OUTLASTS THE WHIPPOORWILL. Macmillan, 1936. Liberty Bond crusades, propaganda, food conservation, in a small Wisconsin farming community during the war.

1818 Odum, Howard. WINGS ON MY FEET. Bobbs, 1929. Negro's narrative of his part in the war.

1819 O'Hara, John. THE EWINGS. Random, 1972. Manners and morals among the well-to-do in industrial Cleveland, just before and during WW I, when fortunes were made by war profiteering.

1820 Paul, Charlotte. HEAR MY HEART SPEAK. Messner, 1950. Story of the rehabilitation of a shell-shocked veteran.

1821 Putnam, Nina Wilcox and Norman Jacobsen. ESMERALDA. Lippincott, 1918. Amusing satire centering around a down-to-earth girl from California who shocks the New York social set into entering war work.

1822 Richmond, Grace Louise. THE WHISTLING MOTHER. Garden City, 1917. Tells of the farewell visit home of a college boy who is leaving for the war.

1823 Scanlon, William. GOD HAVE MERCY ON US. Houghton, 1929. Story of the U.S. Marines at Belleau Wood in 1918.

1824 Sheean, Vincent. BIRD OF THE WILDERNESS. Random, 1941. Reactions to the war by the people of a small town in Illinois, seen by a high-school boy with German-American relations.

1825 Sherwood, Margaret Pollock. A WORLD TO MEND. Little, 1920. Observations of life in a New England village during the war, by a philosophical shoe-mender.

1826 Sinclair, Upton. WORLD'S END. Viking, 1940. Story of the world munitions industry, the war, and the peace conference as seen by the son of an American munitions maker. First in the author's Lanny Budd series. Followed by Between Two Worlds (The Twenties).

1827 Smith, Betty. A TREE GROWS IN BROOKLYN. Harper, 1943. Life of a tenement family in the Williamsburg section of Brooklyn, before and during World War I.

1828 Stallings, Lawrence. PLUMES. Harcourt, 1924. Story of the futility of war, expressed in the life of a college professor completely broken by his war experiences.

1829 Streeter, Edward. DERE MABLE. Stokes, 1918. Humorous letters from a rookie to his girl friend, relating incidents of life in a Southern training camp.

1830 Tilden, Freeman. KHAKI. Macmillan, 1918. Story of a pacifist community jarred out of its complacency and into the war effort by the death, in France, of the rich spinster who was the town's only patriot.

1831 Tucker, Augusta. MISS SUSIE SLAGLE'S. Harper, 1939. Life in a boarding house for medical students at Johns Hopkins, at the time of the war.

1832 Van Doren, Dorothy. DACEY HAMILTON. Harper, 1942. Picture of life in New York City in 1918.

1833 Walker, Mildred. BREWER'S BIG HORSES. Harcourt, 1940. Michigan girl flouts conventions by working as a newspaper-woman and marrying a brewer's son.

1834 Wharton, Edith. THE MARNE. Appleton, 1918. An American boy is shocked at the American attitude of selfish indifference at the beginning of the war; at the second battle of the Marne, he discovers that other Americans love France as he does.

1835 _______. SON AT THE FRONT. Scribner, 1923. Novel of America's participation in the war, showing the feeling of neutrality and isolationism felt by some.

1836 Wharton, James. SQUAD. Coward, 1928. Story of trench warfare experienced by a variety of American youths thrown together by the draft.

1837 Whitehouse, Arch. (pseud.). SQUADRON FORTY-FOUR. Doubleday, 1965. Story of a young American with the Royal Flying Corps; pictures the hazards and excitement of the early days of air warfare.

1838 _______. PLAYBOY SQUADRON. Doubleday, 1970. Aerial combat story. American flyers are trained by British, sent to a French airfield near enemy lines where they earn the DSO making a successful but unauthorized raid on German installations.

1839 Wise, Evelyn. AS THE PINES GROW. Appleton, 1939. Story of a farming community from 1910 to post-war days; centers on the conflict over pacifist and anti-German feeling in the family and in the community.

THE NINETEEN-TWENTIES

1840 Abbe, George. THE WINTER HOUSE. Doubleday, 1957. Son of a small-town minister rebels at a society based on money and social position and turns to socialism during his college days.

1841 Adamic, Louis. GRANDSONS. Harper, 1935. Cross-section of American life in the twenties; story centers around a neurotic war veteran, an Al Capone henchman, and a labor organizer.

1842 Adams, Samuel Hopkins. SIEGE. Boni and Liveright, 1924. Story of the struggles of the labor unions in conflict with benevolent paternalism.

1843 ________. REVELRY. Boni and Liveright, 1926. Social and political life in Washington, based on the scandals during the Harding administration.

1844 Anderson, Sherwood. DARK LAUGHTER. Boni and Liveright, 1925. Story of a newspaperman dissatisfied with the undemanding society of his day, who leaves his job and wife to go drifting.

1845 ________. KIT BRANDON, A PORTRAIT. Scribner, 1936. Depicts the confusion of values in American life in the twenties; factory working conditions, and bootlegging.

1846 Angoff, Charles. THE SUN AT NOON. Yoseloff, 1955. Story of the life and customs of a family of Russian Jews in Boston; 1919-1923. Sequel to In the Morning Light (World War I).

1847 ________. BETWEEN DAY AND DARK. Yoseloff, 1959. Continues the story of family life and customs of a Russian Jewish family in Boston during the 1920's. Followed by Summer Storm (The Thirties).

1848 Arnold, Oren. THE GOLDEN CHAIR. Elsevier, 1954. Texas family life in the twenties, seen through the experiences of two children; centers around the family grocery store.

1849 Atherton, Gertrude. BLACK OXEN. Boni and Liveright, 1923. Story of life in the sophisticated social and literary circles of New York City in 1922.

1850 Bacheller, Irving. THE SCUDDERS. Macmillan, 1923. Contemporary novel which pictures the insecurity of family life of the period.

1851 ________. UNCLE PEEL. Stokes, 1933. Story of the financial boom and of its consequences; Florida real-estate boom.

1852 Backer, George. APPEARANCE OF A MAN. Random, 1966. Story of the career of a Wall Street broker, culminating in the stock market crash in 1929.

1853 Bailey, Temple. ENCHANTED GROUND. Penn, 1933. Story of Florida after the collapse of the land boom.

1854 Banning, Margaret Culkin. SPELLBINDERS. Doran, 1922. Story of the woman suffrage movement in a Midwestern city.

1855 Beals, Charleton. BLACK RIVER. Lippincott, 1934. Story of American oil companies in Mexico; closes with the scandal of Teapot Dome.

1856 Becker, Stephen D. A COVENANT WITH DEATH. Atheneum, 1965. A judge reviews his life as a trial lawyer in the Southwest during the 1920's.

1857 Bellow, Saul. ADVENTURES OF AUGIE MARCH. Viking, 1953. Picture of the lower level of American society of the twenties; set in Chicago.

1858 Benchley, Nathaniel. SPEAKEASY. Doubleday, 1980. Characters that recall Robert Benchley, Dorothy Parker, and the others who met around the table at the Algonquin Hotel to discuss the events of the world and New York's theatrical scene.

1859 Bethea, Jack. BED ROCK. Houghton, 1924. Realistic story of coal mining in Alabama, with conflict arising from bootlegging and sabotage.

1860 Blassingame, Wyatt. THE GOLDEN GEYSER. Doubleday, 1961. Story of the Florida land boom in the early 1920's, and of its consequences for a young couple getting started with a plant nursery.

1861 Block, Libbie. WILD CALENDAR. Knopf, 1946. Story of disillusionment and unrest in Denver in the late twenties.

1862 Brace, Ernest. COMMENCEMENT. Harper, 1924. Picture of the problems and conflicts facing young people emerging from college to face life in the jazz age.

1863 Bradbury, Ray. DANDELION WINE. Doubleday, 1957. One

summer in the life of a 12-year-old boy in a small town in Illinois in 1928.

1864 Brown, Frederic. THE OFFICE. Dutton, 1958. Story of a shy office boy and of the people around him in Cincinnati in the 1920's.

1865 Burgan, John. THE LONG DISCOVERY. Farrar, 1950. Story of the change, from iron-ruled company towns to the union strength of the workers; set in the Pennsylvania coal fields.

1866 Burnett, William Riley. LITTLE CAESAR. Dial, 1929. Story of the rise and fall of a Chicago gangster, based on the life of Al Capone and other gangsters of the Prohibition era.

1867 Burt, Maxwell Struthers. THE DELECTABLE MOUNTAINS. Scribner, 1927. Picture of American life and manners of the day; set in Wyoming.

1868 Carlisle, Helen Grace. MERRY, MERRY MAIDENS. Harcourt, 1937. The story of the life of six girls as they grow up during the post-war twenties.

1869 Carter, John Stewart. FULL FATHOM FIVE. Houghton, 1965. Family portrait of a wealthy Midwestern surgeon.

1870 Caspary, Vera. EVVIE. Harper, 1960. Story of the life of a murdered divorceé during the high-living days of the 1920's in Chicago.

1871 Coker, Elizabeth Boatwright. THE BEES. Dutton, 1968. Charleston, South Carolina in 1924; story centers around the management of the family cotton mill.

1872 Colby, Nathalie Sedgwick. BLACK STREAM. Harcourt, 1927. New York society life in a novel of manners, showing the selfishness, greed, and meaningless activity of the period.

1873 Coleman, Lonnie. KING. McCraw, 1967. Nostalgic story of boyhood diversions in a small town in Georgia in the twenties.

1874 Condon, Richard. MILE HIGH. Dial, 1969. Story of a cold, opportunistic Irish-Sicilian-American, increasing his fortune by promoting the Eighteenth Amendment and profiting from his gangster-controlled Prohibition empire.

1875 Cooley, Leland Frederick. THE RUN FOR HOME. Doubleday, 1958. Story of the squalid conditions prevailing in the U.S. Merchant Marine Service during the twenties.

1876 _______. THE RICHEST POOR FOLKS. Doubleday, 1963. Folksy picture of family life in the Upper Sacramento River valley of California, through the recollection of a ten-year-old boy.

1877 Corbett, Elizabeth. THE HEART OF THE VILLAGE. Appleton, 1963. Story of family life centering around the family bookstore in Greenwich Village.

1878 Corey, Paul. COUNTY SEAT. Bobbs, 1941. Bootlegging; violent stock markets upsets; farm foreclosures; picture of everyday life in an Iowa farming community.

1879 Cowen, William. THEY GAVE HIM A GUN. Smith and Haas, 1936. Story of confused young war veteran who turns to crime; an indictment of post-war American society.

1880 Cunningham, Sara and William. DANNY. Crown, 1953. Adventures of a young cub reporter in a small Oklahoma town.

1881 Curran, Henry. VAN TASSEL AND BIG BILL. Scribner, 1923. Humorous story of New York ward politics.

1882 Cushman, Dan. GOODBYE, OLD DRY. Doubleday, 1959. A quack doctor tries to bolster the economy of a village in Montana in the 1920's.

1883 Davis, Elmer. WHITE PANTS WILLIE. Bobbs, 1932. Story of the Florida boom and Chicago; 1923-24.

1884 Davis, Wesley Ford. THE TIME OF THE PANTHER. Harper, 1958. Story of a boy growing up during the summer he was 14 years old; set in a Florida lumber camp in the 1920's.

1885 De Capite, Raymond. THE COMING OF FABRIZZE. McKay, 1960. Happy story of life in the Italian colony of Cleveland, Ohio in the 1920's; the stock-market crash affects, but does not depress, the characters.

1886 Doner, Mary Frances. THE GLASS MOUNTAIN. Doubleday, 1942. Picture of social and cultural life in the Great Lakes region; influence of the Chautauqua, and shipping on the Great Lakes.

1887 Dos Passos, John. MANHATTAN TRANSFER. Harper, 1925. View of various types of life in New York City.

1888 _______. THE 42ND PARALLEL. Houghton, 1930. Pictures the United States during the period of the twenties.

1889 _______. THE BIG MONEY. Houghton, 1936. Picture of American life in the frenzied boom-days from 1919 to 1929.

1890 _______. ADVENTURES OF A YOUNG MAN. Houghton, 1939. Social and economic problems of American society met by a young man growing up in the twenties until his death in the Spanish Civil War. Hero is sympathetic to communist ideals.

1891 Douglas, Marjory. ROAD TO THE SUN. Rinehart, 1952. Story of south Florida and the Everglades in the days when Miami was growing.

1892 Downes, Anne Miller. UNTIL THE SHEARING. Stokes, 1940. Story of the growing up of a sensitive boy in up-state New York.

1893 _______. THE ANGELS FELL. Stokes, 1941. Greenwich Village and Westchester County from the end of the war through the twenties.

1894 _______. KATE CAVANAUGH. Lippincott, 1958. Story of of a shaky marriage which reflects the spirit of the restless twenties.

1895 Dreiser, Theodore. AN AMERICAN TRAGEDY. Boni and Liveright, 1925. Graphic picture of American society in the twenties.

1896 Dudley, Frank. KING COBRA. Carrick and Evans, 1940. The rise of a national terrorist organization in the twenties.

1897 Dunning, John. DENVER. Times Books, 1979. A newspaper novel, set in Denver, when the Ku Klux Klan had a hand in the police force, the courts, and the Colorado state government.

1898 Eastman, Max. VENTURE. Boni, 1927. Story of a young man, expelled from college, who lives it up in New York, until he becomes interested in the labor movement.

1899 Ehle, John. LAST ONE HOME. Harper, 1984. Chronicles the development of Asheville, North Carolina. The excitement of the growing town led a farm boy to leave the land and become an urban insurance man.

1900 Estes, Winston M. STREETFUL OF PEOPLE. Lippincott, 1972. Accurate renderings of the parades, club meetings, and recitals that made up the happy daily life of a small Texas town in the optimistic pre-Depression years.

1901 Fairbank, Janet Ayer. RICH MAN, POOR MAN. Houghton, 1936. Picture of the American political and social scene from 1912 to 1929; Theodore Roosevelt and the reform movement; women's suffrage; prohibition; the stock-market boom; and the financial crash.

1902 Farrar, Rowena Rutherford. A WONDROUS MOMENT THEN. Holt, 1968. Story of the struggle for women's suffrage in Nashville, Tennessee during and after World War I; events leading to the state's ratification of the Nineteenth Amendment in 1920.

1903 Farrell, James T. JUDGMENT DAY. Vanguard, 1935. Follows the career of Studs Lonigan, growing up in Chicago.

1904 _______. FATHER AND SON. Vanguard, 1940. Story of Danny O'Neill growing up, from the seventh grade through high school; Chicago setting.

1905 _______. MY DAYS OF ANGER. Vanguard, 1943. Follows Danny O'Neill through his college years in the middle twenties.

1906 _______. THE SILENCE OF HISTORY. Doubleday, 1963. Daily life and struggles of a poor young man working his way through the University of Chicago. Followed by What Time Collects.

1907 _______. WHAT TIME COLLECTS. Doubleday, 1964. Story of the married life of a young couple, showing life on Chicago's South Side. Sequel to The Silence of History.

1908 _______. LONELY FOR THE FUTURE. Doubleday, 1966. Picture of the literary and social life of three friends, one a struggling writer, on Chicago's South Side. Sequel to What Time Collects.

1909 Fitch, Albert. NONE SO BLIND. Macmillan, 1924. Story of college life, set in Harvard and Boston; shows effect of democratic ideas of the day clashing with tradition.

1910 Fitzgerald, F. Scott. THE BEAUTIFUL AND DAMNED. Scribner, 1922. Story of a rich playboy and of the downward spiral of his marriage during the wild excesses of the jazz age.

1911 _______. THE GREAT GATSBY. Scribner, 1925. Picture of the jazz-age society of Long Island in the years after World War II.

1912 Fleming, Berry. TO THE MARKET PLACE. Harcourt, 1938. Picture of New York social and economic life in the twenties.

1913 Flint, Margaret. BACK O' THE MOUNTAIN. Dodd, 1940. Story of Maine life in the twenties.

1914 Gann, Ernest. BLAZE OF NOON. Holt, 1946. Story of aviation in the twenties, when barnstorming pilots started carrying the U.S. Mail.

1915 Goodrich, Norma Lorre. THE DOCTOR AND MARIA THERESA. St. Martin's, 1962. Life of a village doctor in rural New England.

1916 Grubb, Davis. THE VOICES OF GLORY. Scribner, 1962. The townspeople of Glory, West Virginia describe their troubles during the early 1920's; centers around the efforts of a U.S. Public Health Service nurse to combat juvenile delinquency and the apathy of the town's conservative element.

1917 _______. SHADOW OF MY BROTHER. Holt, 1966. Story of hate and prejudice in a small Southern town, centering around a lynching witnessed by two young people.

1918 Hale, Nancy. SECRETS. Coward, 1971. Contrasting family life styles in a New England town. The protagonist is a rather lonely child, the daughter of artist parents. Her companions are the children of a social-climbing father. The young people grow up from the period of World War I through the 1920's.

1919 Halper, Albert. THE FOUNDRY. Viking, 1934. Chicago industrial scene, 1928-29; conflict between owners, bosses, and laborers.

1920 Hardman, Ric. FIFTEEN FLAGS. Little, 1968. Story of the American troops in the Siberian Expeditionary Force, patrolling the Trans-Siberian Railway during the counter-revolution of the White Army in Russia in 1920.

1921 Harris, Corra May. FLAPPER ANNE. Houghton, 1926. Story of a typical flapper in the South in the early 1920's.

1922 Hawes, Evelyn. THE HAPPY LAND. Harcourt, 1965. Diary of a high-school girl growing up in a politically oriented family near the Canadian border in the Far West.

1923 Hefferman, William. BRODERICK. Crown, 1980. A novel based on the life of the real Johnny Broderick, a tough city detective in the administration of the flamboyant Mayor Jimmy Walker.

1924 Herbst, Josephine. THE EXECUTIONER WAITS. Harcourt, 1934. Story of a middle-class family caught in the changing times, victims of the economic process; 1919-1929.

1925 Hobart, Alice Tisdale. THE CLEFT ROCK. Bobbs, 1948. Picture of power monopolies and irrigation projects in a California valley in the twenties.

1926 Hoffman, William. THE DARK MOUNTAINS. Doubleday, 1963. Story of a West Virginia coal-mine owner and his battle against unionism and reform.

1927 Hull, Helen Rose. THE HAWK'S FLIGHT. Coward, 1946. Family life in Connecticut in the twenties.

1928 Irwin, Inez Hayes. P. D. F. R. Harper, 1928. Sympathetic view of the self-sufficient life of rich sophisticated youth in New York City.

1929 Jackson, Margaret. FIRST FIDDLE. Bobbs, 1931. Conflict between a war veteran and his career wife.

1930 Jenson, Dwight. THERE WILL BE A ROAD. Doubleday, 1978. Two young men brave the harsh Idaho winter of 1928 in the wilderness, cutting timber into fence posts. They must survive a treck through a blizzard after fire destroys their camp.

1931 Keene, Day and Dwight Vincent. CHAUTAUQUA. Putnam, 1960. Story of the events which occurred in an Iowa town in the summer of 1921 during the visit of the Chautauqua.

1932 Kelland, Clarence Budington. CONTRABAND. Harper, 1923. A girl newspaper editor exposes the murderers and bootleggers in control of her town.

1933 Kelleam, Joseph. BLACKJACK. Sloane, 1948. Story of a decaying Oklahoma town brought back to life by the discovery of oil.

1934 Kelley, Edith Summers. THE DEVIL'S HAND. Southern Illinois University Press, 1974. Originally published in 1925. The economic hardships and politics of Southern California after World War I are depicted in the story of two young women who came to farm in the Imperial Valley.

1935 Kerkbride, Ronald. WINDS, BLOW GENTLY. Fell, 1945. Family life on a run-down plantation in South Carolina; conflict with Southern conservatism on the issues of fair wages and education for Negroes, and diversified crops; activities of the Ku Klux Klan.

1936 Kerr, Sophie. MISS J. LOOKS ON. Farrar, 1935. Picture of a wealthy family hit by the financial crash of 1929.

1937 Keyes, Frances Parkinson. VICTORINE. Messner, 1958. Mystery plot set in the rice-growing country of Louisiana in the mid-1920's, showing the manners and customs of the time.

1938 Killens, John Oliver. YOUNGBLOOD. Trident, 1966. Story of a Negro family in a small Georgia town, pictures the oppression of the Negro in the white man's world, and centers on the rise of a Negro hotel-workers' union. First published in 1954.

1939 Lerman, Rhoda. ELEANOR. Holt, 1979. Eleanor Roosevelt's life from 1918, when Franklin was assistant secretary of the navy and falling in love with Lucy Mercer, to 1921, when he was struck by polio at Campobello.

1940 Levin, Meyer. OLD BUNCH. Viking, 1937. Reunion in Chicago during the World's Fair in 1934; characters review events in their lives since 1921.

1941 ______. COMPULSION. Simon and Schuster, 1956. Fictionized account of the Leopold-Loeb murder case in Chicago in 1925.

1942 Lewis, Sinclair. BABBITT. Harcourt, 1922. Picture of American middle-class life, through the story of a conservative Republican real-estate agent.

1943 ______. ARROWSMITH. Harcourt, 1925. Picture of medical education and practice; story of a doctor, from medical school and general practice as a country doctor to his conflicts with politics in public-health work.

1944 ______. ELMER GANTRY. Harcourt, 1927. An attack on the hypocrisy of the times centering around the story of the sensational rise of an evangelist.

1945 Lloyd, Norris. A DREAM OF MANSIONS. Random, 1962. Story of a year in the life of an adolescent girl; setting is rural Georgia.

1946 Longstreet, Stephen. THE CRIME. Simon & Schuster, 1959. Story of the murder of a minister and his mistress, based on the Halls-Mills murder case in New Jersey in 1922.

1947 ______. REMEMBER WILLIAM KITE? Simon & Schuster, 1966. In the form of a memoir by a dashing, wealthy American World War I flying ace; shows the excitement of life in Europe and America during the 1920's and 1930's.

1948 McGibney, Donald. SLAG. Bobbs, 1922. Story of conflict between management and labor in a steel mill; characters are an arrogant capitalist, a labor agitator, and a society girl experimenting with communism.

1949 McKenna, Richard. THE SAND PEBBLES. Harper, 1963. Story of the crew who manned a U.S. gunboat in Hunan Province, Chica, during the Kuomintang rebellion, 1925-1927.

1950 McKenney, Ruth. JAKE HOME. Harcourt, 1943. Picture of the proletarian struggle from 1912 to the early 1930's; organization of labor, communist activity, and the Sacco-Vanzetti trial.

1951 MacKenzie, Rachel. THE WINE OF ASTONISHMENT. Viking, 1974. Rigid social conventions and moral judgments of a small upstate New York town affect the lives of two spinster sisters after the death of their dominating mother.

1952 McMillion, Bonner. THE LOT OF HER NEIGHBORS. Lippincott, 1953. Pictures the spirit of a Texas town in the twenties.

1953 Marks, Percy. PLASTIC AGE. Century, 1924. Detailed picture of all sides of college life in the post-war years.

1954 Maxwell, William. THE FOLDED LEAF. Harper, 1945. Picture of high-school life in Chicago in the early twenties.

1955 Meagher, Joseph William. TIPPY LOCKLIN. Little, 1960. A story of boyhood and of Catholic family life in Brooklyn in the 1920's.

1956 Millar, Margaret. IT'S ALL IN THE FAMILY. Random, 1948. Story of family life during the year 1925.

1957 Moll, Elick. MEMOIR OF SPRING. Putnam, 1961. Reminiscences of a Jewish boyhood in Brooklyn in the post-World War I era; picture of immigrant workers in the ladies-clothing industry.

1958 Morley, Christopher. PANDORA LIFTS THE LID. Doran, 1924. Adventurous tale of a group of school girls who kidnap a financier and a radical professor; a story of the flapper age.

1959 ________. KITTY FOYLE. Lippincott, 1939. Story of a girl growing up struggling against tradition in an industrial section of Philadelphia in the 1920's and 1930's.

1960 Morris, Wright. THE HUGE SEASON. Viking, 1954. Pictures the problems of the generation of the jazz age, told in flashbacks from the viewpoint of the protagonists in 1952.

1961 Murray, Albert. TRAIN WHISTLE GUITAR. McGraw, 1974. A young black boy grows up in an Alabama hamlet during the 1920's. Much of his education is picked up from songs and stories in the oral tradition of his people.

1962 Nathan, Robert. ONE MORE SPRING. Knopf, 1933. Effect of the financial crash of 1929 on a diverse group who spend the winter in a tool shed in Central Park.

1963 Neff, Wanda Fraiden. LONE VOYAGERS. Houghton, 1929. Story of economic hardships faced by a faculty of a Midwestern university.

1964 Nichols, Edward. DANGER! KEEP OUT. Houghton, 1943. Story of the gas and oil industry in Chicago in the twenties pictures the growth of the automobile industry and conflict between the workers and the industrial plant.

1965 Norris, Charles. PIG IRON. Dutton, 1926. Story of a Massachusetts farm boy's rise from hardware store to success as a financier and iron manufacutrer during the war years; criticism of American society and the effect of industrialization on human relations.

1966 O'Hara, John. LOVEY CHILDS. Random, 1969. A social-sexual whirl through New York and Philadelphia society in the twenties.

1967 Parks, Gordon. THE LEARNING TREE. Harper, 1963. A small town in Kansas in the 1920's is the setting for the story of a year in the life of a teenaged black boy.

1968 Pascal, Ernest. CYNTHIA CODENTRY. Brentano, 1926. Biographical novel of a young woman of the jazz age, set in Long Island and Florida; a satire on the society of the period.

1969 Paterson, Isabel. GOLDEN VANITY. Morrow, 1934. New York City before and during the crash of 1929.

1970 Peck, Robert Newton. A DAY NO PIGS WOULD DIE. Knopf, 1972. Rural Vermont in the 1920's. A boy learns that down-to-earth farm life leaves no room for sentimentality when he has to help slaughter his pet pig.

1971 Perretta, Armando. TAKE A NUMBER. Morrow, 1957. Happy story of boyhood and family life in the Italian section of Hartford, Connecticut.

1972 Powell, Dawn. THE GOLDEN SPUR. Viking, 1962. Satirical view of Greenwich Village life in the 1920's and 1950's as a young man from Ohio searches for his father.

1973 Pratt, Theodore. THE BAREFOOT MAILMAN. Duell, 1943. Picture of the early Florida land booms and politics in and around Palm Beach and Miami.

1974 Prouty, Olive Higgins. LISA VALE. Houghton, 1938. Boston in 1929 is the setting of a story about the social and economic problems of a middle-aged woman and her four grown children.

1975 Puzo, Mario. THE FORTUNATE PILGRIM. Atheneum, 1965. Tragic story of an Italian-American family living in the Chelsea district of New York City from 1928 to World War II.

1976 Rexroth, Kenneth. AN AUTOBIOGRAPHICAL NOVEL. Doubleday, 1966. A literary tall tale of the author's life up to 1927; covers art, radical politics, bootlegging, jazz, Negro life and race relations.

1977 Richter, Conrad. THE GRANDFATHERS. Knopf, 1964. Story of life in the hills of western Maryland in the 1920's.

1978 Riesenberg, Felix. EAST SIDE, WEST SIDE. Harcourt, 1927. Story of the rise of the main character from poverty on the East Side to a position of wealth and power, and the growth of New York City.

1979 Rogers, Samuel. DUSK AT THE GROVE. Little, 1934. Scenes in the lives of three young people as they grew up in the twenties.

1980 Rylee, Robert. ST. GEORGE OF WELDON. Farrar, 1937. Thirty years in the life of a man who drowns in 1929.

1981 Sachs, Emanie N. TALK. Harper, 1924. Story of an insecure marriage threatened by sudden wealth and a flapper-dominated society.

1982 Shenkin, Elizabeth. MIDSUMMER'S NIGHTMARE. Rinehart, 1960. Story of family life at a New York beach resort in 1923.

1983 Shipley, C. L. THE JADE PICCOLO. Atheneum, 1969. Small-town America seen through the eyes of two adolescent boys as they hero-worship the mysterious town bootlegger.

1984 Siebel, Julia. FOR THE TIME BEING. Harcourt, 1961. Family life in a small town in Kansas in the Post-World War I years.

1985 Sinclair, Harold. MUSIC OUT OF DIXIE. Rinehart, 1952. Story of the growth of jazz music in the twenties, from New Orleans' Storyville district to the success of Jelly Roll Morton in New York.

1986 Sinclair, Upton. OIL. Boni, 1927. Oil industry in Southern California, based on the Teapot Dome oil scandals during the Harding administration.

1987 ________. BOSTON. Boni, 1928. Story of the Sacco-Vanzetti trial; condemns the state of mind which permitted their conviction and execution.

1988 ________. THE WET PARADE. Farrar, 1931. Passionate defense of Prohibition-showing the evil effects of alcohol, the ineffective methods of Prohibition agents, and the efforts of the respectable rich to circumvent the law.

1989 ________. BETWEEN TWO WORLDS. Viking, 1941. Political and economic developments in postwar Europe and America from 1919 to 1929; Treaty of Versailles, the rise of Mussolini in Italy, growing Nazi power in Germany, and the stock market crash in 1929. Part of author's Lanny Budd series (see other categories).

1990 ________. ANOTHER PAMELA; OR, VIRTUE STILL REWARDED. Viking, 1950. Satire on the social history of the U.S. in the twenties.

1991 Smith, Betty. TOMORROW WILL BE BETTER. Harper, 1948. Typical family life in Brooklyn in the twenties.

1992 Soles, Gordon H. CORNBREAD AND MILK. Doubleday, 1959. Family and boyhood life on a Kansas farm during the 1920's.

1993 Sorensen, Virginia. ON THIS STAR. Reynal, 1946. Story of Mormon life in Utah in the twenties.

1994 Sprague, Jesse Rainsford. THE MIDDLEMAN. Morrow, 1929. Story of the wholesale merchandising business and its place in the economic system.

1995 Sterret, Frances Roberta. THE GOLDEN STREAM. Penn, 1931. Story of a wealthy family in conflict with a son's wife until her common sense saves them in the financial crash of 1929.

1996 Stone, Alma. THE HARVARD TREE. Houghton, 1954. Story of a happy family life and amiable race relations in a small Texas town.

1997 Stribling, T. S. BACKWATER. Doubleday, 1930. Social and business life in an Arkansas rural community.

1998 ________. THE UNFINISHED CATHEDRAL. Doubleday, 1934. The real-estate boom, and a skyscraper cathedral project in a north Alabama town. Sequel to The Store (Nation Grows Up).

1999 Stuart, Colin. SHOOT AN ARROW TO STOP THE WIND. Dial, 1970. The great-grandson of a Scotsman immigrant and his Blackfoot wife spends a summer with his maternal relatives and learns to appreciate his Indian heritage; the year is 1926.

2000 Suchow, Ruth. THE FOLKS. Farrar, 1934. Family life in a small Iowa town from World War I through the twenties.

2001 Suhl, Yuri. ONE FOOT IN AMERICA. Macmillan, 1950. Humorous story of a Jewish boy and his father, immigrants from Poland; the son becoming Americanized, the father clinging to the old ways.

2002 _______. COWBOY ON A WOODEN HORSE. Macmillan, 1953. Continues the story of a Jewish boy and his problems, from courtship to labor unions. Sequel to <u>One Foot in America</u>.

2003 Tarkington, Booth. CLAIRE AMBLER. Doubleday, 1928. Social life and customs in the jazz age of the 1920's; picture of contemporary flapper society.

2004 _______. MIRTHFUL HAVEN. Doubleday, 1930. Life in a small village in Maine as seen by the daughter of the local rum runner.

2005 Thielen, Benedict. THE LOST MEN. Appleton, 1946. Story of World War I veterans given the job of building a railroad across the Florida Keys.

2006 Train, Arthur Cheney. THE NEEDLE'S EYE. Scribner, 1924. A story of labor union activity in the West Virginia coal fields. Minor character is a society girl with socialistic ideas.

2007 _______. PAPER PROFITS. Liveright, 1930. Plea against stock-market speculation.

2008 Updegraff, Robert Rawls. CAPTAINS IN CONFLICT. Shaw, 1927. Story of the change in business methods from the turn of the century to the twenties as two men compete for control of the company they founded together.

2009 Walker, Charles Rumford. BREAD AND FIRE. Houghton, 1927. A thesis novel dealing with the problems of labor in the steel mill and the growth of the socialist movement.

2010 Watts, Mary Stanbery. THE FABRIC OF THE LOOM. Macmillan, 1924. A story depicting the superficial aspect of materialistic American society in contrast with European culture.

2011 Webber, Gordon. YEARS OF EDEN. Little, 1951. Story of a boy growing up in Michigan in the twenties.

2012 Webster, Henry Kitchell. AN AMERICAN FAMILY. Bobbs, 1923. Story of a contemporary family in Chicago in the postwar years and the early twenties.

2013 Weidman, Jerome. FOURTH STREET EAST. Random, 1970. How it was, growing up in the poorest of Jewish immigrant families on the Lower East Side in the decade following World War I.

2014 ______. LAST RESPECTS. Random, 1972. The same milieu as in Fourth Street East. The mother of the family has died, her returning son recalls her years of struggle.

2015 Welty, Eudora. DELTA WEDDING. Harcourt, 1946. Story of the week before the wedding of one of the girls of a Mississippi Delta family in 1923.

2016 Wharton, Edith. TWILIGHT SLEEP. Appleton, 1927. Novel of social life in the upper levels of society; picture of the optimism and self-indulgence of the jazz age.

2017 Widdemer, Margaret. GALLANT LADY. Harcourt, 1926. Story of flippant irresponsibility among the young-married set in the jazz age.

2018 Wiley, John. THE EDUCATION OF PETER. Stokes, 1924. Story of undergraduate life at Yale in the twenties.

2019 ______. QUEER STREET. Scribner, 1928. Set in New York City, the story of an old family house encroached on by night clubs, speakeasies, and rooming houses.

2020 Williams, Joan. OLD POWDER MAN. Harcourt, 1966. Story of the life of Frank Wynn, who introduced the use of dynamite in Mississippi River valley flood control projects for the U.S. Corps of Engineers.

2021 Williamson, Thames Ross. HUNKY. Coward, 1929. Slavic laborer in a big city, buffeted by a system he cannot understand; social study of a workingman's life in the twenties.

2022 Wilson, Mary B. YESTERDAY'S PROMISE. Penn, 1934. The effect of the 1929 market crash on the country-club set.

2023 Wilson, Mitchell. MY BROTHER, MY ENEMY. Little, 1952. Story of early experiments with television.

2024 Zugsmith, Leane. NEVER ENOUGH. Liveright, 1932. Portrays the extravagance, restlessness, and lack of purpose that characterized much of American life in the twenties.

THE NINETEEN-THIRTIES

2025 Algren, Nelson. A WALK ON THE WILD SIDE. Farrar, 1956. Story of degenerate life in New Orleans during the Depression.

2026 Angoff, Charles. SUMMER STORM. Yoseloff, 1963. Sixth in a series on Russian-Jewish family life covers the period 1933-35; shows effects of Franklin Roosevelt's New Deal policies to combat the Depression, reaction to Father Coughlin's broadcasts, and economic life of the magazine publishing world in Boston. Sequel to Between Day and Dark (The Twenties).

2027 Astor, Brooke. THE BLUEBIRD IS AT HOME. Harper & Row, 1965. New York and Washington social life and fashions in the 1930's.

2028 Athas, Daphne. ENTERING EPHESUS. Viking, 1971. An adolescent girl faces change when her Greek father moves the family from New England to the poorest section of a small Southern town during the Depression. Possessed of an adventurous nature and an iconoclastic intellect, she confounds the town's tradition-bound society.

2029 Atherton, Gertrude. HOUSE OF LEE. Appleton, 1940. Effect of the Depression on the women of an upper-class San Francisco family.

2030 Atwell, Lester. LOVE IS JUST AROUND THE CORNER. Simon & Schuster, 1963. Communist activity in the fashion and advertising world in 1936.

2031 Auchincloss, Louis. THE EMBEZZLER. Houghton, 1966. Picture of the social and financial world of New York City, centering around a scandal on Wall Street during the Depression.

2032 ________. COUNTRY COUSIN. Houghton, 1978. Old families, moneyed and mannerly, but not always trustworthy, in New York City during the first Roosevelt administration.

2033 Baker, Elliott. THE PENNY WARS. Putnam, 1968. Moving story of an adolescent boy experiencing life in a small town in upstate New York as war breaks out in Europe.

2034 Banning, Margaret Culken. MESABI. Harper, 1969. Story of the iron-ore mining business of the Mesabi range; set in and around Duluth, Minnesota in the years before World War II.

2035 Barrett, B. L. LOVE IN ATLANTIS. Houghton, 1969. Story of a teenaged girl's view of the world from a small California town, and of her first innocent love; good feeling for the period of the thirties.

2036 Behrman, S. N. THE BURNING GLASS. Little, 1968. Picture of the world of the theater in Europe, Hollywood, and New York from 1937 to 1940, showing the effect of the growing Nazi menace on the career of a young Jewish playwright.

2037 Bell, Thomas. ALL BRIDES ARE BEAUTIFUL. Little, 1936. Story of a young couple living in the Bronx during the Depression on $25 a week, who determine to be happy in their marriage, and succeed.

2038 Bickham, Jack M. I STILL DREAM ABOUT COLUMBUS. St. Martin's, 1982. The Depression brings poverty, and the Ku Klux Klan make trouble, but the narrator remembers the warmth and love that shaped his childhood in Columbus, Ohio.

2039 Blackwell, Louise. THE MEN AROUND HURLEY. Vanguard, 1957. Story of life in a remote small town in Alabama from the time of the Depression, through the 1930's, to the outbreak of World War II.

2040 Blake, Sally M. WHERE MIST CLOTHES DREAM AND MYTH RUNS NAKED. McGraw, 1965. A Boston slum during the Depression is the setting for this tragedy of an immigrant family in conflict over the old-world Jewish culture and facing the harsh realities of urban poverty.

2041 Boyd, Thomas Alexander. IN TIME OF PEACE. Minton, 1935. Picture of American life in the twenties and thirties, told through the story of a World War I veteran, a newspaper reporter struggling against the economic system and the Depression. Sequel to Through the Wheat (World War I).

2042 Breckenridge, Gerald. THE BESIEGED. Doubleday, 1937. Effect of the Depression on the character of the members of several families.

2043 Brelis, Dean. MY NEW FOUND LAND. Houghton, 1963. Story of a Greek-American family in Newport, Rhode Island in 1932; the father is a shoemaker and part-time bootlegger.

2044 Brody, Catherine. NOBODY STARVES. Longmans, 1932. Story of the Depression among automobile factory workers in and around Detroit.

2045 Brown, Joe David. ADDIE PRAY. Simon and Schuster, 1971. Addie, an eleven-year-old orphan, joins forces with Long Boy, a con man. The two of them live by swindling the gullible in the Depression South.

2046 Browne, Lewis. SEE WHAT I MEAN? Random, 1943. Rise of a subversive movement in southern California in the late thirties; anti-Semitism used as a tool by Nazi sympathizers.

2047 Brush, Katherine. DON'T EVER LEAVE ME. Farrar, 1935. Picture of the hard-drinking, fast-living country-club set, with the fashions, catch-words, and songs of 1932.

2048 Buckles, Eleanor. VALLEY OF POWER. Creative Age, 1945. Story of the T.V.A., its value and meaning, and the reaction of the Tennessee mountain families who must be evicted to make way for it.

2049 Burnett, William Riley. KING COLE. Harper, 1936. Picture of state politics, set around the last six days in a gubernatorial campaign in which the honest governor resorts to a planned riot to help him win reelection.

2050 Burwell, Basil. A FOOL IN THE FOREST. Macmillan, 1964. Story of an actor's first year in summer stock in Cape Cod in 1930.

2051 Caldwell, Janet Taylor. EAGLES GATHER. Scribner, 1940. Brings the story of a Pennsylvania munitions family up to 1938. Sequel to Balance Wheel (World War I).

2052 Callaghan, Morley. THEY SHALL INHERIT THE EARTH. Random, 1935. Effects of the Depression on a group of people in a moderate-sized American city.

2053 Carousso, Dorothee. OPEN THEN THE DOOR. Morrow, 1942. Story of a happy marriage in spite of mothers-in-law and the Depression.

2054 Champagne, Marian Mira. QUIMBY AND SON. Bobbs, 1962. A century-old family grocery company becomes a chain of supermarkets in a story set in New York State in the Depression years.

2055 Chinn, Lawrence Chambers. BELIEVE MY LOVE. Crown, 1962. Chicago during the Depression is the setting for this love story of a Nebraska girl and a Japanese-American engineering student.

2056 Clarke, Tom E. THE BIG ROAD. Lothrop, 1964. Story of a farm boy who leaves home during the Depression to become a hobo. Includes a glossary of hobo terms.

2057 Collins, Max. TRUE DETECTIVE. St. Martin's, 1984. Prohibition in Chicago brought ferment among gangsters, lawmen, and politicians. This story mixes fact with fiction in its action.

2058 Connell, Evan S. MRS. BRIDGE. Knopf, 1969. A quiet story of the social problems on the American scene from the Depression to the years before World War II, in Kansas City.

2059 Cooper, Jamie Lee. THE CASTAWAYS. Bobbs, 1970. Harsh realities of the Depression destroy a family's dreams as they travel the U.S. in an old jalopy, their only home. Only the young son survives.

2060 Corbett, Elizabeth. THE CROSSROADS. Appleton, 1965. Story of a family bookshop in Greenwich Village during the Depression. Sequel to Heart of the Village (The Twenties).

2061 Corey, Paul. ACRES OF ANTAEUS. Holt, 1946. The plight of the farmers when foreclosures and eviction threaten during the hard years of the 1930's.

2062 Corrigan, Barbara. VOYAGE OF DISCOVERY. Scribner, 1945. Sophisticated picture of college life in the 1930's.

2063 Costello, Anthony. JERICHO. Bantam, 1982. Father Coughlin's tirades foment his Irish followers in a Massachusetts mill town. A crusading newspaperwoman and a bitter strike at the mill shift the views of some citizens.

2064 Covert, Alice. RETURN TO DUST. Kinsey, 1939. Dust-bowl conditions and the reaction to government relief in a small Oklahoma community.

2065 ________. THE MONTHS OF RAIN. Kinsey, 1941. Oklahoma farm family fights droughts, storms, and the Depression.

2066 Covin, Kelley. HEAR THAT TRAIN BLOW! Delacorte, 1970. Novel about the nine Negro youths accused, tried, and sentenced to death on charges of rape of two white women in Scottsboro, Alabama in 1931. Depression and the developing war in Europe are in the background of this story of racial injustice.

2067 Curran, Dale. PIANO IN THE BAND. Reynal, 1940. Story of the feverish atmosphere of the world of jazz music in 1933.

2068 Curry, Peggy. OIL PATCH. McGraw, 1959. Story of life

in a Western oil town in the 1930's; a wife rebels against strict company rule.

2069 Daniels, Guy. PROGRESS, USA. Macmillan, 1968. Provincial life in a small Iowa town in the early 1930's, as seen by a teenaged boy.

2070 Davis, Julia. THE SUN CLIMBS SLOW. Dutton, 1942. America at the time of the Spanish Civil War.

2071 Davis, Kenneth. THE YEARS OF THE PILGRIMAGE. Doubleday, 1948. Conflicting philosophies in a Kansas town in the thirties.

2072 Deal, Bordon. DUNBAR'S COVE. Scribner, 1957. Study of the social and economic life in the Tennessee River valley in the thirties; a family's fight with T. V. A. over condemnation of their land for a dam.

2073 ________. THE LEAST ONE. Doubleday, 1967. An ordinary family faces up to the hard times of the Depression.

2074 Deasy, Mary. DEVIL'S BRIDGE. Little, 1952. Politics in a Southern town; 1929-1933.

2075 ________. THE CELEBRATION. Random House, 1963. Story of the rise and fall of a proud family in a Midwestern city in the 1930's.

2076 Doig, Ivan. ENGLISH CREEK. Atheneum, 1984. Everyday life on a Montana ranch in the summer of 1939. Two young men are growing up, and as the story ends on Labor Day, war is breaking out in Europe. Life will never be the same, even in this remote rural land.

2077 Dos Passos, John. NUMBER ONE. Houghton, 1943. Politics and the gullibility of the masses in a story of a Southern demagogue; based on the career of Huey Long.

2078 ________. GRAND DESIGN. Houghton, 1949. Story of New Deal politics in Washington.

2079 Drake, Robert. AMAZING GRACE. Chilton, 1965. Eighteen short stories which combine to present a picture of rural Tennessee in the 1930's and 1940's.

2080 Duncan, David. THE LONG WALK HOME FROM TOWN. Doubleday, 1964. Nostalgic view of boyhood life in a small town in Montana in the early thirties.

2081 Dutton, Mary. THORPE. World, 1967. Southern race relations in Arkansas in the thirties.

2082 Ehle, John. LION ON THE HEARTH. Harper, 1961. Story of a mountain family who move to the outskirts of Asheville, North Carolina, and face the hardships of the Depression.

2083 ______. WINTER PEOPLE. Harper, 1982. Hatred between clans of hill people in North Carolina triggers murder and revenge.

2084 Ellison, Earl. THE DAM. Random, 1941. Story of the construction of a W. P. A. dam near Chicago and its effect on the chief engineer.

2085 Ellison, Ralph. INVISIBLE MAN. Random, 1952. Story of a Negro trying to find himself and of Negro-white relations during the Depression years. Set in a small Southern town and in New York's Harlem.

2086 Epstein, Seymour. THE SUCCESSOR. Scribner, 1961. Portrait of a young Jewish salesman in the business world of a small town in New York from 1935 to 1947.

2087 Estes, Winston M. ANOTHER PART OF THE HOUSE. Lippincott, 1970. Story is told by a ten-year-old boy whose life in Texas in the Depression was made even harder by drought-bred dust storms.

2088 Ethridge, Willie Snow. MINGLED YARN. Macmillan, 1938. Story of a paternalistic Georgia mill owner; welfare plan and social clubs offered as compensation for starvation wages.

2089 Fair, Ronald. WE CAN'T BREATHE. Harper, 1972. Young black escapes the horrors of life in a Chicago ghetto in the hard-times thirties when he discovers other worlds in books, and later becomes an author himself. Autobiographical novel.

2090 Farrell, James T. THE DUNNE FAMILY. Doubleday, 1976. The Dunne family, part of an Irish neighborhood on Chicago's South Side, struggle together through the twenties and the hard times of the thirties.

2091 Fast, Howard. POWER. Doubleday, 1962. Story of the rise of Benjamin R. Holt as a labor leader in the coal-miners union in the mine fields of West Virginia and Illinois in the twenties and thirties.

2092 Faulkner, John. MEN WORKING. Harcourt, 1941. Story of a shiftless family who leave tenant farming to go to work for the W. P. A.

2093 Feibleman, Peter S. A PLACE WITHOUT TWILIGHT. World, 1958. Negro life in New Orleans in the 1930's and 1940's.

2094 Finley, Joseph. MISSOURI BLUE. Putnam, 1976. The terrible poverty of a Missouri farm family serves to strengthen their love for one another, and deepen their appreciation for intangible values.

2095 Fumento, Rocco. TREE OF DARK REFLECTION. Knopf, 1961. Troubled life of an Italian immigrant family in a Massachusetts textile mill town and in an industrial suburb of Boston in the 1930's.

2096 Gallagher, Thomas. THE GATHERING DARKNESS. Bobbs, 1952. Follows the economic ups and downs of a middle-class family in New York; 1929-1942.

2097 Gilbreth, Frank B. LOBLOLLY. Crowell, 1959. Warm and funny story of an eccentric family in Charleston, South Carolina in 1935, bringing in the Depression and the New Deal as background.

2098 Gold, Herbert. THEREFORE BE BOLD. Dial, 1960. Story of a Jewish boy growing up in a non-Jewish suburb of Cleveland, Ohio in the 1930's.

2099 _______. FATHERS. Random, 1967. Story of family life and growing up in a Jewish immigrant family in Cleveland, Ohio and New York City, through the Depression and into World War II.

2100 Granit, Arthur. TIME OF THE PEACHES. Abelard, 1959. Poetic story of Jewish life in the Brownsville section of Brooklyn in the 1930's.

2101 Green, Gerald. TO BROOKLYN WITH LOVE. Trident, 1967. A nostalgic look back on boyhood survival in pre-World War II Brooklyn.

2102 Grubb, Davis. A TREE FULL OF STARS. Scribner, 1965. A sentimental tale of Christmas in a small Ohio town during the Depression.

2103 _______. FOOL'S PARADE. World/NAL., 1969. Adventures of three ex-convicts in the mining country of West Virginia in 1935.

2104 _______. THE BAREFOOT MAN. Simon and Schuster, 1971. Striking miner seeks revenge for the death of a friend at the hands of strikebreakers; West Virginia locale.

2105 Grumbach, Doris. THE SHORT THROAT, THE TENDER MOUTH. Doubleday, 1964. Members of the class of 1939 of the Washington Square Campus of New York State University look back on their student days as rebels and communists.

2106 Guy, Rosa. MEASURE OF TIME. Holt, 1983. A young black girl escapes from Jim Crow Alabama to the alluring glamor of Harlem. In order to share the good life around her, she becomes a whiz at shoplifting.

2107 Gwaltney, Frances I. IDOLS AND AXLE-GREASE. Bobbs, 1974. The idiosyncracies of some of the citizens of an Arkansas hamlet during the Depression. Fictionalized memories of the author.

2108 Halper, Albert. UNION SQUARE. Viking, 1933. Story of a few days in the life of the radicals and the destitute in the tenements in the Union Square area of New York.

2109 ______. THE CHUTE. Viking, 1937. Proletarian novel set in the order department of a Chicago mailing house; theme is the inhuman activity needed to keep the package chute fed.

2110 Hamilton, Harry. RIVER SONG. Bobbs, 1945. Story of two Mississippi River bums after a radio scout discovers their musical talent.

2111 Harnack, Curtis. LOVE AND BE SILENT. Harcourt, 1961. Farm and town life in Iowa is the setting for a story of two brothers and two sisters and their emotional entanglements.

2112 Herbst, Josephine. ROPE OF GOLD. Harcourt, 1939. Continues the story of a middle-class American family through the Depression; 1933-1937. Sequel to The Executioner Waits (The Twenties).

2113 Herrick, William. HERMANOS! Simon and Schuster, 1969. A tale of social unrest and international violence in a review of communist activity in Cuba, the United States, and in the Spanish Civil War.

2114 Heyward, Du Bose. STAR SPANGLED VIRGIN. Farrar, 1939. Story of the Virgin Islands; showing the disintegrating effect of New Deal relief measures on the natives.

2115 Hicks, Granville. ONLY ONE STORM. Macmillan, 1942. World events from 1937 to 1939 as seen by a family who retreated from the pressures of New York City business life.

2116 Hobart, Alice Tisdale. THE CUP AND THE SWORD. Bobbs, 1942. Story of the California grape and wine industries from the 1920's to the beginning of World War II.

2117 Hotchner, A. E. KING OF THE HILL. Harper, 1972. An adolescent boy growing up in St. Louis learns all the tricks of scrimping and scrounging for a hand-to-mouth living in the Depression.

2118 Hubbell, Catherine. FRANCES. Norton, 1950. Picture of life in New York City from the 1920's to the 1940's.

2119 Hudson, Lois Phillips. THE BONES OF PLENTY. Little, 1962. A wheat farmer loses his rented farm as a result of drought, dust storms, wheat smut, and economic depression in a North Dakota wheat-growing community.

2120 ________. REAPERS OF THE DUST. Little, 1965. Episodes based on memories of a farm childhood in the wheat-farming area of North Dakota, suffering from drought and the dust storms of the 1930's.

2121 Hueston, Ethel. A ROOF OVER THEIR HEADS. Bobbs, 1937. Picture of moral disintegration brought on by the Depression; theme is that unemployment forced families together in overcrowded conditions and going on relief was inevitable.

2122 Hulbert, James. THE DISPUTED BARRICADE. Holt, 1966. Story of a young iron worker who rises to power in the labor movement in Gary, Indiana during the Depression.

2123 Hull, Morris. CANNERY ANNE. Houghton, 1936. Picture of life among the migratory workers in a California cannery.

2124 Humphrey, William. A TIME AND A PLACE. Knopf, 1968. Collection of stories depicting the effects of the Depression, oil strikes, and climate on small-town life in Oklahoma and Texas.

2125 Idell, Albert. THE CORNER STORE. Doubleday, 1953. Family life in a run-down section of Philadelphia during the Depression.

2126 Jackson, Margaret. KINDY'S CROSSING. Bobbs, 1934. Story of the rise and fall of an American industrialist family, from wealth and power in the automobile industry to the loss of everything during the Depression.

2127 Jackson, Shirley. THE ROAD THROUGH THE WALL. Farrar, 1948. Picture of American middle-class family life in a California town in 1936.

2128 Janeway, Elizabeth. LEAVING HOME. Doubleday, 1953. Story of the insecurity of three children growing up in Brooklyn in the 1930's.

2129 Johnson, Josephine. NOW IN NOVEMBER. Simon & Schuster, 1934. Story of poor crops, labor troubles, drought, and debt on a Midwestern farm in the years leading up to the Depression.

2130 ________. JORDANSTOWN. Simon and Schuster, 1937. Story of the hopelessness of the poor in a small town, contrasted with the indifference of the financially secure.

2131 Johnson, Robert Proctor. LEGACY OF THORNS. Morrow, 1965. Realistic and grim picture of growing up in a small town near Lake Superior during the Depression.

2132 Jones, Douglas C. WEEDY ROUGH. Holt, 1981. A part-Indian boy in South Dakota gets into real trouble when some worthless friends involve him in a bank robbery.

2133 Jones, Nard. STILL TO THE WEST. Doddy, 1946. Building of the Grand Coulee Dam on the Columbia River.

2134 Kanin, Garson. BLOW UP A STORM. Random, 1959. Story centers around the members, white and Negro, of a small jazz combo in the days of jazz music in the early thirties.

2135 Kaufman, Charles. FIESTA IN MANHATTAN. Morrow, 1939. Story of a Mexican couple lured to New York; stranded by unemployment in the Depression, they turn to the marijuana racket.

2136 Keyes, Frances Parkinson. ALL THAT GLITTERS. Messner, 1941. Picture of social changes in Washington during the period from December 1927 to June 1940.

2137 Kluger, Richard. UNAMERICAN ACTIVITIES. Doubleday, 1982. The radical fringe movements of the thirties from the Harvard Students League to the Communist Party in New York City. The protagonist was for awhile a counselor in a C. C. C. camp; this scene is accurately portrayed.

2138 Kotlowitz, Robert. THE BOARDWALK. Knopf, 1977. A Jewish boy vacations with his parents in Atlantic City during the summer of 1939. They return home as the news of Hitler's invasion of Poland breaks, an event which will change his life forever and alter the course of history.

2139 Kroll, Harry Harrison. THE USURPER. Bobbs, 1941. Conflict between the growers and the sharecroppers of the South, through prosperity and the Depression.

2140 Langley, Adria Locke. A LION IS IN THE STREETS. Whittlesey, 1945. Rise and fall of a demagogue; based on the career of Huey Long.

2141 Lanham, Edwin. THE STRICKLANDS. Little, 1939. Story of the conflict centering around organizing the tenant farmers of Oklahoma into unions after the Depression had changed the system of owner-operated farms.

2142 _______. THUNDER IN THE EARTH. Harcourt, 1941. Story of a Texas oil town in the 1930's; emphasizes that rich natural resources should not be exploited.

2143 Lawrence, Josephine. IF I HAVE FOUR APPLES. Stokes, 1935. Story of a middle-class family trying to live beyond their income in spite of the Depression and of the inevitable consequences of installment buying.

2144 _______. SOUND OF RUNNING FEET. Stokes, 1937. Effects of the Depression on the staff of a real-estate office; picture of home and office life during the period.

2145 _______. BUT YOU ARE YOUNG. Little, 1940. Economic struggles of a young girl forced to support her family through the Depression years.

2146 _______. NO STONE UNTURNED. Little, 1941. Picture of the moral and economic standing of an ordinary American family during the Depression and the recovery.

2147 Lee, Harper. TO KILL A MOCKINGBIRD. Lippincott, 1960. Two children growing up in Alabama in the thirties witness small-town life and violence when their lawyer father defends a falsely accused Negro.

2148 Lewis, Janet. AGAINST A DARKENING SKY. Doubleday, 1943. Family life in the Santa Clara valley near San Francisco during the Depression.

2149 Lewis, Sinclair. ANN VICKERS. Doubleday, 1933. Social satire of a professional feminist, social worker, and prison reformer.

2150 Liederman, Judith. THE MONEYMAN. Houghton, 1979. Manners and customs of New York City from the 1920's to the 1940's. A young man, raised in dreary poverty in Brooklyn, aspires to wealth. He makes it big by controlling the coat-checking concessions in Manhattan's nightspots.

2151 Linn, James Weber. WINDS OVER THE CAMPUS. Bobbs, 1936. Picture of students and faculty life at the University of Chicago.

2152 Littleton, Betty. IN SAMSON'S EYE. Atheneum, 1965. Life in a small town in Oklahoma through the Depression into the 1940's.

2153 Litwak, Leo. WAITING FOR THE NEWS. Doubleday, 1969.

Family life of a Jewish labor leader in Detroit in 1939; the joys of childhood shadowed by violence and the news of Hitler's aggressions against the Jews in Germany.

2154 Longo, Lucas. THE FAMILY ON VENDETTA STREET. Doubleday, 1968. Life in the Italian colony of New York City.

2155 Longstreet, Stephen. DECADE, 1929-1939. Random, 1940. Story of the financial decline of a benevolent old capitalist, from the crash of 1929 to the years preceding World War II.

2156 McCarthy, Cormac. THE ORCHARD KEEPER. Random House, 1965. Picture of life in the Smoky Mountains of East Tennessee in the twenties and thirties, as the characters resist the forces of change.

2157 McIntyre, John Thomas. STEPS GOING DOWN. Farrar, 1936. Novel of underworld life in an American city of the thirties.

2158 _______. FERMENT. Farrar, 1937. Proletarian novel of strikebreaking and labor racketeering in Philadelphia; theme is the futility of the workingman's struggle against the evils of industrialism and fascism.

2159 McKay, Allis. GOODBYE, SUMMER. Macmillan, 1953. Teenager on an apple ranch in the Columbia River valley near Seattle goes from adolescence to manhood working on the Grand Coulee Dam.

2160 Maclean, Norman. A RIVER RUNS THROUGH IT. University of Chicago Press, 1976. Two novellas and a short story set in Montana country picture life in the young U.S. Forest Service, in fishing camps, and with logging crews.

2161 MacLeish, Archibald. CONE OF SILENCE. Houghton, 1944. Story of the United States in the summer of 1933; the growth of fascism in Europe and America.

2162 McWhirter, Millie. HUSHED WERE THE HILLS. Abingdon, 1969. Bits of family life as a widowed school teacher raises her children in the hill country of Tennessee during the Depression.

2163 Maltz, Albert. THE UNDERGROUND STREAM. Little, 1940. Industrial conflict between communists and organized labor on the one hand and fascists on the other.

2164 Markfield, Wallace. TEITLEBAUM'S WINDOW. Knopf, 1970. A lighthearted memoir of a Jewish youth in Brighton Beach, Brooklyn, in prewar days.

2165 Marshall, Catherine. JULIE. McGraw, 1984. A flood-prone steel town in Pennsylvania is hit hard by high water in the 1930's. Its citizens, steel barons, union leaders, a crusading newspaper editor, all manage to cooperate in the crisis.

2166 Martin, Peter. THE BUILDING. Little, 1960. Story of a Russian Jewish family struggling through the Depression in upstate New York, with a background of immigration from Russia in the early 1900's and family and business life to the thirties.

2167 Mayhall, Jane. COUSIN TO HUMAN. Harcourt, 1960. Story of the maturing of a 15-year-old girl in a small town in Kentucky in the mid-thirties.

2168 Meriwether, Louise. DADDY WAS A NUMBERS RUNNER. Prentice, 1970. A twelve year old grows up in a Harlem setting of despair and violence during the Depression; the young Adam Clayton Powell appears in the story.

2169 Merrick, Elliott. FROM THIS HILL LOOK DOWN. Stephen Daye, 1934. Sketches of life in Vermont during the Depression; drought, rain, sick neighbors, and a C. W. A. job make up part of the story.

2170 Moore, Ruth. SPOONHANDLE. Morrow, 1946. Maine coastal town in the middle thirties.

2171 Morreale, Ben. MONDAY, TUESDAY ... NEVER COME SUNDAY. Scribners, 1977. Depression years in Brooklyn recalled by a Sicilian youngster. His father reluctantly gets money by helping a relative in the Mafia. An older streetwise Jewish friend and protector of the boy will leave to join the Spanish freedom fighters.

2172 Morris, Hilda. THE MAIN STREAM. Putnam, 1939. Contrasting picture of life on a farm in New York and life in a factory town.

2173 Newhouse, Edward. YOU CAN'T SLEEP HERE. Furman, 1934. Story centering around the movement for unemployment insurance; a New York reporter joins a squatters' colony and becomes active in the movement after losing his job during the Depression.

2174 Norris, Charles. HANDS. Farrar, 1935. Novel showing how the Depression forced many to go back to the pioneer ways of working with the hands.

2175 ________. FLINT. Doubleday, 1944. Conflict between capital and labor in the shipbuilding industry in San Francisco in the mid-thirties.

2176 North, Jessica Nelson. ARDEN ACRES. Harcourt, 1935. Story of a family in a slum section of Chicago on relief during the Depression.

2177 Oates, Joyce Carol. GARDEN OF EARTHLY DELIGHTS. Vanguard, 1967. Life in a migrant work camp and a small town following the Depression.

2178 O'Hara, John. THE BIG LAUGH. Random, 1962. Centers around theatrical life in New York in the 1920's, and on to Hollywood movie stardom during the Depression.

2179 Olsen, Tillie. YONNONDIO. Delacorte, 1974. The developing mind of a young girl as she witnesses her impoverished family try mining in Wyoming, tenant farming in South Dakota, and finally factory work in Chicago as they struggle through the Depression.

2180 O'Rourke, Frank. THE BRIGHT MORNING. Morrow, 1963. A young teacher is the central character in this pleasant tale of life and love in a small Midwestern town in the 1930's.

2181 Owen, Guy. JOURNEY FOR JOEDEL. Crown, 1970. The thirteen-year-old son of a sharecropper and his Indian wife sets off for his first tobacco auction and encounters prejudice against his Indian blood. Life of the North Carolina tobacco farmer in the 1930's.

2182 Palmer, Artes. THERE'S NO PLACE LIKE NOME. Morrow, 1963. Picture of family life and the construction business in Seattle in the 1930's; when the business fails in the Depression the family takes up bootlegging, and later, gold dredging in Alaska.

2183 Patterson, Harry. DILLINGER. Stein and Day, 1983. Dillinger, as in real life, makes an escape from prison in Indiana. In this fictional story, he flees to Mexico.

2184 Paul, Elliot. THE STARS AND STRIPES FOREVER. Random, 1939. Paternalistic owner opposes the organization of a labor union in his factory.

2185 Pearce, Donn. COOL HAND LUKE. Scribner, 1965. Life on a chain gang in a Florida prison camp.

2186 Perry, Dick. RAYMOND AND ME THAT SUMMER. Harcourt, 1964. Summer adventures of two boys in Cincinnati, Ohio during the Depression.

2187 ________. THE ROUND HOUSE, PARADISE, AND MR. PICKERING. Doubleday, 1966. Story of family life and railroading, in Cincinnati, Ohio, in the heyday of the New York Central.

2188 Pharr, Robert Deane. THE BOOK OF NUMBERS. Doubleday, 1969. Negro life and the numbers racket in the ghetto of a Southern city in the thirties.

2189 Pierce, Noel. THE SECOND MRS. DRAPER. McBride, 1937. Social life among the Long Island sophisticated country-club set in the thirties.

2190 Raines, Howell. WHISKEY MAN. Viking Press, 1977. A young man, the first of his family to get a higher education, returns from college to rural Alabama where bootlegging whiskey is a major source of income during the Depression.

2191 Raymond, Margaret Thomsen. BEND IN THE ROAD. Longmans, 1934. Story of a young girl who leaves home and gets a job in a factory.

2192 ________. SYLVIA, INC. Dodd, 1938. Story of a young girl called home from art school to help her father save his failing pottery business during the Depression.

2193 Rice, Elmer. IMPERIAL CITY. Appleton, 1937. Complex social and financial life of a wealthy family in New York City.

2194 Rickett, Frances. A CERTAIN SLANT OF LIGHT. Putnam, 1968. Politics and family life in a small town in Indiana during the Depression.

2195 Ritner, Ann Katherine. SEIZE A NETTLE. Lippincott, 1961. Story of a household of women and of their efforts to keep going during the Depression.

2196 Roberts, Marta. TUMBLEWEEDS. Putnam, 1940. Unemployment and gradual demoralization of a Mexican couple brought to California as railroad laborers; depicts the fear and dislike of relief agencies by those who need it most.

2197 Robinson, Dorothy. THE DIARY OF A SUBURBAN HOUSEWIFE. Morrow, 1936. Story of a Long Island housewife's courage and resourcefulness in meeting the Depression.

2198 Roe, Wellington. THE TREE FALLS SOUTH. Putnam, 1937. Kansas farmers facing destitution from drought, dust, storms, and the Depression march on the county seat for government aid.

2199 Roth, Arthur J. SHAME OF OUR WOUNDS. Crowell, 1961. A grim realistic picture of New York City in the 1930's, set around the adventures of three boys who run away from a Catholic Home for Boys.

2200 Rothberg, Abraham. THE SONG OF DAVID FREED. Putnam,

1968. Story of cultural and family conflicts as a young Jewish boy grows up in New York City during the Depression.

2201 Rubin, Louis. THE GOLDEN WEATHER. Atheneum, 1961. Nostalgic view of a thirteen-year-old boy's activities in Charleston, South Carolina, before and during the 75th anniversary of the fall of Fort Sumter, in 1936.

2202 Ryan, J. M. MOTHER'S DAY. Prentice, 1969. Based on the life of the Ma Barker outlaw gang, from their wild existence in the Ozarks to their death in a Florida ambush in the "Bonnie and Clyde" tradition.

2203 Sandoz, Mari. CAPITAL CITY. Little, 1939. Picture of sordid political and social life in a Midwestern city; story of conflict between capital and labor; the rise of fascism, the tragedy of dispossessed farmers, unemployment, and graft and corruption in government.

2204 Saxton, Alexander. THE GREAT MIDLAND. Appleton, 1948. Economic class struggle and race relations in Chicago in the thirties; a story of labor unions, race riots, and communist activities.

2205 Scott, Evelyn. BREAD AND A SWORD. Scribner, 1937. Story of a writer compromising his creative integrity to support his family during the Depression.

2206 Scott, Virgil. THE HICKORY STICK. Swallow, 1948. Economic conditions of a young student and teacher in a small Ohio town through the Depression years.

2207 Scowcroft, Richard. FIRST FAMILY. Houghton, 1940. Life in a prosperous middle-class family after the 1929 crash.

2208 Shepherd, Jean. IN GOD WE TRUST, ALL OTHERS PAY CASH. Doubleday, 1966. Memories of childhood in a small Indiana town recall family life and customs, Tom Mix movies, sarsaparilla, and other nostalgia.

2209 Sherburne, James. STAND LIKE MEN. Houghton, 1973. A quasi-documentary about the strife between miner and mine owner, and rival unions during the Kentucky coal war of 1931. Vindictive violence on all sides.

2210 Simon, Charlie May. SHARE-CROPPER. Dutton, 1937. Picture of the economic problems of an Arkansas cotton farmer during the Depression; story of the tenant-farmers' union.

2211 Sims, Marian. THE CITY ON THE HILL. Lippincott, 1940. City solicitor of a small Southern city crusades against slums, political graft, and unjust liquor regulations.

2212 Sinclair, Upton. CO-OP. Farrar, 1936. Development of the farmers' self-help co-operatives in California, 1932-1936.

2213 ______. DRAGON'S TEETH. Viking, 1942. Period between 1929 and 1934; events in France and Germany during the rise of Hitler, Goering, and Goebbels. Imprisonment in Dachau prison; Lanny Budd series. Sequel to Between Two Worlds (The Twenties).

2214 ______. WIDE IS THE GATE. Viking, 1943. Lanny Budd furthers his anti-Nazi activities while posing as a personal friend of Hitler, Goering, and Hess, and witnesses the beginning of the Spanish Civil War. Sequel to Dragon's Teeth.

2215 ______. PRESIDENTIAL AGENT. Viking, 1944. Lanny Budd becomes a secret agent of President Roosevelt reporting on the political situation in Europe from 1937 to 1938 and the Munich Pact between Chamberlain and Hitler. Sequel to Wide is the Gate.

2216 Skidmore, Hubert. THE HAWK'S NEST. Doubleday, 1941. Senate investigation of the deaths of many workers from silica dust on a West Virginia mountain tunnel project in 1931.

2217 Slade, Caroline. THE TRIUMPH OF WILLIE POND. Vanguard, 1940. Ironic story of a family on relief; thesis is that New Deal relief measures treat symptoms rather than causes.

2218 ______. JOB'S HOUSE. Vanguard, 1941. Story of unemployment and relief during Depression years.

2219 Smith, Betty. JOY IN THE MORNING. Harper, 1963. Young married love in a Midwest college town.

2220 Smitter, Wessell. F.O.B. DETROIT. Harper, 1938. Story of the automobile industry, showing the inhuman speedup in the factory, and the workingman's helplessness in the system.

2221 Sondheim, Victor. INHERITORS OF THE STORM. Dell, 1981. A ruined banker kills himself; his children face the hard times of the Depression in diverse ways. One will join the Okies, one works in the Roosevelt administration, another gets an appointment to West Point.

2222 Stallworth, Anne. THIS TIME NEXT YEAR. Vanguard, 1972. Story of a young girl living in a tenant farm in Alabama with her parents, who hold differing, unattainable dreams. The mother longs for a real house in a city; the father, who loves the land, hopes only for a good crop to save him from eviction.

2223 Steinbeck, John. IN DUBIOUS BATTLE. Viking, 1936. Story of a strike among the fruit pickers in the California fruit country during the Depression.

2224 _______. OF MICE AND MEN. Covici, 1937. Life of itinerant ranch workers in California.

2225 _______. THE GRAPES OF WRATH. Viking, 1939. Story of Oklahoma farm families seeking relief from the dust bowl by following the seasonal fruit-picking jobs in California.

2226 Storm, Hans Otto. COUNT TEN. Longmans, 1940. Story of an American trying to find his place in life during the Depression.

2227 Stribling, T. S. THE SOUND WAGON. Doubleday, 1935. Novel of politics; reform candidates opposed to the entrenched political machine and gangsters.

2228 Swarthout, Glendon. LOVELAND. Doubleday, 1968. Lighthearted tale of a young man's summer during the Depression with references to the music and slang of the period.

2229 Taber, Gladys. A STAR TO STEER BY. Macrae, 1938. Wisconsin mill town torn by a strike when a labor organizer incites the workers against the paternalistic mill owners.

2230 Tarkington, Booth. THE HERITAGE OF HATCHER IDE. Doubleday, 1941. Pictures the changes in a respectable Middle West family as a result of the Depression.

2231 Thomas, Dorothy. THE HOME PLACE. Knopf, 1936. Story of a family conflict and hope for better times when drought and the Depression force three brothers to return with their families to the old farm.

2232 Thomas, Mack. GUMBO. Grove, 1965. Sketches of boyhood life in the Texas in the thirties.

2233 Thorp, Duncan. THANKS YER HONOR. Crown, 1963. A college boy and his fundamentalist grandmother live through Prohibition and Depression in Cucamonga, California.

2234 Trilling, Lionel. THE MIDDLE OF THE JOURNEY. Viking, 1947. Life among the summer residents and natives in a farming area in Connecticut in the late 1930's; agitated by community feeling against a communist in their midst.

2234a _______. THE MIDDLE OF THE JOURNEY. Scribner, 1976. A reissue of his 1947 novel with a new introduction by the author. The communist in the story was patterned on Whittaker Chambers.

2235 Tunis, John. SON OF THE VALLEY. Morrow, 1949. Story of T.V.A. and the resentment of the people whose homes would be flooded by the project.

2236 Turner, Steven. A MEASURE OF DUST. Simon and Schuster, 1970. An adolescent lives through the Depression in Bible-thumping Choctaw County, Mississippi. He sees the dichotomy between the religion spouted by those around him and the realities of the lives they lead.

2237 Turpin, Waters Edward. O CANAAN! Doubleday, 1939. Follows the lives of the Negroes who migrated to Chicago in 1916 and after; through prosperity, the crash of 1929, and the Depression.

2238 Villarreal, José Antonio. POCHO. Doubleday, 1959. Childhood of a Mexican migratory worker in the Santa Clara valley of California during the Depression years.

2239 Vogel, Joseph. MAN'S COURAGE. Knopf, 1938. Technicalities and red tape of the New Deal relief system and the chaotic economic conditions faced by a Polish immigrant family in a small American city.

2240 Wagner, Tobias. THE TURBULENT PENDRAYLES. Little, 1937. Family and social life of a Philadelphia locomotive manufacturer after the 1929 crash.

2241 Walker, Alice. COLOR PURPLE. Harcourt, 1982. This novel, in the form of letters, tells of the grimness of life for the Southern blacks, especially black women.

2242 Walker, Mildred. FIREWEED. Harcourt, 1934. Story of life in a lumber mill town in upper Michigan after the Depression closes the mill.

2243 Warren, Robert Penn. ALL THE KING'S MEN. Harcourt, 1946. Story of a demagogue based on the life and death of Huey Long.

2244 Weaver, John. ANOTHER SUCH VICTORY. Viking, 1948. Presents both sides of the veterans' Bonus March against Washington in 1932. MacArthur and Patton appear.

2245 Webber, Gordon. WHAT END BUT LOVE. Little, 1959. Memories of farm life and industrial growth set in the framework of a family reunion on a Michigan farm near the automobile factories in 1934.

2246 Weller, George Anthony. NOT TO EAT, NOT FOR LOVE. Smith and Haas, 1933. Picture of undergraduate life at Harvard University in 1933.

2247 Welty, Eudora. LOSING BATTLES. Random House, 1970. A family reunion on the occasion of the grandmother's minetieth birthday is the focus for this story of life in rural backwater Mississippi in the Depression.

2248 White, Milton. A YALE MAN. Doubleday, 1966. Realistic sketches of student life at Yale during the Depression and New Deal years.

2249 Wickenden, Dan. TOBIAS BRANDYWINE. Morrow, 1948. A story of family life during nine years of the Depression and New Deal relief measures.

2250 _______. THE RED CARPET. Morrow, 1952. New York in 1936 as a young Illinois college graduate found it.

2251 Williams, Ben Ames. TIME OF PEACE. Houghton, 1942. Novel of American life and political thought from 1930 to Pearl Harbor; theme is the changing reaction to the threat of war and the gradual acceptance of Roosevelt's foreign policy.

2252 Wilson, Gregory. THE VALLEY OF TIME. Doubleday, 1967. Story of a fundamentalist teacher pictures life and religion in eastern Tennessee before and during the T. V. A. years.

2253 Wilson, S. J. HURRAY FOR ME. Crown, 1964. Story of Jewish family life and customs as the five-year-old son grows up in Brooklyn during the Depression.

2254 Wolfe, Thomas. YOU CAN'T GO HOME AGAIN. Harper, 1940. Observations on economic and political life from the Depression to the spread of Nazism; set in New York, Brooklyn, England, and Germany.

2255 Wouk, Herman. THE WINDS OF WAR. Little, 1972. The days just before America enters World War II. An American naval officer is posted as attaché to Berlin, where he meets Hitler, Churchill, Stalin. The story also follows his wife at home, their two sons and daughter as war draws closer.

2256 Wright, Richard. NATIVE SON. Harper, 1940. Story of the frustrations and resentment in the life of a young Negro in Chicago in the 1930's.

2257 _______. LAWD TODAY. Walker, 1963. A day in the life of a Negro postal clerk in Chicago during the Depression.

2258 Wright, Sarah E. THIS CHILD'S GONNA LIVE. Delacorte, 1969. Story of the bleak existence of a Negro family in the black ghetto of a small town in rural Maryland.

2259 Yaffe, James. NOBODY DOES YOU ANY FAVORS. Putnam, 1966. Conflict between father and son over the son's lack of interest in the family leather-wear business.

2260 Yount, John. HARDCASTLE. Richard Marek, 1980. Workers in the coal mines of Kentucky are involved in a bitter strike in 1931. A penniless young man hired as a mine guard is sympathetic to the strikers.

2261 Zara, Louis. SOME FOR THE GLORY. Bobbs, 1937. Rise of orphan boy to presidential candidacy; details of ward, state, and national politics.

2262 Zugsmith, Leane. TIME TO REMEMBER. Random, 1936. Story of the conflicts involved in a department-store strike, from the standpoint of the striking clerks.

WORLD WAR II

2263 Adams, Frank Ramsay. WHEN I COME BACK. McBride, 1944. Story of a typical small-town mother trying to keep her seventeen-year-old son out of the army in 1942.

2264 Albrand, Martha. WITHOUT ORDERS. Little, 1943. Story of an American soldier in undercover work for the American army and the Italian underground.

2265 Allen Ralph. THE HIGH WHITE FOREST. Doubleday, 1964. Three allied soldiers cut off by the German offensive at the Battle of the Bulge in 1944.

2266 Appel, Benjamin. FORTRESS IN THE RICE. Bobbs, 1951. Guerrilla warfare in the Philippines after Pearl Harbor.

2267 Arleo, Joseph. THE GRAND STREET COLLECTOR. Walker, 1970. Fictional explanation of the motives for the real murder of the anti-fascist union leader Carlo Tresca, in 1943.

2268 Arnold, Elliott. THE COMMANDOS. Duell, 1942. Story of the purpose, training, and action of commando guerrilla units culminating in a raid in Nazi-occupied Norway.

2269 ________. TOMORROW WILL SING. Duell, 1945. Story of Italian-American relations at a U.S.-bomber base in southern Italy.

2270 ________. WALK WITH THE DEVIL. Knopf, 1950. Advance of the American army in Italy.

2271 Arnow, Harriette. THE DOLLMAKER. Macmillan, 1954. Story of a Kentucky family in wartime Detroit.

2272 Arthur, Phyllis. PAYING GUEST. Samuel Curl, 1945. Conflicts among an unhappy family are straightened out by their roomer, an engineer at the local war plant.

2273 Ashmead, John. THE MOUNTAIN AND THE FEATHER. Houghton, 1961. Story of wartime Hawaii and combat in the South Pacific from 1943 to the Battle of Leyte Gulf.

2274 Atwell, Lester. PRIVATE. Simon and Schuster, 1958. Story of a middle-aged soldier in the Battle of the Bulge and in the invasion of Germany.

2275 August, John. ADVANCE AGENT. Little, 1942. A newspaperman and a soldier expose a secret Nazi organization.

2276 Barr, George. EPITAPH FOR AN ENEMY. Harper, 1958. An American sergeant, leading a group of French villagers to the beach for evacuation, gains new understanding of the enemy as he sees the influence which a humane German commander had on the group.

2277 Bassett, James. HARM'S WAY. World, 1962. A story of U.S. navy life during the first year of war in the Pacific.

2278 _______. COMMANDER PRINCE, USN. Simon and Schuster, 1971. A navy commander proves to himself that he is a courageous man in the Battle of the Coral Sea.

2279 Beach, Edward. RUN SILENT, RUN DEEP. Holt, 1955. Realistic novel of submarine warfare in the Pacific.

2280 _______. DUST ON THE SEA. Holt, 1972. Submarines battle to destroy Japanese shipping. Authentic details of underwater warfare. Sequel to Run Silent, Run Deep.

2281 Bergamini, David. THE FLEET IN THE WINDOW. Simon and Schuster, 1960. Story of the guerrilla fighting in the Philippines and life in a Japanese internment camp as experienced by the young son of an American missionary doctor.

2282 Berk, Howard. THE HERO MACHINE. New American Library, 1967. Life in a U.S. air base in the China-Burma-India theater in World War II.

2283 Beverley-Giddings, Arthur Raymond. BROAD MARGIN. Morrow, 1945. An American flier, wounded with the R.A.F. recuperates in Tidewater Virginia.

2284 Bonner, Paul Hyde. EXCELSIOR! Scribner, 1955. Scion of a Swiss banking family faces conflicting loyalties in America at the outbreak of the war.

2285 Bowman, Peter. BEACH RED. Random, 1945. Picture of a landing assault on a Pacific island through the thoughts and feelings of a soldier in the hour before his death.

2286 Boyd, Dean. LIGHTER THAN AIR. Harcourt, Brace and World, 1961. Humorous tale of the blimp service in the war.

2287 Boyle, Kay. HIS HUMAN MAJESTY. Whittlesey, 1949. Ski troopers training in Colorado in 1944.

2288 Brelis, Dean. THE MISSION. Random, 1958. Story of an

O.S.S. agent operating behind the Japanese lines in Burma in 1943.

2289 Bridge, Ann. A PLACE TO STAND. Macmillan, 1953. Daughter of an American businessman becomes involved with a family of Polish refugees and witnesses the brutality of the Nazis when they march into Budapest in 1941.

2290 Bright, Robert. THE LIFE AND DEATH OF LITTLE JO. Doubleday, 1944. Story of the effect of the war on a young Spanish-American from a village in New Mexico.

2291 Brinkley, William. DON'T GO NEAR THE WATER. Random, 1956. Comedy of a U.S. navy public relations unit on a Pacific island during the war.

2292 ______. THE NINETY AND NINE. Doubleday, 1966. Life on an LST landing craft at the time of the Anzio Beachhead in Italy.

2293 Bromfield, Louis. MR. SMITH. Harper, 1951. An American major on a Pacific island reviews his fruitless life.

2294 Brown, Eugene. THE LOCUST FIRE. Doubleday, 1957. Fast-paced action story of an Air Transport Command pilot in China during World War II.

2295 Brown, Harry. WALK IN THE SUN. Knopf, 1944. Story of a squad of American soldiers on a beachhead in Italy.

2296 Brown, Joe David. KINGS GO FORTH. Morrow, 1956. Story of two American artillery observers in action against the Germans in Italy and southern France.

2297 Buck, Pearl. COMMAND THE MORNING. Day, 1959. Story of the scientists who developed the first atomic chain reaction at the University of Chicago, December 2, 1942; set in Chicago, Oak Ridge, Washington, and Los Alamos.

2298 Burnett, William Riley. TOMORROW'S ANOTHER DAY. Knopf, 1945. A gay young gambler returns from the war and settles down in the restaurant business.

2299 Busch, Niven. THEY DREAM OF HOME. Bobbs, 1944. Story of five U.S. marines who face the problems of adjusting to civilian life in Los Angeles after action in the Pacific.

2300 Cahill, Susan. EARTH ANGELS. Harper, 1976. A Catholic girlhood in New York City during World War II; good picture of that time and place.

2301 Caiden, Martin. WHIP. Houghton, 1976. Story of the Death's Head Brigade, a U.S. bomber group based secretly in New Guinea.

2302 Caldwell, Janet Taylor. THE FINAL HOUR. Scribner, 1944. Conflict in the Pennsylvania munitions dynasty from 1939 to 1942; some want to do business with Hitler. Sequel to Eagles Gather (The Thirties).

2303 Calmer, Ned. THE STRANGE LAND. Scribner, 1950. Story of an unsuccessful Allied offensive in Europe in 1944.

2304 Camerer, David. THE DAMNED WEAR WINGS. Doubleday, 1958. Personality conflicts among a group of U.S. pilots on an air base in Italy; bombing missions over the Ploesti oil fields.

2305 Camp, William Henry. SKIP TO MY LOU. Doubleday, 1945. Story of an itinerant Arkansas Ozark hill family who migrate to the California shipyards during the war.

2306 Camp, William Martin. RETREAT, HELL! Appleton, 1943. Story of the U.S. Marines fighting in Shanghai and at Cavite, Bataan, and Corregidor in the Philippines on December 6, 1941.

2307 Carleton, Marjorie. THE SWAN SANG ONCE. Morrow, 1947. A soldier, released from Japanese prison camp, seeks proof that his wife was a traitor during the war.

2308 Carse, Robert. FROM THE SEA AND THE JUNGLE. Scribner, 1951. Episode on an island in the West Indies involving an ex-gangster, German submarines, and the sinking of American ships.

2309 Caspary, Vera. THE ROSECREST CELL. Putnam, 1967. Story centers around the activities of a communist group in a Connecticut town from the 1930's into World War II.

2310 Chamales, Tom. NEVER SO FEW. Scribner, 1957. Guerrilla activity in Burma in World War II.

2311 Chambliss, William C. BOOMERANG. Harcourt, 1944. Story of a new U.S. Navy ship in the South Pacific.

2312 Charyn, Jerome. AMERICAN SCRAPBOOK. Viking, 1969. Story of life in the concentration camps for Japanese-Americans set up in California during the war.

2313 ________. THE FRANKLIN SCARE. Arbor House, 1977. The White House and Washington in 1944, when America expressed intense wartime patriotism. Eleanor Roosevelt is an active First Lady. Seeds of such troubles of the future as black rage and an imperial presidency are there, but as yet hard to discern.

2314 Chidester, Ann. NO LONGER FUGITIVE. Scribner, 1943.

Story of a draft dodger whose experiences give him the conviction he needs to take his part in the war effort.

2315 Clagett, John. THE SLOT. Crown, 1958. Story of a PT boat and its crew assigned to guard the busy channel between Guadalcanal and the Solomon Islands in World War II.

2316 Clarke, Arthur C. GLIDE PATH. Harcourt, 1963. Story of the early development of radar with American and British scientists and technicians stationed at an air base in Cornwall, England.

2317 Clavell, James. KING RAT. Little, 1962. Picture of the sordid life of American prisoners-of-war in a Japanese prison camp in Singapore.

2318 Cochrell, Boyd. THE BARREN BEACHES OF HELL. Holt, 1959. Story of a young marine private, through the invasions of Tarawa, Saipan, and Tinian, and occupation duty at Nagasaki, Japan.

2319 Coleman, William Lawrence. THE GOLDEN VANITY. Macmillan, 1962. Struggle for power aboard a cargo ship during the last stages of the war in the Pacific.

2320 Connell, Evan S. THE PATRIOT. Viking, 1960. Story of the training of a naval air cadet, of his life as a seaman, and of his postwar art studies at the University of Kansas.

2321 Cook, Fannie. MRS. PALMER'S HONEY. Doubleday, 1946. Story of the war work and labor-union activity of a lovable black girl in St. Louis.

2322 Cotler, Gordon. BOTTLETOP AFFAIR. Simon and Schuster, 1959. A humorous story of the search for a lone Japanese holdout on a small Pacific island during the war.

2323 Covert, Alice. THE ETERNAL MOUNTAIN. Doubleday, 1944. Romance in which a young man takes a job in a war plant and gets in shape for the army.

2324 Cozzens, James Gould. GUARD OF HONOR. Harcourt, 1948. Tribulations of the commanding officer of an air base in Florida.

2325 Crowley, Robert T. NOT SOLDIERS ALL. Doubleday, 1967. Story of medics under fire during the Italian campaign.

2326 Dailey, Janet. SILVER WINGS, SANTIAGO BLUE. Poseidon, 1984. Story of quasi-military Women's Air Force Service Pilots on stateside duty, flying missions that were often dangerous despite their noncombatant status.

2327 D'Angelo, Lou. WHAT THE ANCIENTS SAID. Doubleday, 1971. Life during World War II in a Sicilian neighborhood in New York where the elders evoked the culture and mores of their homeland.

2328 Daniels, Sally. THE INCONSTANT SEASON. Atheneum, 1962. A young girl recalls her childhood in western New York State during World War II.

2329 Davis, Clyde Brion. THE STARS INCLINE. Farrar, 1946. Career of a Denver newspaperman from the Spanish Civil War to the campaigns in Africa and Europe in World War II.

2330 ________. PLAYTIME IS OVER. Lippincott, 1949. Day-to-day life on a small Arkansas farm during the war.

2331 Davis, Paxton. TWO SOLDIERS. Simon and Schuster, 1956. Two novelettes showing the war in the China-Burma-India theater.

2332 Deighton, Len. GOODBYE MICKEY MOUSE. Knopf, 1982. United States Air Force pilots based in England, flying combat missions over Europe.

2333 De Pereda, Prudencio. WINDMILLS IN BROOKLYN. Atheneum, 1960. Story of a young boy growing up in the Spanish colony of Brooklyn during the World War II years.

2334 Dibner, Martin. THE DEEP SIX. Doubleday, 1953. Life aboard a navy cruiser during the war.

2335 Dixon, Clarice M. THE DEVIL AND THE DEEP. Scribner, 1944. Stories of life in the U.S. Merchant Marine in 1941-1942.

2336 Dodson, Kenneth. AWAY ALL BOATS. Little, 1954. Amphibious warfare in the Pacific from the campaigns in the Gilbert Islands to Okinawa.

2337 ________. STRANGER TO THE SHORE. Little, 1956. Adventurous story centered around a U.S. Merchant Marine sailor and a German raider in the waters off Chile in 1942.

2338 Dunlap, Katharine. ONCE THERE WAS A VILLAGE. Morrow, 1941. Story of Americans involved in war mobilization in a French village at the beginning of the war.

2339 Eastlake, William. CASTLE KEEP. Simon and Schuster, 1965. Story of a group of American soldiers and their relations with the aristocratic owners of the castle in which they are quartered in Germany.

2340 Eddy, Roger. BEST BY FAR. Doubleday, 1966. Reminiscences of World War II veterans at a reunion on the site of a battlefield in Italy.

2341 Edmiston, James. HOME AGAIN. Doubleday, 1955. Story of Japanese-Americans in California and their life in relocation camps during the war.

2342 Ellison, James Whitifield. THE FREEST MAN ON EARTH. Doubleday, 1958. Story of what happens when a conscientious objector refuses to answer a call by the draft board.

2343 Estes, Winston M. HOMEFRONT. Lippincott, 1976. Busy routines of the members of the Holley family, left at home in small-town Georgia, as they conduct first-aid classes, lead War Bond drives, practice drills for possible air raids, and entertain the boys in uniform.

2344 Eyster, Warren. FAR FROM THE CUSTOMARY SKIES. Random, 1953. Life cycle of an American destroyer from training cruise through action at Guadalcanal and New Guinea to its sinking in a battle.

2345 Facos, James. THE SILVER LADY. Atheneum, 1972. Two Americans with very different backgrounds develop a real friendship under pressure as they fly together on bombing raids over Germany.

2346 Falstein, Louis. FACE OF A HERO. Harcourt, 1950. Story of hate, fear, and boredom among the men who flew American bombers based in Italy.

2347 Fast, Howard. THE WINSTON AFFAIR. Crown, 1959. Story of the trial of an American soldier for the killing of a British soldier in the Far East.

2348 Fleming, Berry. COLONEL EFFINGHAM'S RAID. Duell, 1943. Story of a retired army man and a young newspaperman fighting local corrupt politics in a Georgia town, until the reporter joins the National Guard on the way to war.

2349 ________. THE LIGHTWOOD TREE. Lippincott, 1947. A Georgia teacher, exempt from the draft, works to defend liberty at home when local politicians use undemocratic action in arresting a student.

2350 Forester, C. S. THE GOOD SHEPHERD. Little, 1955. Tale of four U.S. Navy ships escorting a merchant-marine convoy from America to England, in the face of repeated German submarine attacks.

2351 Fosburgh, Hugh. VIEW FROM THE AIR. Scribner, 1953. Story of the crew of a bomber on forty missions over Truk in the South Pacific.

2352 Frizell, Bernard. TEN DAYS IN AUGUST. Simon and Schuster, 1956. A romance set against the German occupation of Paris, as the underground Resistance movement prepares for the advancing Allies.

2353 Frye, Pearl. THE NARROW BRIDGE. Little, 1947. Story of the tension and antagonism in Honolulu after the attack on Pearl Harbor.

2354 Gabriel, Gilbert Wolf. I GOT A COUNTRY. Doubleday, 1944. Story of three U.S. Army soldiers stationed in Alaska.

2355 Gaffney, Robert. A WORLD OF GOOD. Dial, 1970. Story points up the terrible effects of the inherent brutality of war on the young, still immature American G.I.'s.

2356 Gallico, Paul. THE LONELY. Knopf, 1949. A young U.S. flyer must decide between an English girl and his girl back home.

2357 Garth, David. BERMUDA CALLING. Putnam, 1944. Spy story of World War II.

2358 ________. WATCH ON THE BRIDGE. Putnam, 1959. The capture of the Remagen Bridge over the Rhine in March, 1945, is the central element in a love story of an American soldier and a German girl.

2359 Gilpatric, Guy. ACTION IN THE NORTH ATLANTIC. Dutton, 1943. Action with the U.S. Merchant Marine on the run to Murmansk.

2360 Gilroy, Frank Daniel. PRIVATE. Harcourt, 1970. Illustrated with snapshot images, the story tells of a young man's initiation, often painful, into the realities of war.

2361 Gionannitti, Len. THE PRISONERS OF COMBINE D. Holt, 1957. Story of six American airmen in a German prison camp in 1944-45.

2362 Glaspell, Susan. JUDD RANKIN'S DAUGHTER. Lippincott, 1945. Story of wartime family life; a war-shocked son; isolationist editor in Iowa.

2363 Goertz, Arthemise. DREAM OF JUJI. McGraw, 1958. Story of a group of Americans interned in Japan at the outbreak of the war.

2364 Goethals, Thomas. CHAINS OF COMMAND. Random, 1955. Strategists at the rear headquarters of a U.S. Army unit ignore warnings of a German offensive shortly before the Battle of the Bulge.

2365 Goldhurst, Richard. THE CHANCES WE TAKE. Richard W. Baron, 1970. Fictional characters developed around a real incident, the tragic 1944 Ringling Brothers and Barnum and Bailey circus fire in Hartford, Connecticut.

2366 Goodman, Mitchell. THE END OF IT. Horizon, 1961. Story of a field artillery unit of the Fifth Army in Italy.

2367 Guthrie, A. B. THE LAST VALLEY. Houghton, 1975. The fifth of the author's Northwestern chronicles; tells of the changing community of Arfive, Montana from the late 1930's through World War II, as observed by the local newspaper editor.

2368 Gwaltney, Francis Irby. THE DAY THE CENTURY ENDED. Rinehart, 1955. Story of the brutality of the war in the Philippines which ended on the day the atom bomb was dropped at Hiroshima.

2369 Habe, Hans (pseud.). THE MISSION. Coward, 1966. Story of the conference of 32 nations at Evian-les-Bains on Lake Geneva called by President Roosevelt to discuss the rescue of Jews in Nazi Germany.

2370 Haines, William Wister. COMMAND DECISION. Little, 1947. The air war over Europe as seen by the commanding officer of a bomber division based in England.

2371 Hall, James Norman. LOST ISLAND. Little, 1944. Pictures the destruction of the natives' way of life when an army of American experts prepare to build an air base on a small Pacific island.

2372 Hanson, Robert P. A GLIMPSE OF CANAAN. Morrow, 1966. A veteran returns home to Vermont after his wife leaves him. He reminisces about his war experiences and about his family background, through three generations in Vermont.

2373 Hardy, William M. U.S.S. MUDSKIPPER. Dodd, 1967. A U.S. submarine crew off the coast of Japan plan a raid to destroy a freight train which runs along the coast.

2374 ________. THE SHIP THEY CALLED THE FAT LADY. Dodd, 1969. Story of the crew of the fictional U.S.S. Rigel, battling the Japanese from December 8, 1941 to the fall of Corregidor.

2375 Hawkins, John and Ward Hawkins. THE PILEBUCK. Dutton, 1943. Indictment of labor-union racketeers and slackers in a wartime shipyard in the Northwest where an FBI spy is sent to investigate sabotage.

2376 Haydn, Hiram. MANHATTAN FURLOUGH. Bobbs, 1945. Story of a young soldier, depressed over the death of a friend in training camp, on leave in New York City.

2377 Hayes, Alfred. GIRL ON THE VIA FLAMINIA. Harper, 1949. The last year of the war in Italy; love affair between an American G.I. and an Italian girl.

2378 Heggen, Thomas. MISTER ROBERTS. Houghton, 1946. Story of life on a cargo ship in the Pacific and the reaction of the crew to the dullness of their duty.

2379 Heller, Joseph. CATCH-22. Simon & Schuster, 1961. A comical novel about a young bombardier stationed in Italy and his efforts to avoid flying missions.

2380 Hemingway, Leicester. THE SOUND OF THE TRUMPET. Holt, 1953. Two American cameramen record the invasion on the Normandy beaches on D-Day.

2381 Herber, William. TOMORROW TO LIVE. Coward, 1958. Set in Hawaii and Saipan in 1944; story of the U.S. Marines engaged in island fighting.

2382 Hersey, John. THE WAR LOVER. Knopf, 1959. Life of an American Flying Fortress crew on missions and on a bomber base in England.

2383 Heyliger, William. HOME IS A ONE-WAY STREET. Westminster, 1945. Story of a wounded soldier and his problems in readjusting to his wife, job, and family.

2384 Heym, Stefan. THE CRUSADERS. Little, 1948. Follows an American division from the Normandy invasion through France, Germany, the liberation of Paris, the Battle of the Bulge, and the occupation of the Ruhr.

2385 Hicks, Granville. BEHOLD TROUBLE. Macmillan, 1944. Story of a conscientious objector and the consequences of his stand against the draft board.

2386 Higginbotham, Robert E. WINE FOR MY BROTHERS. Rinehart, 1946. Story of the trip of an oil tanker from Texas to New York in January 1942.

2387 Hillyer, Laurie. TIME REMEMBERED. Macmillan, 1945. Story of normal life disrupted by the war when a son is caught in the attack on Pearl Harbor; the mother represents pacifist sentiment.

2388 Hilton, James. THE STORY OF DR. WASSELL. Little, 1943. Fictionized account of the heroic efforts of Dr. Corydon Wassell to rescue the wounded men from the

H. M. S. Marblehead and lead them from Java to Australia in 1942.

2389 ________. NOTHING SO STRANGE. Little, 1947. Story of a young American scientist viewing the war in Europe and England.

2390 Hoffman, William. THE TRUMPET UNBLOWN. Doubleday, 1955. Experiences of an American soldier in a field hospital during the Battle of the Bulge.

2391 ________. YANCEY'S WAR. Doubleday, 1966. A sharp operator profits from his deals in the service until he dies a hero's death.

2392 Homewood, Harry. SILENT SEA. McGraw, 1981. A realistic picture of submarine forces fighting in the Pacific. They had to overcome the increased danger caused by malfunctioning torpedoes in the first years of the war.

2393 ________. O GOD OF BATTLES. Morrow, 1983. Two brothers from Chicago compete for navy honors in the Pacific. One is a submariner, the other a fighter pilot. The battle scenes are gripping in their realism.

2394 Hough, Henry Beetle. ROOSTER CROW IN TOWN. Appleton, 1945. A Maine coastal town during 1942-43 and the effect on the lives of the people of the fear of invasion, civil defense dimouts, amphibious forces practicing in the neighborhood, price control, rationing, and general war fever.

2395 Howard, Clark. THE DOOMSDAY SQUAD. Weybright and Talley, 1970. Pacific campaign. Six men volunteer for a dangerous assignment as decoys so the Americans can make a hit-and-run strike against a strategic Japanese-occupied island.

2396 Howe, George. CALL IT TREASON. Viking, 1949. Story of the training and action of three German prisoners dropped behind German lines as a U.S. Army intelligence team.

2397 Hueston, Ethel. MOTHER WENT MAD ON MONDAY. Bobbs, 1944. Family and home life in a small town in New York during the war; son reported missing; teenaged daughter has romance with an army flier.

2398 Hunt, Howard. EAST OF FAREWELL. Knopf, 1942. Story of a destroyer on convoy duty in the Atlantic.

2399 ________. LIMIT OF DARKNESS. Random, 1944. Story of 24 hours in the lives of a group of American fliers based on Guadalcanal.

2400 Jessey, Cornelia. TEACH THE ANGRY SPIRIT. Crown, 1949. Life in the Mexican quarter of Los Angeles during the war.

2401 Jonas, Carl. BEACHHEAD ON THE WIND. Little, 1945. Picture of cleanup operations after a landing on a beachhead in the Aleutian Islands.

2402 Jones, James. FROM HERE TO ETERNITY. Scribner, 1951. Pre-Pearl Harbor army life in Hawaii, ending with the Japanese attack.

2403 _______. THE PISTOL. Scribner, 1958. Follows the actions of a soldier who finds a pistol during the attack on Pearl Harbor through the plots to take it from him.

2404 _______. THE THIN RED LINE. Scribner, 1962. Story of the campaign and battle to recapture Guadalcanal in 1942-43.

2405 _______. WHISTLE. Delacorte, 1978. Completes a wartime trilogy with From Here to Eternity and The Thin Red Line. Story concerns the difficulties of three wounded survivors of the battle for Guadacanal as they are returned to stateside hospitals.

2406 Jones, Nard. THE ISLAND. Sloane, 1948. Pictures the conditions and problems typical of American communities during the war in the story of three men in Seattle.

2407 Kadish, M. R. POINT OF HONOR. Random, 1951. Story of an American artillery battalion in the Italian campaign.

2408 Kantor, MacKinlay. HAPPY LAND. Coward, 1943. A father saddened by news of his son's death reviews the boy's life.

2409 _______. GLORY FOR ME. Coward, 1945. Story in verse form of three veterans with bitter war memories who find themselves misfits in their home town.

2410 Kata, Elizabeth. SOMEONE WILL CONQUER THEM. St. Martin's, 1962. American girl married to a Japanese in Tokyo in 1944 hides an American airman, shot down in a bombing raid; life in wartime and occupation in Japan.

2411 Kay, Terry. THE YEAR THE LIGHTS CAME ON. Houghton, 1976. Electricity is brought to the poor side of a Georgia hamlet in the early 1940's. The lights symbolize blurring of old social distinctions in the changing wartime society. The protagonist in the story is a young boy living on the wrong side of the highway.

2412 Keefe, Frederick L. THE INVESTIGATING OFFICER.

Delacorte, 1966. Suspenseful story of the inquest into the killing of two German prisoners of war by an American officer.

2413 Kehoe, Karon. CITY IN THE SUN. Dodd, 1946. Story of a Japanese-American family in California and in a relocation camp during the war.

2414 Keith, Agnes Newton. BELOVED EXILES. Little, 1972. An American woman, married to a British colonial official, lives in Borneo from the 1930's through the Japanese occupation during World War II. Contrasts the American and British attitudes to colonialism.

2415 Kelly, Jack. THE UNEXPECTED PEACE. Gambit, 1969. Story of an army infantry unit in the Philippines during the war and in Japan as part of the occupation forces.

2416 Kendrick, Baynard H. LIGHTS OUT. Morrow, 1945. Reaction of a blinded soldier to his rehabilitation to daily routine living, and to his discovery that two of his new friends are a Negro and a Jew.

2417 Keyes, Frances Parkinson. ALSO THE HILLS. Messner, 1943. Story of the war effort in a New Hampshire village.

2418 Killens, John Oliver. AND THEN WE HEARD THE THUNDER. Knopf, 1963. A Negro from New York City encounters racial discrimination in the army; story leads up to a bloody race riot in Australia.

2419 Klaas, Joe. MAYBE I'M DEAD. Macmillan, 1955. Story of the forced march of 10,000 prisoners-of-war from a German prison camp, just before the liberation in 1945.

2420 Knowles, John. A SEPARATE PEACE. Macmillan, 1959. Story of life at a New Hampshire boarding school in 1942, showing the restlessness caused by the war.

2421 Kolb, Avery. JIGGER WITCHET'S WAR. Simon and Schuster, 1959. Humorous story of a black soldier in England and behind the German lines in France in World War II.

2422 Kubeck, James. THE CALENDAR EPIC. Putnam, 1956. Life aboard a U.S. Merchant Marine ship in World War II; emphasis on amorous adventures during shore leave.

2423 Lamott, Kenneth. THE STOCKADE. Little, 1952. Pictures the inhuman treatment of 5,000 Okinawans and Koreans in an American prison camp on a Pacific island near the end of the war.

2424 Landon, Joseph. ANGLE OF ATTACK. Doubleday, 1952.

Story of air warfare and the effects of an unethical act on the crew of a bomber based in Italy.

2425 Lasswell, Mary. HIGH TIME. Houghton, 1944. Three beer-drinking, warmhearted old ladies contribute to the war effort.

2426 Lawrence, Josephine. THERE IS TODAY. Little, 1942. A story of the wartime home front representing typical types; the young couple who marry in spite of the draft, the glory-seeking volunteer worker, and the middle-aged patriotic veteran.

2427 ______. A TOWER OF STEEL. Little, 1943. Story of women in wartime, represented by four young women who work in a law office.

2428 Lay, Beirne and Sy Bartlett. TWELVE O'CLOCK HIGH. Harper, 1948. Story of a demoralized bomber group based in England in 1942; pictures the strain and tension of the war in the air.

2429 Leckie, Robert. ORDAINED. Doubleday, 1969. Story of a Catholic priest, ordained in 1936, who serves as an army Chaplain in the Pacific theater.

2430 Leeming, John. IT ALWAYS RAINS IN ROME. Farrar, 1961. A light-hearted tale revolving around the question of whether or not to destroy an ancient bridge in Italy.

2431 Leffland, Ella. RUMORS OF PEACE. Harper, 1979. A young girl's reaction to the war, from Pearl Harbor which is attacked when she is a junior-high student in a small northern California town, to the bombing of Hiroshima.

2432 Leggett, John. WHO TOOK THE GOLD AWAY. Random, 1969. Story of two Yale roommates from college days in 1938 through the war and to success and failure in the electronics industry.

2433 Leonard, George. SHOULDER THE SKY. McDowell, 1959. Story of two young flight instructors assigned to a Georgia base instead of being sent into combat duty in 1944; picture of the training of bomber pilots.

2434 Lewisohn, Ludwig. BREATHE UPON THESE. Bobbs, 1944. Story of a typical American family shocked into awareness of the world by the experiences of a German-refugee scientist.

2435 Long, Margaret. LOUISVILLE SATURDAY. Random, 1950. Story of eleven girls and the crises they meet one Saturday night in Louisville, Kentucky, in 1942.

2436 Loomis, Edward. END OF A WAR. Ballantine, 1957. Follows an infantry man, from training in France through the Belgian offensive in the winter of 1944 and the occupation of Germany.

2437 MacCuish, David. DO NOT GO GENTLE. Doubleday, 1960. Story of a young man who grows up in a Montana mining town; joins the Marine Corps, and, after boot camp, survives the heavy fighting on Guadalcanal.

2438 McGivern, William P. SOLDIERS OF '44. Arbor House, 1979. GI's of a gun section are trapped on a snowy mountain in the Ardennes by a surprise German attack. Cut off from their headquarters, they must struggle to survive.

2439 Mackay, Margaret. FOR ALL MEN BORN. John Day, 1943. Story of life at Pearl Harbor on the day of the Japanese attack.

2440 McLaughlin, Robert. THE SIDE OF THE ANGELS. Knopf, 1947. The reactions of two brothers to their army experiences in the Mediterranean area.

2441 MacLeish, Archibald and Robert De San Marzano. INFERNAL MACHINE. Houghton, 1947. Satire of official Washington during the war.

2442 McMahon, Thomas. PRINCIPLES OF AMERICAN NUCLEAR CHEMISTRY. Little, 1970. The son of an atomic scientist accompanies his father to Oak Ridge and Los Alamos. Then, those involved thought that their invention would make war impossible, but the story tells of the inevitable end of that confidence.

2443 Mailer, Norman. THE NAKED AND THE DEAD. Rinehart, 1948. Picture of amphibious assault and jungle fighting in the capture of a Japanese-held island in the Pacific.

2444 Mandel, George. THE WAX BOOM. Random, 1962. Story of an American platoon in the forefront of the December, 1944 offensive against Germany.

2445 Mandel, Paul, and Sheila Mandel. THE BLACK SHIP. Random, 1969. An American PT-boat crew assigned to a British base on the North Sea survive a sinking and join the Dutch underground.

2446 Marmur, Jacland. ANDROMEDA. Holt, 1947. An American freighter, one of the last to leave Singapore before the Japanese arrive, carries a young romantic girl and an American who turns out to be a Japanese agent.

2447 Marquand, J. P. SO LITTLE TIME. Little, 1943. Satire

of the contemporary scene of theatrical and literary life centering around a World War I veteran whose son is nearing draft age.

2448 _______. REPENT IN HASTE. Little, 1945. Story of the marital problems of a flier in the Pacific.

2449 Master, Dexter. THE ACCIDENT. Knopf, 1955. Novel about the making and using of the atomic bomb, told during the eight days it takes a young atomic scientist to die from exposure to radiation; setting is Los Alamos in 1946.

2450 Matheson, Richard. THE BEARDLESS WARRIORS. Little, 1960. Story of the battle experiences of a squad of U.S. riflemen made up chiefly of eighteen-year-old replacements; set in Germany in December, 1944.

2451 Matthiessen, Peter. RADITZER. Viking, 1961. Character study of two noncombatant sailors, set in Honolulu during World War II.

2452 Mayerson, Evelyn W. NO ENEMY BUT TIME. Doubleday, 1983. Set in wartime Miami. The protagonists are children of workers at the Hotel Flamingo. The resort hotels have been commandeered for barracks, flotsam from torpedoed ships appear on the beaches, and schools give lessons in bomb dousing, but the times are remembered with nostalgia.

2453 Mayo, Eleanor R. TURN HOME. Morrow, 1945. Story of a veteran trying to find a place in his home town.

2454 Merrick, Gordon. THE STRUMPET WIND. Morrow, 1947. Story of an American intelligence officer working with the French underground.

2455 Miller, Dallas. FATHERS AND DREAMERS. Doubleday, 1966. Life in a small town near Cleveland, Ohio in 1943 reflects the feeling of the period; F.D.R., ration books, slang, and the things boys talked about as they reached maturity.

2456 Miller, Merle. ISLAND 49. Crowell, 1945. Picture of the home background and the action of a group of men attacking a coral atoll in the Pacific.

2457 Moon, Bucklin. THE DARKER BROTHER. Doubleday, 1943. Story of a Southern Negro facing Northern intolerance; Pearl Harbor makes him aware of his country, and he goes willingly to fight for it.

2458 Morris, Terry. NO HIDING PLACE. Knopf, 1945. Story of the problems faced by wives who follow their husbands in the army.

2459 Mydans, Shelley. THE OPEN CITY. Doubleday, 1945. Picture of life in Santo Tomas prison camp in Manila, after the Japanese invaded the Philippines.

2460 Myrer, Anton. THE BIG WAR. Appleton, 1957. Story of the U.S. Marines in action in the Pacific, and in love on the home front.

2461 Newhafer, Richard L. THE LAST TALLYHOO. Putnam, 1964. Story of five U.S. Navy pilots and their exploits in the war.

2462 Nichols, John Tredwell. THE WIZARD OF LONELINESS. Putnam, 1966. Life of a lonely eleven-year-old boy spending the last year of the war with his grandparents in a small Vermont town.

2463 Nordhoff, Charles and Norman Hall. THE HIGH BARBAREE. Little, 1945. Iowa farm-boy pilot shot down in the Pacific finds his dream island, but it is only in death that he has found his dream.

2464 Ogilvie, Elisabeth. STORM TIDE. Crowell, 1945. Life of lobster fishermen on an island off the Maine coast; the coming of war brings the submarine menace. Sequel to <u>High Tide at Noon</u>.

2465 ________. EBBING TIDE. Crowell, 1947. Bennett's Island off the coast of Maine during the war. Sequel to <u>Storm Tide</u> (above).

2466 O'Rourke, Frank. 'E' COMPANY. Simon and Schuster, 1945. Formation, training, and action of an infantry company from December 17, 1941 to first action in Africa a year later.

2467 Patterson, Mary. THE IRON COUNTRY. Houghton, 1965. A young couple matures in the Minnesota mining country during World War II.

2468 Paul, Louis. THIS IS MY BROTHER. Crown, 1943. Story of five U.S. soldiers, their thoughts and feelings, as they await death as spies after capture by the Japanese.

2469 Perrin, Ursula. GHOSTS. Knopf, 1967. Memories of life in a small mill town in upstate New York in 1945.

2470 Plagemann, Bentz. THE STEEL COCOON. Viking, 1958. Story of a ship and its crew at war in the Pacific.

2471 Popkin, Zelda. THE JOURNEY HOME. Lippincott, 1945. A train wreck forces a combat veteran to reconsider his ideas about the civilians with whom he had been traveling.

2472 Powell, Richard. THE SOLDIER. Scribner, 1960. Story of the heroic evacuation of U.S. forces from a small unstrategic island in the Pacific.

2473 Pratt, Rex. YOU TELL MY SON. Random, 1958. Story of the annihilation of a Regular Army platoon during a patrol action in the South Pacific and of the survivors' efforts to whip the inexperienced Guard unit, to which they were assigned, into shape for the coming battle.

2474 Pratt, Theodore. MR. WINKLE GOES TO WAR. Duell, 1943. Humorous story of a hen-picked husband who is drafted and returns home a hero.

2475 Raucher, Herman. SUMMER OF '42. Putnam, 1971. Nostalgic memories of a summer during World War II spent on an island off the New England coast, where romance bloomed for the adolescent hero and a young war widow.

2476 Reed, Kit. AT WAR AS CHILDREN. Farrar, 1964. Picture of the daily life and routine of three children whose fathers are away at war in the submarine service.

2477 Ripperger, Henrietta. 112 ELM STREET. Putnam, 1943. Story of family life on the home front; father works in a war plant, one son is in the army, and the family is keeping a young English boy for the duration.

2478 Robertson, Don. THE GREATEST THING SINCE SLICED BREAD. Putnam, 1965. Authentic feeling of the period, based on the gas explosion in Cleveland, Ohio in 1944; nostalgic references to sports, music, movies. Followed by <u>The Sum and Total of Now</u> (Turbulent Years).

2479 Robinson, Wayne. BARBARA. Doubleday, 1962. Follows the fortunes of a U.S. Army tank battalion from the landing in Normandy to the fall of Berlin.

2480 Rosenhaupt, Hans. THE TRUE DECEIVERS. Dodd, 1954. Story of a German-born intelligence officer in the American army, assigned the job of interrogation German prisoners of war.

2481 Ross, James E. THE DEAD ARE MINE. McKay, 1963. The lone survivor of a squad decimated in the Anzio beachhead refuses further combat duty and is assigned to a graves registration unit.

2482 Routsong, Alma. A GRADUAL JOY. Houghton, 1953. Story of a World War II veteran and his ex-Wave wife, and of their life in a trailer camp while attending Michigan State College.

2483 Rubinstein, S. Leonard. THE BATTLE DONE. Morrow, 1954. Prisoners, guards, and camp personnel in a prisoner-of-war camp in South Carolina shortly after the war.

2484 Rylee, Robert. THE RING AND THE CROSS. Knopf, 1947. Racial philosophies of democracy and fascism in a Texas town during World War II.

2485 Santos, Bienvenido. SCENT OF APPLES. University of Washington Press, 1980. Collection of short stories about immigrant Filipino men in the United States, usually alone, and feeling displaced in the unfamiliar society.

2486 Sapieha, Virgilia Peterson. BEYOND THIS SHORE. Lippincott, 1942. Story of an American girl married to a Polish count, who, after fleeing the Germans in Austria and Poland, finds Americans indifferent to the Nazi threat.

2487 Saroyan, William. THE HUMAN COMEDY. Harcourt, 1943. Story of family life in wartime; one son away in the army and the young ones working at odd jobs.

2488 Saxton, Alexander. BRIGHT WEB IN THE DARKNESS. St. Martin's, 1958. Story of the San Francisco shipyards, centering around the labor issues involving Negroes in war work.

2489 Searls, Hank. THE HERO SHIP. World, 1969. Story centers around an act of cowardice on a U.S. Navy aircraft carrier in the final days of the war against Japan; scenes of navy flight training, of Pearl Harbor on December 7, 1941, and the final destruction of the ship; based on the actual loss of the U.S.S. Franklin.

2490 Shapiro, Lionel. SIXTH OF JUNE. Doubleday, 1955. An American paratrooper and an English commander take part in the D-Day invasion of Normandy.

2491 Shaw, Charles. HEAVEN KNOWS, MR. ALLISON. Crown, 1952. After the fall of Bataan, a nun and a marine are marooned on an island behind Japanese lines.

2492 Shaw, Irwin. THE YOUNG LIONS. Random, 1948. Two Americans and a German seen in their prewar life and in episodes of army training and on war duty.

2493 Sheean, Vincent. A CERTAIN RICH MAN. Random, 1947. Story of the wartime experiences, as a bomber pilot, of a rich man and of its effect on his home life and social responsibility after the war.

2494 Sinclair, Upton. DRAGON HARVEST. Viking, 1945. Lanny

Budd in Europe as the secret agent of President Roosevelt, meets Hitler and Chamberlain, and takes part in the evacuation of Dunkirk. Sequel to Presidential Agent (The Thirties).

2495 ______. A WORLD TO WIN. Viking, 1946. As agent of President Roosevelt, Lanny Budd reports on German plans to attack Russia, is tutored by Einstein for a mission to learn about German atomic-energy research, and lands in Hong Kong at the outbreak of the war. Covers the years 1940-1942. Sequel to Dragon Harvest.

2496 ______. PRESIDENTIAL MISSION. Viking, 1947. Lanny Budd acts as Roosevelt's secret agent in Africa, before the American invasion, and later, in Germany. Sequel to A World to Win.

2497 ______. ONE CLEAR CALL. Viking, 1948. Lanny Budd, as Roosevelt's secret agent, operates in Italy, France, Spain, and Germany, from the invasion of Sicily to the invasion of France; story ends with Roosevelt's reelection in 1944. Sequel to Presidential Mission.

2498 ______. O SHEPHERD, SPEAK! Viking, 1949. Lanny Budd takes part in the Nuremberg war trials in 1946, acts as President Truman's representative in Moscow, and uses his trust fund to promote world peace. Sequel to One Clear Call.

2499 Sire, Glen. THE DEATHMAKERS. Simon and Schuster, 1960. Story of war and death during General Patton's armored battalion push into Bavaria in the last days of the war.

2500 Skidmore, Hubert Douglas. VALLEY OF THE SKY. Houghton, 1944. Story of the experiences of a youthful bomber crew in the South Pacific.

2501 Slaughter, Frank G. A TOUCH OF GLORY. Doubleday, 1945. Army medical officer returns home to find an industrial boom town; forms group-medicine plan in opposition to a compensation racket.

2502 ______. SURGEON, U.S.A. Doubleday, 1966. Romantic story about a heart surgeon who volunteers after Pearl Harbor and serves in the army during World War II.

2503 Slavitt, David R. RINGER. Dutton, 1982. Plot inspired by historical fact. In 1942 a submarine landed German saboteurs on Long Island. This is the embroidered story of their pursuit and capture by the F.B.I.

2504 Slote, Alfred. STRANGERS AND COMRADES. Simon and

Schuster, 1964. Pictures various aspects of life on the homefront and in the service from Pearl Harbor to the end of the war.

2505 Smith, William Dale. NAKED IN DECEMBER. Bobbs, 1968. Events in the lives of three families, with a background of the period leading up to the American entry into the war.

2506 Sparks, Dorothy Elizabeth. NOTHING AS BEFORE. Harper, 1944. Isolationist sympathies in a small Illinois town, shattered by the attack on Pearl Harbor.

2507 Starbird, Kaye. THE LION IN THE LEI SHOP. Harcourt, 1970. Differing perceptions of the war on the part of a military wife and her young daughter as they see Pearl Harbor bombed, are evacuated to the States on a troopship, and wait out the war in New England.

2508 Statham, Leon. WELCOME, DARKNESS. Crowell, 1950. Guerrilla warfare in the Philippines.

2509 Stein, Gertrude. BREWSIE AND WILLIE. Random, 1946. Postwar responsibilities of young Americans brought out in the form of bull sessions among a group of soldiers in France after the armistice.

2510 Stephens, Edward. ROMAN JOY. Doubleday, 1965. Story of a jazz drummer and draft-dodger in the music and big-band business during the war.

2511 Stevens, William. THE GUNNER. Atheneum, 1968. Story of the adventures of a young aerial gunner with the Fifteenth Air Force in Italy in 1944, who goes A. W. O. L. after seeing too much action.

2512 Stong, Philip. ONE DESTINY. Reynal, 1942. Story of a rural Iowa community awakening to world events; farmer's son gives up his medical education to become a pilot.

2513 Swarthout, Glendon. THE EAGLE AND THE IRON CROSS. New American Library, 1966. Story of two German prisoners-of-war who escape from an Arizona prison camp and join an Indian tribe on the reservation.

2514 Syers, William Edward. THE SEVEN. Duell, 1960. Story of the action of a U.S. Navy submarine-chaser off the coast of Central America and in the Pacific.

2515 Taylor, Ward. ROLL BACK THE SKY. Holt, 1956. Story of a member of a B-29 bombing crew based on Saipan. Tense picture of low-level bombing missions over Japan.

2516 Thatcher, Russell. THE CAPTAIN. Macmillan, 1951.

Pressures and frustrations of the commander of a landing craft in the Pacific.

2517 Tillett, Dorothy. ANGRY DUST. Doubleday, 1946. Story of conflict between management and labor in a metal-working plant in New York, where the C. I. O. is trying to strengthen its position.

2518 Tregaskis, Richard. STRONGER THAN FEAR. Random, 1945. Picture of street-fighting tactics in the story of an army patrol clearing out Nazi snipers.

2519 Uris, Leon. BATTLE CRY. Putnam, 1953. Life among the U.S. Marines at Guadalcanal, Tarawa, and Saipan.

2520 Van de Water, Frederic. THE SOONER TO SLEEP. Duell, 1946. Story of women without men in a Vermont town during the war.

2521 Van Praag, Van. DAY WITHOUT END. Sloane, 1949. Story of an exhausted platoon in the hedgerows of Normandy.

2522 Wakefield, Dan. UNDER THE APPLE TREE. Delacorte, 1982. An eleven year old promises to keep an eye on his soldier-brother's girlfriend. He grows up as the war proceeds, and his story illustrates the mores of a small Midwestern town in a more innocent era.

2523 Wallace, Francis. EXPLOSION. Morrow, 1943. Story of the heroism of men trapped in a mine explosion and of retribution when the Nazi agent responsible for the explosion is identified.

2524 Warrick, LaMar. YESTERDAY'S CHILDREN. Crowell, 1943. Story of a family with a draft-age son in college as the war approaches; set in a suburb of Chicago.

2525 Weismiller, Edward. THE SERPENT SLEEPING. Putnam, 1962. Activities of an American intelligence unit stationed in Cherbourg, France in late 1944; story involves action with German spies and French collaborators.

2526 Wendt, Lloyd. A BRIGHT TOMORROW. Bobbs, 1945. Pacifist sentiment in rural South Dakota in 1940-1941.

2527 Wernick, Robert. THE FREEBOOTERS. Scribner, 1949. Adventures of three soldiers in an American unit in North Africa and Italy.

2528 Westheimer, David. SONG OF THE YOUNG SENTRY. Little, 1968. Story of two American airmen as prisoners of war, after being shot down over Italy in 1942.

2529 Wharton, William. MIDNIGHT CLEAR. Knopf, 1982. A clerical error has sent into combat a group of very young, very smart men intended as a special reserve. Christmas Eve, 1944 finds them in an abandoned chateau, an observation post in the Ardennes.

2530 White, Theodore. THE MOUNTAIN ROAD. Sloane, 1958. Story of an American demolition squad assigned to delay a Japanese advance in China in 1944.

2531 Wilder, Margaret. SINCE YOU WENT AWAY. Whittlesey, 1943. Letters from a wife to her soldier-husband, telling of life on the home front.

2532 Wilhelm, Gale. THE TIME BETWEEN. Morrow, 1942. Story of the ten days' leave of a heroic American flyer, after hospitalization, before he returns to the war.

2533 Williams, George. THE BLIND BULL. Abelard, 1952. An American major in a Saipan hospital reviews his past life and his battle experiences.

2534 Williams, Thomas. WHIPPLE'S CASTLE. Random, 1969. Home life in a small town in New Hampshire in the 1940's.

2535 Williams, Wirt. THE ENEMY. Houghton, 1951. Story of the tedium and detail of life aboard a warship during wartime.

2536 Wouk, Herman. THE CAINE MUTINY. Doubleday, 1951. Life aboard a minesweeper in the Pacific under a tyrannical skipper.

2537 ________. WAR AND REMEMBRANCE. Little, 1978. Sequel to Winds of War. The Henry family is enveloped by the war. Pug and his wife, apart for long periods, almost end their marriage. Their sons are both in navy combat, while their Jewish daughter-in-law tries to flee the Nazis in Europe.

2538 Wylie, James. THE HOMESTEAD GRAYS. Putnam, 1977. A squadron of black fighter pilots battle valiantly against the Germans; they must also battle the racism of their allied colleagues.

2539 Yates, Richard. A SPECIAL PROVIDENCE. Knopf, 1969. Story of an eighteen-year-old soldier reaching maturity in training camp and in action in Belgium.

THE TENSE YEARS--1945 TO 1959

2540 Abbey, Edward. FIRE ON THE MOUNTAINS. Dial, 1962. Story of a New Mexico rancher and his struggles to prevent government confiscation of his land to expand the White Sands Proving Grounds.

2541 Albrand, Martha. NIGHTMARE IN COPENHAGEN. Random, 1954. An American scientist attempts to thwart the Russians from getting a secret explosive recovered from a German submarine sunk off Denmark in World War II.

2542 Aldridge, James. GOODBYE UN-AMERICA. Little, 1979. In 1941 two men are working for Time magazine. One later falsely accuses the other of working for the Communist Party. The McCarthyism that led to the accusation is shown to have wrecked both lives.

2543 Anania, Michael. RED MENACE. Thunder's Mouth Press, 1984. A teenager grows up in Omaha when fear of communism was rampant. This novel pokes fun at the universal concern and recreates the manners, cars, and clothes of the young.

2544 Anders, Curtis. THE PRICE OF COURAGE. Sagamore Press, 1957. Realistic battle scenes as experienced by an infantry company in the Korean War.

2545 Anderson, Thomas. YOUR OWN BELOVED SONS. Random, 1956. Authentic setting and military detail revolving around a dangerous mission by six volunteers in the Korean War.

2546 Annixter, Jane and Paul. PEACE COMES TO CASTLE OAK. Longmans, 1961. Story of family life in the Carolina and Georgia coastal lowlands, complicated by the return of the eldest son from the Korean War and the encroachment of hill people in the area.

2547 Baker, Elliot. AND WE WERE YOUNG. Times Books, 1979. Story of three young ex-servicemen, home again in an America being reshaped by the air of political menace, and the new medium of television.

2548 Barbeau, Clayton. THE IKON. Coward, 1961. Story of a young American soldier who undergoes a religious conversion during the Korean War.

2549 Bartholomew, Cecilia. THE RISK. Doubleday, 1958. Story of the tragic effect on the family of a man who is declared a security risk because of his friendship with a known subversive. Recreates the uncertainties and suspicions of the McCarthy era in the early 1950's.

2550 Beaumont, Charles. THE INTRUDER. Putnam, 1959. Story of events in a Southern city when a few courageous citizens react to the trouble stirred up by an outside rabble-rouser who came in to form a prosegregation organization.

2551 Boles, Paul Darcy. DEADLINE. Macmillan, 1957. Story of a Southern newspaperman's decision to take a stand against segregation, and of the effects of his decision.

2552 Bonner, Paul Hyde. SPQR. Scribner, 1952. Sophisticated romance centering around a first secretary of the American Embassy in Rome, involving a spy hunt.

2553 ________. HOTEL TALLEYRAND. Scribner, 1953. Story of American diplomatic personnel in Paris in 1950; background is the American effort to check the growth of communism in Europe.

2554 Botsford, Keith. THE MARCH-MAN. Viking, 1964. Picture of life in southern California in the 1940's as viewed by an Italian of a traditional background.

2555 Boyle, Kay. GENERATION WITHOUT FAREWELL. Knopf, 1959. Story of the relationship between victor and vanquished, set in the American occupation zone of Germany in 1948.

2556 Brooks, Gwendolyn. MAUD MARTHA. Harper, 1953. Story of a black girl growing up from childhood to motherhood, facing discrimination on the South Side of Chicago during the 1940's.

2557 Brown, Frank London. TRUMBULL PARK. Regnery, 1959. Fictional account of the race riots in Trumbull Park, a Chicago housing development in the 1950's.

2558 Brown, Kenneth H. THE NARROWS. Dial, 1970. Teenage life in the Bay Ridge section of Brooklyn in the 1950's. The dress, language, and mores of that place and time are recalled. The kids find their security in clubs and gangs.

2559 Bryan, C.D.B. P. S. WILKINSON. Harper, 1965. Adventures of an army lieutenant set against the background of events from the Korean War to the Berlin Blockade.

2560 Buckley, David. PRIDE OF INNOCENCE. Holt, 1957. Story

of the moral and intellectual disillusionment of a young American soldier on occupation duty in Germany after World War II.

2561 Burgess, Jackson. THE ATROCITY. Putnam, 1961. Story of a brutal incident and its effect on one U.S. soldier in an ordnance company stationed in Italy at the end of World War II.

2562 Burnett, Hallie. WATCH ON THE WALL. Morrow, 1965. An American girl visiting in Berlin becomes involved in a plot to help an East German escape to the West over the Berlin Wall.

2563 Carruth, Haydn. APPENDIX A. Macmillan, 1963. Experiences of the editor of a literary magazine depict the publishing and social world of Chicago in the 1950's.

2564 Chatterton, Ruth. THE BETRAYERS. Houghton, 1953. Story of the investigation by a congressional committee of a young scientist suspected of subversive activity.

2565 Chevalier, Haakon Maurice. THE MAN WHO WOULD BE GOD. Putnam, 1959. An F. B. I. agent is won over to the Communist Party by the scientist he is investigating; the scientist, cleared for atomic bomb research, changes his convictions.

2566 Conover, Robert. THE PUBLIC BURNING. Viking, 1977. Set in the early years of the Eisenhower administration. Vice President Nixon appears in this satirical look at the American culture at the time when two convicted Russian spies were given death sentences.

2567 Coon, Gene L. MEANWHILE, BACK AT THE FRONT. Crown, 1961. Humorous account of life in the public information unit of the First Marine Division in the Korean War.

2568 Coppel, Alfred. A LITTLE TIME FOR LAUGHTER. Harcourt, 1969. Follows the fortunes of three friends from graduation in 1940 through World War II, the McCarthy era of the 1950's, and into settled lives in the 1960's.

2569 Crawford, William. GIVE ME TOMORROW. Putnam, 1962. Story of a U.S. Marine officer in the Korean War; flashbacks show the discrimination faced by Mexican-Americans in El Paso, Texas, and the public apathy toward the war.

2570 Daniels, Lucy. CALEB, MY SON. Lippincott, 1956. Tragic story of the effect of segregation upon a family of Southern blacks.

2571 Davis, Christopher. FIRST FAMILY. Coward, 1961. Story

of the effects of a white suburban community when a black family moves into the neighborhood.

2572 Davis, Dorothy. THE EVENING OF THE GOOD SAMARITAN. Scribner, 1961. A review of recent history from the 1930's to the 1950's; story centers on a liberal professor, and atomic scientist, and a "professional" Jew in a large Midwestern city.

2573 Drury, Allen. ADVISE AND CONSENT. Doubleday, 1959. Picture of the workings of the U.S. Senate; story of political and personal conflicts set in motion as the Senate debates confirmation of the president's nomination for secretary of state; at issue is the nominee's association with a student communist group.

2574 Duncan, Julia. HALFWAY HOME. St. Martin's, 1979. Two little girls, one white, one black, are friends in a Southern town, just before the civil rights movement gained impetus. When a black church is bombed, the white family's reaction is morally right, not dictated by their caste role.

2575 Dunne, John Gregory. TRUE CONFESSIONS. Dutton, 1977. An Irish policeman and his brother, a priest, must try to shape their lives in the political corruption of the city of Los Angeles, in the years just after World War II.

2576 Durkin, Barbara Wernecke. OH, YOU DUNDALK GIRLS, CAN YOU DANCE THE POLKA? Morrow, 1984. Adolescence means adjustment for a girl who moves from rural Wisconsin to Baltimore's Dundalk section. Local color infuses life there, even in the period when Elvis would burst onto teenagers everywhere.

2577 Dybeck, Stuart. CHILDHOOD AND OTHER NEIGHBORHOODS. Viking, 1980. Stories of young blacks, growing up poor in a Chicago ghetto.

2578 Edwards, Anne. SHADOW OF A LION. Coward McCann, 1971. The hysteria surrounding the House Un-American Activities Committee's investigation of the movie industry convinces one man to capitulate and report his friends for the sake of his own career.

2579 Edwards, Junius. IF WE MUST DIE. Doubleday, 1963. Story of what happened when a young black Korean veteran tries to vote in an unidentified Southern town.

2580 Elman, Richard. FREDI & SHIRL & THE KIDS. Scribner, 1972. Autobiographical novel about a boy growing up in a Jewish family living in Brooklyn after World War II, finding himself at odds with his parents' culture.

2581 Fleming, Thomas J. ALL GOOD MEN. Doubleday, 1961. Realistic picture of big-city politics, party machinery, and petty ward heelers in an Eastern city in 1951.

2582 Flood, Charles Bracelen. A DISTANT DRUM. Houghton, 1957. Story of a young man, graduate of Harvard's Class of 1951, writing a first novel and growing to maturity; he enlists in the army at the time of the Korean War and goes through basic training before discharge because of a congenital defect.

2583 ________. MORE LIVES THAN ONE. Houghton, 1967. Hardships of life in a communist prisoner-of-war camp in the Korean War contrasted with life going on normally back home.

2584 Ford, Norman R. THE BLACK, THE GRAY, AND THE GOLD. Doubleday, 1961. Picture of the pressures of life at West Point, based on the cheating scandal at the Academy in 1951.

2585 Frank, Pat. HOLD BACK THE NIGHT. Lippincott, 1952. Story of a U.S. Marine unit in Korea, covering the retreat from the Changjin Reservoir to Hungnam on the coast.

2586 Frankel, Ernest. BAND OF BROTHERS. Macmillan, 1958. A story of the marine retreat from the Yalu River to Hungnam when the Chinese entered the war in Korea.

2587 ________. TONGUE OF FIRE. Dial, 1960. Story of a crusading congressman who achieves quick fame through his congressional-committee investigation of communist activity; patterned after the career of Joseph McCarthy.

2588 Franklin, Edward Herbert. IT'S COLD IN PONGO-NI. Vanguard, 1965. Combat novel of the Korean War.

2589 Gallico, Paul. TRIAL BY TERROR. Knopf, 1952. Story of an American newspaperman captured behind the Iron Curtain and tried as a spy.

2590 Gann, Ernest. SOLDIER OF FORTUNE. Sloane, 1954. Picture of communist China as seen by two Americans searching for the photographer-husband of one of them.

2591 Garrett, George. WHICH ONES ARE THE ENEMY? Little, 1961. Set in Trieste after World War II, this is a love story told against a background of U.S. occupation forces and the underground of soldier-gangsters and black marketeers.

2592 Garwood, Darrell. THE ARBAUGH AFFAIR. Macrae, 1970. An atomic scientist who had worked on the Manhattan

Project is given an Atomic Energy Commission post after the war, but in the 50's fails to get security clearance when it is discovered that he supported the Spanish Loyalists in the 30's, and that his college girl friend was a communist.

2593 Geer, Andrew Clare. RECKLESS, PRIDE OF THE MARINES. Dutton, 1955. Story of a mule mascot of the Fifth U.S. Marines who became famous as an ammunition carrier and morale builder in the Korean War.

2594 Giardina, Anthony. MEN WITH DEBTS. Knopf, 1984. An insurance man has realized his American dream with a wife and children in a suburban home. In mid-life he understands that it is not enough to satisfy his psyche.

2595 Gilden, K. B. (pseud.). HURRY SUNDOWN. Doubleday, 1965. Two World War II veterans, a black man and his white neighbor, work together to save their farms from the avaricious citizens of their small Georgia community.

2596 Gilman, Peter. DIAMOND HEAD. Coward, 1960. Recreates the historical background and the struggle for Hawaiian statehood, from the viewpoint of a present-day family.

2597 Gordon, Arthur. REPRISAL. Simon and Schuster, 1950. Story of race violence in a Georgia town when a young black man, whose wife had been murdered, takes things into his own hands.

2598 Greene, Harris. THE "MOZART" LEAVES AT NINE. Doubleday, 1960. A U.S. Army security service chief in American-occupied Austria is busy keeping track of surviving Nazis and Russian agents in the year after the end of World War II; story of the effect of the U.S. decision to return a Russian defector.

2599 Gregor, Manfred. TOWN WITHOUT PITY. Random, 1961. Story of German-American relations in a small German town, still occupied by American troops in the late 1950's.

2600 Groniger, William. RUN FROM THE MOUNTAIN. Rinehart, 1959. Story of the army experiences of a young American soldier in occupied Japan from 1946 to 1949.

2601 Gurney, Hal. FIFTH DAUGHTER. Doubleday, 1957. Story of the interactions of the Okinawans and Americans during the occupation following World War II.

2602 Gwaltney, Francis Irby. THE NUMBER OF OUR DAYS. Random, 1959. A World War II veteran leads a revolt against radical segregationists in his home town in Arkansas, following the Supreme Court decision in 1954.

2603 Haas, Ben. LOOK AWAY, LOOK AWAY. Simon and Schuster, 1964. Story of racial strife in a Southern community, told through the experiences of three World War II veterans, once boyhood friends; one is a politician, one a black who turns to nonviolent protest, and one a newspaperman who suffers because of his editorial against racism.

2604 Habe, Hans. OFF LIMITS. Fell, 1957. Story of the relations between Americans and Germans in the U.S. occupied zone of West Berlin, 1945-1951.

2605 Hannibal, Edward and Robert Boris. BLOOD FEUD. Ballantine, 1979. For Robert Kennedy, putting Jimmy Hoffa behind bars was the primary goal of life after he dropped out of the McCarthy investigations. This is the story of the lengthy legal battles between the two powerful men.

2606 Harrison, Jim. FARMER. Viking, 1976. Realistic portrait of the life of a bachelor farmer and schoolteacher living in a tiny community in upper Michigan in the 1950's.

2607 Hersey, John. A BELL FOR ADANO. Knopf, 1944. Story of the efforts of an understanding American occupation administrator to rebuild a devastated Italian village according to his own democratic ideals.

2608 Hill, Weldon. THE LONG SUMMER OF GEORGE ADAMS. McKay, 1961. Picture of ordinary, everyday events of life in a small Oklahoma town in the 1940's and 1950's.

2609 Hoffman, William. A PLACE FOR MY HEAD. Doubleday, 1960. A small-town Virginia lawyer successfully defends a black's insurance claim but finds the man had hoped to lose as a propaganda weapon for racial agitation.

2610 Hooker, Richard. M.A.S.H. Morrow, 1968. Story of the staff of a mobile army surgical hospital unit in action and in play during the Korean War.

2611 Horowitz, Gene. LADIES OF LEVITTOWN. Marek, 1980. The good life in the suburbs was the goal of the children of the Depression; their children find it life in a gilded cage and escape by any route they can.

2612 Jackson, Felix. SO HELP ME GOD. Viking, 1955. Story of a young lawyer who sends a letter to a congressional committee, anonymously accusing himself of being a communist, in order to expose the dangers of condemning on hearsay evidence.

2613 Jones, Leroi. THE SYSTEM OF DANTE'S HELL. Grove, 1965. Grim story of childhood and adolescence in the Negro slums of Newark, experiences as a serviceman in a small Southern town, and, later, scenes of black life in New York City.

2614 Kaplan, Arthur. HOTEL DE LA LIBERTE. Dutton, 1964. Sketches of the humorous activities of American students living in Paris under the G. I. Bill in the late 1940's.

2615 Karp, David. THE LAST BELIEVERS. Harcourt, 1964. Story of a playwright, portraying the history of communism in the U.S. from the 1920's to the Hollywood blacklisting of the 1950's.

2616 Kavanaugh, Paul. NOT COMIN' HOME TO YOU. Putnam, 1974. Story of a violent murder rampage by a crazed young gunman and a lonely girl he attracted. Based on the 1958 Starkweather-Fugate killings.

2617 Kern, Alfred. THE WIDTH OF WATERS. Houghton, 1959. Story of the preparations for a sesquicentennial celebration in a Pennsylvania town, and of the effect of news that one home-town boy had been killed and another had become a turncoat in the Korean War.

2618 Kerouac, Jack. BIG SUR. Farrar, 1962. Autobiographical novel of a leader of the beat generation, groping for meaning and a role in life.

2619 ______. DESOLATION ANGELS. Coward, 1965. Philosophical novel of life in the beat generation in the 1950's; New York and San Francisco.

2620 ______. VISIONS OF CODY. McGraw, 1972. Written in 1951-52 and published posthumously. This is an account of the travels of two itinerant members of the beat generation, holding long philosophical conversations in diners, dingy bars, and cheap hotels across the land.

2621 Kiker, Douglas. THE SOUTHERNER. Rinehart, 1957. Story of a school-segregation case in a fictional Southern city.

2622 Laurents, Arthur. THE WAY WE WERE. Harper, 1972. A former member of the Young Communist League, who marries and lands in Hollywood, suffers during the McCarthy era's blacklisting of movie-makers.

2623 Lorraine, John. MEN OF CAREER. Crown, 1960. Story of the U.S. State Department diplomatic corps in Vienna in 1953; how the members of the Foreign Service reacted to the McCarthy loyalty investigations.

2624 Lynch, Michael. AN AMERICAN SOLDIER. Little, 1969. Story of the horrors of war as seen by a sensitive army corporal in the Korean War.

2625 McCaig, Donald. BUTTE POLKA. Dial, 1980. A stoker at a copper mine disappears in 1946. The man was hated by the owners for his radical ideas. This story uncovers a murder, and also pictures grim and dangerous conditions for the mine workers.

2626 McGivern, William P. ODDS AGAINST TOMORROW. Dodd, 1957. Story of two bank robbers, one white, one black, and of their friendship, growing out of enmity during their flight and refuge in an isolated farmhouse.

2627 McGovern, James. THE BERLIN COURIERS. Abelard, 1960. Story of a U.S. intelligence agent in Berlin during the East German uprising of 1953, sent to interview a defecting scientist; captured by the Russians, he escapes with important documents.

2628 McIlwain, William. THE GLASS ROOSTER. Doubleday, 1960. Story of violence following the false accusation that a young black had raped a white woman; set around a survey of white and black recreational facilities in a Southern town.

2629 MacInnes, Helen. I AND MY TRUE LOVE. Harcourt, 1953. A Washington hostess and a communist Czech official are caught between communist spies and the hysterical fear of communists in government.

2630 Madden, David. BIJOU. Crown, 1974. Film images shape the perceptions of the world around him for a movie-struck teenager in a small Tennessee town in the late 1940's.

2631 Maddux, Rachel. ABEL'S DAUGHTER. Harper, 1960. Story of a Northern couple who move to a small Southern town during World War II and come to understand the practical aspects of the color question in the South through friendship with the leader of the black community.

2632 Maillard, Keith. CUTTING THROUGH. Beaufort Books, 1982. Sequel to The Knife in My Hands. An unsettled man searches for his psychological roots as he travels the South in the early 1960's. The end of the decade finds him in Boston, a Vietnam War draft dodger in hiding, working for an underground newspaper.

2633 Malliol, William. A SENSE OF DARK. Atheneum, 1968. Story of combat in the Korean War and of training with U.S. Marines at Parris Island.

2634 Mankiewicz, Don. TRIAL. Harper, 1955. Story of the trial of a young Mexican in a West Coast city; communists exploit the possibilities of racial prejudice.

2635 Marquand, J. P. STOPOVER: TOKYO. Little, 1957.

American intelligence agents attempt to break up a communist plot to stage anti-American riots in Japan.

2636 Marshall, Paule. BROWN GIRL, BROWNSTONES. Random, 1959. Story of a black girl coming to grips with herself and with life and its prejudices in Brooklyn.

2637 Mayfield, Julian. THE GRAND PARADE. Vanguard, 1961. Story of the racial crisis in a Southern city, centering on the school segregation issue.

2638 Mercer, Charles. THE MINISTER. Putnam, 1969. Story follows a rebellious Protestant minister in the Civil Rights movement, in jail, in relief work with a Catholic priest in Korea, and on to his break with the organized church; at the time of the Korean War.

2639 Michener, James. BRIDGES AT TOKO-RI. Random, 1953. Story of a U.S. Navy aircraft-carrier task force assigned to bomb enemy supply lines in the Korean War.

2640 Miller, Warren. THE SLEEP OF REASON. Little, 1960. A satire on politics in Washington during the McCarthy era; story of a young man hired to ferret out subversion for a Senate investigating committee.

2641 ________. FLUSH TIMES. Little, 1962. Picture of life in the American colony in Cuba as they witness the change from Batista to Castro.

2642 Moll, Elick. SEIDMAN AND SON. Putnam, 1958. Picture of the New York dress industry following the Korean War.

2643 Morris, Edita. THE FLOWERS OF HIROSHIMA. Viking, 1959. An American realizes the full horror of the atomic bomb when he discovers that the Japanese family with whom he is lodging lost the wife and mother in the bombing raid in 1945 and that the father is now dying of radiation sickness.

2644 Morrison, Toni. THE BLUEST EYE. Holt, 1970. A poor and ugly black girl, pregnant by her father, unable to move out of the misery engendered by a racist society, can only wish for blue eyes--to her, symbols of unattainable happiness and beauty; 1940's.

2645 Newman, Charles. NEW AXIS. Houghton, 1966. Family life in the suburbs of a Midwestern city following the Korean War; shows the American reaction to the launching of the first Russian satellite.

2646 Pollini, Francis. NIGHT. Houghton, 1961. Life of American prisoners captured by the Chinese during the Korean War; centers around the efforts at brainwashing.

2647 Polonsky, Abraham. A SEASON OF FEAR. Cameron, 1956. Story of the conflicts arising out of the signing of a loyalty oath by a civil engineer. Convincing picture of the fear and suspicion made possible by the climate of opinion in the early 1950's, at the time of the McCarthy investigations.

2648 Powers, John. THE LAST CATHOLIC IN AMERICA. Saturday Review Press, 1973. A fictionalized memoir of a boyhood in an Irish section of Chicago; the author recalls parochial elementary school where sin was easily defined, and rewards and punishments meted out in no-nonsense fashion.

2649 Press, Sylvia. CARE OF DEVILS. Beacon, 1958. Story of the efforts of a woman agent in Washington to clear her name from the accusations made against her in a security investigation.

2650 Rauch, Earl Mac. NEW YORK, NEW YORK. Simon, 1977. Love story of a girl singer and a band leader. Milieu and music of the big-band era of the late 1940's.

2651 Renek, Morris. HECK. Harper's Magazine Press, 1971. A veteran returns from World War II, ambitious and street-sharp. Frustrated and bitter at the dead-end jobs he can obtain, he decides to rob a bank.

2652 Robertson, Don. A FLAG FULL OF STARS. Putnam, 1964. Story of politics, family and home life in 1948 on the day Truman defeated Dewey.

2653 Rogers, Lettie Hamlett. BIRTHRIGHT. Simon and Schuster, 1957. Story of the reactions when a teacher in a small Southern town praises the Supreme Court decision of 1954.

2654 Romulo, Carlos P. THE UNITED. Crown, 1951. Picture of international diplomacy at work in the United Nations; story of a U.S. delegate standing up for his principles against the arguments of a newspaper columnist and a Boston Brahmin.

2655 Roripaugh, Robert A. A FEVER FOR LIVING. Morrow, 1961. Tragic love story set in occupied Japan, giving details of life in an army camp.

2656 Ross, Glen. THE LAST CAMPAIGN. Harper, 1962. Adventures of an army bandsman in the first year of the Korean War.

2657 Ross, Walter. COAST TO COAST. Simon and Schuster, 1962. Story of the Senate investigation into the 1959 television quiz-show payola scandals.

2658 Roth, Philip. LETTING GO. Random, 1962. Story of Jewish family life and the college scene in the 1950's; set in New York City and at the University of Chicago.

2659 Rubin, Michael. WHISTLE ME HOME. McGraw-Hill, 1967. Story of Jewish family life in Brooklyn, from 1946 to 1953.

2660 Russell, Ross. THE SOUND. Dutton, 1961. Story of a black trumpeter and the jazz and drug scene in the years following World War II.

2661 Rutman, Leo. FIVE GOOD BOYS. Viking, 1982. A novelization of a real sports scandal at C. C. N. Y. in the 1950's. The young players are treated with compassion here, shown to be in over their heads in a point-spread fix, run by professional gamblers.

2662 Salter, James. THE ARM OF FLESH. Harper, 1961. Vivid picture of life of the members of a fighter squadron in an American air base in occupied Germany after World War II.

2663 Scott, Robert L. LOOK OF THE EAGLE. Dodd, 1955. Story of jet warfare in the Korean War, and of a scheme to fly a Russian jet out of North Korea.

2664 Shaw, Bynum. DAYS OF POWER, NIGHTS OF FEAR. St. Martin's, 1980. Sam Bradford, a senator who closely resembles the real Joseph McCarthy, begins his red-baiting as a reelection ploy he hopes will deflect attention from his lackluster first term.

2665 Shaw, Irwin. THE TROUBLED AIR. Random, 1951. Story of the disastrous results when a radio program director is ordered to fire five actors suspected of being communists.

2666 Sheehan, Edward R. F. THE GOVERNOR. World, 1970. Politics and scandal in public office in Massachusetts in the 1950's, during the incumbency of an Irish Catholic governor.

2667 Sheldon, Walter. TOUR OF DUTY. Lippincott, 1959. Story of Japanese-American relations in occupied Japan after World War II; set on a U.S. Air Force base near a small Japanese village.

2668 Sidney, George. FOR THE LOVE OF DYING. Morrow, 1969. A pessimistic antiwar novel centering around a U.S. Marine unit in the last days of the Korean War.

2669 Silko, Leslie Marmon. CEREMONY. Viking, 1977. The bitterness of the Indian over the white man's larceny and deceit is expressed in this story of a Navaho veteran of World War II, coming home to a New Mexico reservation.

2670 Sinclair, Jo. THE CHANGELINGS. McGraw, 1955. Story of a Jewish community in a Midwestern city being pressed by a growing black population; teenagers lead their parents toward tolerance and understanding.

2671 Sinclair, Upton. RETURN OF LANNY BUDD. Viking, 1953. Events after World War II bring Lanny Budd back to government service; the growth of the Russian menace takes him to trouble spots in Europe from 1946 to 1949.

2672 Singer, Howard. WAKE ME WHEN IT'S OVER. Putnam, 1959. Humorous story of an air force radar man who, in his off duty hours, builds an island resort hotel for servicemen on leave from the Korean War.

2673 Slaughter, Frank G. SWORD AND SCALPEL. Doubleday, 1957. Story of an American army officer in the Korean War; his experiences in battle, as a prisoner of the Chinese, and on trial for collaborating with the communists.

2674 Smith, William Dale. A MULTITUDE OF MEN. Simon and Schuster, 1960. Conflict between a company union and outside labor organizers in a West Virginia steel mill in the period after the Korean War.

2675 Sneider, Vern. THE TEAHOUSE OF THE AUGUST MOON. Putnam, 1951. Humorous story of an American occupation team and its efforts to "rehabilitate" and democratize Okinawa after the war.

2676 _______. A PAIL OF OYSTERS. Putnam, 1953. Story of an American newspaperman on Formosa, determined to find the facts behind official camouflage.

2677 Spencer, Elizabeth. THE VOICE AT THE BACK DOOR. McGraw, 1956. Story of life in a small Mississippi community, showing changing patterns in race relations.

2678 Stallone, Sylvester. PARADISE ALLEY. Putnam, 1977. Three Italian-American brothers hustle for a living in Hell's Kitchen area of New York City in 1946. One becomes a wrestler, the others serve as his trainer and manager.

2679 Stark, Irwin. THE SUBPOENA. New American Library, 1966. A shrill recreation of the McCarthy witch hunts of the 1950's.

2680 Stephens, Edward. BLOW NEGATIVE. Doubleday, 1962. Story of the development of the nuclear submarine; fictional treatment of the career of Admiral Rickover, and the navy's opposition to his ideas.

2681 Thayer, Charles Wheeler. MOSCOW INTERLUDE. Harper, 1962. Story of life in the U.S. Embassy in Moscow in Stalin's era, plagued by Soviet red tape and spies.

2682 Ullman, James Ramsey. WINDOM'S WAY. Lippincott, 1952. An American doctor in a hospital near a rubber plantation in Southeastern Asia sympathizes with the natives in a strike over their need for more rice land; official opposition drives some into the communist camp.

2683 Uris, Leon. ARMAGEDDON. Doubleday, 1964. Story of the American occupation forces in Berlin from the end of World War II to the Berlin airlift in 1948.

2684 Voorhees, Melvin. SHOW ME A HERO. Simon and Schuster, 1954. Story of the Korean War, framed in the story of the moral dilemmas faced by three men; a general, a private, and a newspaperman.

2685 Wallis, Arthur, and Charles Blair. THUNDER ABOVE. Holt, 1956. Story of adventure behind the Iron Curtain when an American plane in the Berlin airlift is shot down.

2686 Weeks, William Rawle. KNOCK AND WAIT AWHILE. Houghton, 1957. Story of American counterespionage in postwar Europe, involving the efforts of an American girl, a reporter, to hide behind the Iron Curtain.

2687 Wheeler, Keith. SMALL WORLD. Dutton, 1958. Story revolves around international events as they affect two American foreign correspondents; World War II, Korean War, Cold War periods.

2688 ________. PEACEABLE LANE. Simon and Schuster, 1960. Story of prejudice in a suburban community near New York when neighbors unite in an effort to block the sale of a house to blacks.

2689 Witherspoon, Mary Elizabeth. THE MORNING COOL. Macmillan, 1972. The McCarthy era; the middle-aged heroine, living in a peaceful Tennessee farmhouse, fears a subpoena from the Un-American Activities Committee because she worked with a group of young radicals in the 1930's.

2690 Wooley, Brian. TIME AND PLACE. Dutton, 1977. In 1952 a polio epidemic hits a small Texas town. Two young men find their lives changed, as one is crippled and the other trapped by a hasty marriage.

2691 Wouk, Herman. YOUNGBLOOD HAWKE. Doubleday, 1962. Picture of the publishing and entertainment worlds of New York and Hollywood; 1949-1951.

2692 Wright, Richard. THE OUTSIDER. Harper, 1953. Story of a black's search for an ethical identity; Chicago.

2693 _______. THE LONG DREAM. Doubleday, 1958. Story of a black's boyhood in a Mississippi town; his father had achieved importance by cooperation with corrupt officials; in the end the son takes flight to France.

2694 Young, Jefferson. A GOOD MAN. Bobbs, 1953. Story of the trouble aroused when a Mississippi black tenant farmer decided to paint his house white.

2695 Zarubica, Mladin. SCUTARI. Farrar, 1967. An American C.I.A. agent faces the Chinese communists at a missile base in Albania.

THE TURBULENT YEARS--1960 TO 1977

2696 Albert, Mimi. THE SECOND STORY MAN. The Fiction Collective, 1975. A young woman dropout from the middle class surrenders her independence to support the alcoholic second-story man of the title; Greenwich Village, 1960's.

2697 Anderson, Patrick. THE APPROACH TO KINGS. Doubleday, 1970. The story of a speechwriter and confidant to the president offers a realistic picture of congressmen, cabinet members, and others in the inner circle of government in the Washington of the 1970's.

2698 ________. ACTIONS AND PASSIONS; Doubleday, 1974. A young aide to John F. Kennedy moves through his political career to become a senator. The book offers a realistic picture of senators in the 1960's, and of the women's liberation movement, through the story of the wife of the protagonist.

2699 Anderson, William C. THE GOONEY BIRD. Crown, 1968. Pictures the lighter side of life for an American helicopter crew, a female war correspondent, and some friendly natives in Vietnam.

2700 Arnold, Elliott. CODE OF CONDUCT. Scribner, 1970. A novel of international intrigue built around a search for the real explanation of the "*Pueblo* affair."

2701 Barry, Jane. GRASS ROOTS. Doubleday, 1968. Story of a political campaign for a congressional seat in which the issues of the 60's--Vietnam, civil rights, and big government versus private enterprise--are discussed.

2702 Bergstein, Eleanor. ADVANCING PAUL NEWMAN. Viking, 1973. The story of two young women, campaign workers preparing for an appearance by Paul Newman for candidate Eugene McCarthy in the 1968 campaign; culminates in the horror of Robert Kennedy's assassination.

2703 Betts, Doris. THE RIVER TO PICKLE BEACH. Harper, 1972. Violence and unrest as experienced by a married couple managing a resort on the East Coast; reflects the violence of the nation at the time of Robert Kennedy's assassination.

2704 Birmingham, John. THE VANCOUVER SPLIT. Simon and Schuster, 1973. Two young dropouts from society, drug users, hitchhike from New York to San Francisco. One finally returns to his home, and at the end of the book the narrator commits himself to a hospital for treatment.

2705 Bittle, Camilla R. A SUNDAY WORLD. Coward. 1966. Picture of life in a small Southern university town faced with rapid social and economic changes.

2706 Bourjaily, Vance. THE MAN WHO KNEW KENNEDY. Dial, 1967. A story set in the early 1960's showing the effect of the assassination of President Kennedy on the leading character.

2707 Boyle, Kay. THE UNDERGROUND WOMAN. Doubleday, 1975. A middle-aged widow and professor joins the ranks of anti-war protestors in California, is arrested and jailed. Her contact with the other prisoners leads her to sympathize with the feminist movement.

2708 Bradford, Richard. SO FAR FROM HEAVEN. Lippincott, 1973. Set in New Mexico. A light approach to the serious problems of the chicano and gringo in the story of the Tafoya family's efforts to win back farmland for the Mexican-Americans' use.

2709 Bradley, David. SOUTH STREET. Grossman, 1975. An authentic picture of the inhabitants of a black slum in Philadelphia as observed by a newcomer, Adlai Stevenson Brown.

2710 Breasted, Mary. I SHOULDN'T BE TELLING YOU THIS. Harper, 1983. The ambitions and intrigues of rival newspaper reporters. Set in 1976, the story is clearly about the New York Times, here called just "The Newspaper."

2711 Briley, John. THE TRAITORS. Putnam, 1969. Story of five GI's captured by the Viet Cong, and of the consequences of their anti-war campaign.

2712 Briskin, Jacqueline. CALIFORNIA GENERATION. Lippincott, 1970. The Peace Corps and the Watts riot are just two of the major events of the sixties reflected in the stories of eight members of the graduating class of a California high school.

2713 Bristow, Robert O'Neil. NIGHT SEASON. Morrow, 1970. A young white liberal and a bitter black separatist are two characters appearing in the story of Toby Snow, a Southern black man who finds some escape from the effects of poverty and racism in alcohol.

2714 Brown, John E. INCIDENT AT 125TH STREET. Doubleday,

1970. A New Yorker comes to the aid of an elderly victim of a mugging. When one of the attackers dies after falling from a train platform, the rescuer is charged with manslaughter.

2715 Browning, Patricia Griffith. THE FUTURE IS NOT WHAT IT USED TO BE. Simon and Schuster, 1970. A middle-class girl's conflicts with her father lead her to life in an urban ghetto where she sees the problems of the 1960's reflected in alcohol, drugs, hunger, and hopelessness.

2716 Bryant, Dorothy. ELLA PRICE'S JOURNAL. Lippincott, 1972. A middle-aged wife and mother returns to college. The book is her class-assigned journal, reflecting her growing doubts about her role as she observes the student unrest and the peace movement.

2717 Bunting, Josiah. THE LIONHEADS. Braziller, 1972. An ambitious and callous commanding general needlessly risks the lives of his men in order to win a promotion during the Tet offensive of 1968 in Vietnam.

2718 Burke, Alan Dennis. FIRE WATCH. Little, 1980. Education does not happen at an urban high school under forced desegregation in the 1970's. The teachers feel only futility faced with undisciplined students and overwhelming social problems.

2719 Burke, James Lee. TO THE BRIGHT AND SHINING SUN. Scribner, 1970. Story of the plight of the coal miners in Kentucky. Labor unions cannot solve the problem of not enough work. One young miner is offered hope by the Job Corps, but the death of his father means he must return and struggle at home to help his fiercely independent family.

2720 Cain, George. BLUESCHILD BABY. McGraw, 1971. A black basketball star has succumbed to drugs. He struggles back with the aid of the woman who loves him. Good picture of Harlem life, the street scene.

2721 Calisher, Hortense. STANDARD DREAMING. Arbor House, 1972. The son of a plastic surgeon has disappeared from college and from his father's life. The stricken father joins a group of parents in similar circumstances, and eventually leaves his lucrative practice to rehabilitate children in Chinatown.

2722 Chandler, David. ¡HUELGA! Simon and Schuster, 1970. Story of the rise of Daniel García, who organizes agricultural workers in California. Based on the real-life leader Cesar Chavez. Sympathetic to the workers, but the viewpoint of the farm owners is also presented.

2723 _______. CAPTAIN HOLLISTER. Macmillan, 1973. Novel of the Vietnam War; an American captain, assigned to write letters to the families of deceased soldiers, suffers a breakdown in this antiwar story.

2724 Chastain, Thomas. JUDGMENT DAY. Doubleday, 1962. Documentary story of a Southern town torn by racial violence following a lynching. A white minister attempts to lead his congregation in constructive action proposed by a black militant leader.

2725 Chaze, Eliott. TIGER IN THE HONEYSUCKLE. Scribner, 1965. Story of a civil rights demonstration in a small Mississippi town, as witnessed by a white newspaper reporter.

2726 Clark, Alan. THE LION HEART. Morrow, 1969. Raw picture of life and action in the Vietnam War.

2727 Cobb, William. AN INCH OF SNOW. Blair, 1964. Political satire of the 1960 presidential campaign in a Southern town.

2728 Collingwood, Charles. THE DEFECTOR. Harper, 1970. C.I.A. persuades an American reporter to travel to North Vietnam and seek out a government official who may defect.

2729 Connolly, Edward. DEER RUN. Scribner, 1971. Locals misunderstand and mistrust young outsiders who come to establish a commune on a Vermont farm; eventually the farmhouse at the commune is burned.

2730 Conroy, Pat. LORDS OF DISCIPLINE. Houghton, 1980. The first black cadet has been admitted to a Southern military academy at the time of the Vietnam War. The narrator is assigned the job of helping the black through his first year.

2731 Corley, Edwin. LONG SHOTS. Doubleday, 1981. A film director is called to testify before the House Un-American Activities Committee. Flashbacks show him in the thirties in Hollywood, in the forties filming the Russian army for the War Department, and then seeing his Japanese-American cameraman being forced into an internment camp.

2732 Cottonwood, Joe. FRANK CITY (GOODBYE). Delacorte, 1981. A picture of pure-spirited hippies who are too mixed-up to succeed for long at living in the heyday of Haight-Ashbury.

2733 Craddock, William J. BE NOT CONTENT. Doubleday, 1970. A young man searches for identity after hearing poet Allen Ginsberg; depicts the subculture of the flower children in Haight-Ashbury from their earliest gathering to 1970.

2734 Decker, William. HOLDOUTS. Little, 1979. Cattle-raising and meat-packing as practiced in 1968, and the nitty-gritty of life for the modern cowhand.

2735 Dobler, Bruce. LAST RUSH NORTH. Little, 1976. A reporter went to Alaska to write the story of the pipeline, and, after going broke, ends up a worker himself. High pay was a clarion call, but the harsh dark winter and danger make the work onerous.

2736 Doctorow, E. L. BOOK OF DANIEL. Random House, 1971. The troubled lives of the now-grown children of two spies executed in the McCarthy era for selling atomic secrets to the Russians. Based on the Rosenberg case.

2737 Dodge, Ed. DAV. Berkley, 1984. Vivid battle scenes are drawn in this story of a helicopter crew member in Vietnam, and of the mental havoc he suffers as a veteran.

2738 Douglas, Michael. DEALING. Knopf, 1971. A Harvard student travels to Berkeley to pick up 10 kilos of grass; a manic view of undergraduate life oriented toward the marijuana culture.

2739 Dykeman, Wilma. THE FAR FAMILY. Holt, 1966. Story of race relations in the southern Appalachians; with flashbacks to life in the South Carolina highlands in an earlier day.

2740 Ehrlichman, John. THE COMPANY. Simon and Schuster, 1976. A story of C.I.A. shenanigans, directed from President Richard Monckton's administration; ends with a "Watergate" in the making.

2741 _______. WHOLE TRUTH. Simon, 1979. The President, the C.I.A., and the Senate are involved in a plot and its coverup. Uruguay is the country entailed, but the action of the politicians evokes the Watergate manipulations.

2742 Elegant, Robert S. A KIND OF TREASON. Holt, 1966. Story of intrigue and suspense in Saigon, set against a background of the Vietnam War in 1964.

2743 Fair, Ronald L. HOG BUTCHER. Harcourt, 1966. Life in a black ghetto in Chicago, seen through the eyes of two ten-year-old boys.

2744 Fairbairn, Ann. FIVE SMOOTH STONES. Crown, 1966. Story of the struggle of a New Orleans black man who works his way through Harvard Law School and returns to work in the civil rights movement.

2745 _______. THAT MAN CARTWRIGHT. Crown, 1970. An

editor new to a California community fights the local establishment when his paper prints the views of the migrant workers who are trying to organize.

2746 Fast, Howard. OUTSIDER. Houghton, 1984. A rabbi in a Connecticut town has only a few Jews in his community, so he often represents a minority view as the residents wrestle with the large moral issues of the 1960's.

2747 Ford, Jesse Hill. THE LIBERATION OF LORD BYRON JONES. Little, 1965. Story of racial conflict and crisis in a Tennessee town.

2748 ________. THE FEAST OF SAINT BARNABAS. Little, 1969. Race relations in a small town in Florida in 1966, as tension mounts, leading up to a race riot.

2749 Frankel, Charles. A STUBBORN CASE. Norton, 1972. A college professor, returning to a U.S. campus after captivity by guerrillas in Uruguay, is appalled by student revolution. The confrontations in the novel resemble those at Columbia University in 1968.

2750 Friedland, Ronald. BRINGING IT ALL BACK HOME. Lippincott, 1971. Students at a black college in North Carolina stage an angry strike aimed at the administration they label "Uncle Tom." Violence and tragedy follow when the college president brings police in to subdue the rebelling students.

2751 Gaine, Ernest J. A GATHERING OF OLD MEN. Knopf, 1983. In the 1970's in Louisiana, a Cajun has been shot, and a black man accused. The elderly men of the black community take a heroic stand against the sheriff, both protecting the accused and atoning for the past when blacks were made scapegoats.

2752 Garfield, Brian. THE LAST BRIDGE. McKay, 1966. Story of a combat team on a suicide mission in the Vietnam War.

2753 ________. THE THREEPERSONS HUNT. Evans, 1974. The problems of present-day Indian life are presented in this story of a Navajo state trooper assigned to hunt an Apache prison escapee. Another theme is the battle for water rights between the Indians and the white ranchers.

2754 Good, Paul. ONCE TO EVERY MAN. Putnam, 1970. White college students from Yale, a black organizer representing Martin Luther King, and a TV reporter all converge on a northern Florida city for a Freedom March in 1963.

2755 Gould, Peter. BURNT TOAST. Knopf, 1971. Picture of life at a Vermont commune in the 1960's. Expresses the feeling of living with nature, the hazy dreaminess of the marijuana users, the rites celebrating human connections.

2756 Graham, Lorenz. NORTH TOWN. Crowell, 1965. Story of a black family that escapes from the violent racial bigotry of the South to face the subtle bigotry of the North.

2757 Graves, Wallace. TRIXIE. Knopf, 1969. Diary of a young girl from Watts who lives hidden in a Los Angeles college building; covers the few years between the assassinations of John Kennedy and Martin Luther King.

2758 Green, Gerald. AN AMERICAN PROPHET. Doubleday, 1977. Roman â clef about Joseph Wood Krutch. Story of a retired professor living in Arizona and battling for the preservation of the desert land.

2759 Groom, Winston. BETTER TIMES THAN THESE. Simon, 1978. In Vietnam, Bravo Company suffers long jungle campaigns with too few breaks, often under incompetant leaders.

2760 Haas, Ben. THE LAST VALLEY. Simon and Schuster, 1966. A veteran of World War II and the Korean War fights to save his Appalachian valley from destruction when a power company proposes to construct a hydroelectric dam.

2761 Halberstam, David. ONE VERY HOT DAY. Houghton, 1967. Story of a small American unit in Vietnam during one day of very heavy fighting.

2762 Hall, Richard. LONG GEORGE ALLEY. Delacorte, 1972. Set in a Freedom House in a small Mississippi town in that period of the 1960's when white liberals and black militants cooperated in the civil rights struggle.

2763 Hannah, Barry. GERONIMO REX. Viking, 1972. Story of an eccentric young man in Dream of Pines, Louisiana, an impoverished area stripped of its timber by greedy paper mills, and now facing the beginnings of the black liberation movement.

2764 Hardy, William. THE JUBJUB BIRD. Coward, 1966. A good-humored account of a civil rights drive in a Southern college town, involving white and black liberals, segregationists, militants, and a student from the North.

2765 Harris, Marilyn. HATTER FOX. Random House, 1973. Tragic story of a young Indian girl in prison, a victim of harsh treatment as an incorrigible. A doctor in the Indian service is touched by her plight and tries to rehabilitate her.

2766 Hasford, Gustav. THE SHORT-TIMERS. Harper, 1979. A marine combat reporter in Vietnam resists promotion to sergeant and persists in wearing a peace button on his uniform. The noise and stench of battle are made real and terrifying.

2767 Hathaway, Bo. A WORLD OF HURT. Taplinger, 1980. At first an eager soldier, the hero of this story rebels against the war after his beloved sergeant dies.

2768 Hempstone, Smith. A TRACT OF TIME. Houghton, 1966. Story of the war in Vietnam in 1963, written by a correspondent for the Chicago Daily News.

2769 Hercules, Frank. I WANT A BLACK DOLL. Simon and Schuster, 1968. Tragic story of the mixed marriage of a white girl from Kentucky and a black medical student.

2770 Higgens, George V. A CITY ON A HILL. Knopf, 1975. Post-Watergate politics in Washington, D. C. A Congressman from Cape Cod and his assistant try to marshal influential support for the presidential campaign of a New England senator.

2771 Hoffman, Roy. ALMOST FAMILY. Dial, 1983. A liberal white matron and her black maid of many years are parted when the civil rights movement forces each of them to reappraise old roles.

2772 Holland, William E. LET A SOLDIER DIE. Delacorte, 1984. A story of American helicopter forces in Vietnam, in constant danger as they must touch down and evacuate casualties in the midst of battle.

2773 Horwitz, Julius. THE W. A. S. P. Atheneum, 1967. A sordid story of Negro-white relations in Harlem.

2774 ________. DIARY OF A. N. Delta Books, 1971. The diary of a fifteen-year-old girl reveals in vivid personal terms the horrors of life in a ghetto slum, the dehumanizing effect of the welfare system, the temptation of an easy escape via drugs. The diary writer is intelligent and perceptive and may find a real way out.

2775 Huggett, William Turner. BODY COUNT. Putnam, 1973. This naturalistic war novel depicts a marine platoon in Vietnam experiencing the tense monotony of waiting for action, the bad decisions of the top command, and the vivid horror of combat.

2776 Humphrey, William. PROUD FLESH. Knopf, 1973. Racial prejudice, the weakening of clan ties, and the conflict between generations are exposed by a family crisis as the matriarch of a rural Texas clan lies dying. Ten children gather, but the mother is bitter over the absence of a run-away son.

2777 Hunter, Evan. LOVE, DAD. Crown, 1981. A father finally disowns his daughter, whose long trip into the hippie culture's self-destruction has also destroyed her parents' marriage.

2778 Jessup, Richard. A QUIET VOYAGE HOME. Little, 1970. Sixteen-hundred students returning from Europe on the S. S. New York are incited to mutiny by a young hippie.

2779 Jones, Madison. CRY OF ABSENCE. Crown, 1971. A wealthy Southern matron is forced to cope with integration in the New South when the hatred of the poor whites for the blacks erupts into violence, involving her son.

2780 Jordan, Robert. THANKSGIVING. Dutton, 1971. A group of angry young radicals, filled with loathing of America's Vietnam policy and contempt for a society they perceive as uncaring and greedy, plan to bomb a Long Island country club as a symbol of protest.

2781 Just, Ward. STRINGER. Little, 1974. An antiwar novel. The protagonist is an unsuccessful American journalist in Southeast Asia, sunk in the spiritual morass of the protracted war.

2782 Kennedy, Jay Richard. FAVOR THE RUNNER. World, 1963. Story of a liberal activist involved in various movements, from the Spanish Civil War to the civil rights movement.

2783 Killens, John Oliver. 'SIPPI. Trident, 1967. Negro life in the rural South before and after the Supreme Court decision of 1954; civil rights movement, Ku Klux Klan, Southern liberals, and Northern hippies.

2784 King, Larry L. THE ONE-EYED MAN. New American Library, 1966. Picture of Southern politics centering on the efforts of a demagogic governor to cope with integration at the state university.

2785 Kingman, Lee. PETER PAN BAG. Houghton, 1970. An objective look at the motives of young people who left home for the hippie scene; told in the story of one seventeen-year-old girl who joined a community of flower children in the Beacon Hill area of Boston.

2786 Kirkwood, James. SOME KIND OF HERO. Crowell, 1975. The tribulations of a returned POW from Vietnam who comes home to a failed marriage. He turns to making money by crime before deciding on a new direction for his life.

2787 Knebel, Fletcher. THE ZINZIN ROAD. Doubleday, 1966. Story of Peace Corps volunteers in Africa.

2788 Kolpacoff, Victor. THE PRISONERS OF QUAI DONG. New American Library, 1967. The brutalizing effect of war, shown by the treatment of a prisoner at a military base in Vietnam.

2789 Leonard, Frank. BOX 100. Harper, 1972. An exposé of incompetent, uncaring bureaucrats dealing with the victims of urban decay and poverty in New York City.

2790 Levine, Faye. SPLENDOR AND MISERY. St. Martin's, 1983. A memoir of Harvard in the 1960's, as experienced by a coed who arrived on campus as a naive freshman from Iowa.

2791 Lurie, Alison. THE WAR BETWEEN THE TATES. Random House, 1974. The student confrontation provoked by the Vietnam War is a backdrop for the personal problems of a professor and his wife who face a failing marriage and rebellion on the part of their own teenaged children.

2792 McCarthy, Abigail. CIRCLES. Doubleday, 1977. A political story based on the 1972 presidential campaign. A senator seeks his party's nomination; accurate picture of the role of the politicians' wives in the Washington scene.

2793 McConkey, James. A JOURNEY TO SAHALIN. Coward, 1971. Campus upheaval of the 1960's. The protagonist is a dean at a fictional New York university where the students strike.

2794 McHale, Tom. FARRAGAN'S RETREAT. Viking, 1971. A father is provoked to act, when, faced with a long-haired, draft-evading son, he is goaded by his flag-waving brother and sister.

2795 McInerny, Ralph. THE PRIEST. Harper, 1973. In 1968, a young priest returns from study in Rome to a small Ohio town where he is caught in the conflict between conservative and liberal parishioners.

2796 McLaughlin, Robert and Phil Foran. NOTHING TO REPORT. Little, 1975. Realities of life in the career of a present-day policeman in New York City who encounters bad cops, local pols on the make, and organized crime, as he moves from rookie to captain.

2797 MacLeish, Roderick. A CITY ON THR RIVER. Dutton, 1973. The book mixes fiction and nonfiction sections which together show the operations of our federal government. The story, about a president-elect taking over the reins, suggests that Washington fails to perceive the needs of the people.

2798 McLendon, James. DEATHWORK. Lippincott, 1977. The story examines the rights and wrongs of the death penalty. A writer visits a Florida prison where four men are executed after the most recent Supreme Court ruling.

2799 Meiring, Desmond. THE BRINKMAN. Houghton, 1965. A story of American involvement in Vietnam and Laos.

2800 Mills, James. REPORT TO THE COMMISSIONER. Farrar, 1972. A rookie cop blunders into the involvement of members of the Narcotics Bureau with the drug trade, and is made a scapegoat in the investigation he triggers; New York City.

2801 Moore, Col. Gene D. THE KILLING AT NGO'THO. Norton, 1967. Story of the life and actions of a U.S. army colonel sent as an advisor to the Vietnamese army early in the war.

2802 Moore, Robin. THE GREEN BERETS. Crown, 1965. Sketches of combat life with the U.S. Special Forces in Vietnam.

2803 Morgan, Al. THE WHOLE WORLD IS WATCHING. Stein and Day, 1972. A television producer and his crew watch and report the terrible confrontations between the establishment and the protestors at the scene of the 1968 Democratic Convention in Chicago. Many real participants appear as characters.

2804 Morressy, John. THE ADDISON TRADITION. Doubleday, 1968. Story of a student rebellion at a small liberal arts college, showing the student unrest and revolt of the sixties.

2805 Morris, Willie. THE LAST OF THE SOUTHERN GIRLS. Knopf, 1973. A good picture of life on Capitol Hill is shown in the story of an Arkansas debutante who sweeps onto the Washington social scene and takes as her lover a congressman on his way up.

2806 Moynahan, Julian. GARDEN STATE. Little, 1973. The politics and economics of land use are the theme of this novel. A New Jersey nurseryman tries to preserve land for a potential community recreation area, in the face of greedy developers.

2807 O'Donnell, M. K. YOU CAN HEAR THE ECHO. Simon and Schuster, 1966. Follows the activities of the members of one family in a small town near Dallas, Texas on the day President Kennedy was assassinated.

2808 Ogburn, Charlton. WINESPRING MOUNTAIN. Morrow, 1973. A young man is sent to work instead of college by his father, a coal-company president. He learns to love the mountains of West Virginia, and joins the conservationists fighting to end strip-mining operations

2809 Pelfrey, William. THE BIG V. Liveright, 1972. The experiences of a young draftee in Vietnam, emphasizing tentative but important camaraderie developed in the face of death.

2810 Pharr, Robert Deane. S. R. O. Doubleday, 1971. Life in a rundown single-room-occupancy hotel in Harlem, where stubborn vitality and humanity mitigate the lonely poverty of the residents.

2811 Piercy, Marge. SMALL CHANGES. Doubleday, 1973. A middle-class wife opts out of her marriage and tries life in several types of women's communes.

2812 ________. VIDA. Summit Books, 1979. Vida has been a fugitive for nine years, since she took part in the bombing that climaxed a radical antiwar protest. She and her fellow revolutionaries were convinced that only total destruction could force a just society.

2813 Powell, Richard. DON QUIXOTE, U. S. A. Scribner, 1966. A comic novel about the life of a Peace Corps volunteer sent to a Caribbean island.

2814 Pratt, John Clark. THE LAOTIAN FRAGMENTS. Viking, 1974. The book, documentary in form, questions the American involvement in Laos. The story is of an official investigation of a former hero of the Vietnam War, now serving as a civilian air controller in Laos in the early 1970's.

2815 Price, Richard. THE WANDERERS. Houghton, 1974. Story of twelve members of a street gang in an Italian section of the Bronx; 1960's.

2816 Quammen, David. TO WALK THE LINE. Knopf, 1970. Story of a tentative cooperation between young white liberals and distrustful black militants, all of whom want to attack landlord abuses in a Chicago ghetto during the summer after Martin Luther King's assassination.

2817 Reston, James, Jr. TO DEFEND, TO DESTROY. Norton, 1970. An officer in Vietnam, sickened by the war, sabotages intelligence missions, is tried for treason and convicted in this antiwar novel.

2818 Rex, Barbara. VACANCY ON INDIA STREET. Norton, 1967.

Story of middle-class suburban life, and how it is when a black family moves into the neighborhood.

2819 Reybold, Malcolm. THE INSPECTOR'S OPINION. Saturday Review Press, 1975. The book uses the device of a fictional retired Scotland Yard man, hired to deduce the true story from news accounts, to present the author's theories about Kennedy and Chappaquiddick.

2820 Riggan, Rob. FREE FIRE ZONE. Norton, 1984. A combat medic in Vietnam becomes a disaffected loner in response to the carnage and death he must deal with every day.

2821 Robertson, Don. THE SUM AND TOTAL OF NOW. Putnam, 1966. Picture of family life in a small Ohio town as a teenager adjusts to the death of his grandmother. Sequel to The Greatest Thing Since Sliced Bread (World War II).

2822 Rossner, Judith. LOOKING FOR MR. GOODBAR. Simon and Schuster, 1975. Psychological novel based loosely on the real murder, in 1973, of Roseann Quinn, a schoolteacher who found lovers in singles bars.

2823 Sanguinetti, Elise. McBEE'S STATION. Holt, 1971. The reshaping of the relationships between blacks and whites in an isolated Georgia hamlet, told in the story of an elderly widow and her son, a would-be writer who finds a meeting of minds with an educated black woman.

2824 Savage, Marc. THE LIGHT OUTSIDE. Harper, 1976. A young war protester, released from prison after serving a three-year term for refusing induction, goes to search for a cousin who has dropped out to become a hippie.

2825 Sayles, John. UNION DUES. Little, 1977. A young West Virginian, the son of a coal miner, runs away to Boston. His father comes to search for him, supporting himself by day labor. Pictures of union halls and shop floors, the life of working men in the 1960's.

2826 Scott-Heron, Gil. THE NIGGER FACTORY. Dial, 1972. The students at an all-black college, with a don't-rock-the-boat president, press for change.

2827 Settle, Mary Lee. KILLING GROUND. Farrar, Straus, 1984. This fifth novel of her quintet explains that the premature death of her brother led the author to understand what had gone before, and thus to write the West Virginia novels. See also O Beulah Land (Colonial America), Know Nothing (Civil War--Old South), and Scapegoat (Nation Grows Up).

2828 Silver, Joan and Linda Gottlieb. LIMBO. Viking, 1972. Three wives of MIA's in Vietnam struggle with world political facts as they try to discover whether their husbands survive as prisoners of war.

2829 Sloan, James Park. WAR GAMES. Houghton, 1971. A would-be writer in search of material enlists and volunteers for combat patrol in Vietnam. The rapaciousness of his fellow soldiers leads him to kill them, but his actions are misinterpreted and he is mistakenly decorated for heroism.

2830 Smith, C. W. THIN MEN OF HADDAM. Grossman, 1974. A Mexican-American ranch foreman, raised and educated by a Texas cattleman, is pulled between the chicano and white cultures.

2831 Smith, Daniel. A WALK IN THE CITY. World, 1971. A youth in a black ghetto surmounts the psychological damage threatening him when a coach encourages him to a sports career and an older Black Muslim instills pride of race.

2832 Smith, Edgar. A REASONABLE DOUBT. Coward, 1970. This story about the investigation of a murder questions the equality of the American system of justice.

2833 Smith, Lee. FANCY STRUT. Harper, 1973. A small Alabama town in the 1960's; the citizens are planning their sesquicentennial while absorbing the changes of becoming part of the new South.

2834 Smith, Robert Kimmel. RANSOM. McKay, 1971. Angry black revolutionists kidnap children of wealthy citizens to raise, in ransom, large sums of money for the poor.

2835 Smith, Steven Phillip. AMERICAN BOYS. Putnam, 1975. This war novel follows four young American soldiers in Vietnam, feeling the tensions bred by the constant threat of sudden death.

2836 Stallworth, Annie Nall. GO, GO, SAID THE BIRD. Vanguard, 1984. A mulatto boy in a small Southern town struggles to find a niche in a society composed of two separate races, even as the civil rights movement is changing some of the rules.

2837 Stern, Daniel. FINAL CUT. Viking, 1975. A former aide to President Kennedy comes to Hollywood to help market a movie based on the Woodstock Festival of the late sixties.

2838 Stone, Robert. DOG SOLDIERS. Houghton, 1974. An American journalist and an expatriate woman living in Saigon in the waning days of the war become involved in the trafficking of heroin.

2839 Styron, William. THE LONG MARCH. Random, 1968. Story of life in a U.S. Marine training base in South Carolina, centering on the effects of a forced march on officers and men.

2840 Tauber, Peter. THE LAST BEST HOPE. Harcourt, 1977. A young scientist is the protagonist in this saga of the troubled sixties that includes Kent State, the moon shot, the McCarthy campaign, and My Lai.

2841 Taylor, Thomas. A PIECE OF THIS COUNTRY. Norton, 1970. A black soldier in Vietnam volunteers for dangerous duty, bitterly aware that he can better help his family in Vietnam than he could by being with them at home in Maryland.

2842 Tiede, Tom. COWARD. Trident, 1968. Story of soldiers at war in Vietnam, a war of cruelty, blundering, and sudden death.

2843 Tinker, Barbara W. WHEN THE FIRE REACHES US. Morrow, 1970. The inhabitants of one small black neighborhood in Detroit observe the slow progress of civil rights through the sixties when the partial, hard-won, legislative progress seemed doomed to end in the violent riots of 1967.

2844 Von Hoffman, Nicholas. TWO, THREE, MANY MORE. Quadrangle, 1969. Based on the student rebellion and riots in American universities in the sixties; similar to the Columbia University affair in 1968.

2845 Walker, Alice. THE THIRD LIFE OF GRANGE COPELAND. Harcourt, 1972. Many years before, a despairing Southern black had abandoned wife and family and fled north. Returning at last, disappointed by life in New York, he finds his grown son imprisoned. He takes custody of his small granddaughter and finds hope in his love for her.

2846 Waller, Leslie. THE BRAVE AND THE FREE. Delacorte, 1979. The members of the 1964 class of an Ohio high school will experience social and political turbulence in the following decade.

2847 Wambaugh, Joseph. THE NEW CENTURIONS. Little, 1971. Story of three Los Angeles policemen through their training and rookie years, ending with the Watts riot of 1965; explains what "law and order" means to those enforcing it.

2848 Webb, James. FIELDS OF FIRE. Prentice, 1978. A platoon of marines in Vietnam doggedly endure months of jungle combat with its inevitable horrors. Although morale often sags, the comradeship peculiar to war is a sustaining force.

2849 ________. A SENSE OF HONOR. Prentice, 1981. The midshipmen at Annapolis train with missionary zeal in 1968, while the Tet offensive takes a terrible toll, and their peers protest the war in ever-growing numbers.

2850 Wersba, Barbara. RUN SOFTLY, GO FAST. Atheneum, 1970. The artistic son of a self-made businessman leaves home for the free life of Greenwich Willage. Only when his father dies does he begin to appreciate the old man's values.

2851 West, Morris. THE AMBASSADOR. Morrow, 1965. Story based on U.S. political and military involvement in Vietnam in 1963.

2852 Williams, John A. CLICK SONG. Houghton, 1982. A bitter look at racism directed at black writers, by publishers who lionized them for a time in the socially conscious sixties but then reverted to rejections.

2853 Wilson, John Rowan. THE SIDE OF THE ANGELS. Doubleday, 1968. Story of a Russian scientist who defects to the United States.

2854 Wilson, William. THE L. B. J. BRIGADE. Apocalypse, 1965. Antiwar story of a recent college graduate who is drafted and sent to Vietnam.

2855 Wooley, Brian. NOVEMBER 22. Seaview, 1983. The title refers to the day of John Kennedy's assassination. The book juxtaposes the activities of many citizens of Dallas as the day passes.

2856 Wright, Stephen. MEDITATIONS IN GREEN. Scribners, 1983. A soldier in an intelligence unit endeavors to survive Vietnam by maintaining a careful detachment. His efforts fail, and, home again, he struggles to make some sense of his experiences.

2857 Yount, John. THE TRAPPER'S LAST SHOT. Random House, 1973. The story is set in rural Georgia in 1960, as the uneducated whites fear the civil rights movement. One such young man hopes for social mobility through a college education, while his brother longs to own land; both find their goals elusive.

CHRONICLES

2858 Aaron, Chester. ABOUT US. McGraw, 1967. Story of a Jewish family life in a coal-mining town near Pittsburgh, from the Depression through WW II.

2859 Adelson, Ann. THE LITTLE CONQUERORS. Random, 1960. Story of an Italian-American family settling and growing up in a New England town dominated by Irish politicians; time is the 1930's to the 1950's.

2860 Aldrich, Bess Streeter. MISS BISHOP. Appleton, 1933. Story of an English teacher in a Midwestern college facing life from the 1880's to the 1930's.

2861 Andrews, Raymond. APPALACHEE RED. Dial, 1978. Red is the illegitimate son of the most influential citizen of a small Georgia town, born to his black maid. Many years later Red returns to Appalachee to take revenge against his father and to protest the racial injustice of society.

2862 Appel, Benjamin. A BIG MAN, A FAST MAN. Morrow, 1961. Story of a labor leader's interviews with a public-relations man hired to project a better public image of him; ranges from the drives to organize labor in the 1930's to the era of the big unions in the 1950's.

2863 Arnout, Susan. THE FROZEN LADY. Arbor House, 1983. Interactions between the Eskimo and the white settlers of Alaska, from the days of the gold rush in the 1890's to statehood in 1959.

2864 Aronson, Harvey. GOLDEN SHORE. Putnam, 1982. In 1911 a Quaker sets out to build modest family cottages on Miami Beach. His children team up with land developers, and by the story's close in 1949 the mangroves and crocodiles have been displaced by casinos and resort hotels.

2865 Auchincloss, Louis. HOUSE OF FIVE TALENTS. Houghton, 1960. Family chronicle of the rich in Newport and New York from 1873 to 1948; pictures mansions on Fifth Avenue, garden parties, the opera, and architecture.

2866 ________. PORTRAIT IN BROWNSTONE. Houghton, 1962. Social and business life in New York City from 1901 to 1951.

2867 _______. THE WINTHROP COVENANT. Houghton, 1976. Fictional picture of generations of the Winthrop family from the time of the trial of Anne Hutchinson to the Vietnam War, all shaped by or reacting to the Puritan ethic.

2868 Bacon, Josephine. ROOT AND THE FLOWER. Appleton, 1936. Development of the position of women in American life from 1860 to the 1930's.

2869 Banister, Margaret. TEARS ARE FOR THE LIVING. Houghton, 1963. Panorama of one hundred years in the life of a Virginia town, from before the Civil War to the 1950's.

2870 Banning, Margaret Culkin. THE QUALITY OF MERCY. Harper, 1963. Story of a Midwestern family and of their involvement in various charitable organizations--Red Cross, U.N.R.R.A., and volunteer hospital work--from 1910 through WW II.

2871 Barolini, Helen. UMBERTINA. Seaview, 1979. Umbertina and her husband arrive in America from Calabria, Italy in the 1860's. Years of hard work bring them a fine home in upstate New York for their seven children. Umbertina's grandchildren and great grandchildren continue the story.

2872 Benjamin, Harold. THE SAGE OF PETALUMA. McGraw, 1965. Autobiographical novel of a schoolteacher and administrator, from childhood through his teaching career from pre-WW I days to the 1960's.

2873 Birmingham, Stephen. AUERBACH WILL. Little, 1984. Flashbacks from the sickbed of a wealthy philanthropist and businessman. They reveal the struggles he and his wife had developing a great mail-order catalog business.

2874 Blassingame, Wyatt. LIVE FROM THE DEVIL. Doubleday, 1959. Story of the Florida cattle country and the development of the modern cattle industry from 1900 to the 1950's.

2875 Blondell, Joan. CENTER DOOR FANCY. Delacorte, 1972. Autobiographical story of life in a family of troupers in the last years of vaudeville, the daughter's later movie career, and eventual stardom.

2876 Boles, Paul Darcy. GLENPORT, ILLINOIS. Macmillan, 1956. Portrays average community life in a small town near Chicago from 1929 to 1944; the son of an Irish baker grows up to be a successful bandleader, until his death in World War II.

2877 Bourjaily, Vance. THE VIOLATED. Dial, 1958. Follows the lives of four Americans from the prosperous twenties, through the Depression and World War II to prosperity's return in the fifties.

2878 Boyd, James. ROLL RIVER. Scribner, 1935. Story of four generations of a Pennsylvania river-town family.

2879 Brace, Gerald Warner. THE GARRETSON CHRONICLE. Norton, 1947. Story of three generations of a New England family in a village not far from Boston.

2880 Bradley, David. CHANEYSVILLE INCIDENT. Harper, 1981. A black history professor returns to western Pennsylvania to learn of his grandfather's role in the Underground Railroad, and of the thirteen escaped slaves who chose death over recapture.

2881 Brandon, Evan. GREEN POND. Vanguard, 1955. Story of the medical profession, set in the Carolina red-lands, from the Civil War to the 1950's.

2882 Bromfield, Louis. THE FARM. Harper, 1933. Ohio farm and small-town life from 1815 to 1915; depicts the changing manners and patterns of rural social life and the development of a small Midwestern industrial town.

2883 Brown, Cecil. LIFE AND LOVES OF MR. JIVEASS NIGGER. Farrar, 1969. A black man assumes many aliases in the course of his life, first in the South, a period in Harlem, expatriate years in Copenhagen; he finally returns to the United States, which he both loves and hates.

2884 Brown, Dee. CREEK MARY'S BLOOD. Holt, 1980. A grandson of Creek Mary tells his family story to a reporter in 1905. His grandmother was a Muskogee chief's daughter before the American Revolution. She and her two sons experience the deceptive and destructive policies of the new nation toward its native peoples.

2885 Burdett, David Llewellyn. HIX NIX STIX PIX. Seymour Lawrence, 1984. A movie actor's life from the eve of the World War I to the eve World War II. His Hollywood roles are in sharp contrast to his off-screen life, as he fights in the trenches of Europe, supports Upton Sinclair's role in California politics, and tours with the Federal Theatre Project in the Depression.

2886 Burlingame, Roger. THREE BAGS FULL. Harcourt, 1936. Panorama of life in the Mohawk valley of New York from the days of the Holland Land Company to the present; picture of the change from the log cabin of pioneer days to mansion and town house as communities developed.

2887 Carleton, Jetta. THE MOON FLOWER VINE. Simon and Schuster, 1963. History of a family in rural Missouri, from 1900 to the Korean War; father is a teacher, the youngest child becomes a television writer in New York City.

2888 Carroll, Gladys Hasty. DUNNYBROOK. Macmillan, 1943. Fictional biography of the author's family from Revolutionary War days. Setting is a Maine village.

2889 ______. SING OUT THE GLORY. Little, 1957. Panorama of United States history, from the turn of the century, as it affects an isolated community in Maine.

2890 ______. NEXT OF KIN. Little, 1974. A young man brings his pregnant lover to a neglected farm belonging to his family. A neighbor befriends the young couple and relates the young man's family history from the Indian Wars of 1698 on; set in Maine.

2891 Carroll, James. MORTAL FRIENDS. Little, 1978. A fictional Irish immigrant plays a role in Boston politics, from the Depression years of the 1930's to the time of Kennedy's election.

2892 Catling, Patrick Skene. JAZZ, JAZZ, JAZZ. St. Martin's, 1982. Lives and careers of two New Orleans jazz musicians who grew up together at the turn of the century. One of them is the son of a well-to-do white family, the other the son of their black cook.

2893 Caudill, Harry M. THE SENATOR FROM SLAUGHTER COUNTY. Little, 1974. The story of the career of a Kentucky senator shows the social ferment in the coal mining area from the 1930's to the 1970's; the story also traces his family from the arrival of the first settlers of the region in 1789.

2894 Cavanaugh, Arthur. LEAVING HOME. Simon and Schuster, 1971. The focus is on the youngest son in this story of a happy Irish-American family living in Brooklyn; from the Depression through WW II and the 1950's.

2895 Charters, Samuel. JELLY ROLL MORTON'S LAST NIGHT AT THE JUNGLE INN. M. Boyars, 1984. Subtitled An Imaginary Memoir. The famous jazz man recalls his childhood in New Orleans in the 1890's and his early professional success in Florida.

2896 Cheever, John. THE WAPSHOT CHRONICLE. Harper, 1957. Picture of family life in an old New England town from the turn of the century to the 1950's.

2897 Cheuse, Alan. THE BOHEMIANS. Applewood, 1982. The life story of John Reed, a journalist and author, who moved from being something of a playboy as a youth to a radical in politics and a sympathetic reporter of the Russian Revolution.

2898 Childress, Alice. A SHORT WALK. Coward, 1979. The

sojurn of a black woman born in 1900 in the rural South, her move to Harlem, and marriage to an earnest devotee of Marcus Garvey, who works for his cause at the expense of providing for his family.

2899 Clad, Noel. LOVE AND MONEY. Random, 1959. Chronicle of the social and economic history of the United States from 1917 to 1948; includes anti-German feeling during World War I, the growing movie industry, the jazz age, the Florida boom, the Depression, the rise of Hitler, World War II, the housing boom following the war, and the congressional investigations of the McCarthy era.

2900 Clune, Henry. BY HIS OWN HAND. Macmillan, 1952. Story of a small segment of American society from 1906 through the 1920's and 1930's.

2901 Collier, Peter. DOWNRIVER. Holt, 1978. A Berkeley radical journeys with his dying father to the family's South Dakota homestead. The story covers recent politics, and, in flashbacks, "Custer's Last Stand" and the Homestead Steel strike in 1892.

2902 Coomer, Joe. DECATUR ROAD. St. Martin's, 1983. The Parks' family farm fronts on the road to the Kentucky county seat. They watch the road improve and its travelers change, from the 1920's through the years of the great Depression and the second World War.

2903 Cuomo, George. FAMILY HONOR. Doubleday, 1983. The history of the American labor movement in the twentieth century is recreated in the life of a union leader from the Bronx.

2904 Davis, Paxton. THE SEASON OF HEROES. Morrow, 1967. Three generations of a Virginia family, from the Civil War to 1912, when the children witness a lynching.

2905 Deal, Babs H. HIGH LONESOME WORLD. Doubleday, 1969. Story of the life and death of a country-music star; based on the life of Hank Williams.

2906 De Blasis, Celeste. THE PROUD BREED. Coward, 1978. A family saga which reflects California history from the Spanish culture of the early nineteenth century, through the gold rush, and the development of San Francisco as a great commercial center.

2907 Delmar, Viña. THE BIG FAMILY. Harcourt, 1961. Story of the Slidell family and of the social and political events of the country, from the Revolutionary War through the 1870's; centers on John Slidell, Southern political leader and Confederate representative to France during the Civil War.

2908 Dos Passos, John. MID-CENTURY. Houghton, 1961. A panoramic documentary of the labor movement in the United States, tracing the growth of big unions; includes short biographies of representative people in the movement.

2909 ______. CENTURY'S EBB. Gambit, 1975. The last of the author's contemporary chronicles of American life in this century, published posthumously. Much of the tone is despairing, but he seems to find some hopeful events, among them the moon walk that closes the book; covers the 1930's to the late 1960's.

2910 Douglas, Ellen. A FAMILY'S AFFAIRS. Houghton, 1962. Story of simple family customs, births, and deaths in three generations of a Creole family in a small Mississippi town, from the early 1900's to post-World War II days.

2911 Downes, Anne Miller. THE EAGLE'S SONG. Lippincott, 1949. Story of a strong-willed family clan and a growing community in the Mohawk River valley of New York from the Revolution to World War I.

2912 Dubus, Elizabeth. CAJUN. Seaview, 1983. Two Louisiana families, both with roots in France, have a role in area politics from 1755 to 1916. The Cajun family arrived in 1755, the other line descended from a French aristocrat who settled there in 1780.

2913 Edwards, Anne. THE HESITANT HEART. 1974. A novel about the solitary life of the poet Emily Dickinson; theorizes about the identity of the man she loved.

2914 Elliott, George. MURIEL. Dutton, 1972. The atmosphere of small-town America over four decades; the story is of the disintegration of one family, with a bitterly small-minded and controlling woman in the role of wife and mother; the 1930's on.

2915 Epps, Garrett. THE SHAD TREATMENT. Putnam, 1977. A native Virginian comes home from Harvard in the late 1960's to work for a new-style politician. Part of the book tells the story of his Virginia ancestors, from the time of the Civil War.

2916 Espey, John Jenkins. THE ANNIVERSARIES. Harcourt, 1963. Pictures the rapid growth of southern California, through the story of three generations of a Pasadena family.

2917 Farb, Peter. YANKEE DOODLE. Simon and Schuster, 1970. A retrospective look at our whole history. The protagonist wanders through a Connecticut town one afternoon in 1963. Disturbed by the scene, he ponders, in stream-of-consciousness style, historical events from 1663 on, finding some flawed roots in the American heritage.

2918 Ferber, Edna. AMERICAN BEAUTY. Doubleday, 1931. Chronicle of the build-up, the gradual disintegration, and the rejuvenation of a large estate in Connecticut from 1700 to 1930.

2919 _______. COME AND GET IT. Doubleday, 1935. Story of the rise and fall of the lumber industry in Wisconsin and Michigan from 1850 to the 1930's.

2920 _______. GIANT. Doubleday, 1952. Sweeping story of land- and oil-rich Texans; 1920's to the 1950's.

2921 _______. ICE PALACE. Doubleday, 1958. Tale of Alaska from pioneering days to the movement for statehood.

2922 Fields, Jonathan. THE MEMOIRS OF DUNSTAN BARR. Coward, 1959. Picture of the changing patterns of farm and small-town life and the growth of small business in Illinois, from 1890 to the stock-market crash of 1929.

2923 Gaines, Ernest J. THE AUTOBIOGRAPHY OF MISS JANE PITTMAN. Dial, 1971. Story of one black American woman who witnessed, in her long life, all of the violent struggle for equality for her race, from slavery to the fight to integrate public places in the South.

2924 Garvin, Richard M. and Edmond G. Addeo. MIDNIGHT SPECIAL. Geis, 1971. Story of the extraordinary guitarist called Leadbelly. Born in Texas, circa 1888, he spent years on chain gangs before being discovered and brought to New York by Lomax, the famous folklorist. His life ended in the psychiatric ward of Bellevue hospital in 1949.

2925 Gavin, Catherine. SUNSET DREAM. St. Martin's, 1984. Four generations of the Estrada family, who settled in the Sonoma valley of California in the 1840's. They stayed through Fremont's wresting control from the Spanish, through the gold rush, and saw San Francisco change from a cluster of tents and shacks to a modern city.

2926 Gerson, Noel B. THE CRUSADER. Little, 1970. A novel about Margaret Sanger, the first crusader for birth control as a right of women, and the reaction of scandalized horror her ideas roused in many segments of society.

2927 _______. CLEAR FOR ACTION. Doubleday, 1970. A biographical novel about David Farragut's naval career, from the time he was a midshipman at the tender age of ten to its climax when he became an admiral during the Civil War.

2928 Goddard, Gloria. THESE LORD'S DESCENDANTS. Stokes, 1930. Story of changing American life, from colonial times to World War I, through the fortunes of the descendants of an English migrant to the colonies.

2929 Grau, Shirley Ann. THE KEEPERS OF THE HOUSE. Knopf, 1964. Story of three generations of Negro-white relationships in a Southern community.

2930 Green, Gerald. CHAINS. Seaview, 1980. Story of Jewish "shtarkers" in Brooklyn. These strongmen moved from the honorable intent of protecting Jews and their property from rival Irish rowdies and preventing injury to the garment workers as they formed unions to profiting from racketeering and bootlegging.

2931 Green, Hannah. THE DEAD OF THE HOUSE. Doubleday, 1972. The mingling of past and present for a young girl living in Ohio before and after World War II. Her grandfather brings history alive with ancestral stories of the days of Anthony Wayne and Tecumseh.

2932 Gross, Joel. HOME OF THE BRAVE. Seaview, 1982. In 1640 an indentured servant, Virginia Taylor, married John Collins, a trapper. The story of their descendants in in Connecticut is told in episodes of the years 1715, 1855, and 1930.

2933 Hebson, Ann. THE LATTIMER LEGEND. Macmillan, 1961. Story of the break-up of a marriage in the post-Korean War period, with a flashback to the Civil War on the West Virginia border when a Gettysburg widow is won over by one of Morgan's Raiders.

2934 Heidish, Marcy. SECRET ANNIE OAKLEY. New American Library, 1983. A novelization of the life of the sharpshooter. The story explores her childhood misery in Ohio, and the years when her shows brought the excitement of the legendary Old West to staid Eastern communities.

2935 Hergesheimer, Joseph. THE LIMESTONE TREE. Knopf, 1931. Chronicle of Kentucky family life, from the time of Daniel Boone through the Civil War to the 1890's.

2936 Holt, Isabella. THE GOLDEN MOMENT. Random, 1959. Story of a woman's marriages, set against a background of American political life from the 1920's through the Roosevelt era and World War II to the 1950's.

2937 Horgan, Paul. MEMORIES OF THE FUTURE. Farrar, 1966. Story of two sisters married to U.S. navy men, and of their lives from World War I through the 1920's and 1930's to World War II.

2938 Horwitz, Gene. HOME IS WHERE YOU START FROM. Norton, 1966. Story of a Jewish family in New York City, from the early 1920's through the Depression to World War II.

2939 Hough, Henry Beetle. LAMENT FOR A CITY. Atheneum, 1960. Reporter and editor of a New England newspaper, from 1900, describes the decline of his paper.

2940 Hummel, George Frederick. JOSHUA MOORE, AMERICAN. Doubleday, 1943. Episodes in American history from colonization, the Revolution, settling in Ohio, antislavery riots in Kansas, and expansion in California.

2941 Humphrey, William. THE ORDWAYS. Knopf, 1965. Story of four generations of a Tennessee family adapting to a new environment in an east Texas border town.

2942 Hunter, Evan. SONS. Doubleday, 1969. Story of three generations of a Wisconsin family, set against a background of participation in World War I, World War II, and the Vietnam War, by a grandfather, father, and son.

2943 Hunter, Rodello. A HOUSE OF MANY ROOMS. Knopf, 1965. Episodes in the life of a Mormon family in Utah, from the 1890's to post-World War I days.

2944 Jaffe, Rona. FAMILY SECRETS. Simon and Schuster, 1974. A Russian immigrant arrives in the United States, penniless, in 1902. He becomes rich and acquires a secluded estate as a haven for his children. The members of the third generation find the estate and their ancestral culture confining.

2945 Jakes, John. THE BASTARD. Pyramid, 1974. This is the first of seven published titles in a series, first called the Bicentennial Series, and now titled the Kent Family Chronicles. Each is a sequel to the title before, and will be listed here by the dates the story covers. This opening title covers the years 1770-1775.

2946 _______. THE REBELS. Pyramid, 1974. Covers 1775-1781.

2947 _______. THE SEEKERS. Pyramid, 1975. Covers 1794-1814.

2948 _______. THE FURIES. Pyramid, 1976. Covers 1836-1852.

2949 _______. THE TITANS. Pyramid, 1976. Covers 1860-1862.

2950 _______. THE WARRIORS. Pyramid, 1977. Covers 1864-1868.

2951 _______. THE LAWLESS. Jove, 1978. Covers 1869-1877.

2952 Jenks, Almet. THE SECOND CHANCE. Lippincott, 1950.

Story of a man who missed fighting in World War I, entered Wall Street in the 1920's, recovered from financial near-disaster during the 1930's, and was killed in action during World War II.

2953 Jessup, Richard. SAILOR. Delacorte, 1966. Life and times of a career sailor, from his early life in Savannah, Georgia, during World War I, through the Depression to World War II, when his freighter is sunk by a German U-Boat.

2954 Jourdain, Rose. THOSE THE SUN HAS LOVED. Doubleday, 1978. The saga of a prosperous American black family, established in 1772 when Jacques Clavier arrived in New Bedford from the West Indies and became a sea captain and shipowner.

2955 Kern, Alfred. MADE IN U.S.A. Houghton, 1966. Portrait of a union leader and of his drive to the top.

2956 Keyes, Frances Parkinson. CRESCENT CARNIVAL. Messner, 1942. New Orleans from the 1890's to the 1940's; details of the carnival season, Louisiana lottery, firemen's parade, architecture, and social and political life.

2957 ________. THE RIVER ROAD. Messner, 1945. Picture of political, financial, and social conditions in the bayou country of Louisiana, from World War I through World War II.

2958 ________. STEAMBOAT GOTHIC. Messner, 1952. Family chronicle which reflects fluctuations in the economic life and describes the customs and manners of plantation and river life on the lower Mississippi River from 1870 to 1930.

2959 King, Joan. IMPRESSIONIST. Beaufort, 1983. Story of Mary Cassatt, the artist whose painting expressed her American youth, even though she lived her adult life as an expatriate in France.

2960 Knickerbocker, Charles H. THE DYNASTY. Doubleday, 1962. A realistic medical novel which follows a young doctor through medical school and through most of her professional life.

2961 Kornfield, Anita Clay. VINTAGE. Simon and Schuster, 1980. A tale of the Donati family, Italian immigrant vintners in the Napa Valley, from 1894 to 1960.

2962 Kriegel, Leonard. QUITTING TIME. Pantheon, 1982. The story of Jewish labor unions, centered on an idealistic young organizer who fought the gangsters who led unions.

His ideals led him to embrace communism, and in the "red scare" of 1950 he is forced out of leadership.

2963 Levin, Benjamin H. TO SPIT AGAINST THE WIND. Citadel, 1970. Fictional account of the life of Thomas Paine; his early life in England, his important part in pressing for the Revolution in the colonies, and his lonely old age when the antireligious views he expressed in Age of Reason isolated him.

2964 Lockridge, Ross. RAINTREE COUNTY. Houghton, 1948. Story of an Indiana county from 1844 to 1892, showing current events as the hero saw them on his visits home.

2965 Longman, M. B. (pseud.). THE POWER OF BLACK. Globus, 1961. Epic story of three generations of a Southern family that loses everything in the Civil War, begins over in the Texas oil fields; follows the fluctuations in the oil industry through the post-World War I era.

2966 Longstreet, Stephen. THE BANK. Putnam, 1976. Fiscal adventures of a banker who started his financial empire during the Civil War, profited from cornering the gold market with Jay Gould, and weathered two stock-market crashes before his death in 1930.

2967 McConkey, James. CROSSROADS. Dutton, 1967. Recollections of childhood in the Depression and service in World War II, and how they affect the present life of an ordinary family man.

2968 McCunn, Ruthanne Lum. THOUSAND PIECES OF GOLD. Design Enterprises, 1981. A story of a remarkable real woman, who was born in China, sold into slavery, sent to a brothel in San Francisco, purchased by a saloon-keeper in Idaho, and found love and happiness with a man who won her in a poker game. The rest of her life was spent on his remote and lovely claim on the Salmon River.

2969 Maier, William. THE TEMPER OF THE DAYS. Scribner, 1961. A slow-moving novel, set in New England, shows the feelings of the times from the flamboyant 1920's through the Depression and its aftermath.

2970 Marquand, J. P. HAVEN'S END. Little, 1933. Chronicle of a New England town through three generations of a family whose prosperity was based on slave-running.

2971 ________. THE LATE GEORGE APLEY. Little, 1937. Life story of a member of a Beacon Hill family. Pictures the life and customs of aristocratic Boston in the period from the 1880's to 1933.

2972 _______. SINCERELY, WILLIS WADE. Little, 1949. Story of the rise of a successful industrialist, picturing the impact of changes in the American economic scene from the turn of the century to the 1940's.

2973 Meaker, M. J. HOMETOWN. Doubleday, 1967. Three generations of a family in the grocery business in a small town in the New York Finger Lakes district from 1914 to 1941.

2974 Mercer, Charles E. GIFT OF LIFE. Putnam, 1963. Picture of a small town in Pennsylvania, from World War I to World War II; story of a determined woman raising her illegitimate daughter.

2975 Michener, James. HAWAII. Random, 1959. An epic history of the Hawaiian Islands, from ancient times to the successful struggle for statehood.

2976 _______. CENTENNIAL. Random, 1974. Mixed fiction and fact; explores the history of a Colorado town from archeological development to 1976; looks at animals, aborigines, settlers, railroads, cattle and sheep men, and recent environmental problems.

2977 _______. CHESAPEAKE. Random, 1978. An epic history of the Maryland shore, spanning four centuries. Indians, white settlers, slaves, Irish and immigrants all played roles, most of them drawing on the resources of the sea.

2978 _______. SPACE. Random, 1982. Americans in space, from the beginnings in WW II to N.A.S.A.'s triumphs in the 1980's. Real historical characters interact with fictional people in the plot.

2979 Mills, Charles. THE ALEXANDRIANS. Putnam, 1952. Panorama of the changing patterns of life in a small Georgia town, from its first settlement in 1839 until the day of its centennial celebration in 1939.

2980 Milton, David Scott. SKYLINE. Putnam, 1982. The sons of two Lower East Side families, Irish and Jewish, are members of rival gangs of adolescents in the 1920's. One becomes a boxer, and then gets into city politics. The other is hired by L. B. Mayer. They meet again in middle age when a business deal brings them together.

2981 Moody, Minnie Hite. LONG MEADOW. Macmillan, 1941. Chronicle of the Hite family, from 1705 to the 1860's, when two of the cousins died in the Civil War, one fighting for the South, the other for the North.

2982 Moore, Ruth. SPEAK TO THE WINDS. Morrow, 1956.

Three generations of the families who, in 1844, developed a town on an island off the Maine coast to exploit the granite found there.

2983 _______. THE GOLD AND SILVER HOOKS. Morrow, 1969. Story of a New England woman and her family problems from the early 1900's through the Prohibition era of the twenties, when her husband is involved in rum-running.

2984 Morris, Hilda. THE LONG VIEW. Putnam, 1937. A three-generation family chronicle showing the changing patterns of life from the Civil War through the Depression; New Jersey, rural New York, Indiana, Chicago, and Europe.

2985 Morris, Wright. PLAINS SONG; FOR FEMALE VOICES. Harper, 1980. Three generations of the women of a Nebraska family. The life of the grandmother was spent on the farm, and all of her energies went into its improvement; she spent almost no time in town. Her granddaughter, by contrast, lives in the town, uninterested in the homestead, now empty, neglected, and threatened by the growing suburbs.

2986 Morrison, Toni. SULA. Knopf, 1974. The lives of two black women living in the Negro section of a fictional Ohio city; spans forty years, from their girlhoods to maturity, and also tells the life stories of their parents and grandparents.

2987 Myrer, Anton. ONCE AN EAGLE. Holt, 1968. Saga of army life, from World War I through World War II and after; story of a career soldier as he rises from private to general.

2988 _______. THE LAST CONVERTIBLE. Putnam, 1978. Stories of several Harvard men who enter college in 1940, bent on enjoying their youth. War ends their carefree days, and one by one they enter military service. The story follows their postwar lives, which bring them disillusionment.

2989 Noble, Marguerite. FILAREE. Random, 1979. A long life, remembered by a ninety-year-old woman. She was trapped in her first marriage by poverty and drudgery, burdened with small children, and moving from one shabby house to another in rural Arizona. Her husband finally deserted the family, and when her children grew up she was free for the first time to settle on her own pursuits.

2990 Norris, Frank. TOWER IN THE WEST. Harper, 1957. Picture of American social and economic life from the twenties to World War II, through the life history of a revolutionary skyscraper hotel in St. Louis; Prohibition, the stock-market crash of 1929, the Depression, recovery, and prosperity.

2991 O'Hara, John. FROM THE TERRACE. Random, 1958. Study of the life of a member of the wealthy class, from boyhood through service in World War I, a career in the early aviation industry and in Wall Street financial circles, and government service in World War II.

2992 Ozick, Cynthia. TRUST. New American Library, 1966. Intellectual, political, and social life of the rich in Europe and New York from the 1930's to the 1960's.

2993 Peck, Richard. THIS FAMILY OF WOMEN. Delacorte, 1983. Lena Wheatley came to California in a covered wagon in 1850. The four generations of daughters descended from her play parts in California history; to the beginning of World War II.

2994 Petrakis, Harry Mark. THE ODYSSEY OF KOSTAS SOLAKIS. McKay, 1963. An account of life in the Greek-American community of Chicago from 1919 to 1954.

2995 Powell, Richard. THE PHILADELPHIAN. Scribner, 1956. Story of social life and customs seen through four generations of a Philadelphia family from 1857 to the 1950's.

2996 ________. I TAKE THIS LAND. Scribner, 1963. Social and business life, railraod building, land booms, and the orange-growing business in southwest Florida from the 1890's to the 1920's.

2997 Price, Reynolds. THE SURFACE OF THE EARTH. Atheneum, 1975. Lives of three generations of two families united by marriage, living in rural North Carolina and Virginia from 1903 to 1944.

2998 Rawlings, Marjorie Kinnan. THE SOJOURNER. Scribner, 1953. Life on a farm in upstate New York from 1880 to World War II.

2999 Rejan, Edwin. ONE CLEAR CALL. Macmillan, 1962. Recollections by an eighty-two-year old priest of his forty-five years in a Brooklyn parish; covers events during the polio epidemic of 1916, World Wars I and II, the New York dock strike of 1936, and the migration of Puerto Ricans into the neighborhood.

3000 Robinson, Henry Morton. WATER OF LIFE. Simon and Schuster, 1960. American social and political events from the Reconstruction period through Prohibition form the background for this story of the whiskey industry.

3001 Rollins, Kelly. FIGHTER PILOTS. Little, 1981. Autobiographical story of a fighter pilot's long dangerous career, from battling the Luftwaffe in WW II through the wars in Korea and Vietnam.

3002 Rooney, Frank. THE COURTS OF MEMORY. Vanguard, 1954. Story of modern family life from the 1930's to the 1950's; set in Los Angeles and New York.

3003 Sanchez, Thomas. RABBIT BOSS. Knopf, 1973. Story of four generations of Washo Indians in the California Sierras, each generation suffering from its relations with the white man.

3004 Sandburg, Carl. REMEMBRANCE ROCK. Harcourt, 1948. Panorama of American history from the days of the Pilgrims to the end of World War II.

3005 Santmeyer, Helen. AND LADIES OF THE CLUB. Putnam, 1984. Life in a small Ohio town, from the Civil War to the 1930's. The story focuses on the women members of a literary study club.

3006 Saunders, Winifred Crandall. TO SPAN A CONTINENT. Caxton, 1965. Family saga of a New York State farmer who wanders westward to the Pacific in 1839; after settling on an Illinois homestead his sons are active in the Underground Railroad and fight in the Civil War; pictures family and social customs, frontier life, and the abolition movement.

3007 Scanlon, John. DAVIS. Doubleday, 1969. Biography of a military genius from his days as a West Point cadet, before the second World War, through action in the Burma campaign with Wingate's Raiders, promotion between wars, and to his death in the Korean War.

3008 Seeman, Ernest. AMERICAN GOLD. Dial, 1978. This story of the rise of a North Carolina tobacco town, from the 1880's to the mid-twentieth century captures the folkways, atmosphere, and the local idiom.

3009 Seton, Anya. THE HEARTH AND EAGLE. Houghton, 1948. Story of Marblehead, Massachusetts from its earliest settlement to the 1950's.

3010 Shaw, Irwin. VOICES OF A SUMMER DAY. Delacorte, 1956. The son of immigrant Russian parents looks back on his family life from 1927 to the 1960's.

3011 Siebel, Julia. THE NARROW COVERING. Harcourt, 1965. Life in a small town in Kansas from before World War I to the years following Pearl Harbor.

3012 Sigal, Clancy. GOING AWAY. Houghton, 1961. Memoir of an angry young man experiencing the changes, reforms, and leftist agitation in American society; 1930's to 1950's.

3013 Simmons, Herbert. MAN WALKING ON EGGSHELLS. Houghton, 1962. Story of the economic and social struggles of a black family, from the 1920's to the 1950's.

3014 Skimin, Robert. CHIKARA! St. Martin's, 1984. Story of a Japanese who came to the U.S. in 1907 with his wife and one of their sons. The son fights in WW I but is denied citizenship. Covers the Nisei internment during the next war and the subsequent rise of Japan's economic might, affecting American life.

3015 Sorrentino, Gilbert. STEELWORK. Pantheon, 1971. Vignettes of lives in a white working-class neighborhood in Brooklyn, from the 1930's to the 1950's.

3016 Sourian, Peter. THE GATE. Harcourt, 1965. Three generations of an Armenian-American family whose son becomes a successful architect.

3017 Stegner, Wallace. THE BIG ROCK CANDY MOUNTAIN. Duell, 1943. Life in the Far West and in Saskatchewan, from 1906 to 1942.

3018 Stern, Richard Martin. BROOD OF EAGLES. New American Library, 1969. Story of a family and their business empire in the aircraft industry from before World War I to the 1960's.

3019 Stevens, Louis. DAYS OF PROMISE. Prentice, 1948. Panorama of American society from the Civil War to the 1940's told through the chronicle of a Kansas newspaper-owner's family.

3020 Stewart, Fred Mustard. ELLIS ISLAND. Morrow, 1983. Five immigrants arrive at Ellis Island in 1907. They are fleeing the Old World's pogroms, military conscriptions, and hunger. Their lives in the new world will illustrate major events in the U. S. history of the early twentieth century.

3021 Streeter, Edward. HAM MARTIN, CLASS OF '17. Harper, 1969. Success story of a Harvard graduate, through World War I, the Depression, and World War II, who sees his son become the creative writer he had wished to be.

3022 Stuart, Colin. WALKS FAR WOMAN. Dial, 1976. A 90-year-old Blackfoot Indian woman recounts her life story to her grandson and his white fiancée. Historic events such as the Battle of Little Big Horn are in her memory, as are details of Indian customs and tradition.

3023 Sulkin, Sidney. THE FAMILY MAN. Luce, 1962. A Russian-Jewish immigrant struggles for financial success from the Depression years of the 1930's to the 1950's.

3024 Swados, Harvey. STANDING FAST. Doubleday, 1970. Story traces a group of radical socialists from their activist years in the 1930's and 1940's to the time of John Kennedy's assassination, when a new generation is seeking new ways to remedy social ills.

3025 Thorp, Roderick. WESTFIELD. Crown, 1977. Saga of four generations of a New York family. A slum orphan adopted in the 1870's amasses wealth which is lost by his sons in the period of gangsters and Prohibition. The last inheritor of the family mantle is a bewildered veteran of the Vietnam War.

3026 Tute, Warren. LEVIATHAN. Little, 1959. A story of the steamship industry; the building and operation of a great liner from its launching in the 1930's to its sinking while serving as a troop carrier in World War II.

3027 Uhnak, Dorothy. LAW AND ORDER. Simon and Schuster, 1973. The men of the O'Malley family in New York are policemen. Three generations are covered in this story from a hardboiled cynical cop in the 1940's to an idealistic rookie, back from Vietnam in the late 1960's.

3028 Vasquez, Richard. CHICANO. Doubleday, 1970. The Sandoval family fled bandit-ridden Mexico in the early years of this century. Their sons prospered in the U. S., but their grandsons suffer from bigotry in a Los Angeles barrio.

3029 Vidal, Gore. WASHINGTON, D. C. Little, 1967. Private life and politics of a U. S. senator from the early days of the New Deal to the period of the Cold War.

3030 Walker, Mildred. CURLEW'S CRY. Harcourt, 1955. Picture of ranch life in Montana from 1905 to the 1940's.

3031 Watson, Virginia. MANHATTAN ACRES. Dutton, 1934. Depicts the growth of New York City; chronicle of a Dutch family from the 1630's to 1933.

3032 Weeks, Jack. SOME TRUST IN CHARIOTS. McGraw, 1964. Three-generation saga of a family empire growing with the automobile industry, from the invention of a gas buggy in 1895 to the 1940's.

3033 Weidman, Jerome. A FAMILY FORTUNE. Simon, 1978. Story of Max and Ida Lessing, who came to America in the 1920's and settled in Minneapolis. Max is now a respected businessman and a wealthy man, but his first years in this country were spent in the underworld of bootleggers.

3034 Wescott, Glenway. THE GRANDMOTHERS. Harper, 1927. Chronicle of a Wisconsin family, one of those that helped settle the frontier; from the 1840's to the turn of the century.

3035 White, William Allen. A CERTAIN RICH MAN. Macmillan, 1909. Story of a millionaire industrialist and the growth of his Kansas town, from the Civil War to the turn of the century.

3036 Wight, Frederick. CHRONICLE OF AARON KANE. Farrar, 1936. Story of the long life of a Scotch-Irish Cape Cod sailor, from 1838 through the years after the Civil War.

3037 Wilder, Robert. THE SUN IS MY SHADOW. Putnam, 1960. Story of a woman's career in newspaper work; economic and political events from the late 1920's through the Depression, the Roosevelt era, the rise of Hitler, and World War II.

3038 ______. THE SEA AND THE STARS. Putnam, 1967. Saga of the growth of Florida from undeveloped scrub land through the boom days of World War I and the twenties, the collapse of the bubble, and rebuilding the fruit and truck farms, the tourist industry, and the building of new communities.

3039 Williams, Ben Ames. THE STRANGE WOMAN. Houghton, 1941. Story of a wicked beautiful woman, extending in time from the War of 1812 through the Civil War; set in Maine.

3040 Williams, John. STONER. Viking, 1965. Life of a poor Missouri farm boy who worked his way through the University of Missouri and stayed on as a teacher until driven away by a scandal; 1891 to 1956.

3041 Williams, John A. CAPTAIN BLACKMAN. Doubleday, 1972. A polemic on the unfair treatment of the black military man throughout our history; Captain Blackman, an Everyman, wounded in Vietnam, drifts in and out of a coma, envisioning black soldiers in every American war.

3042 Williams, Lawrence. I, JAMES McNEILL WHISTLER. Simon and Schuster, 1972. Life story of the famous nineteenth-century American painter, who spent much of his career in Europe.

3043 Wilson, Mitchell. LIVE WITH LIGHTNING. Little, 1949.

Story of the career of a physicist, from his years as a laboratory assistant during the Depression, to industrial scientist, to atomic researcher during World War II and after.

3044 Wilson, William Edward. EVERYMAN IS MY FATHER. Saturday Review Press, 1973. The chronicle of the Clayburne family, from colonial New England to the 1970's, reviews the thoughts, feelings, and ways of life for typical Americans at varying points in history.

3045 Winston, Daoma. FALL RIVER LINE. Marek, 1984. The Fall River Line of luxury steamers was a proud sector of transportation in this country for 137 years. The lives of all the characters in this nostalgic saga touched and were touched by the ships.

3046 Woiwode, Larry. BEYOND THE BEDROOM WALL. Farrar, 1975. Shows the changes in culture in heartland America through the story of a family whose ancestors arrived in North Dakota in the days of the sodbusters.

3047 Yglesias, José. THE TRUTH ABOUT THEM. World, 1972. Story of a clan of Cubans in the United States. The first to arrive is the aristocratic grandmother who came to Tampa in 1890. She is undaunted by her sudden social fall as she becomes a cigar-factory worker. Relatives drift to New York during the Depression, and the story ends with the narrator visiting Castro's Cuba.

3048 Zollinger, Norman. RIDERS TO CIBOLA. Museum of New Mexico Press, 1978. Life and work on a cattle ranch in the Southwest, over a three-generation span, after a ten-year-old Mexican boy flees the revolutionary chaos in his home village and is taken in at the McAndrews ranch.

AUTHOR-TITLE INDEX

SUBJECT INDEX